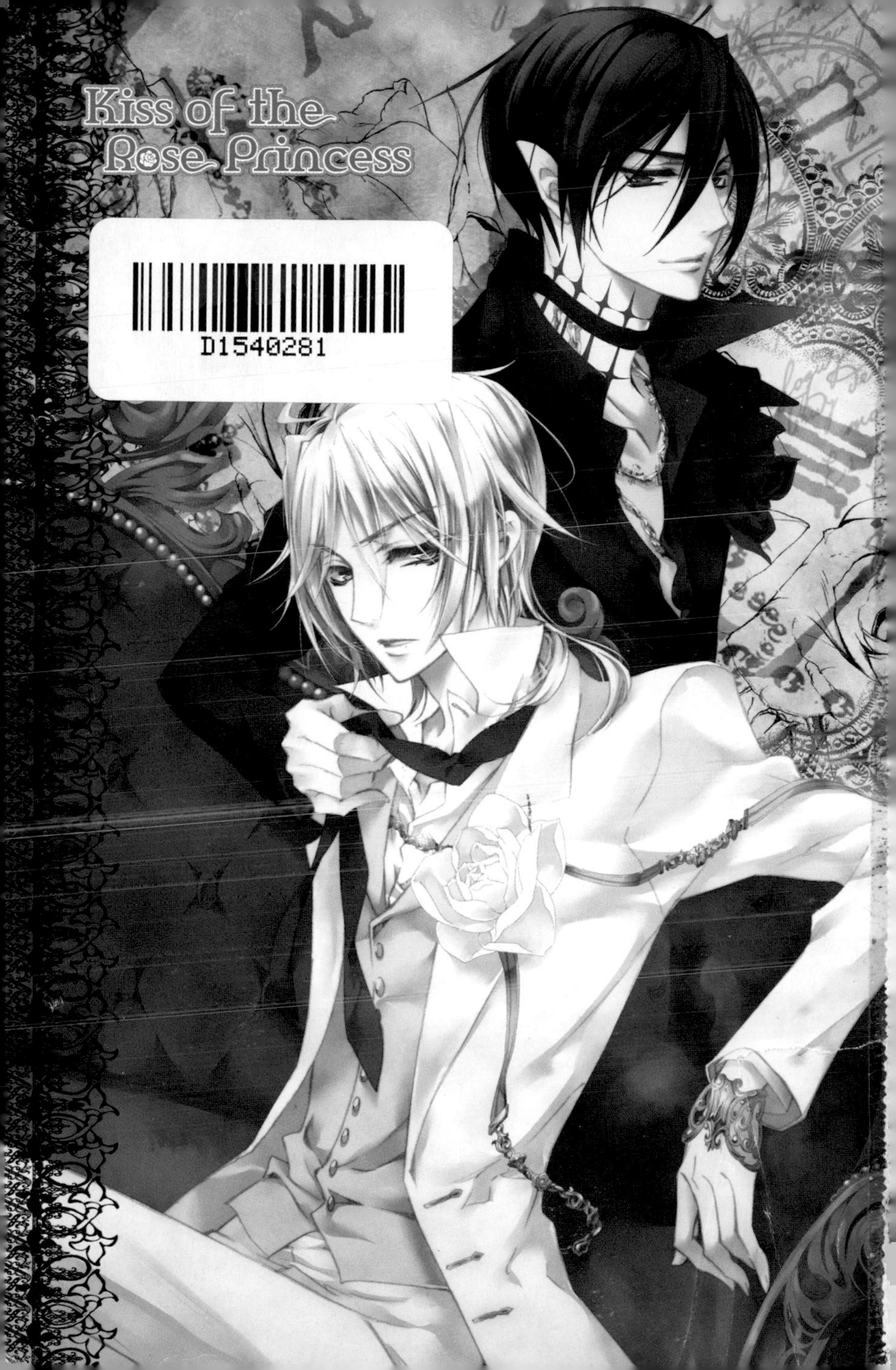
Kiss of the Rose Princess

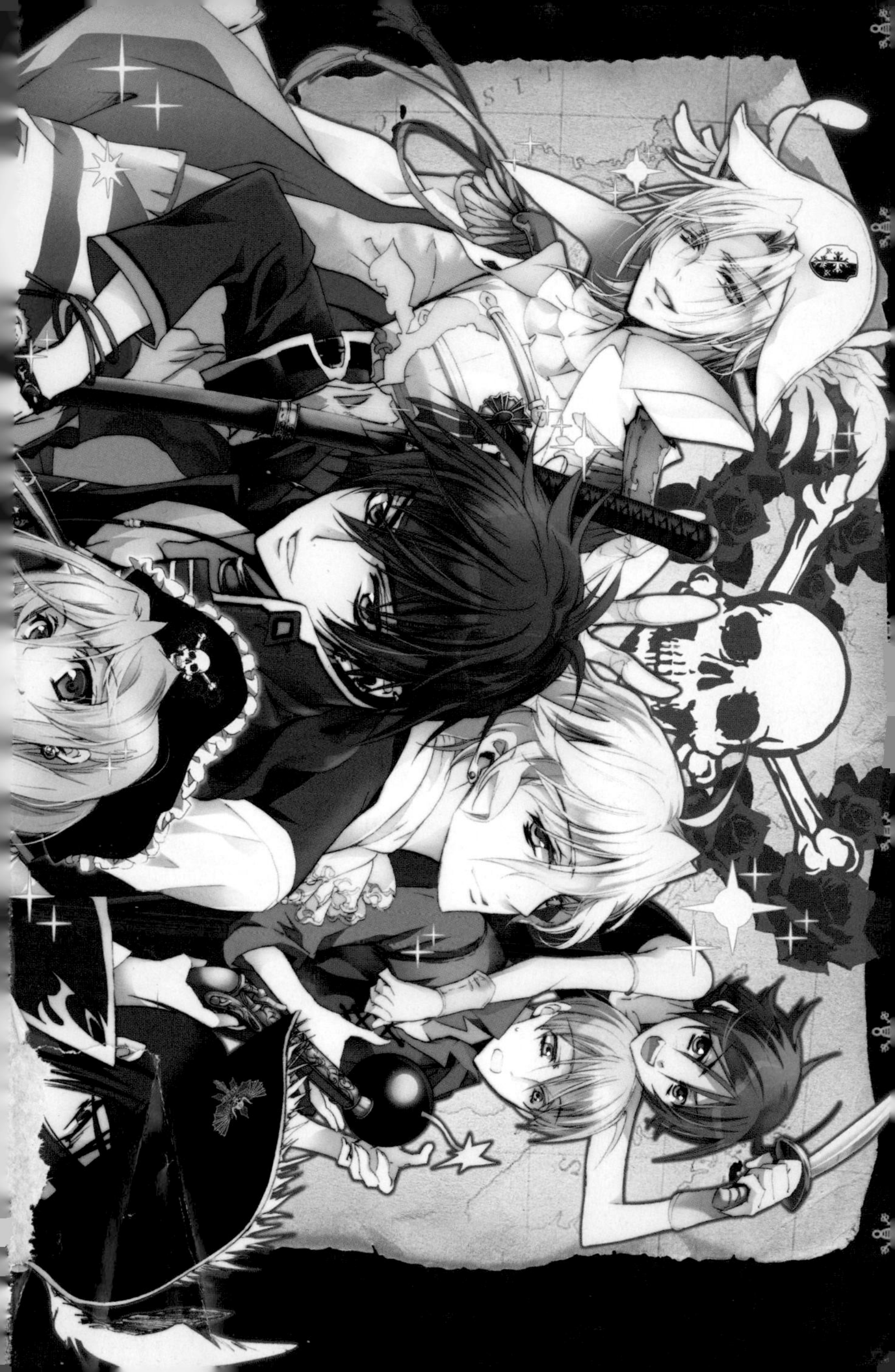

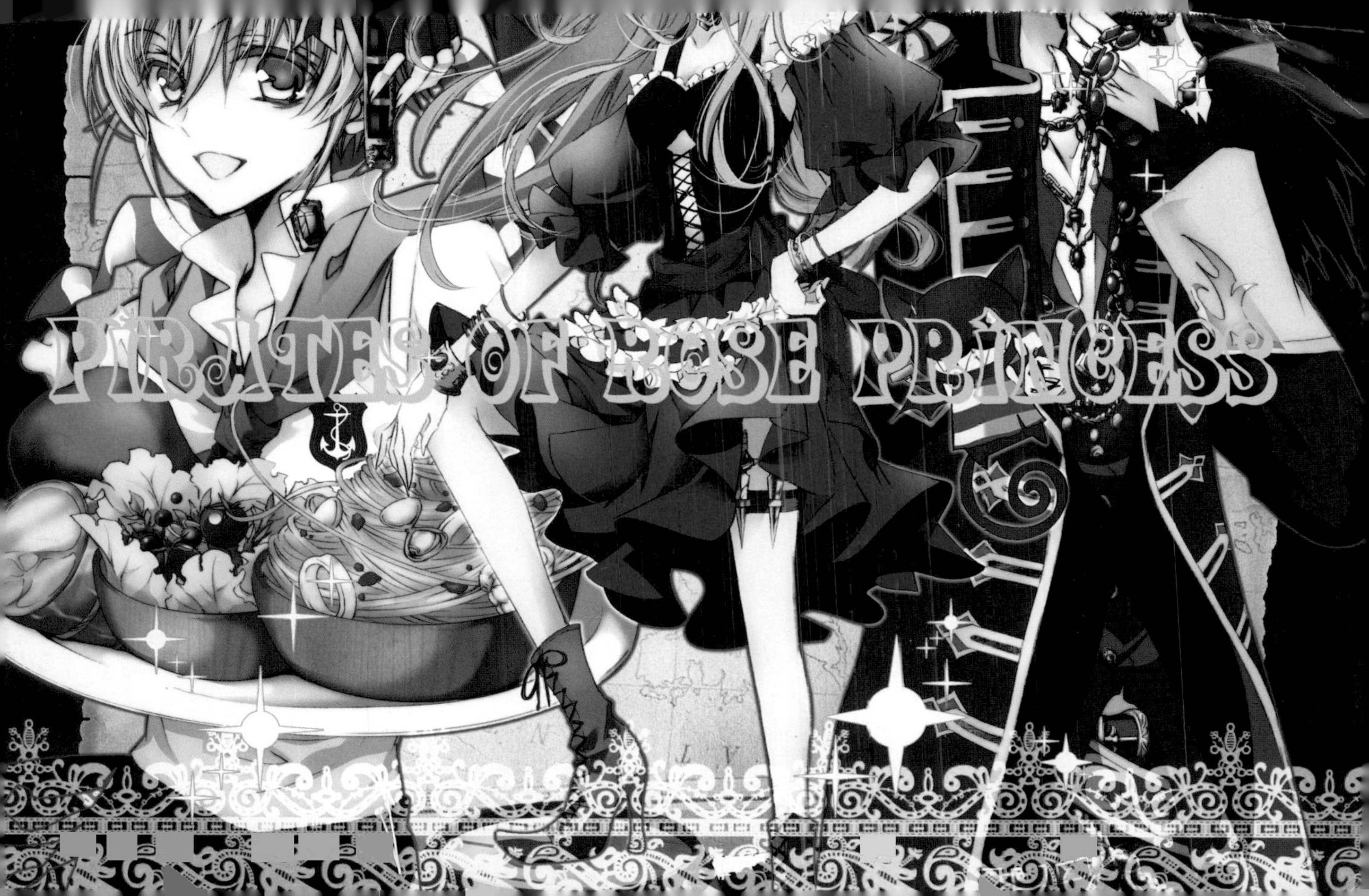
PIRATES OF ROSE PRINCESS

Kiss of the Rose Princess

Contents

Characters

Rose Knights

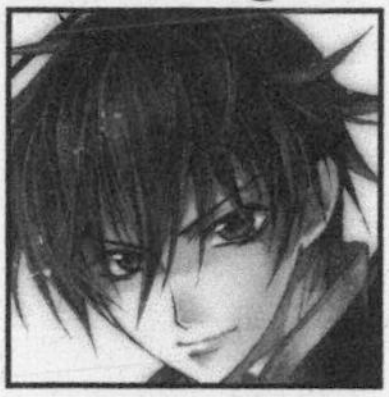

Kaede Higa (Red Rose)

Anise's classmate. He is an excellent athlete who often teases Anise.
Specialty: Offence

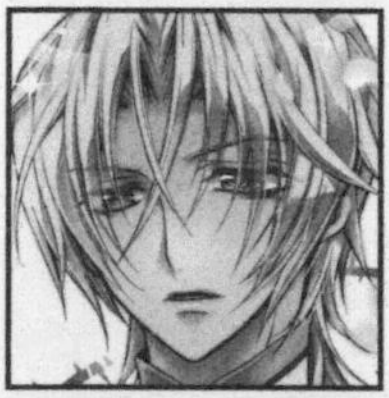

Mitsuru Tenjo (White Rose)

Third-year and Student Council President. He is revered by both male and female students. Super-rich.
Specialty: Healing, Defense

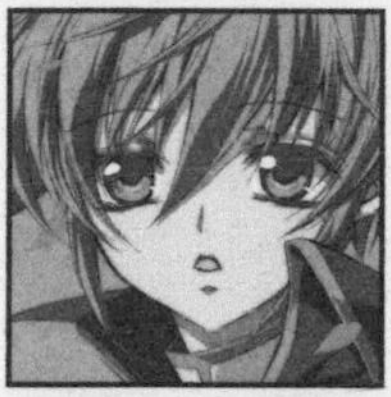

Seiran Asagi (Blue Rose)

First-year. This boy is cuter than any girl at school, and he doesn't know he's the school idol. He's well-versed in a wide range of topics.
Specialty: Alchemy, Science

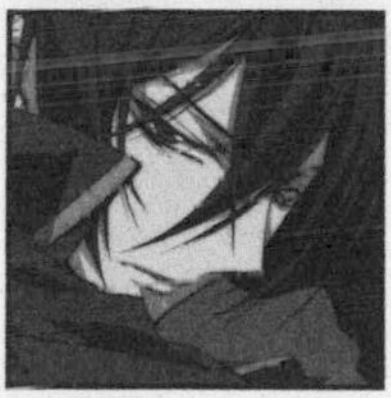

Mutsuki Kurama (Black Rose)

Second year. There are many frightening rumors about this mysterious student. Apparently he lives in the basement of Tenjo's house.
Specialty: Discovery, Capture

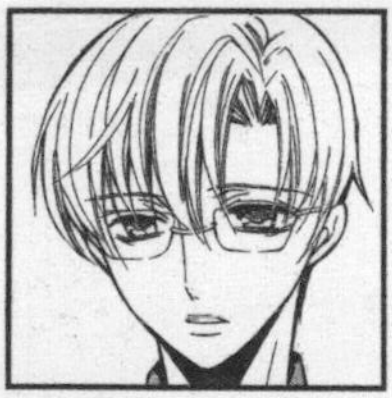

Itsushi Narumi (Classics Teacher)

He is the most knowledgeable about the "Sovereign," her "Rose Knights" and the "Rose Contract" that binds them...

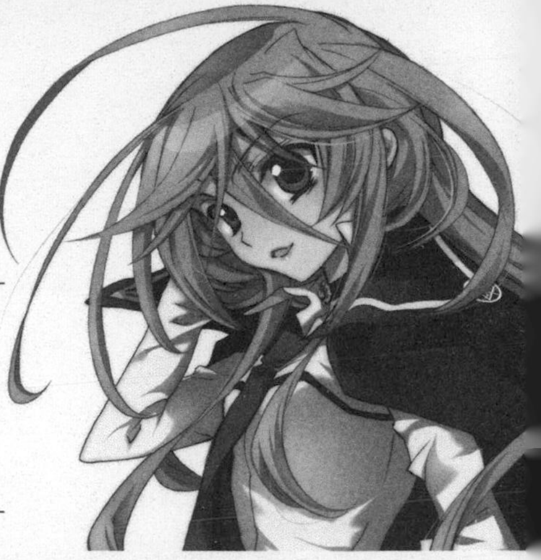

Anise Yamamoto

First-year at Shobi Academy. She was an ordinary girl who became the Rose Princess after her choker was removed from her neck.

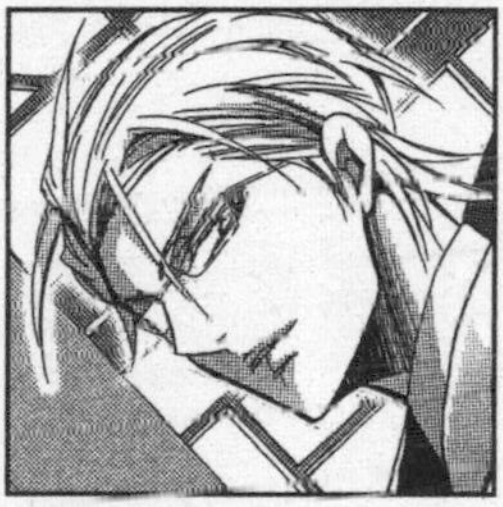

Schwarz Yamamoto

Anise's father. It seems he had a motive in putting the rose choker on Anise.

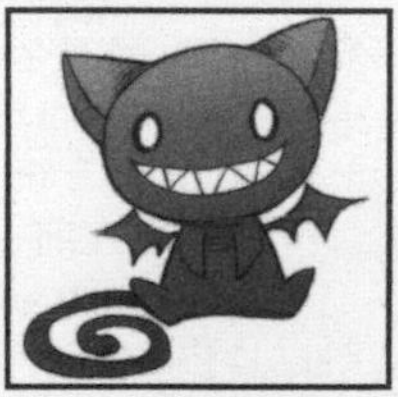

Ninufa (Guardian)

The guardian who has been protecting the cards since ancient times.

Characters

Fake Rose Princess

Ella

She has a strong obsession with Anise. She commands four Fake Rose Knights.

Fake Rose Knights

Shiden Fujinomiya (Purple Rose)

A loyal follower of Ella. He controls water to attack his enemies.

Yocto (Gray Rose)

Mutsuki's older brother. His dream is to reestablish Dark Stalkers in the world.

Rhodecia

Idel Suzumura (Orange Rose)

An active and optimistic student at Shobi Academy. He can attack using sound waves.

Yako Hasuzaki (Lime Rose)

A student at Shobi Academy. He uses the power of scent to hypnotize people.

Story Thus Far

Anise and the Rose Knights are invited to the Academy Foundation Gala held on the anniversary of the day Shobi Academy was established. They are all dressed up and enjoying the dance when a blackout occurs during a lightning storm. Suddenly Anise finds herself being kissed by Mutsuki! Before Anise is able to come to terms with what has happened, Idel of Rhodecia appears and asks her for help. After listening to Idel's story, Anise makes up her mind to face her father, Schwarz, in order to save Yako!

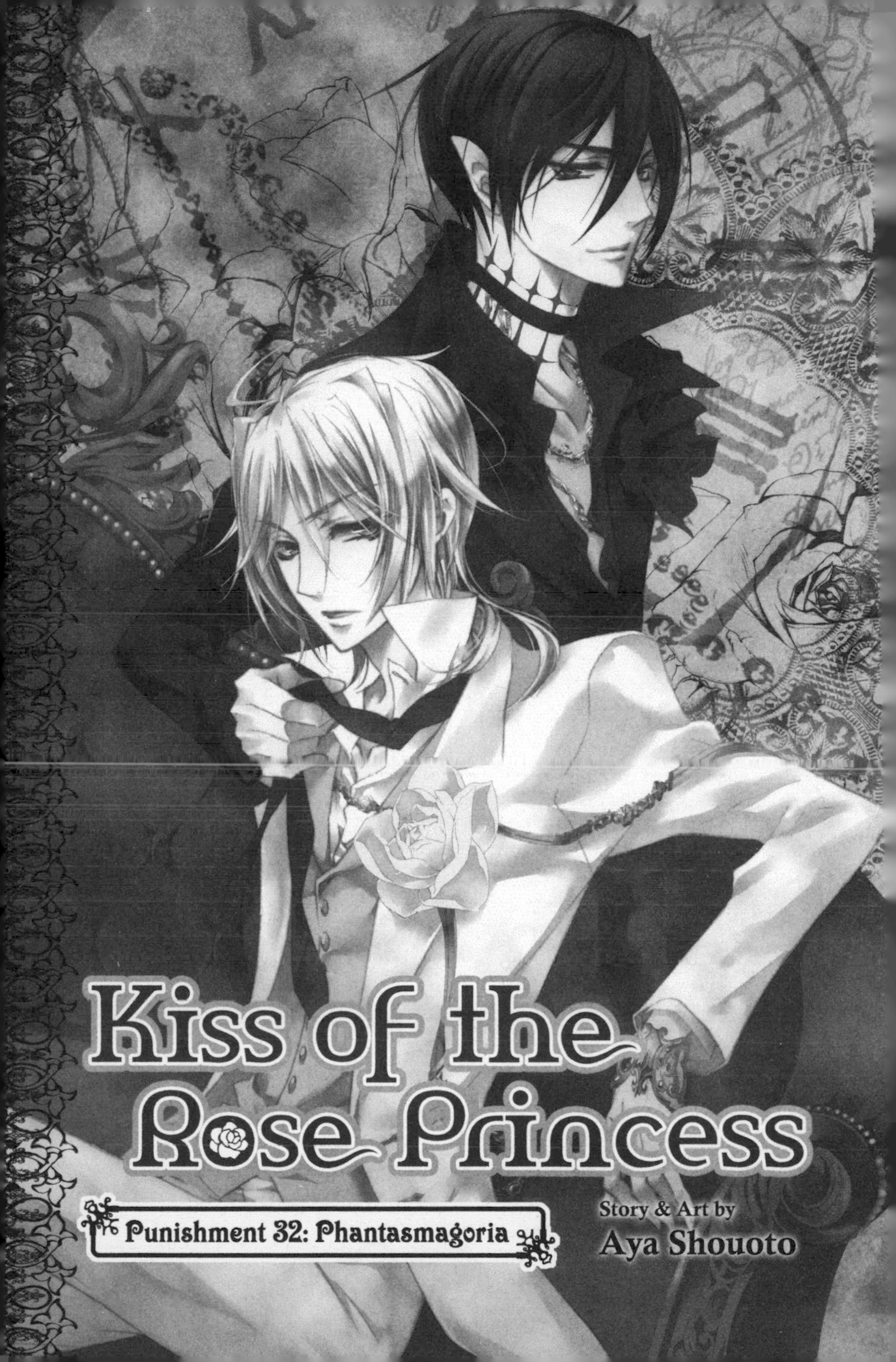
Kiss of the Rose Princess
Punishment 32: Phantasmagoria
Story & Art by
Aya Shouoto

Kiss of the Rose Princess

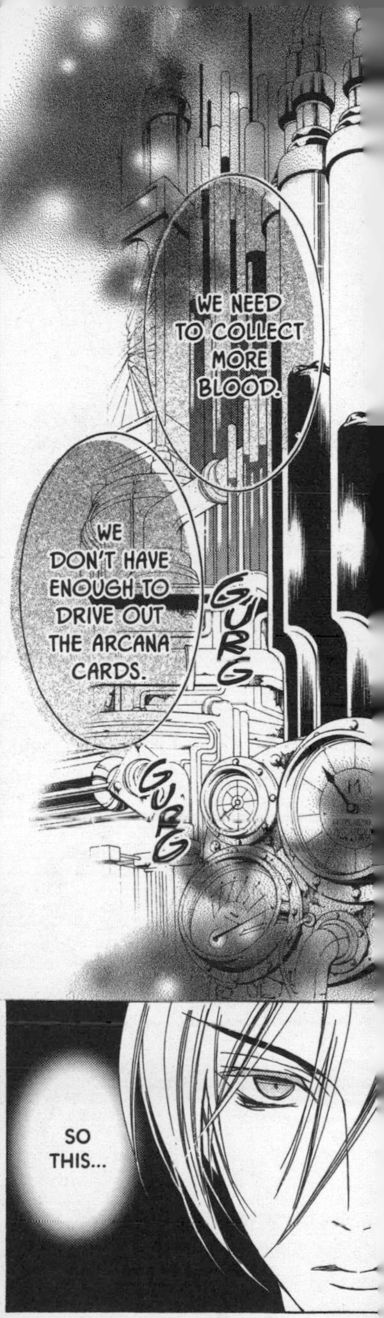
WE NEED TO COLLECT MORE BLOOD.
WE DON'T HAVE ENOUGH TO DRIVE OUT THE ARCANA CARDS.
GURG
GURG
SO THIS...

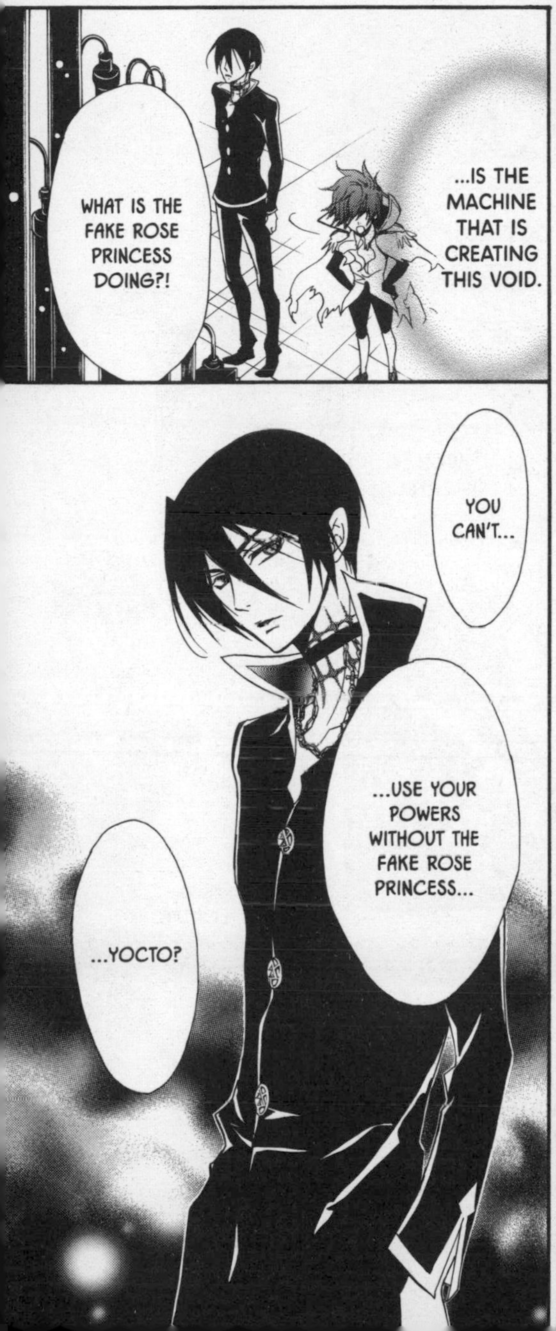
...IS THE MACHINE THAT IS CREATING THIS VOID.
WHAT IS THE FAKE ROSE PRINCESS DOING?!
YOU CAN'T...
...USE YOUR POWERS WITHOUT THE FAKE ROSE PRINCESS...
...YOCTO?

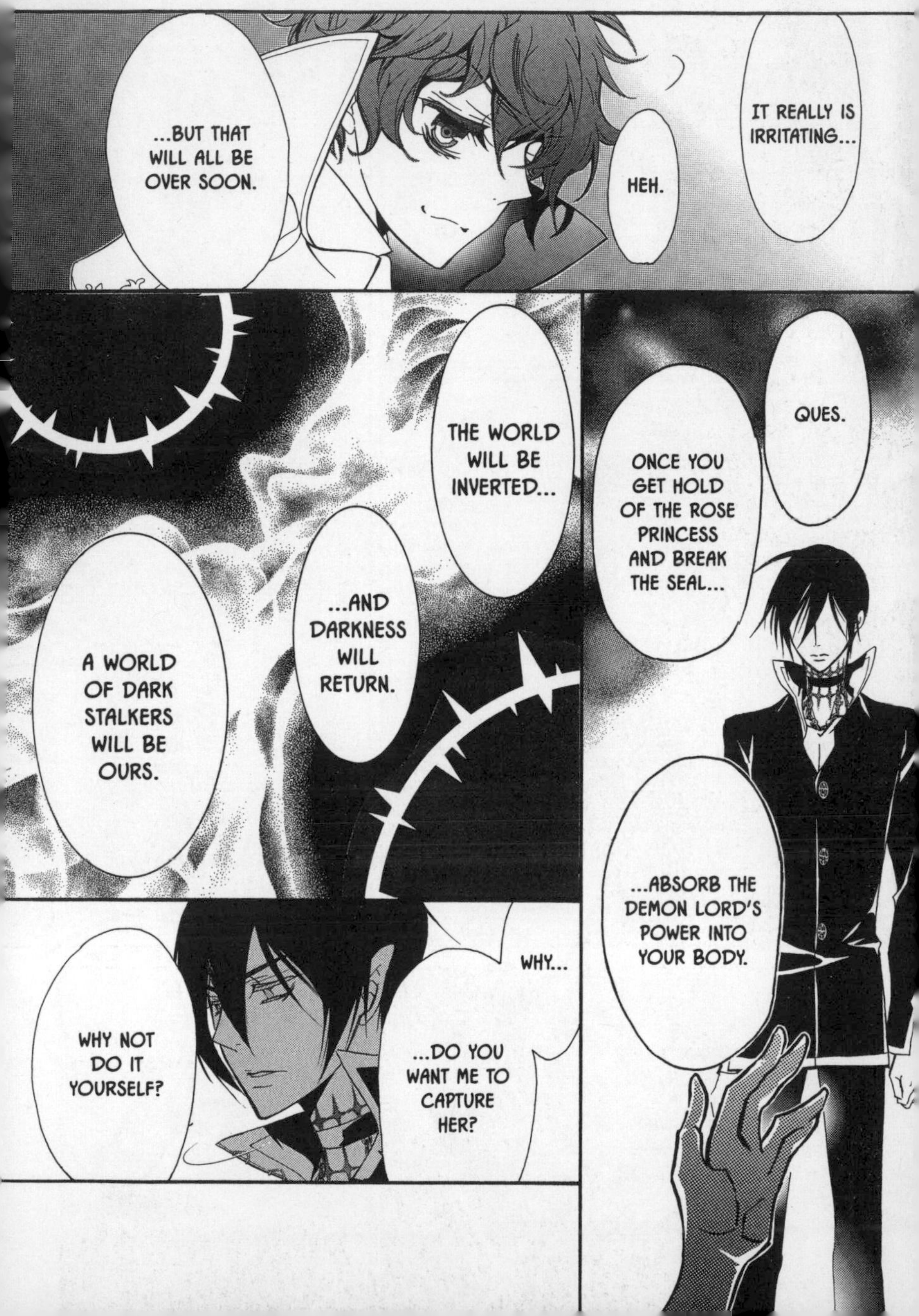
IT REALLY IS IRRITATING...
HEH.
...BUT THAT WILL ALL BE OVER SOON.
QUES.
ONCE YOU GET HOLD OF THE ROSE PRINCESS AND BREAK THE SEAL...
...ABSORB THE DEMON LORD'S POWER INTO YOUR BODY.
THE WORLD WILL BE INVERTED...
...AND DARKNESS WILL RETURN.
A WORLD OF DARK STALKERS WILL BE OURS.
WHY...
...DO YOU WANT ME TO CAPTURE HER?
WHY NOT DO IT YOURSELF?

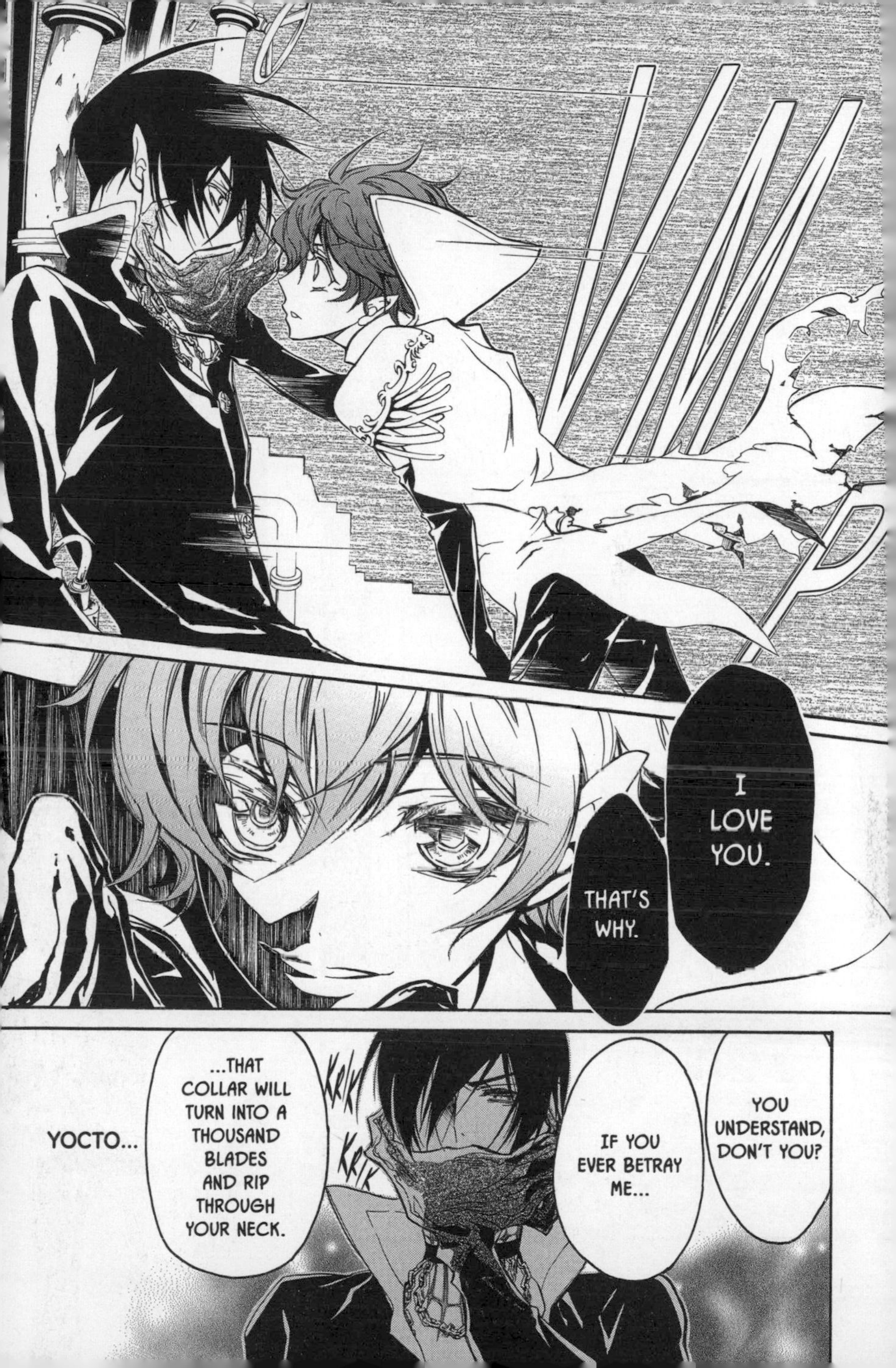

I LOVE YOU.
THAT'S WHY.
YOU UNDERSTAND, DON'T YOU?
IF YOU EVER BETRAY ME...
KRIK
KRIK
...THAT COLLAR WILL TURN INTO A THOUSAND BLADES AND RIP THROUGH YOUR NECK.
YOCTO...

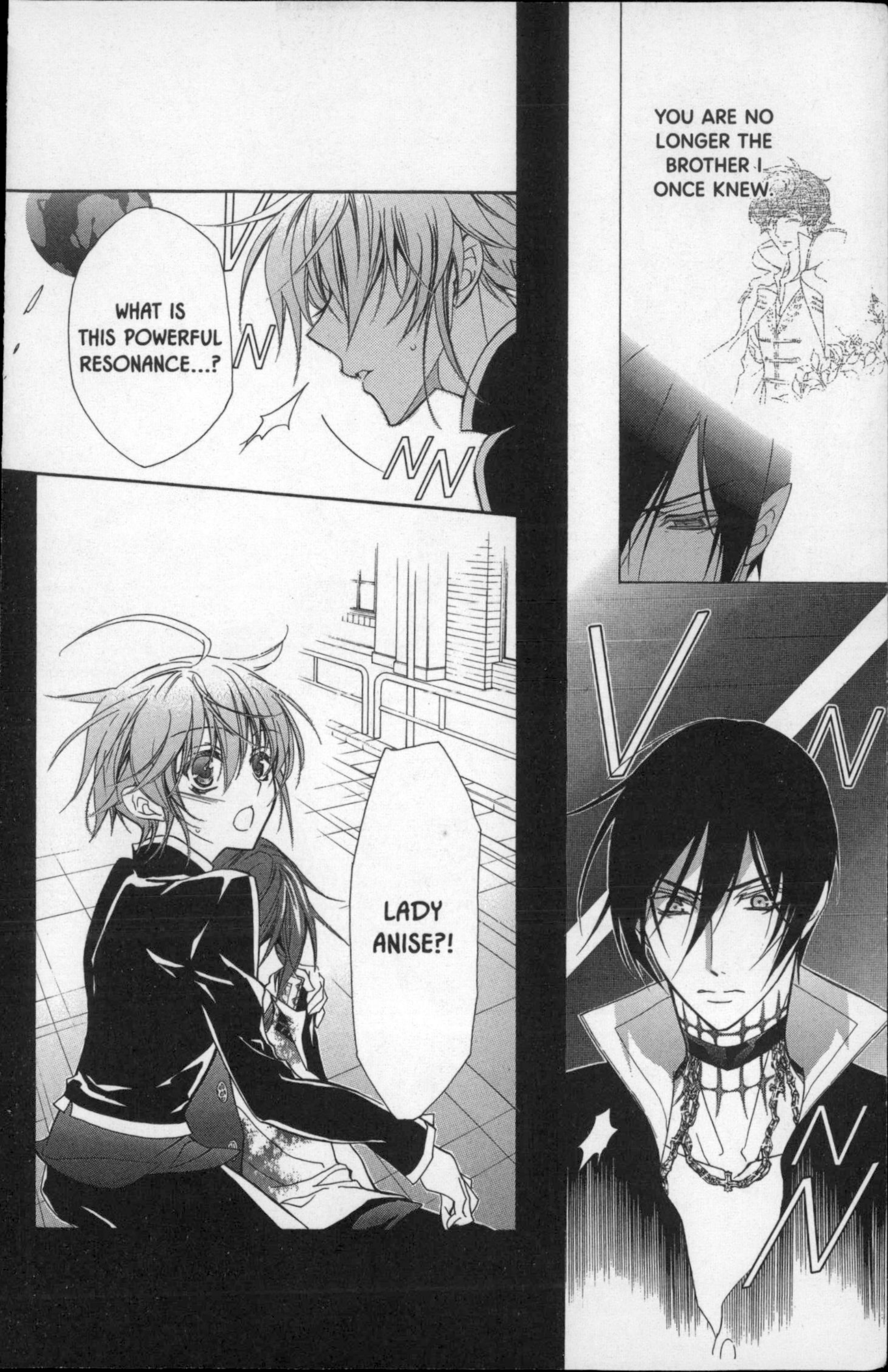

YOU ARE NO LONGER THE BROTHER I ONCE KNEW.
V
N
N
N
WHAT IS THIS POWERFUL RESONANCE...?
V
N
NN
LADY ANISE?!

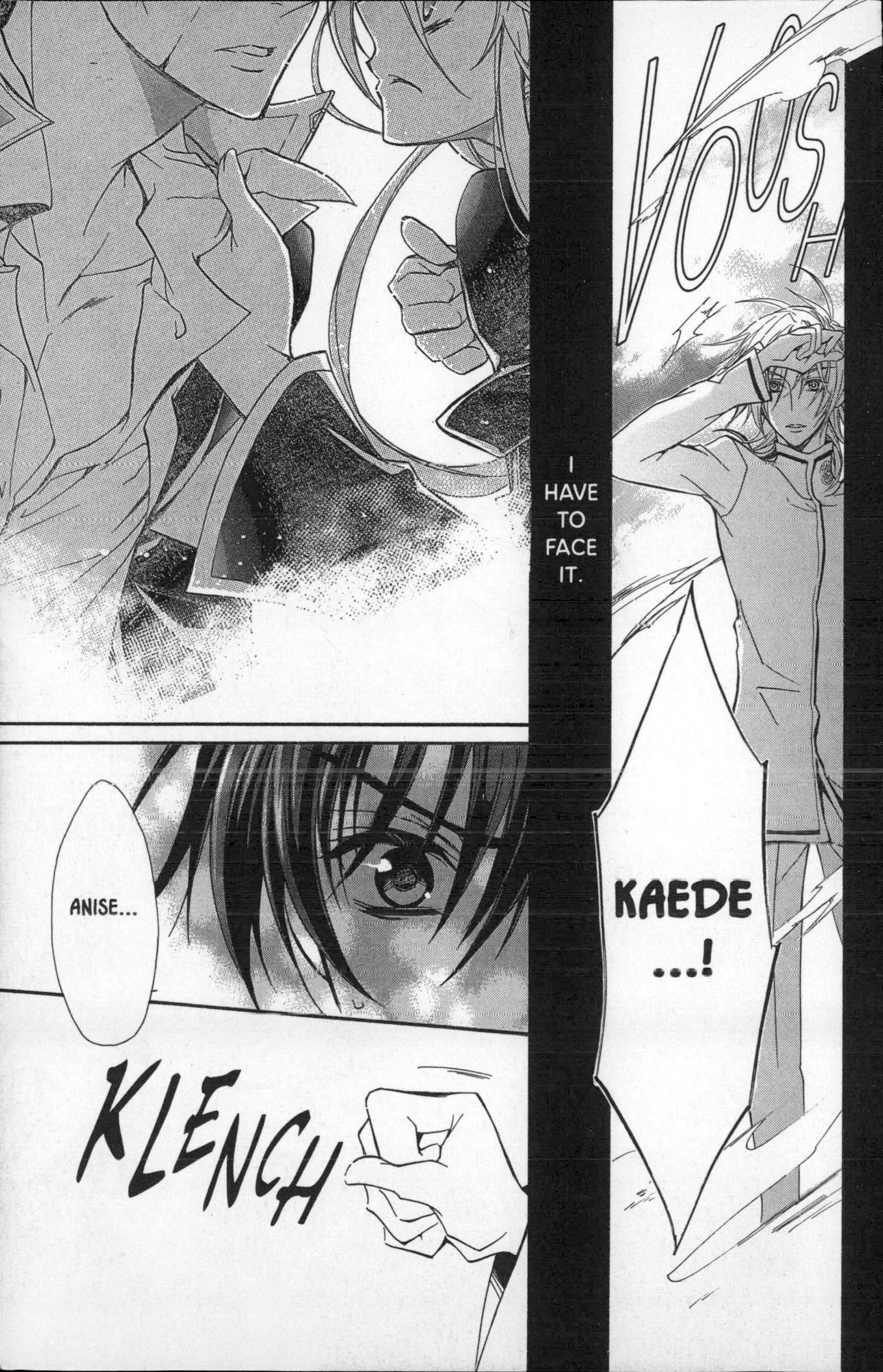
VOUSH
KAEDE ...!
I HAVE TO FACE IT.
ANISE...
KLENCH

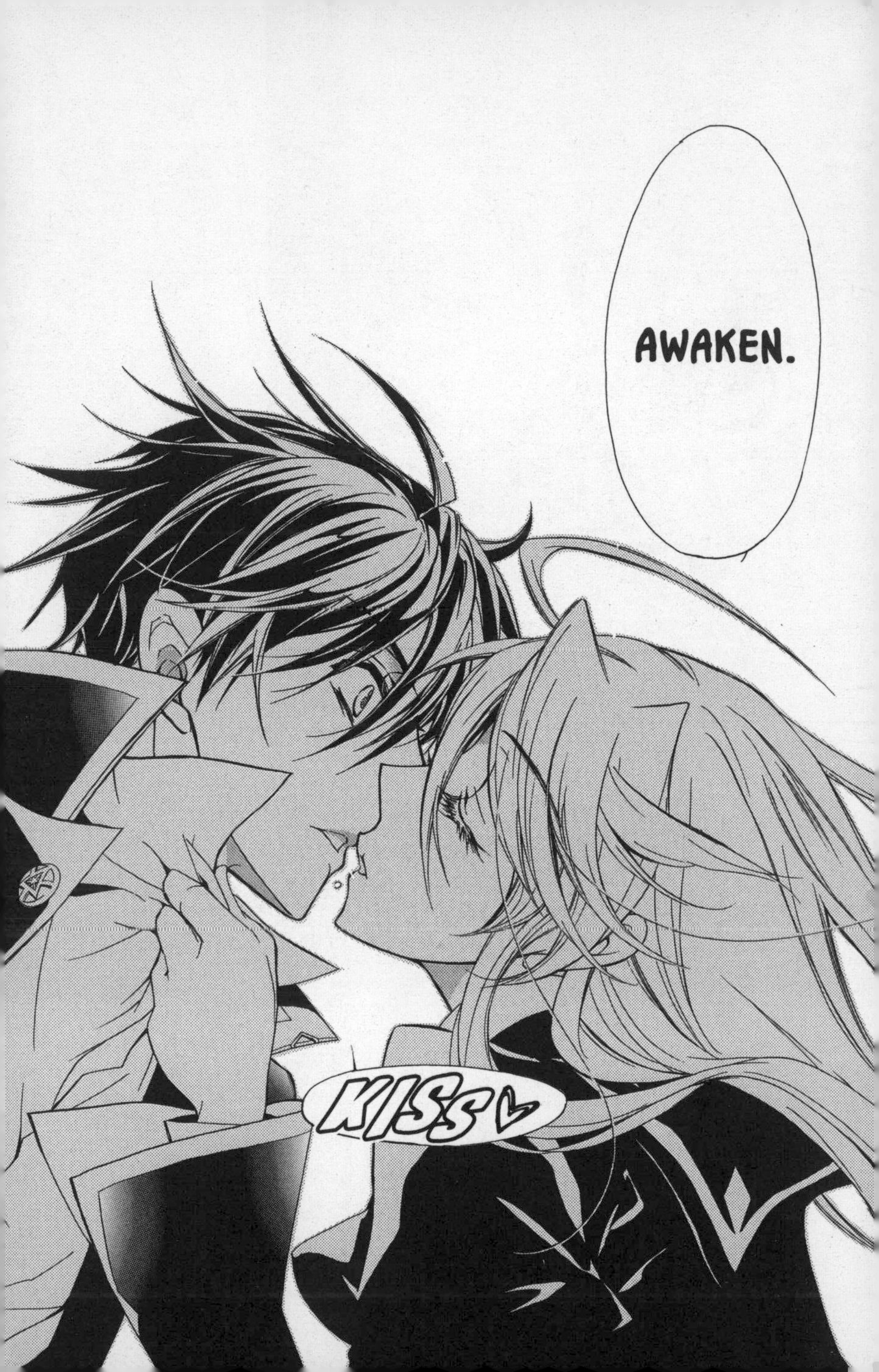
AWAKEN.
KISS♡

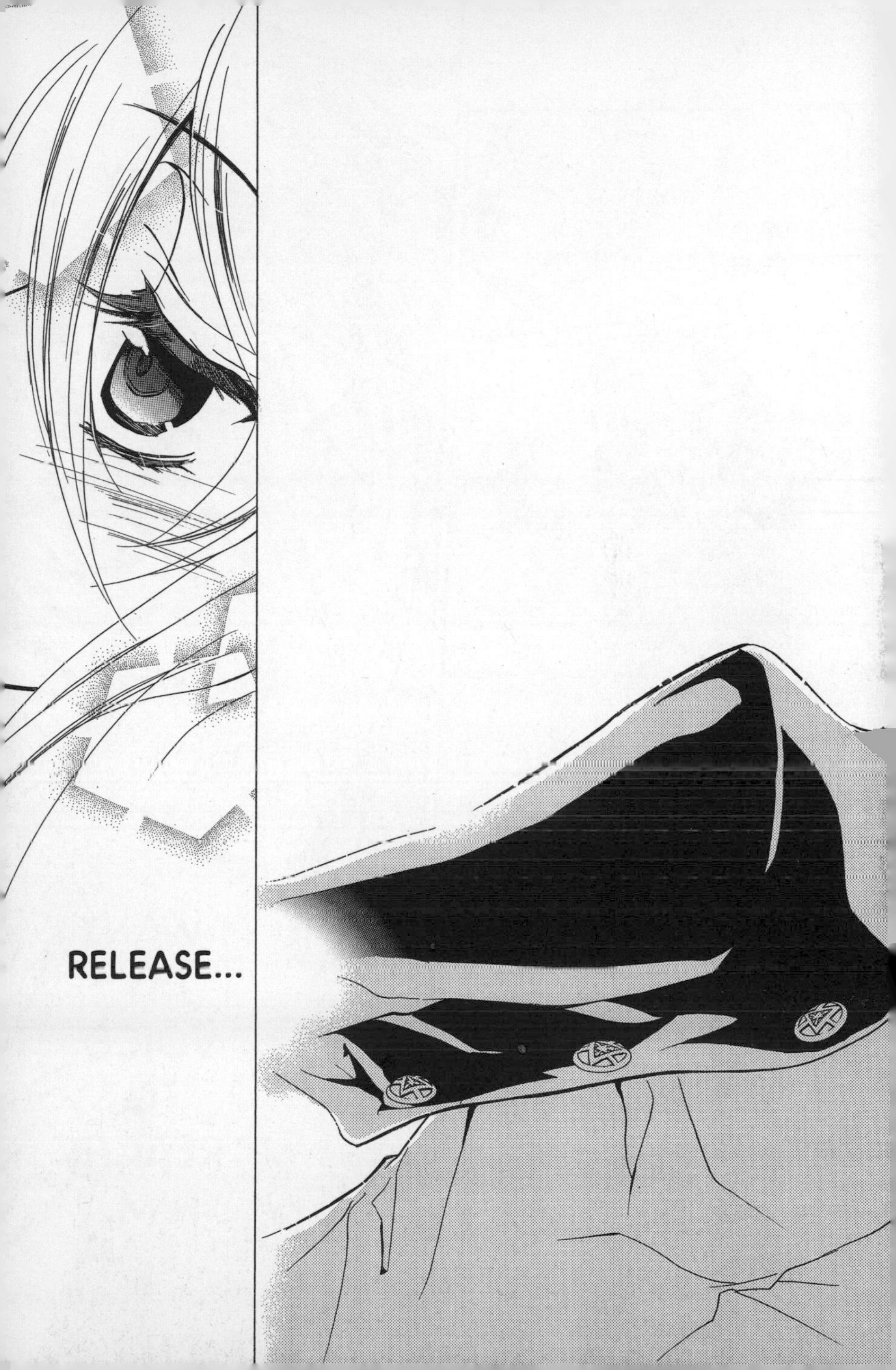
RELEASE...

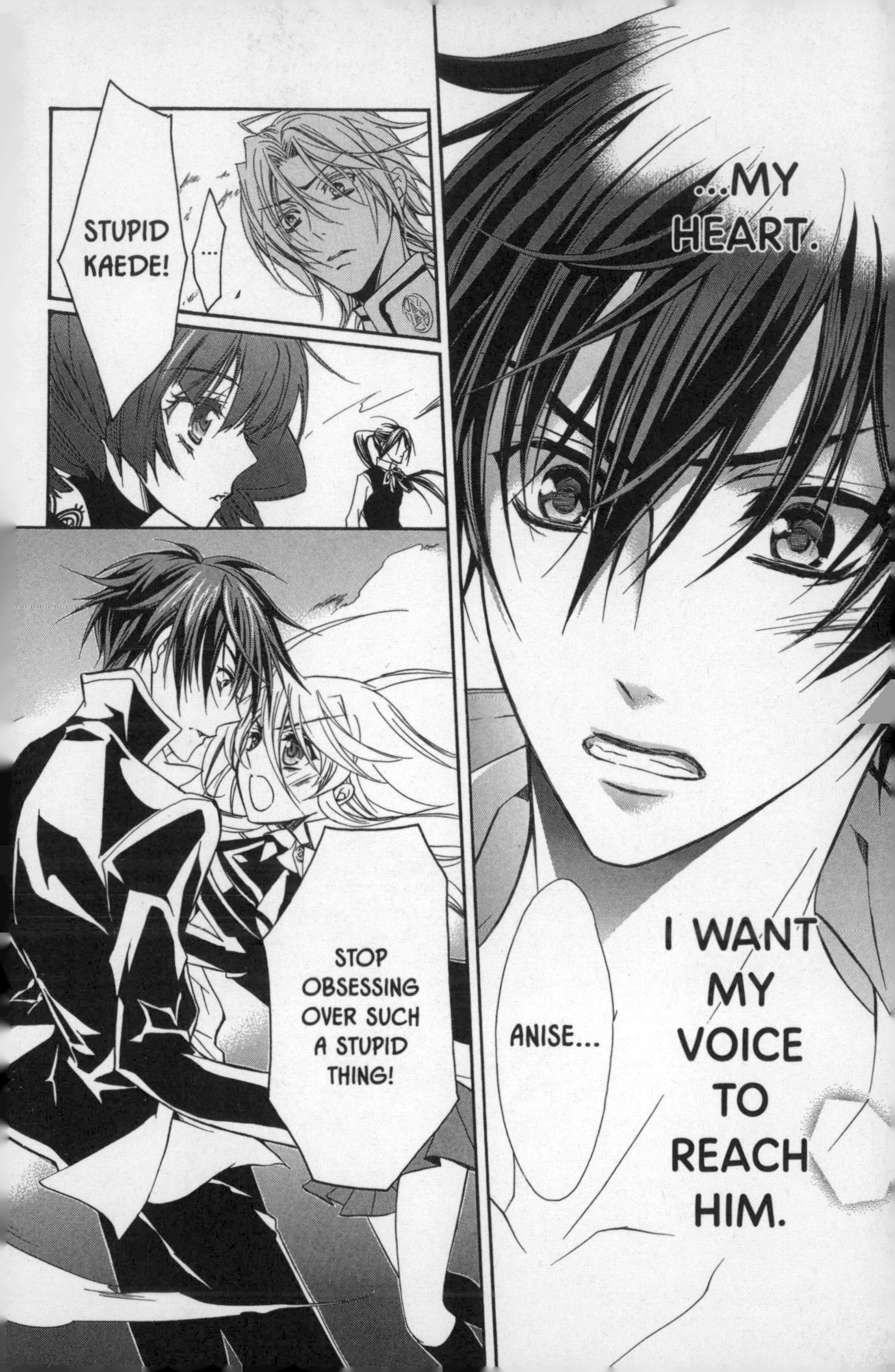

...MY HEART.
I WANT MY VOICE TO REACH HIM.
ANISE...
...
STUPID KAEDE!
STOP OBSESSING OVER SUCH A STUPID THING!

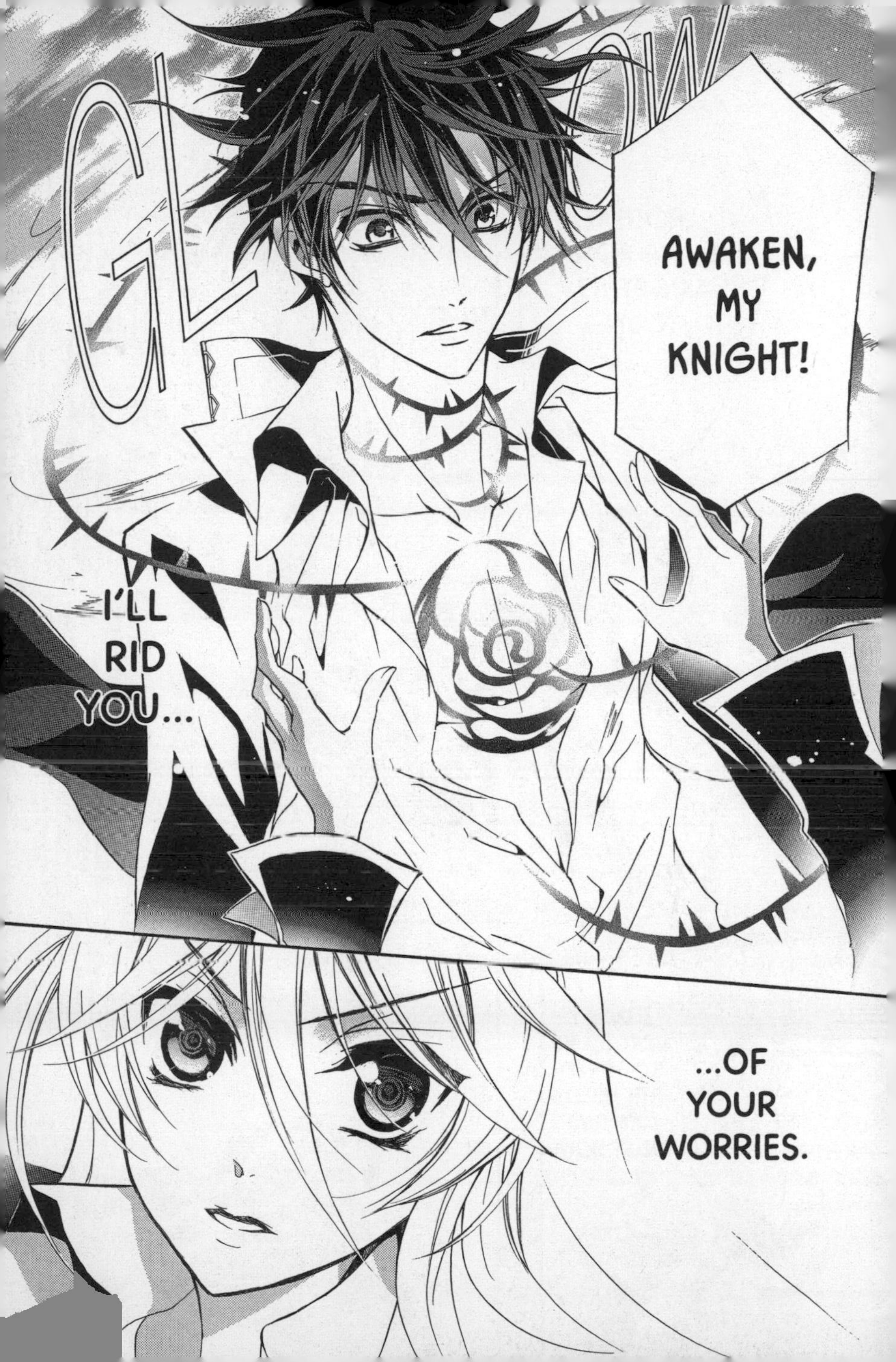
GLOW
AWAKEN, MY KNIGHT!
I'LL RID YOU...
...OF YOUR WORRIES.

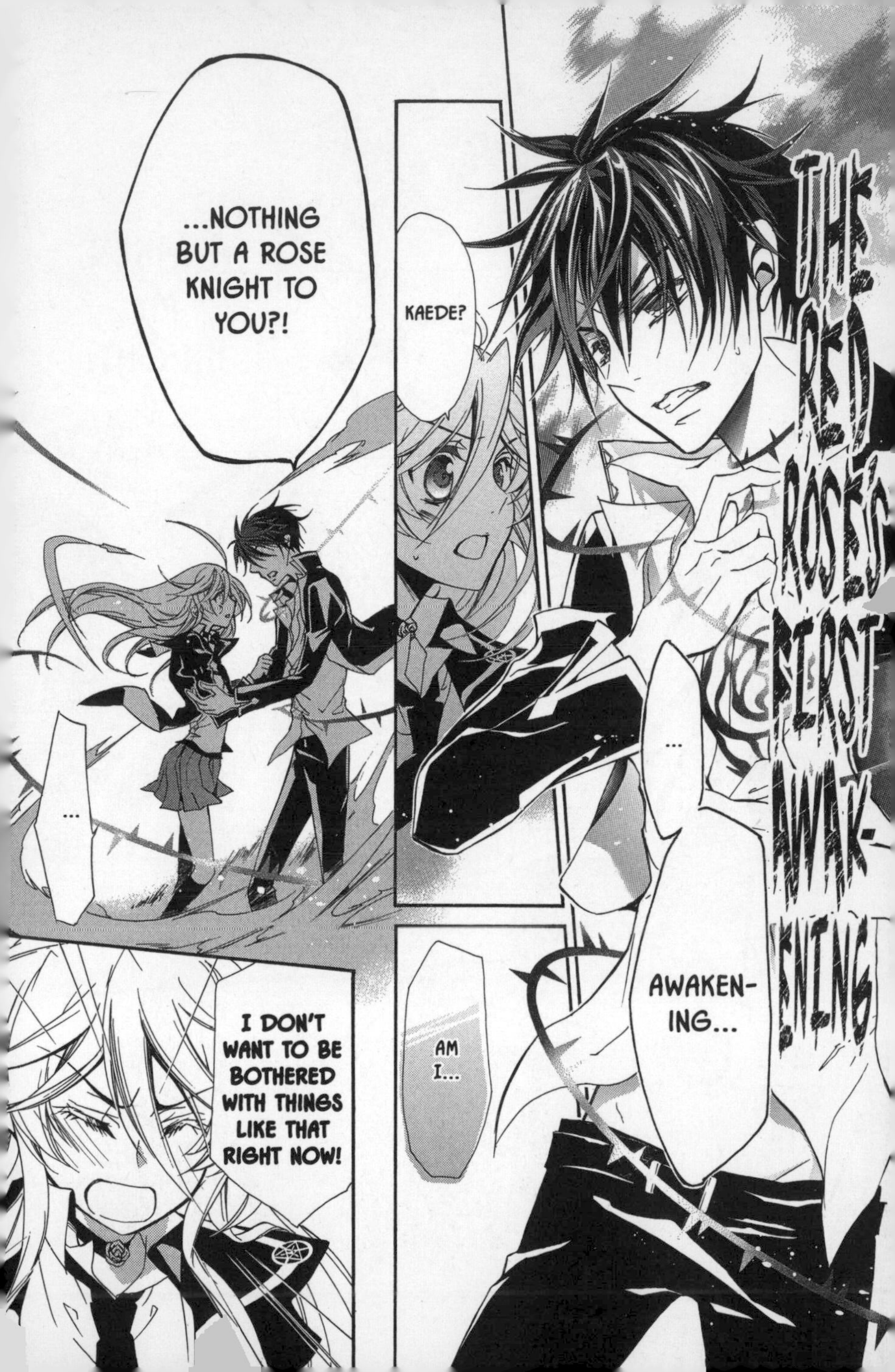
THE RED ROSE'S FIRST AWAK-ENING
...
AWAKEN-ING...
KAEDE?
...NOTHING BUT A ROSE KNIGHT TO YOU?!
...
AM I...
I DON'T WANT TO BE BOTHERED WITH THINGS LIKE THAT RIGHT NOW!

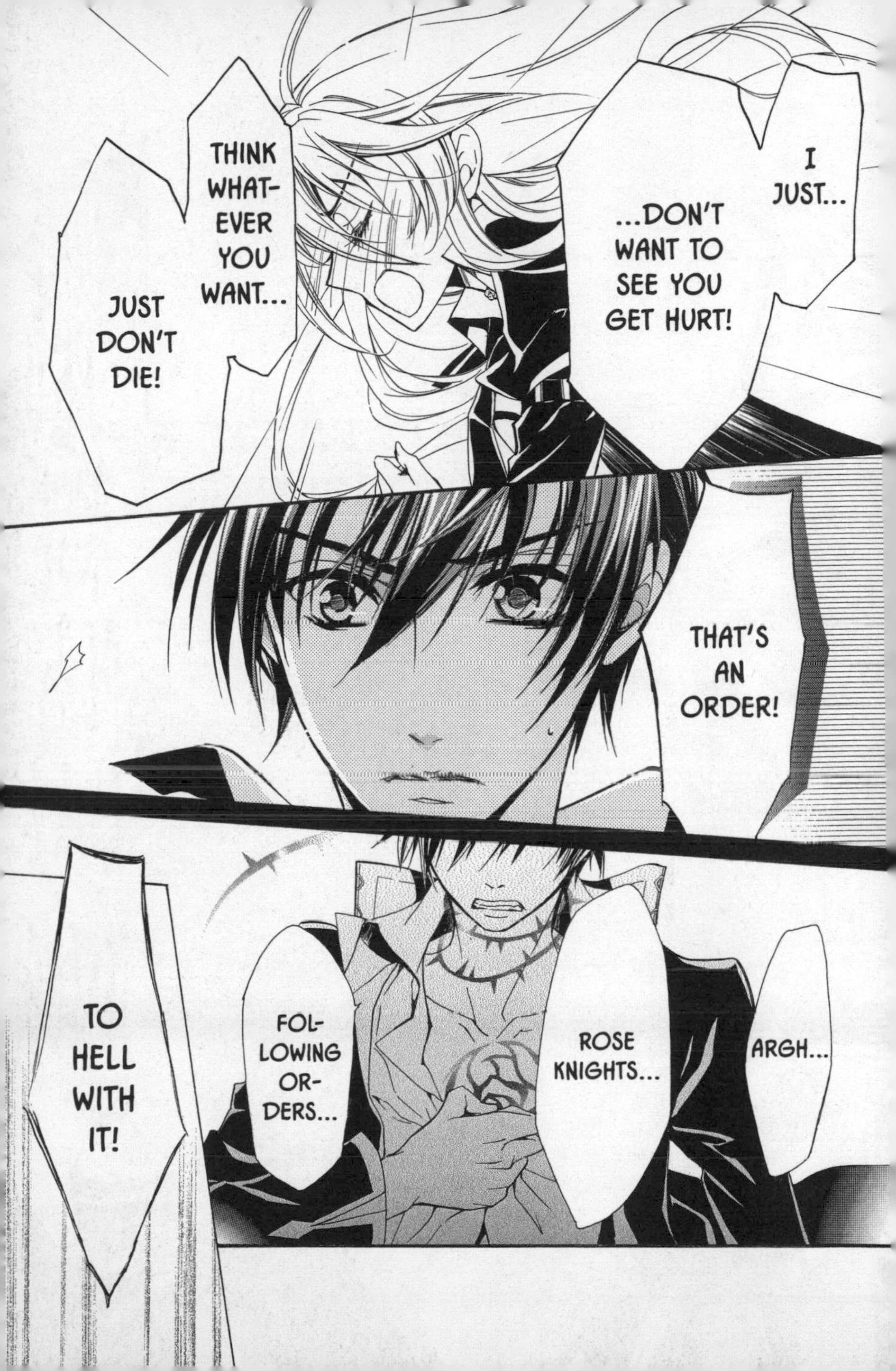
I JUST...
...DON'T WANT TO SEE YOU GET HURT!
THINK WHATEVER YOU WANT...
JUST DON'T DIE!
THAT'S AN ORDER!
ARGH...
ROSE KNIGHTS...
FOLLOWING ORDERS...
TO HELL WITH IT!

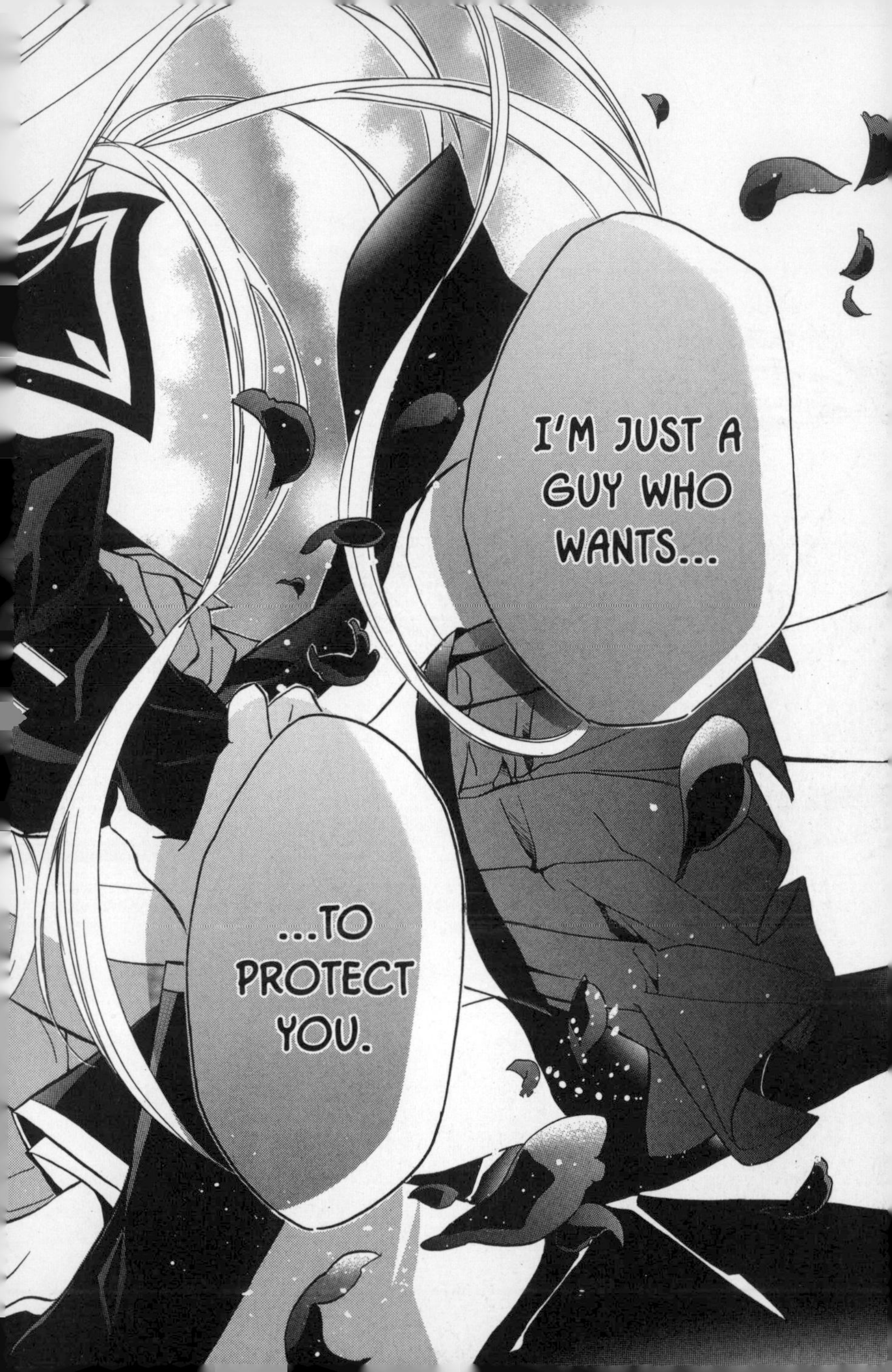
I'M JUST A GUY WHO WANTS...
...TO PROTECT YOU.

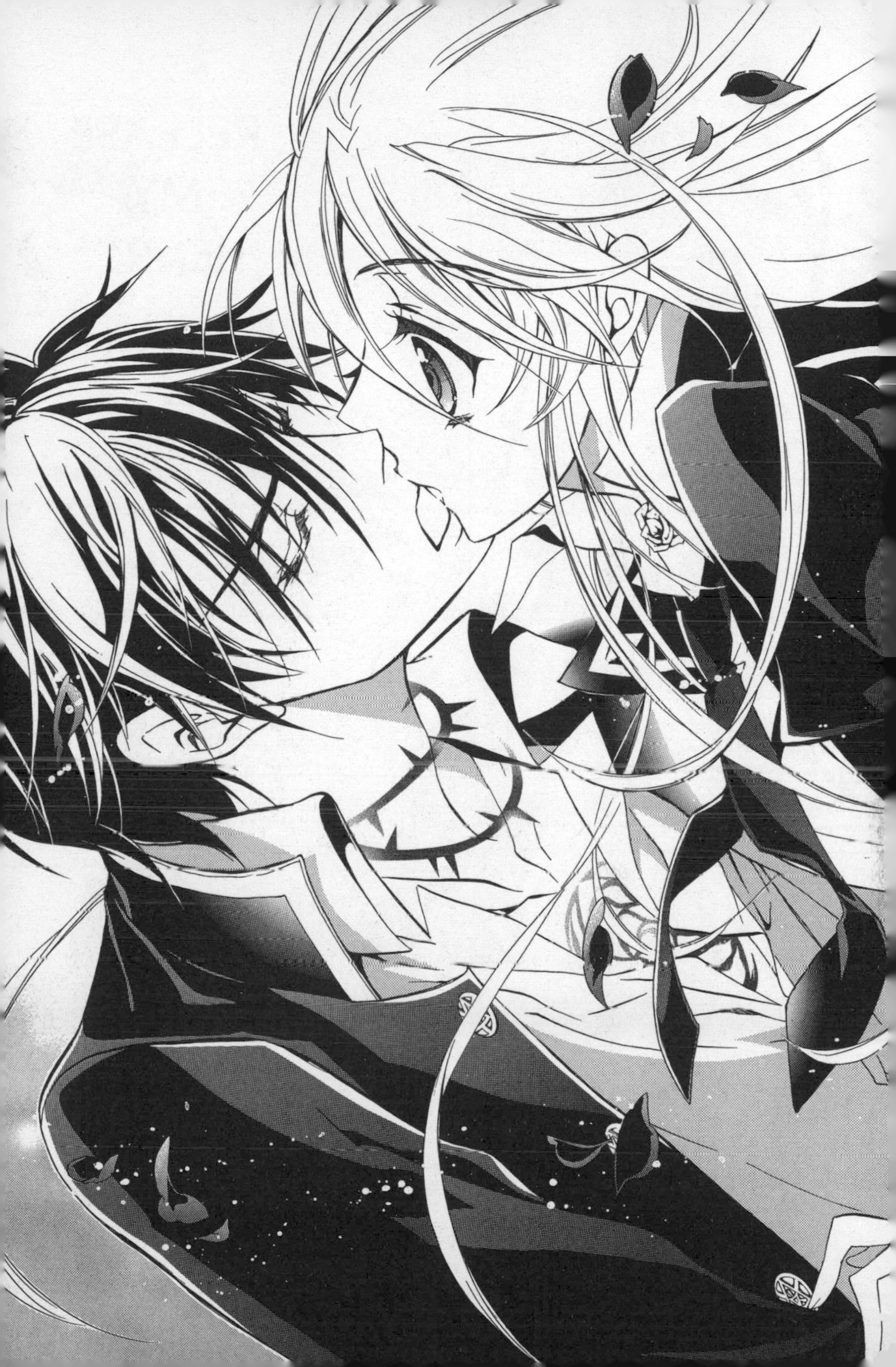

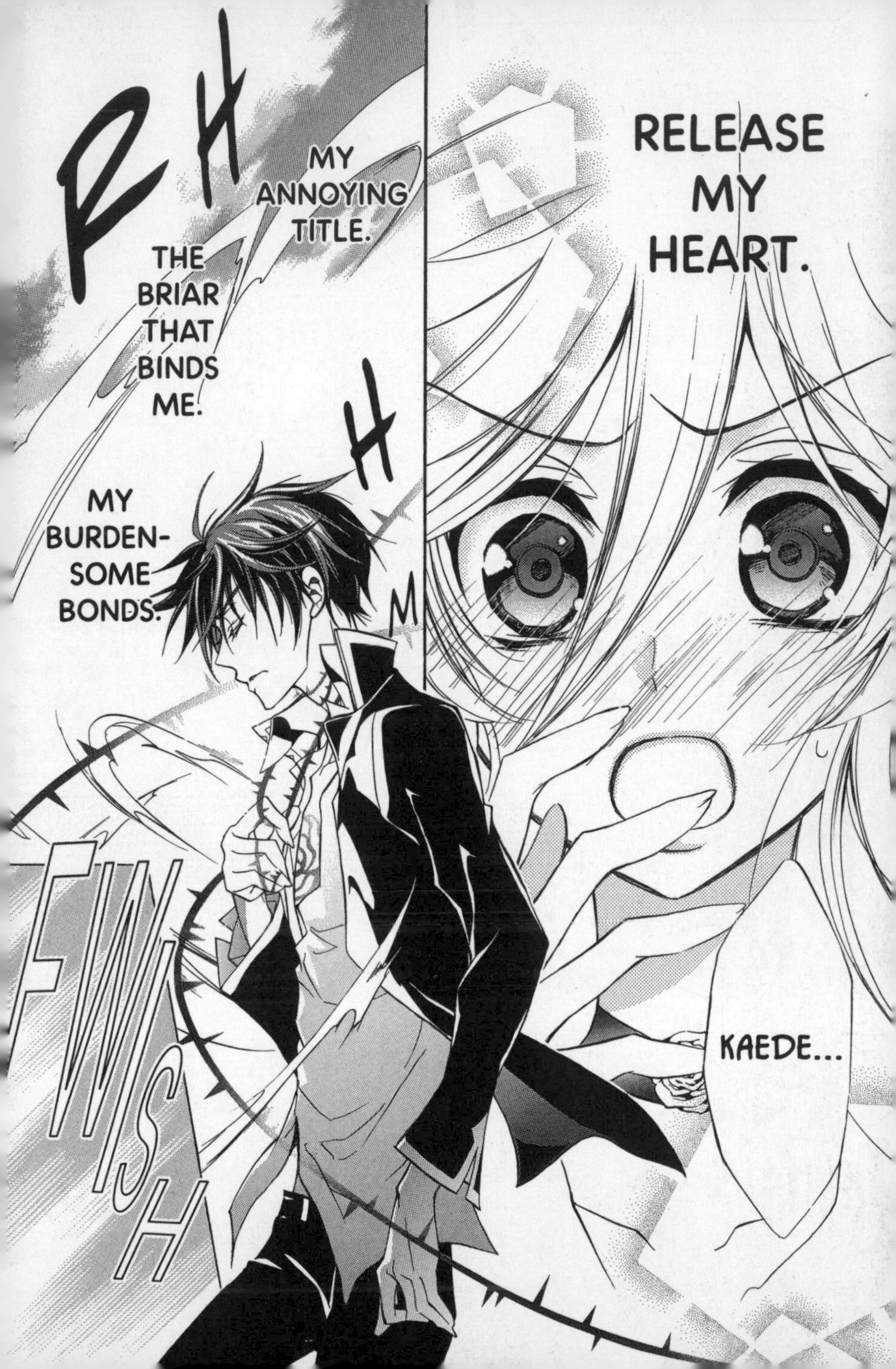
RELEASE MY HEART.
KAEDE...
MY ANNOYING TITLE.
THE BRIAR THAT BINDS ME.
MY BURDEN-SOME BONDS.
RHHM
FWISH

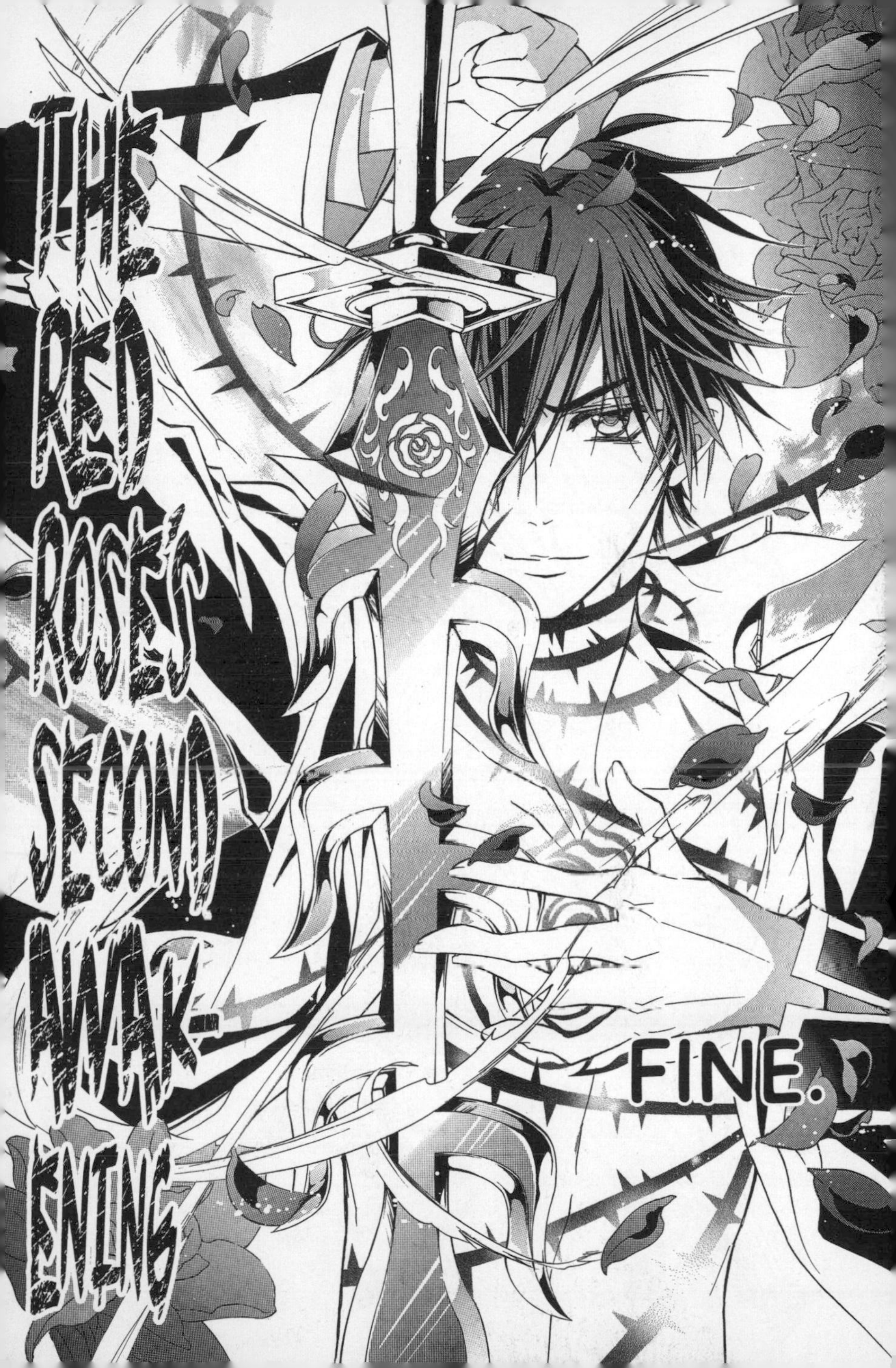
THE RED ROSE'S SECOND AWAKENING
FINE.

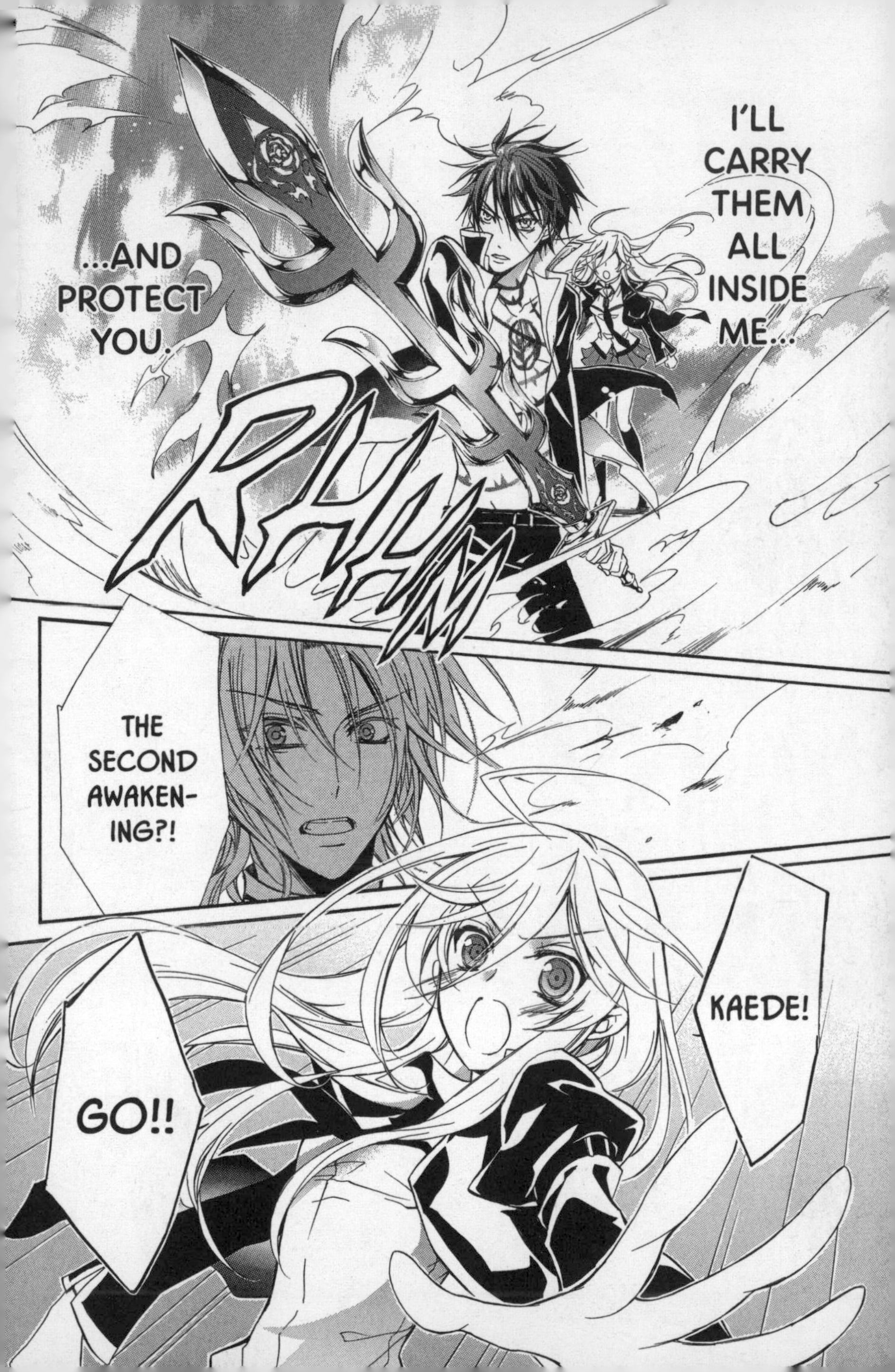
I'LL CARRY THEM ALL INSIDE ME...
...AND PROTECT YOU.
THE SECOND AWAKEN-ING?!
KAEDE!
GO!!

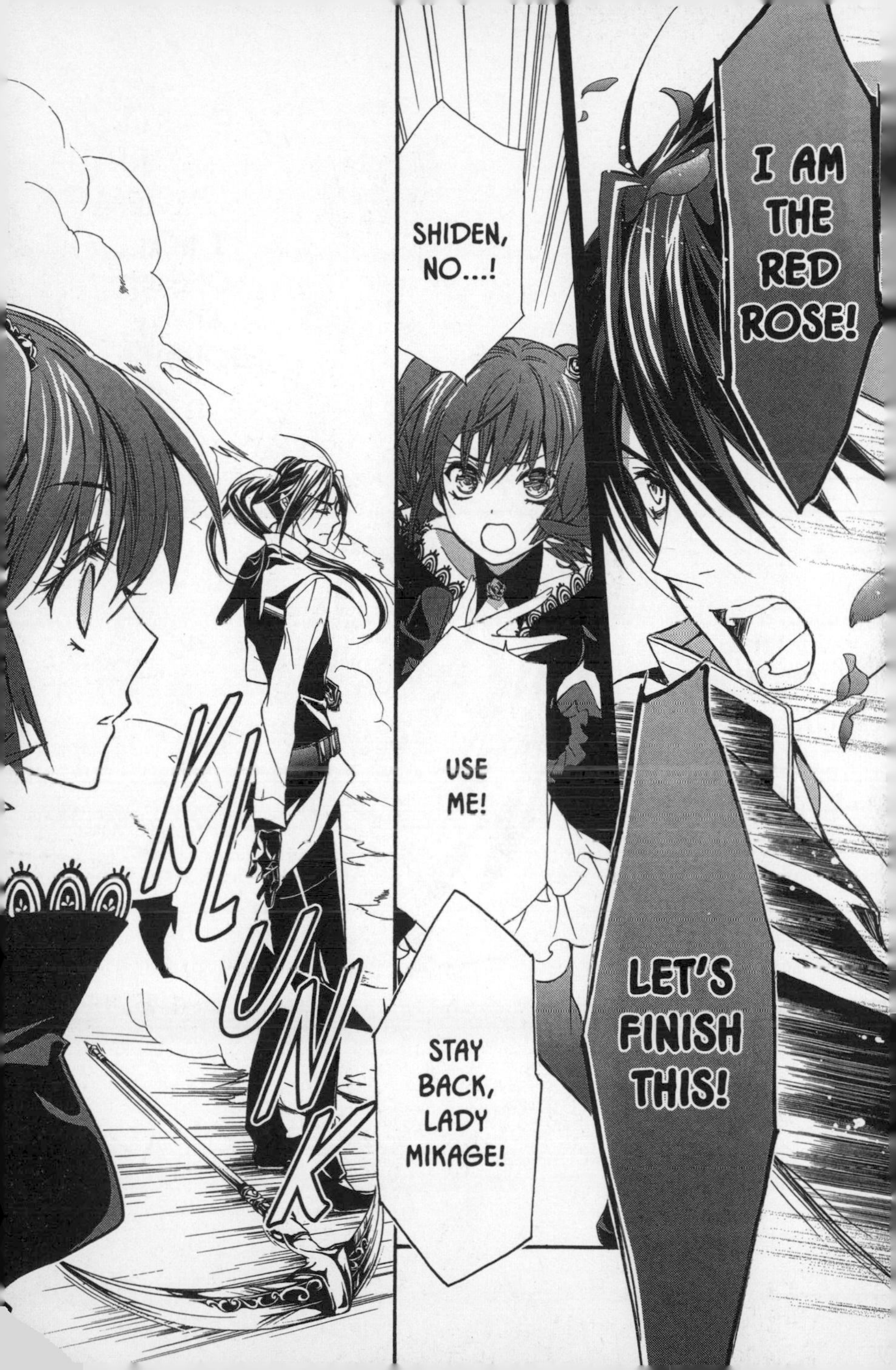
I AM THE RED ROSE!
LET'S FINISH THIS!
SHIDEN, NO...!
USE ME!
STAY BACK, LADY MIKAGE!
KLUNK

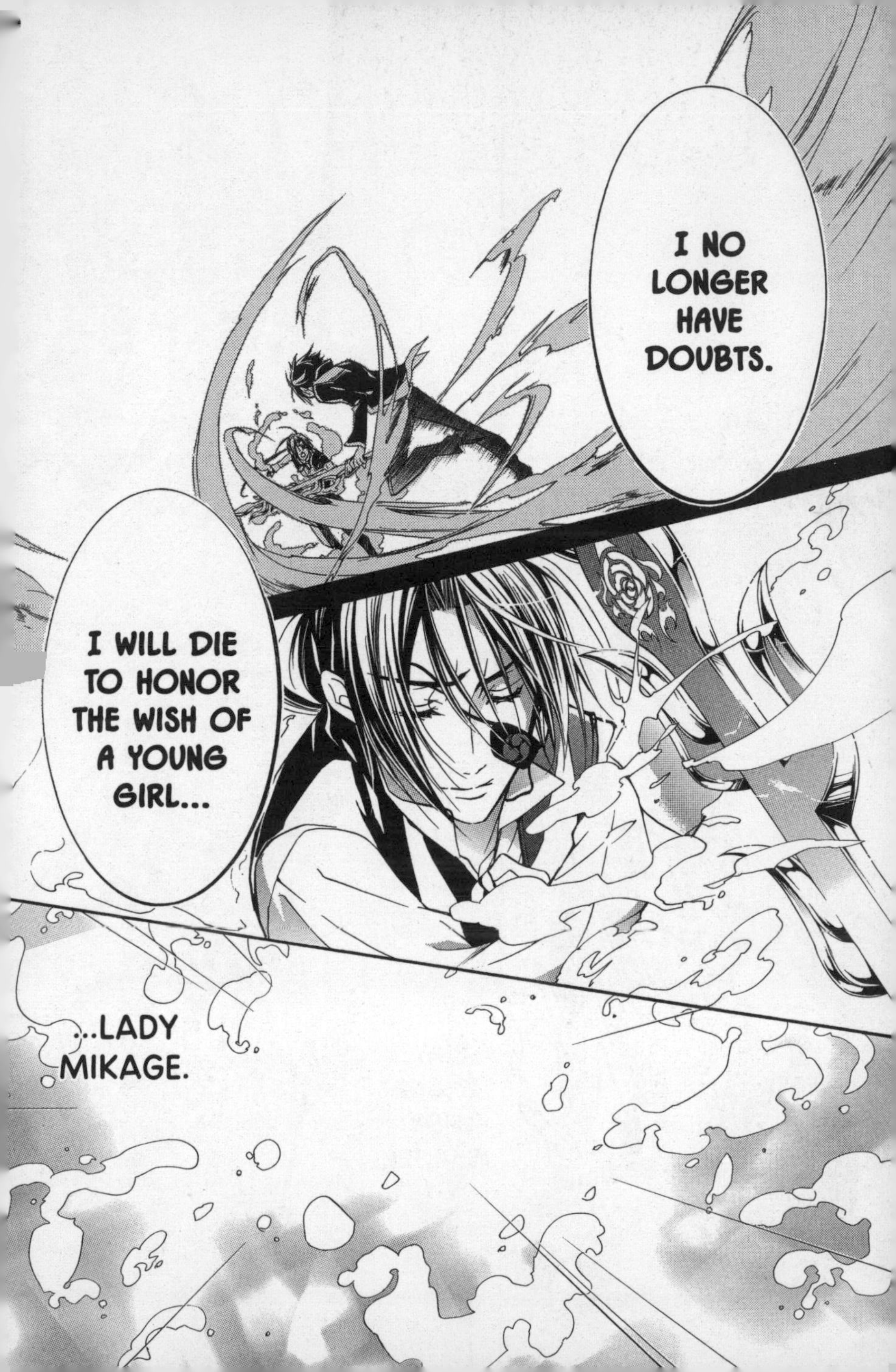
I NO LONGER HAVE DOUBTS.
I WILL DIE TO HONOR THE WISH OF A YOUNG GIRL...
...LADY MIKAGE.

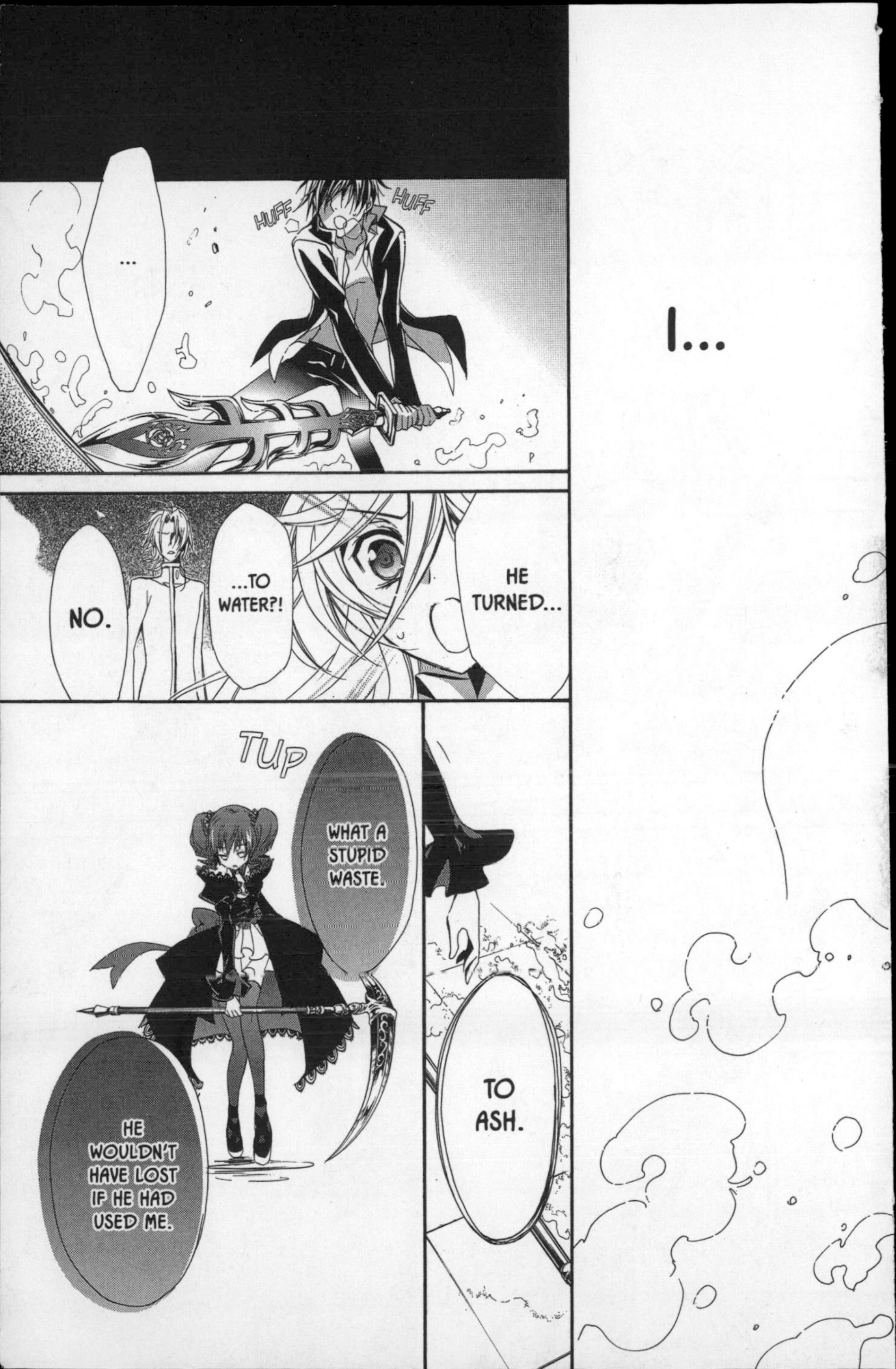
I...
HUFF HUFF
...
HE TURNED...
...TO WATER?!
NO.
TO ASH.
TUP
WHAT A STUPID WASTE.
HE WOULDN'T HAVE LOST IF HE HAD USED ME.

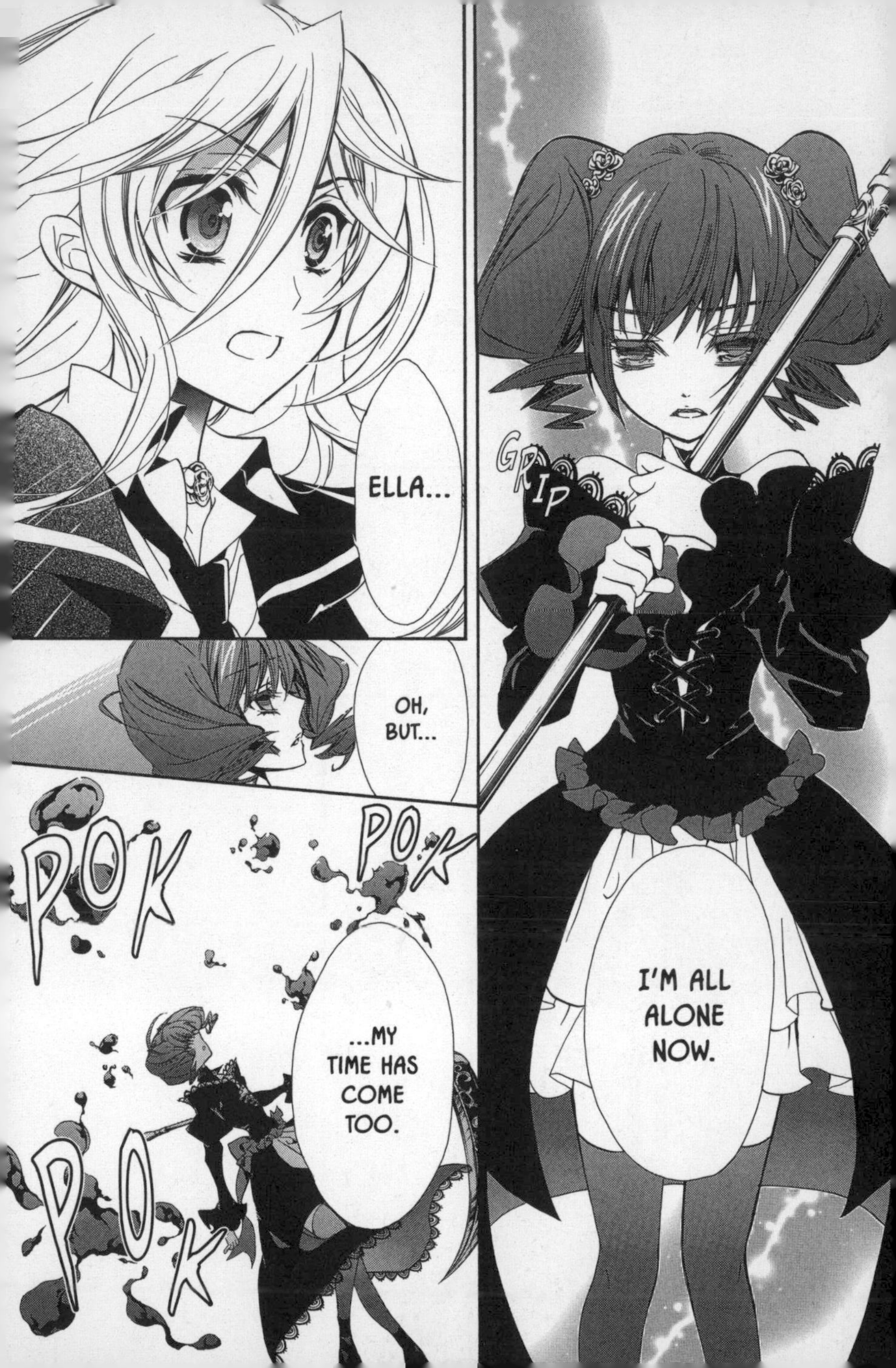
GRIP
I'M ALL ALONE NOW.
ELLA...
OH, BUT...
POK
POK
...MY TIME HAS COME TOO.
POK

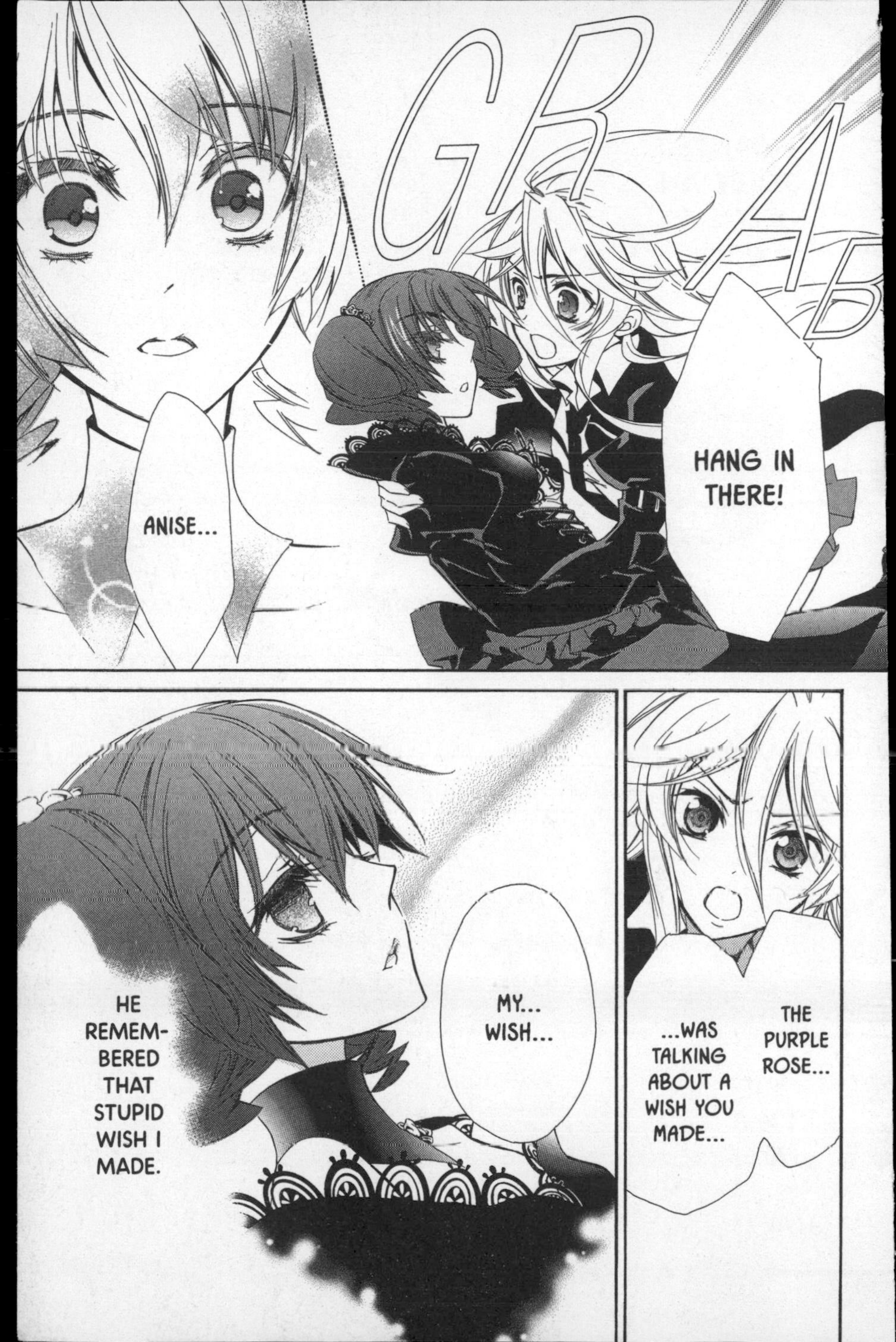
GRAB
HANG IN THERE!
ANISE...
THE PURPLE ROSE...
...WAS TALKING ABOUT A WISH YOU MADE...
MY... WISH...
HE REMEMBERED THAT STUPID WISH I MADE.

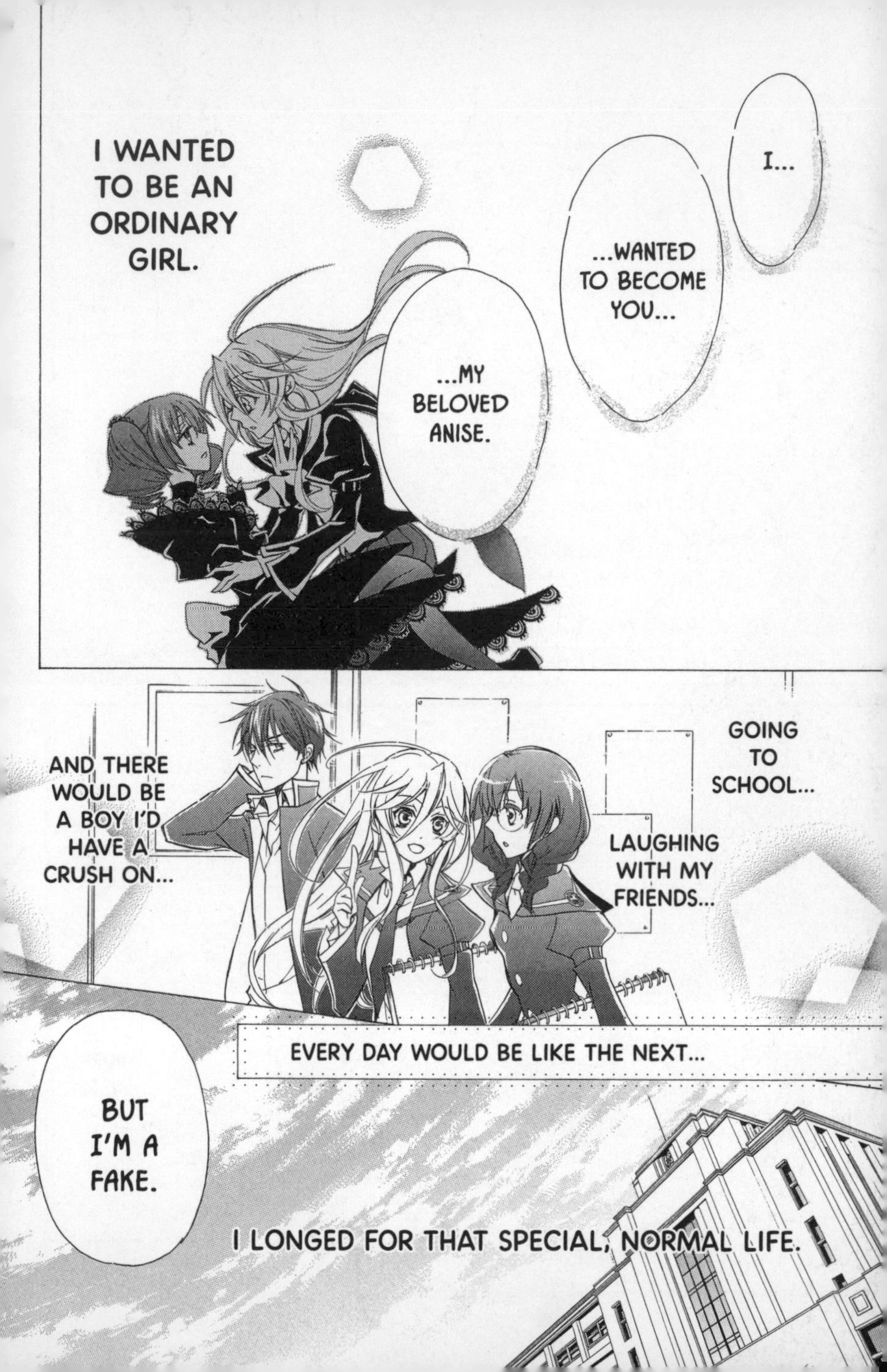
I...
...WANTED TO BECOME YOU...
...MY BELOVED ANISE.
I WANTED TO BE AN ORDINARY GIRL.
GOING TO SCHOOL...
LAUGHING WITH MY FRIENDS...
AND THERE WOULD BE A BOY I'D HAVE A CRUSH ON...
EVERY DAY WOULD BE LIKE THE NEXT...
I LONGED FOR THAT SPECIAL, NORMAL LIFE.
BUT I'M A FAKE.

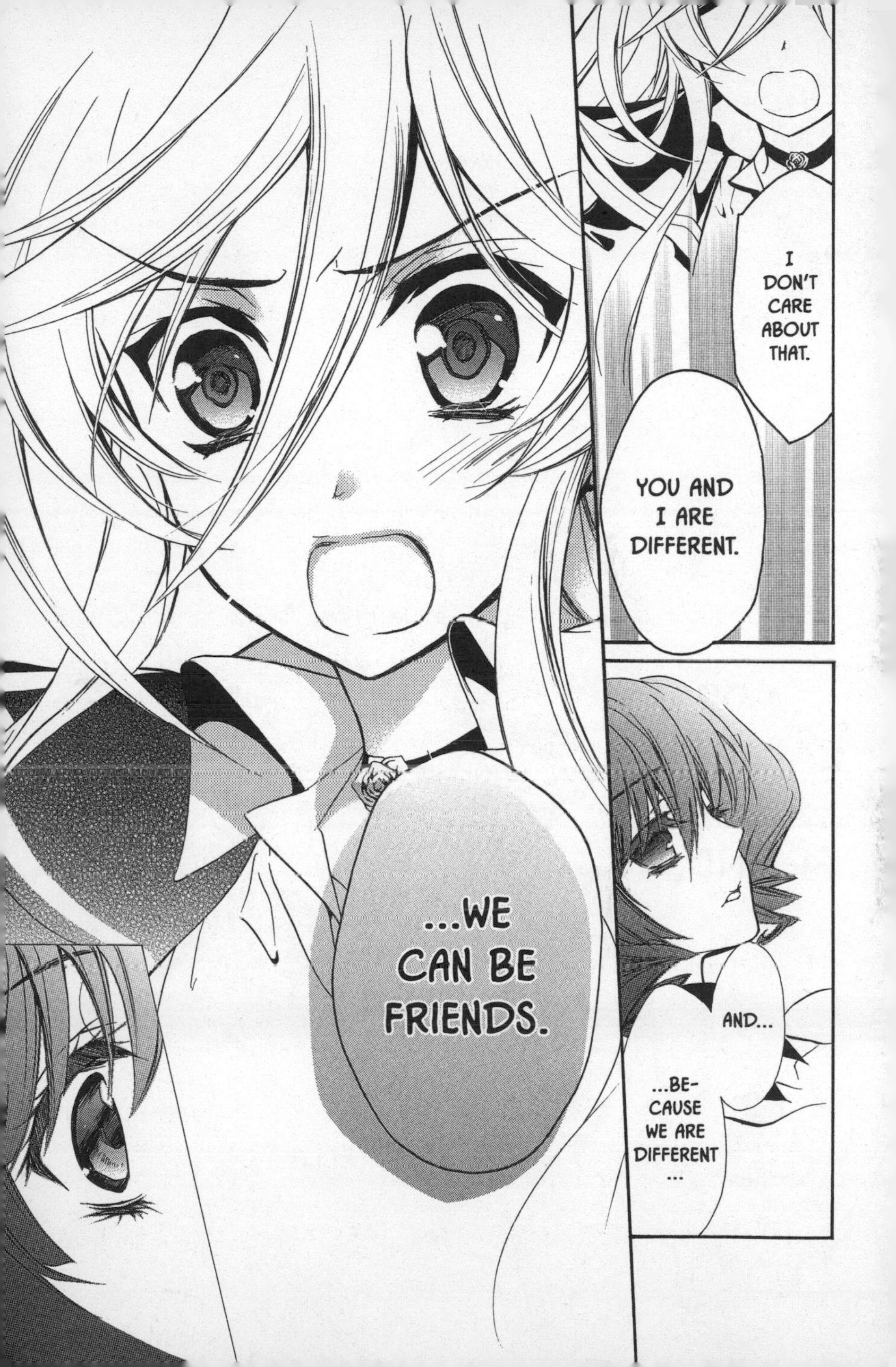
I DON'T CARE ABOUT THAT.
YOU AND I ARE DIFFERENT.
AND...
...BE-CAUSE WE ARE DIFFERENT...
...WE CAN BE FRIENDS.

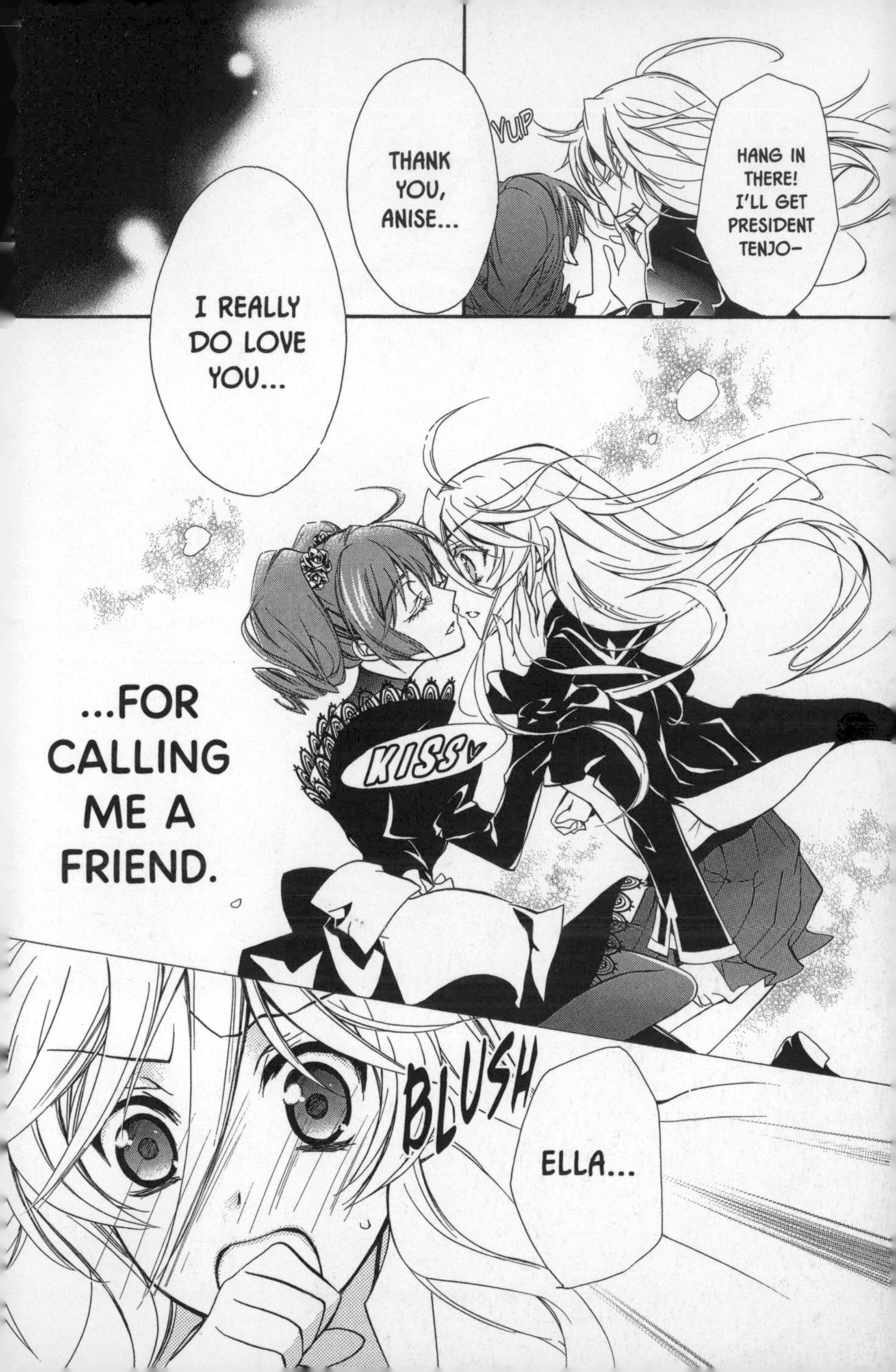
HANG IN THERE! I'LL GET PRESIDENT TENJO–
YUP
THANK YOU, ANISE...
I REALLY DO LOVE YOU...
...FOR CALLING ME A FRIEND.
KISS♥
BLUSH
ELLA...

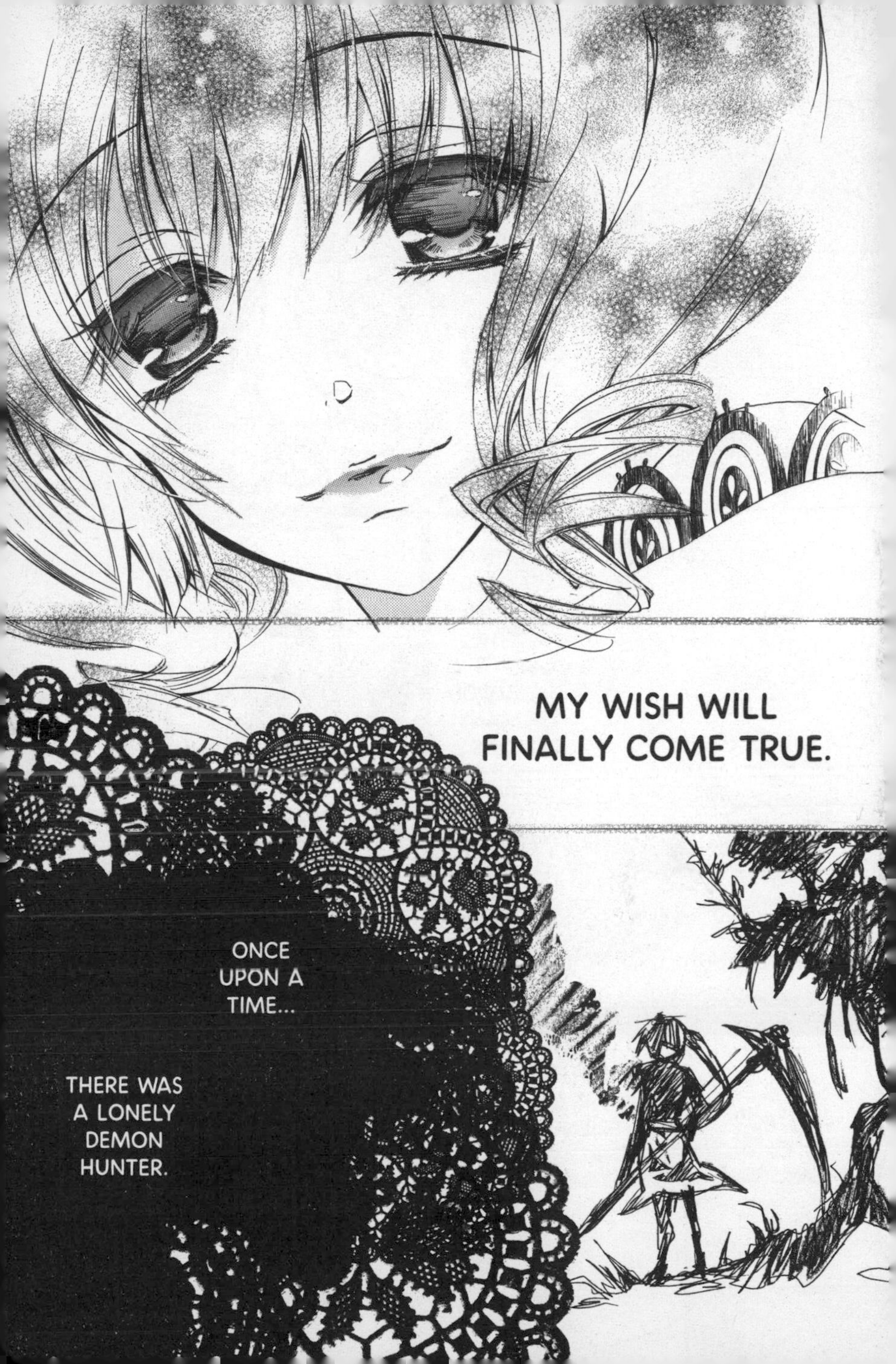
MY WISH WILL FINALLY COME TRUE.
ONCE UPON A TIME...
THERE WAS A LONELY DEMON HUNTER.

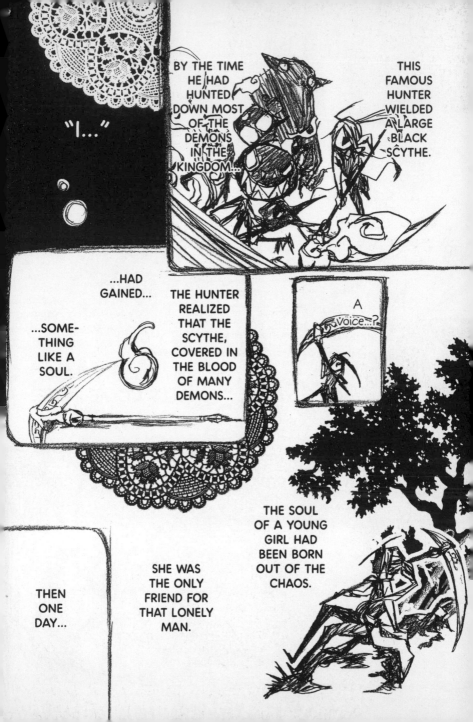

"I..."

THIS FAMOUS HUNTER WIELDED A LARGE BLACK SCYTHE.

BY THE TIME HE HAD HUNTED DOWN MOST OF THE DEMONS IN THE KINGDOM...

...HAD GAINED...

THE HUNTER REALIZED THAT THE SCYTHE, COVERED IN THE BLOOD OF MANY DEMONS...

...SOMETHING LIKE A SOUL.

A voice...?

THE SOUL OF A YOUNG GIRL HAD BEEN BORN OUT OF THE CHAOS.

SHE WAS THE ONLY FRIEND FOR THAT LONELY MAN.

THEN ONE DAY...

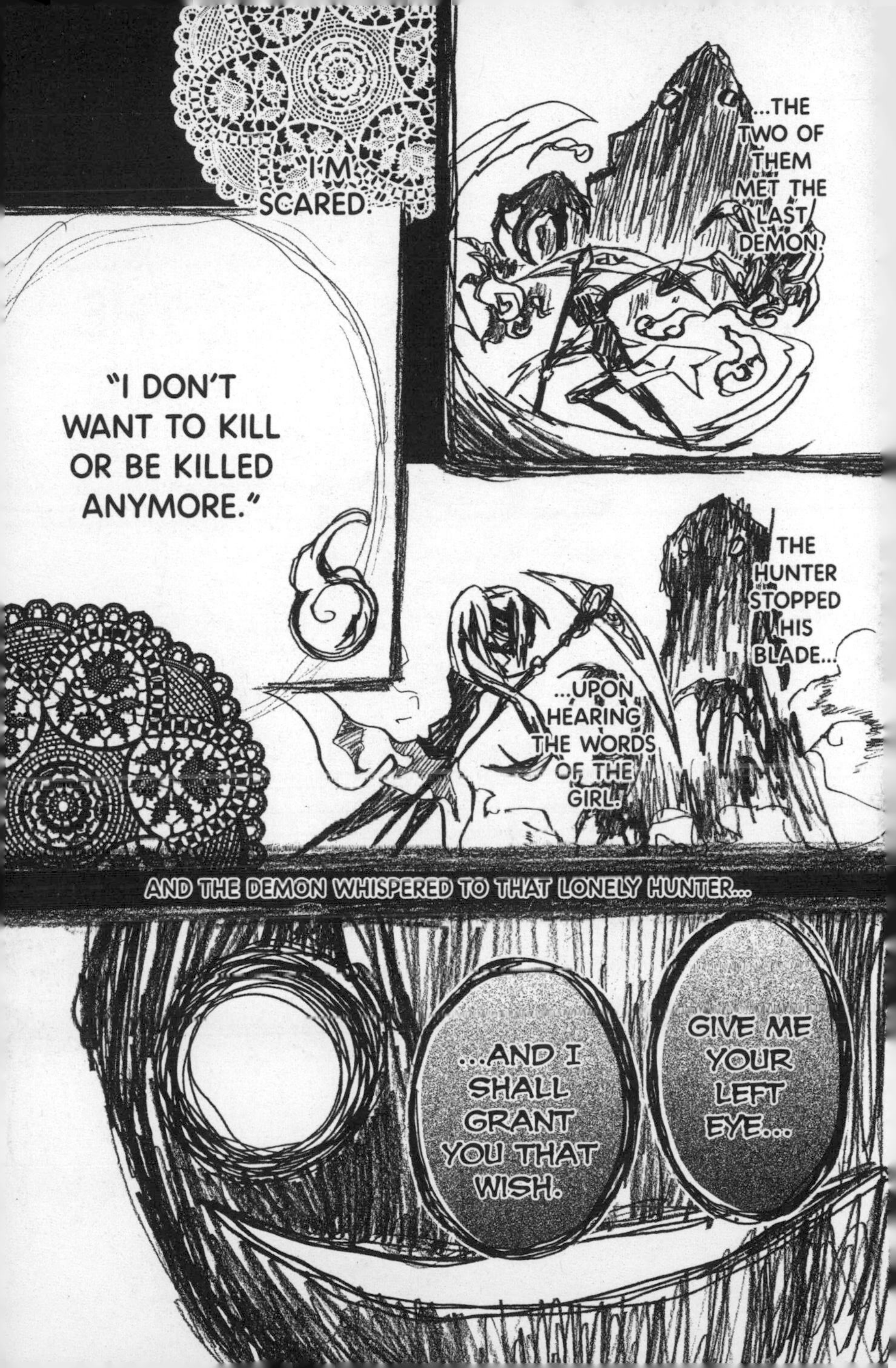
...THE TWO OF THEM MET THE LAST DEMON.
I'M SCARED.
"I DON'T WANT TO KILL OR BE KILLED ANYMORE."
THE HUNTER STOPPED HIS BLADE...
...UPON HEARING THE WORDS OF THE GIRL.
AND THE DEMON WHISPERED TO THAT LONELY HUNTER...
GIVE ME YOUR LEFT EYE...
...AND I SHALL GRANT YOU THAT WISH.

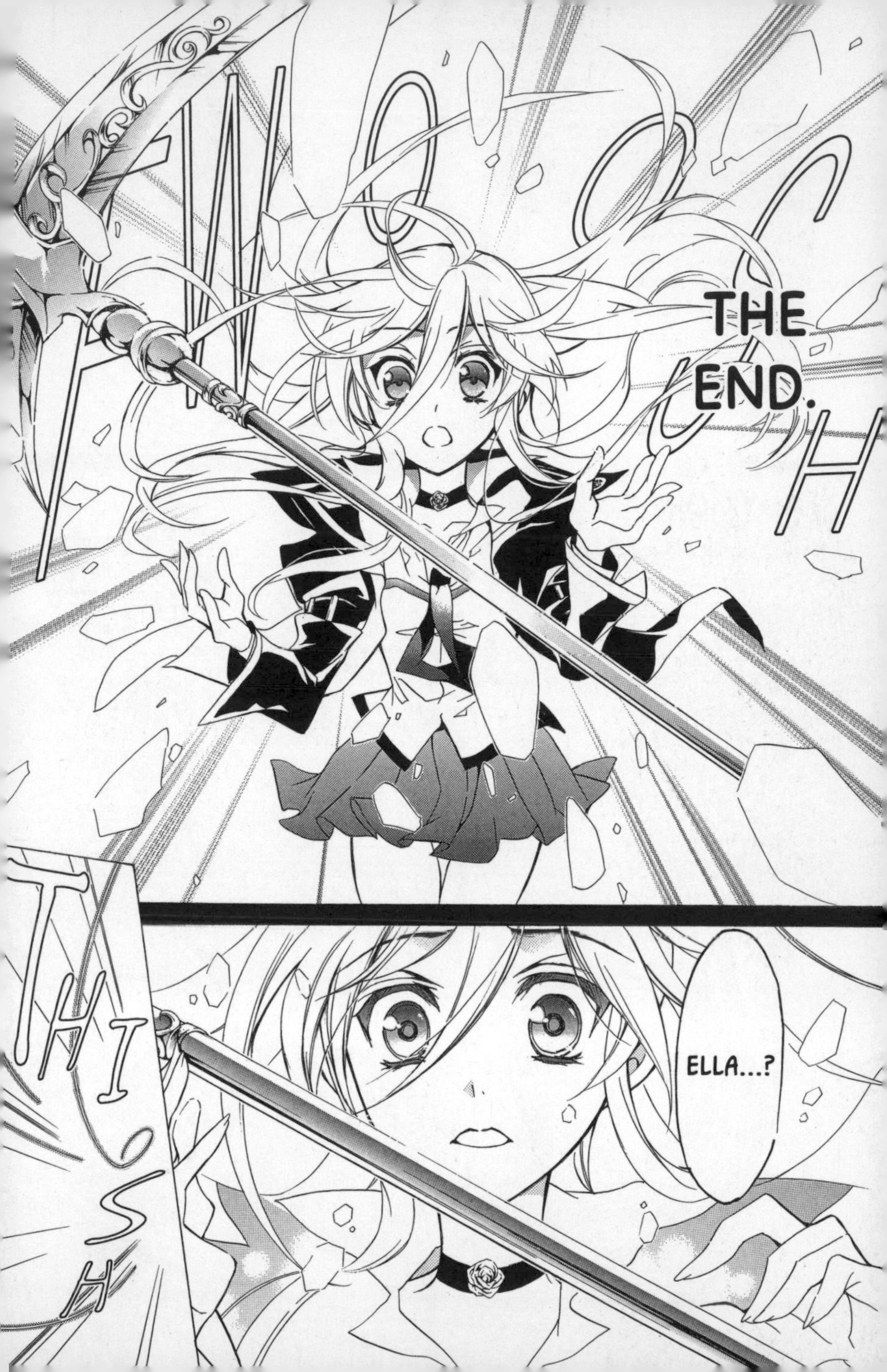
THE END.
ELLA...?

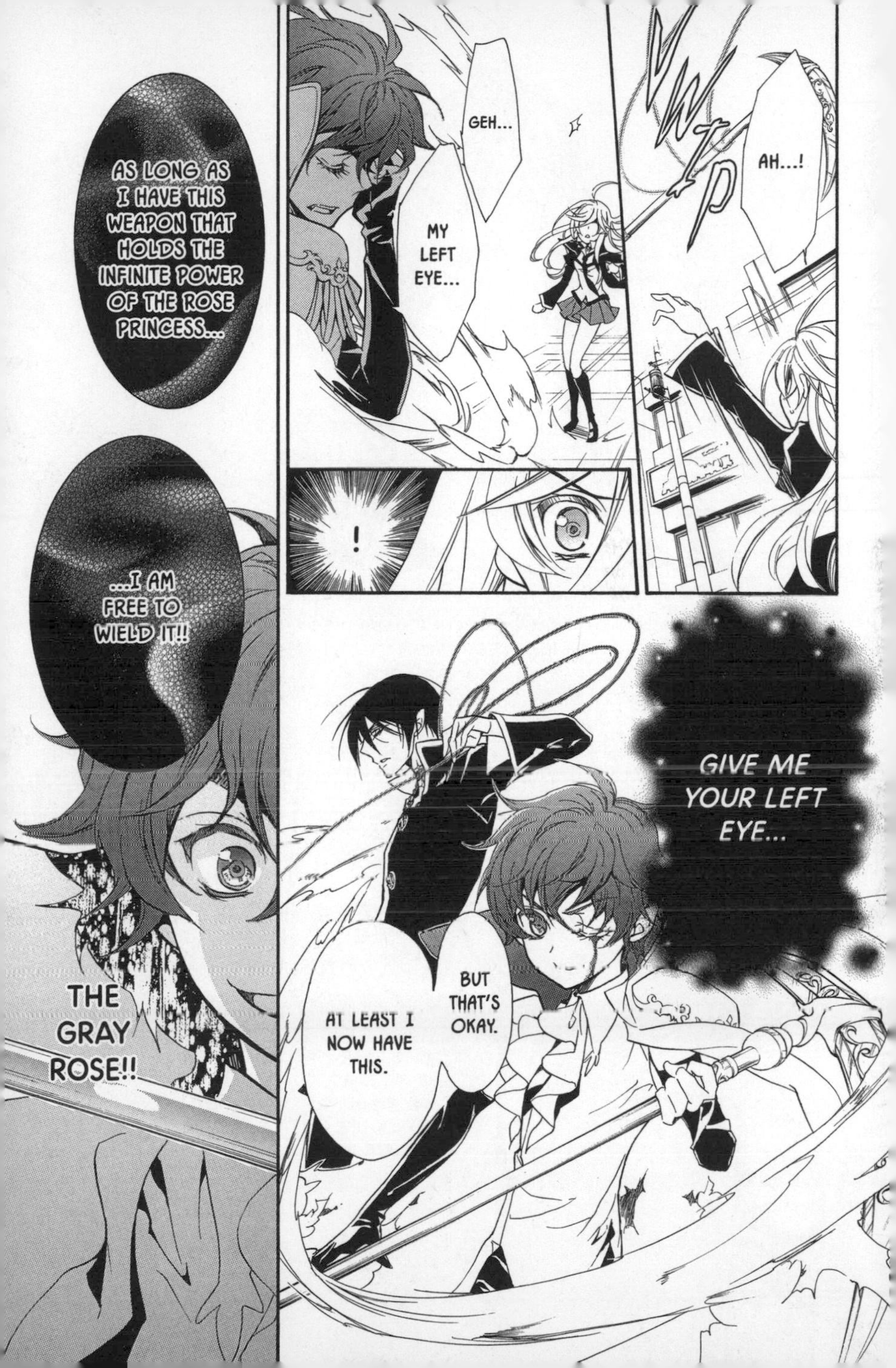

VWIP
AH...!
GEH...
MY LEFT EYE...
!
GIVE ME YOUR LEFT EYE...
BUT THAT'S OKAY.
AT LEAST I NOW HAVE THIS.
AS LONG AS I HAVE THIS WEAPON THAT HOLDS THE INFINITE POWER OF THE ROSE PRINCESS...
...I AM FREE TO WIELD IT!!
THE GRAY ROSE!!

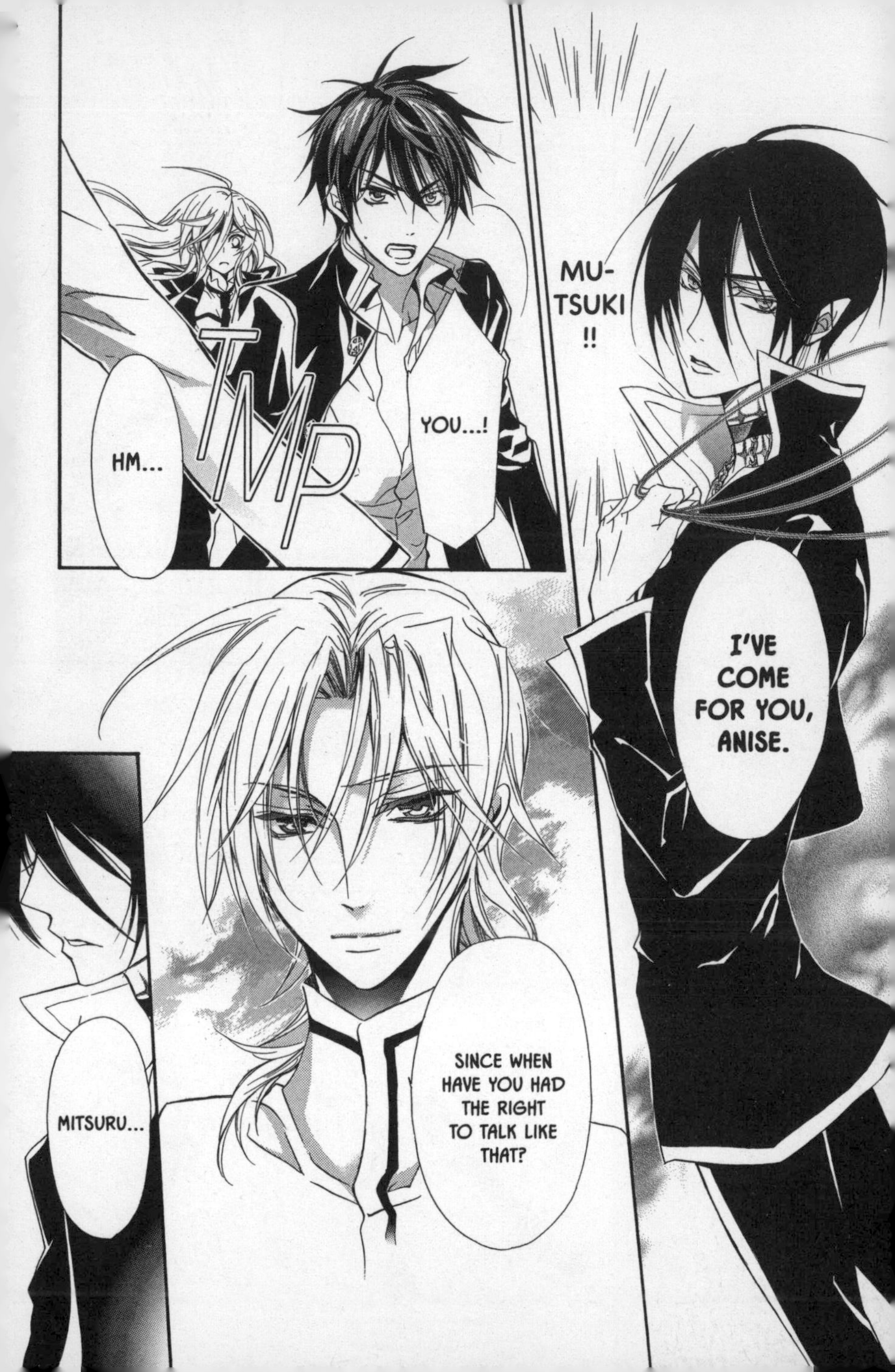

MU-TSUKI!!
I'VE COME FOR YOU, ANISE.
YOU...!
TMP
HM...
SINCE WHEN HAVE YOU HAD THE RIGHT TO TALK LIKE THAT?
MITSURU...

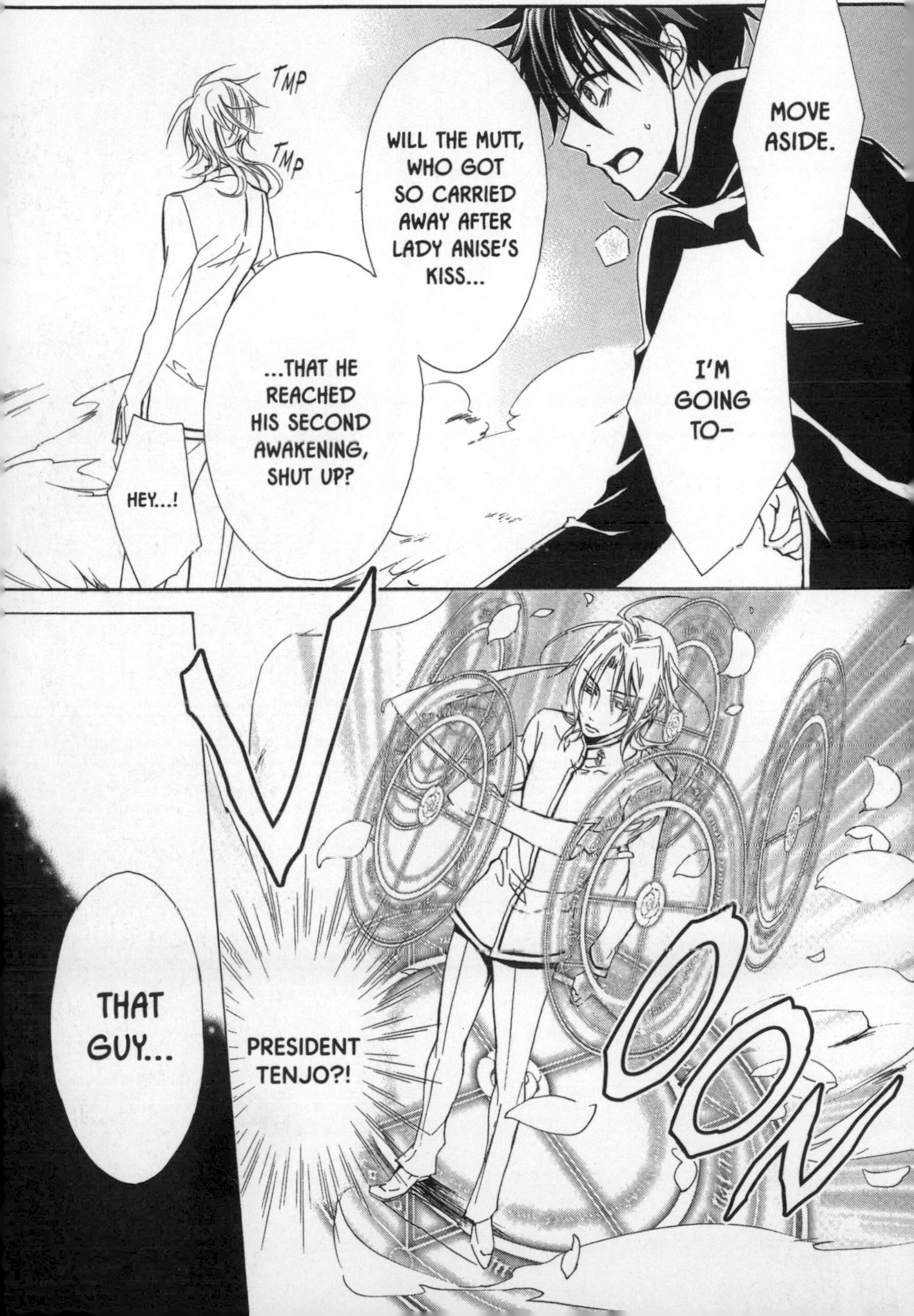
MOVE ASIDE.
I'M GOING TO-
WILL THE MUTT, WHO GOT SO CARRIED AWAY AFTER LADY ANISE'S KISS...
...THAT HE REACHED HIS SECOND AWAKENING, SHUT UP?
TMP
TMP
HEY...!
VOOON
PRESIDENT TENJO?!
THAT GUY...

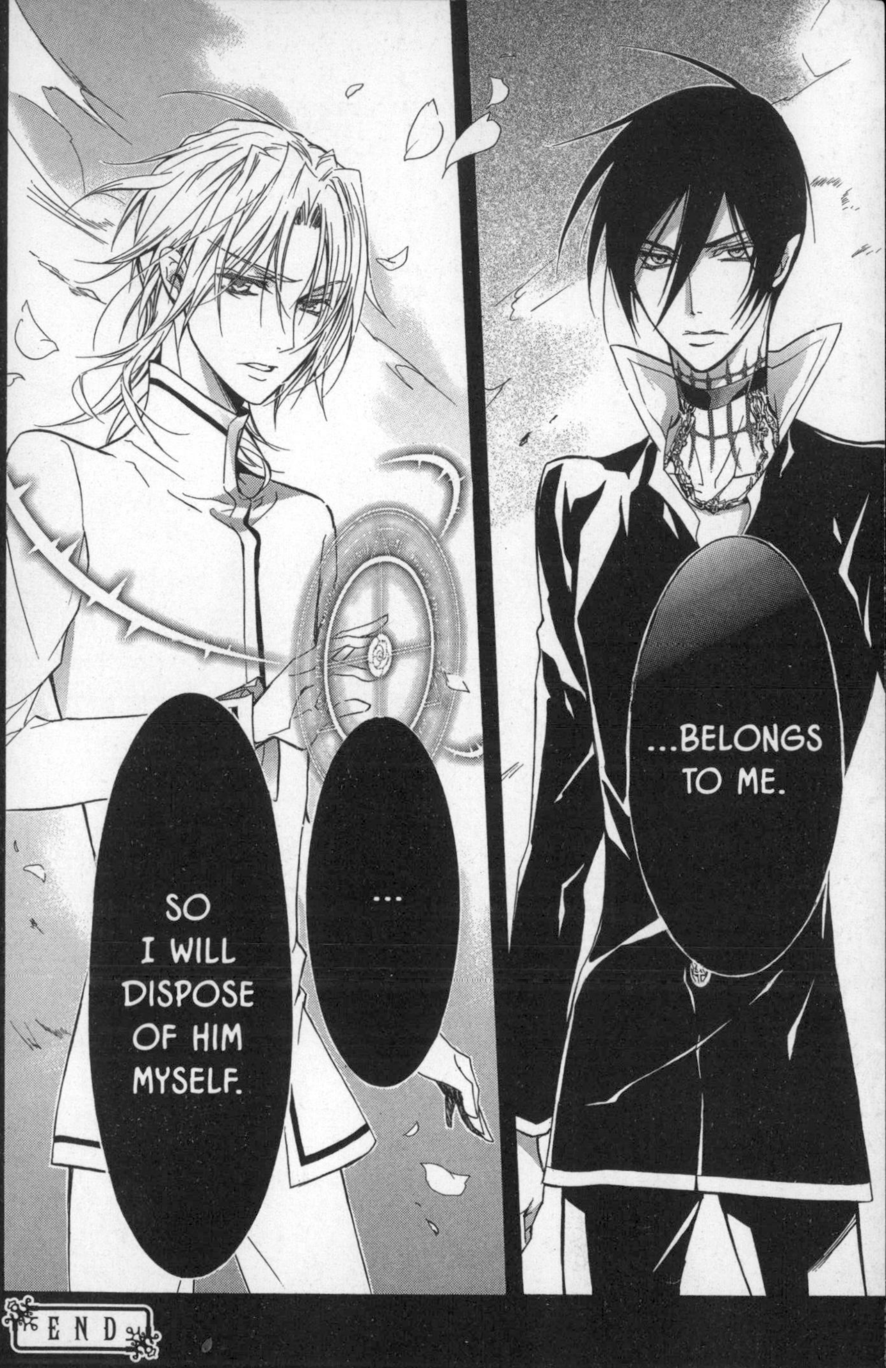
...BELONGS TO ME.
...
SO I WILL DISPOSE OF HIM MYSELF.
END

Kiss of the Rose Princess

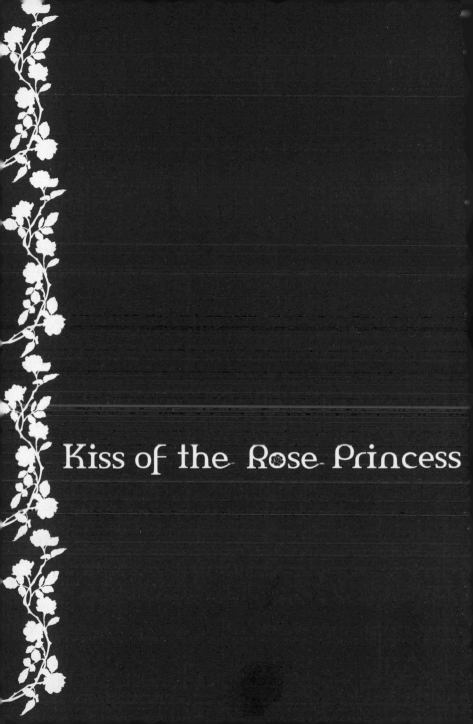

Kiss of the Rose
Princess

Punishment 33

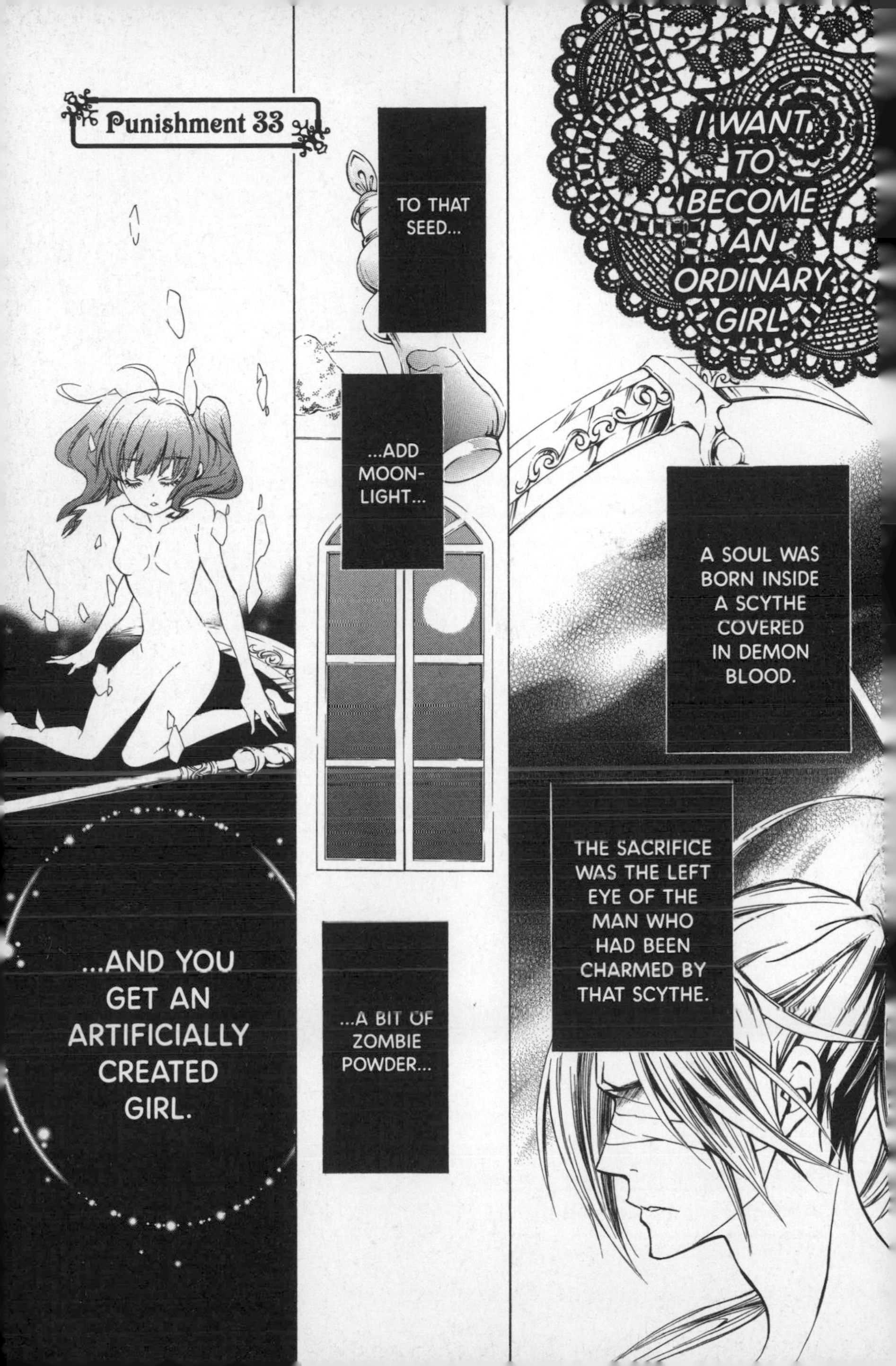
I WANT TO BECOME AN ORDINARY GIRL.
A SOUL WAS BORN INSIDE A SCYTHE COVERED IN DEMON BLOOD.
THE SACRIFICE WAS THE LEFT EYE OF THE MAN WHO HAD BEEN CHARMED BY THAT SCYTHE.
TO THAT SEED...
...ADD MOON-LIGHT...
...A BIT OF ZOMBIE POWDER...
...AND YOU GET AN ARTIFICIALLY CREATED GIRL.

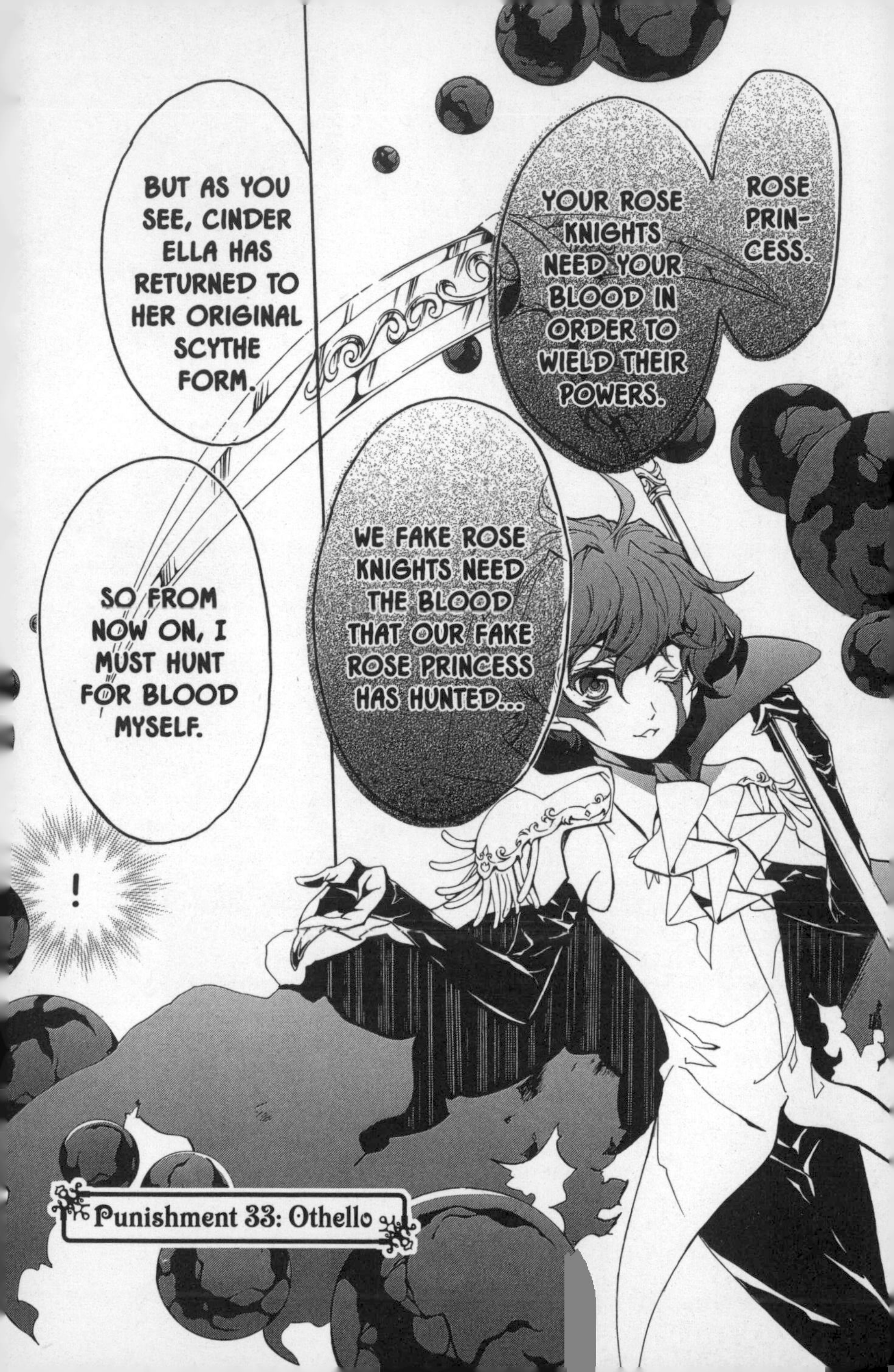
ROSE PRIN-CESS.
YOUR ROSE KNIGHTS NEED YOUR BLOOD IN ORDER TO WIELD THEIR POWERS.
WE FAKE ROSE KNIGHTS NEED THE BLOOD THAT OUR FAKE ROSE PRINCESS HAS HUNTED...
BUT AS YOU SEE, CINDER ELLA HAS RETURNED TO HER ORIGINAL SCYTHE FORM.
SO FROM NOW ON, I MUST HUNT FOR BLOOD MYSELF.
!
Punishment 33: Othello

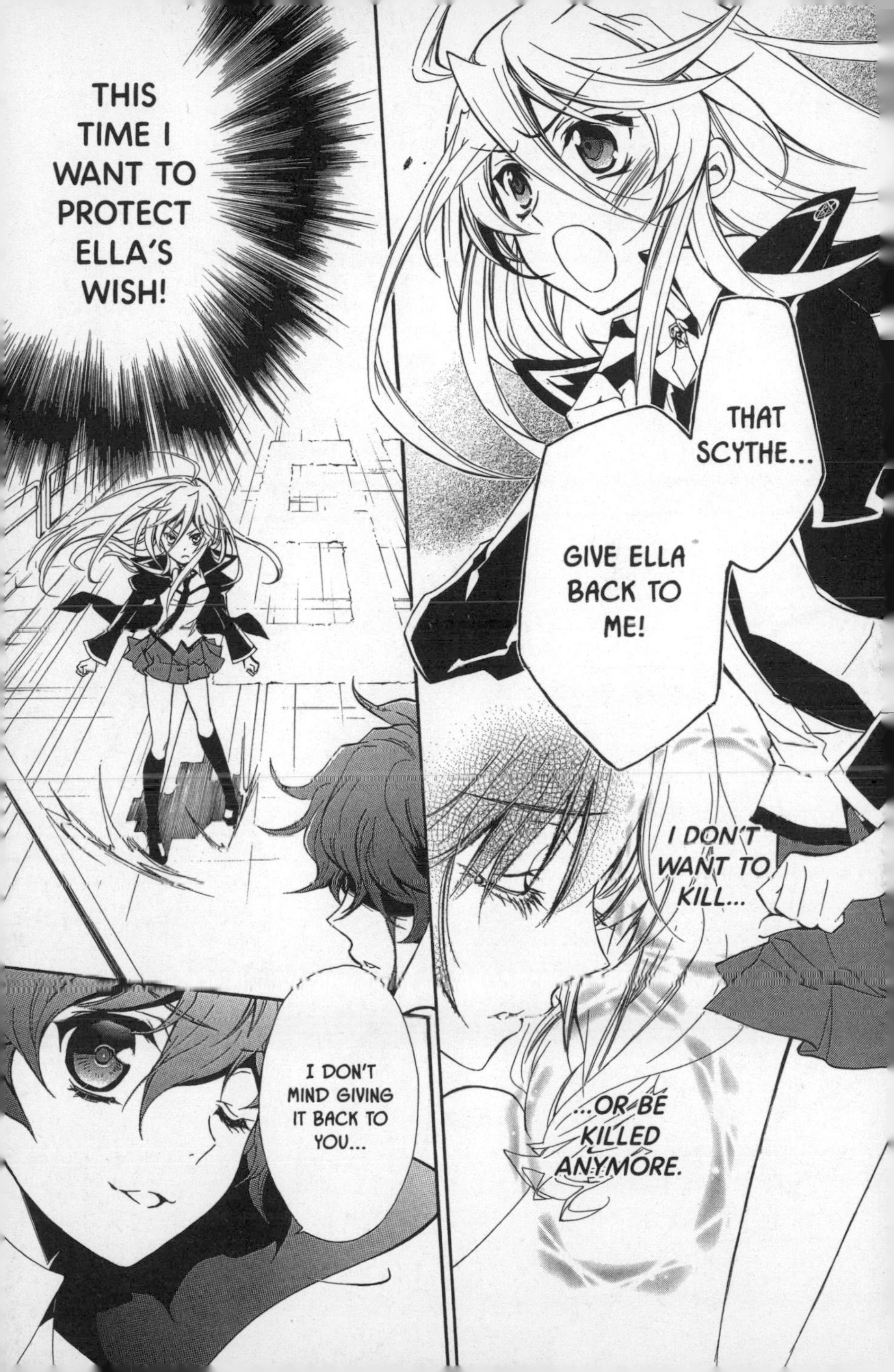
THAT SCYTHE...
GIVE ELLA BACK TO ME!
THIS TIME I WANT TO PROTECT ELLA'S WISH!
I DON'T WANT TO KILL...
...OR BE KILLED ANYMORE.
I DON'T MIND GIVING IT BACK TO YOU...

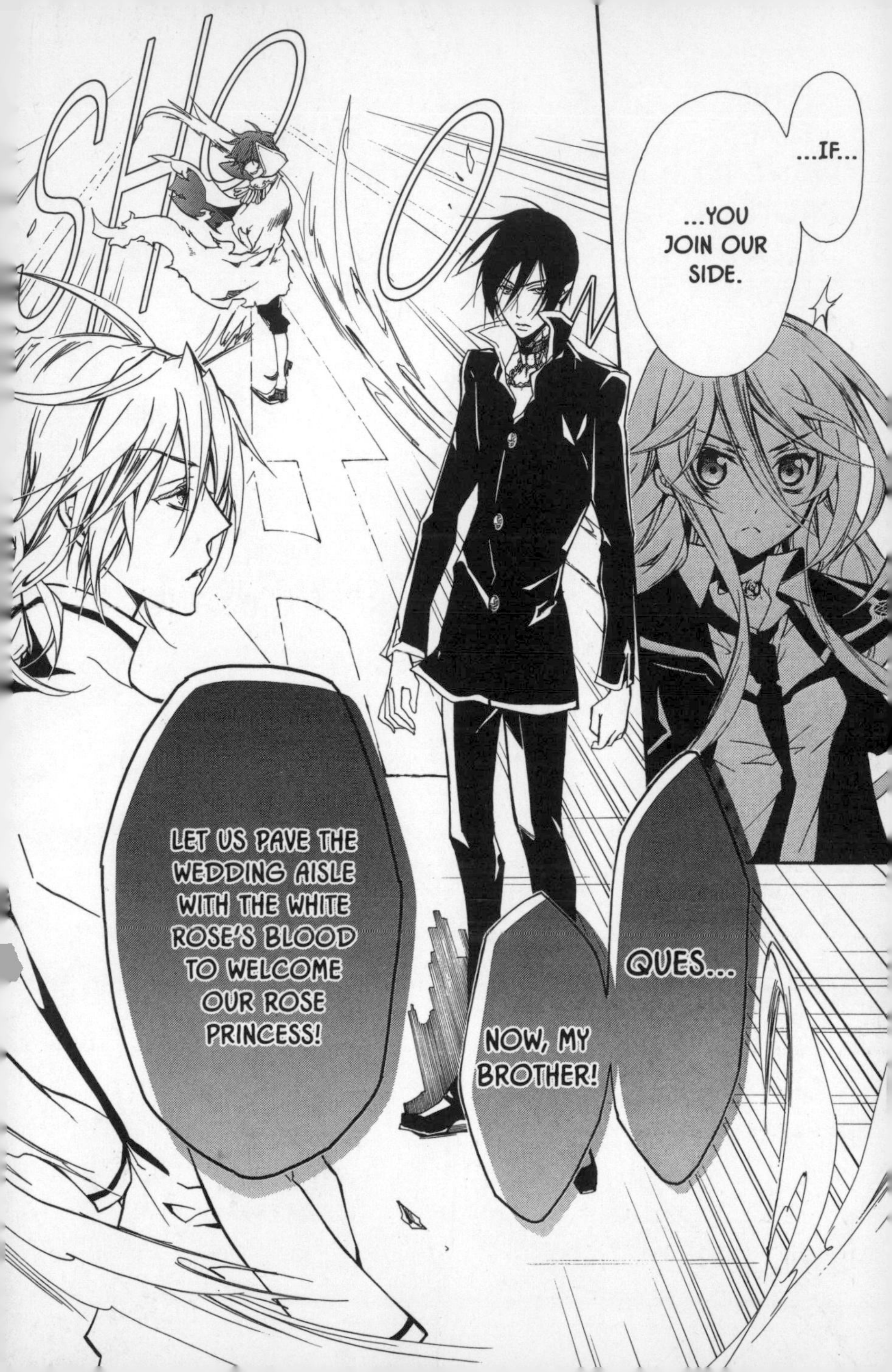
...IF...
...YOU JOIN OUR SIDE.
QUES...
NOW, MY BROTHER!
LET US PAVE THE WEDDING AISLE WITH THE WHITE ROSE'S BLOOD TO WELCOME OUR ROSE PRINCESS!

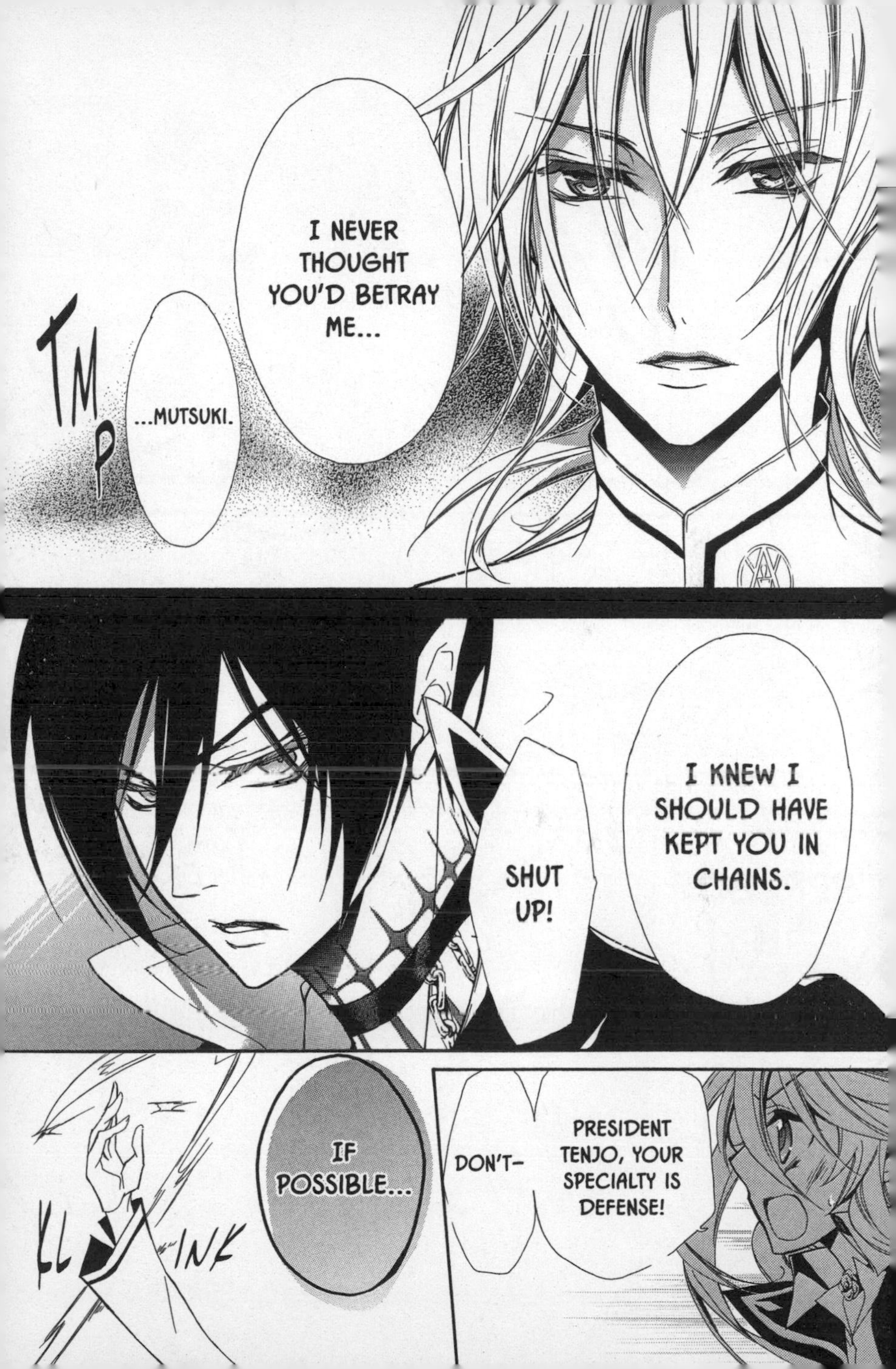

I NEVER THOUGHT YOU'D BETRAY ME...
...MUTSUKI.
TMP
I KNEW I SHOULD HAVE KEPT YOU IN CHAINS.
SHUT UP!
PRESIDENT TENJO, YOUR SPECIALTY IS DEFENSE!
DON'T-
IF POSSIBLE...
KLINK

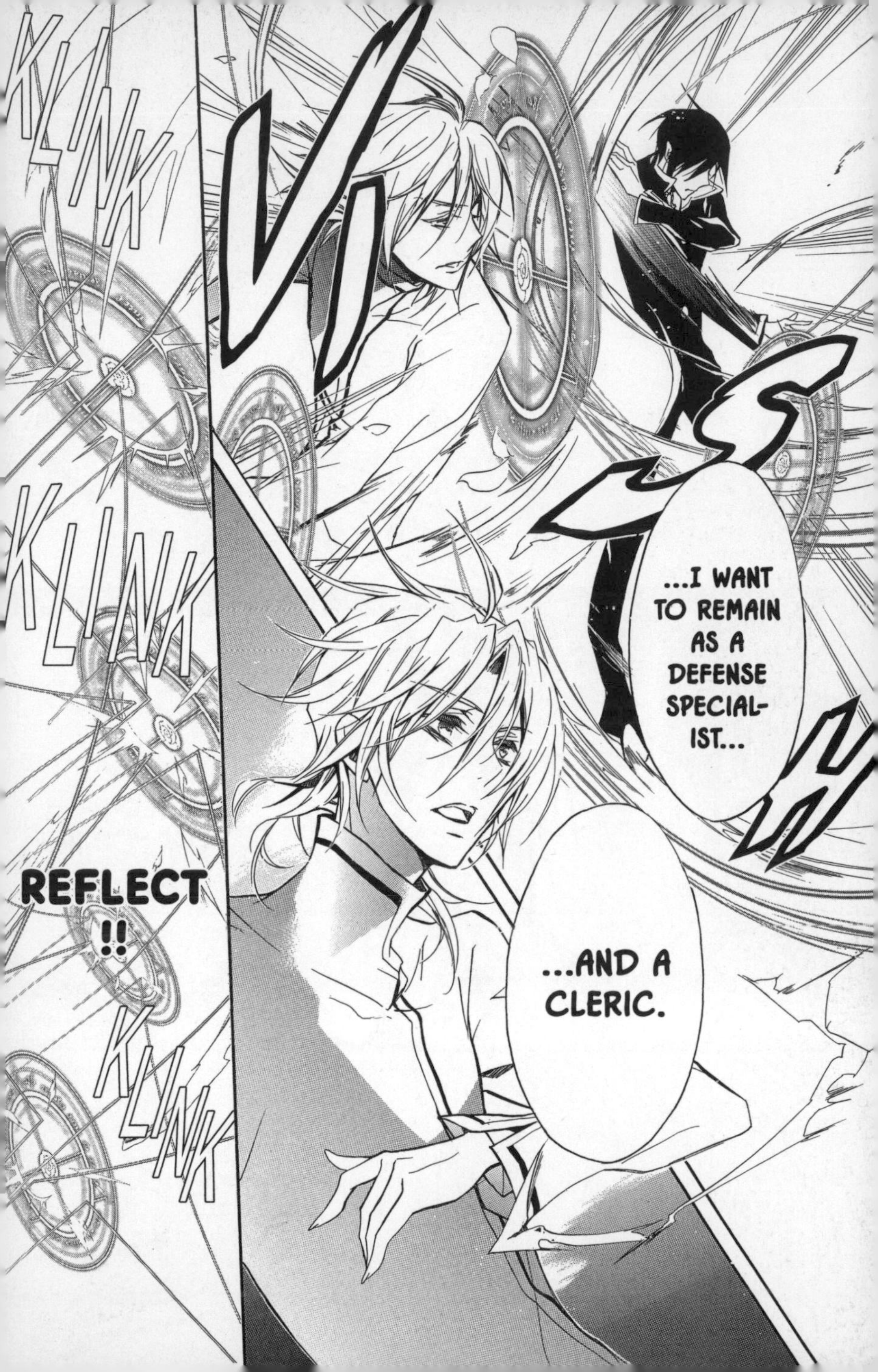
VSSH
...I WANT TO REMAIN AS A DEFENSE SPECIAL-IST...
...AND A CLERIC.
KLINK
KLINK
REFLECT!!
KLINK

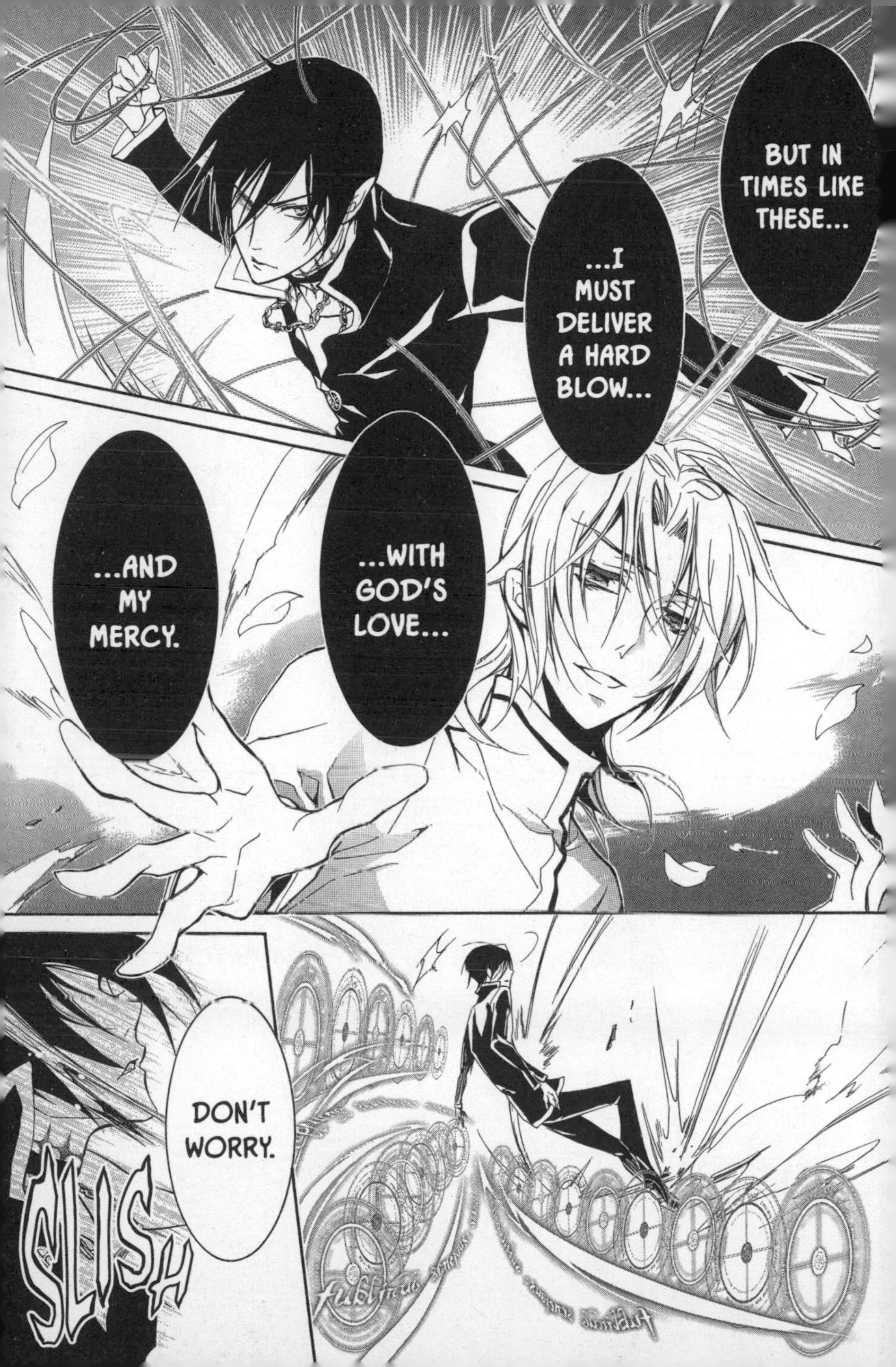
BUT IN TIMES LIKE THESE...
...I MUST DELIVER A HARD BLOW...
...WITH GOD'S LOVE...
...AND MY MERCY.
DON'T WORRY.
SLISH

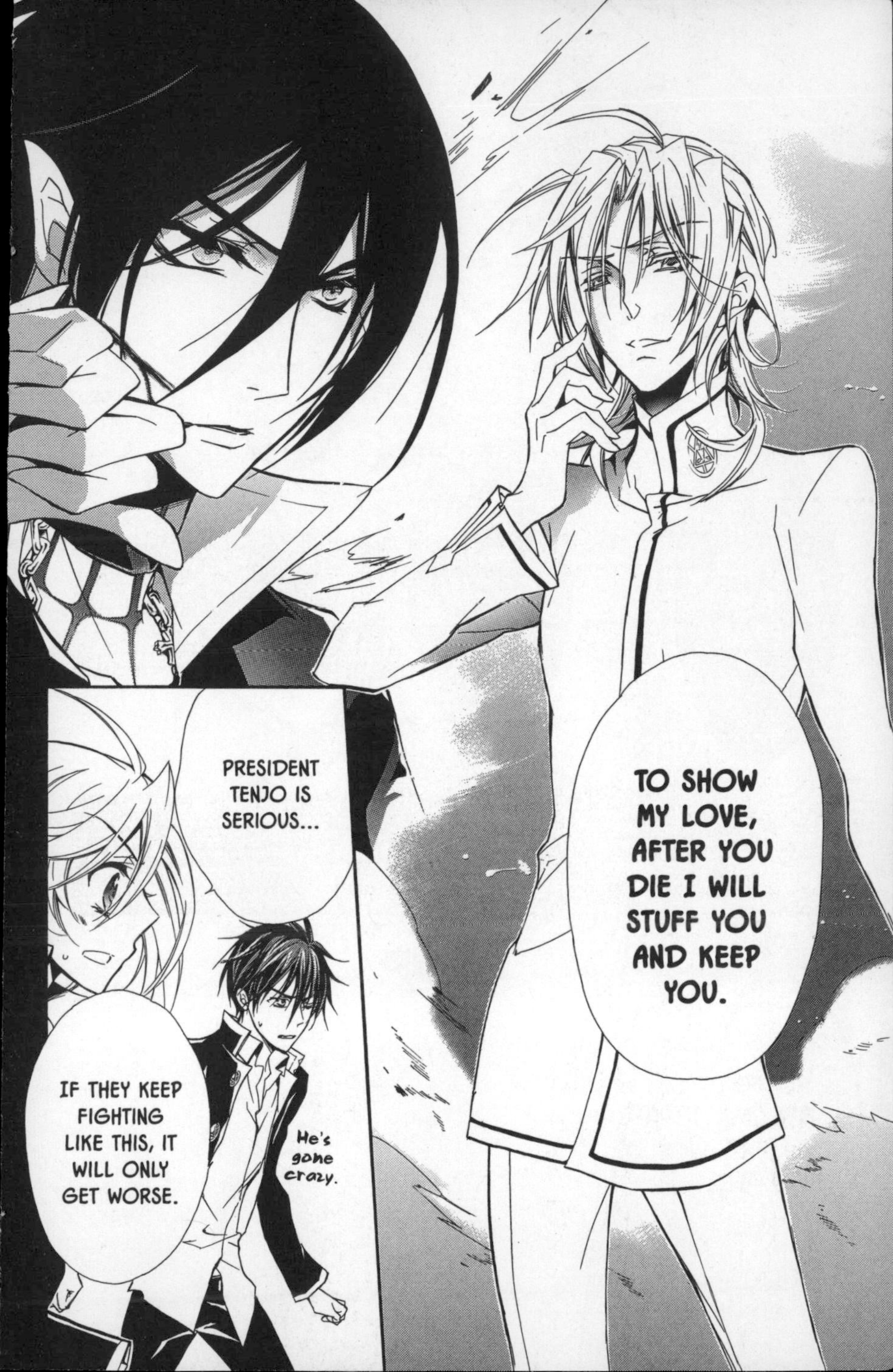
TO SHOW MY LOVE, AFTER YOU DIE I WILL STUFF YOU AND KEEP YOU.
PRESIDENT TENJO IS SERIOUS...
He's gone crazy.
IF THEY KEEP FIGHTING LIKE THIS, IT WILL ONLY GET WORSE.

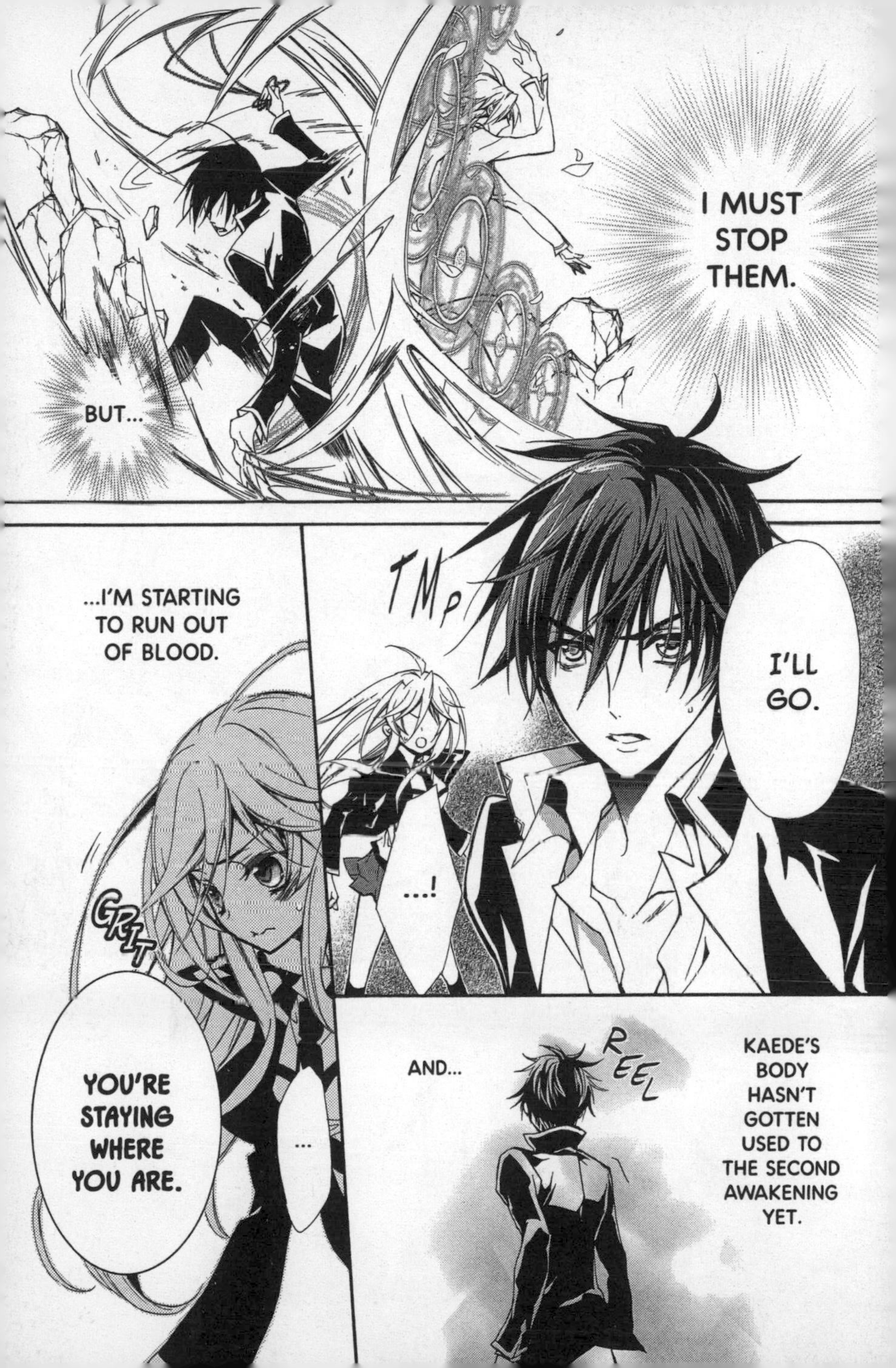
I MUST STOP THEM.
BUT...
TMP
I'LL GO.
...!
KAEDE'S BODY HASN'T GOTTEN USED TO THE SECOND AWAKENING YET.
REEL
AND...
...I'M STARTING TO RUN OUT OF BLOOD.
GRIT
...
YOU'RE STAYING WHERE YOU ARE.

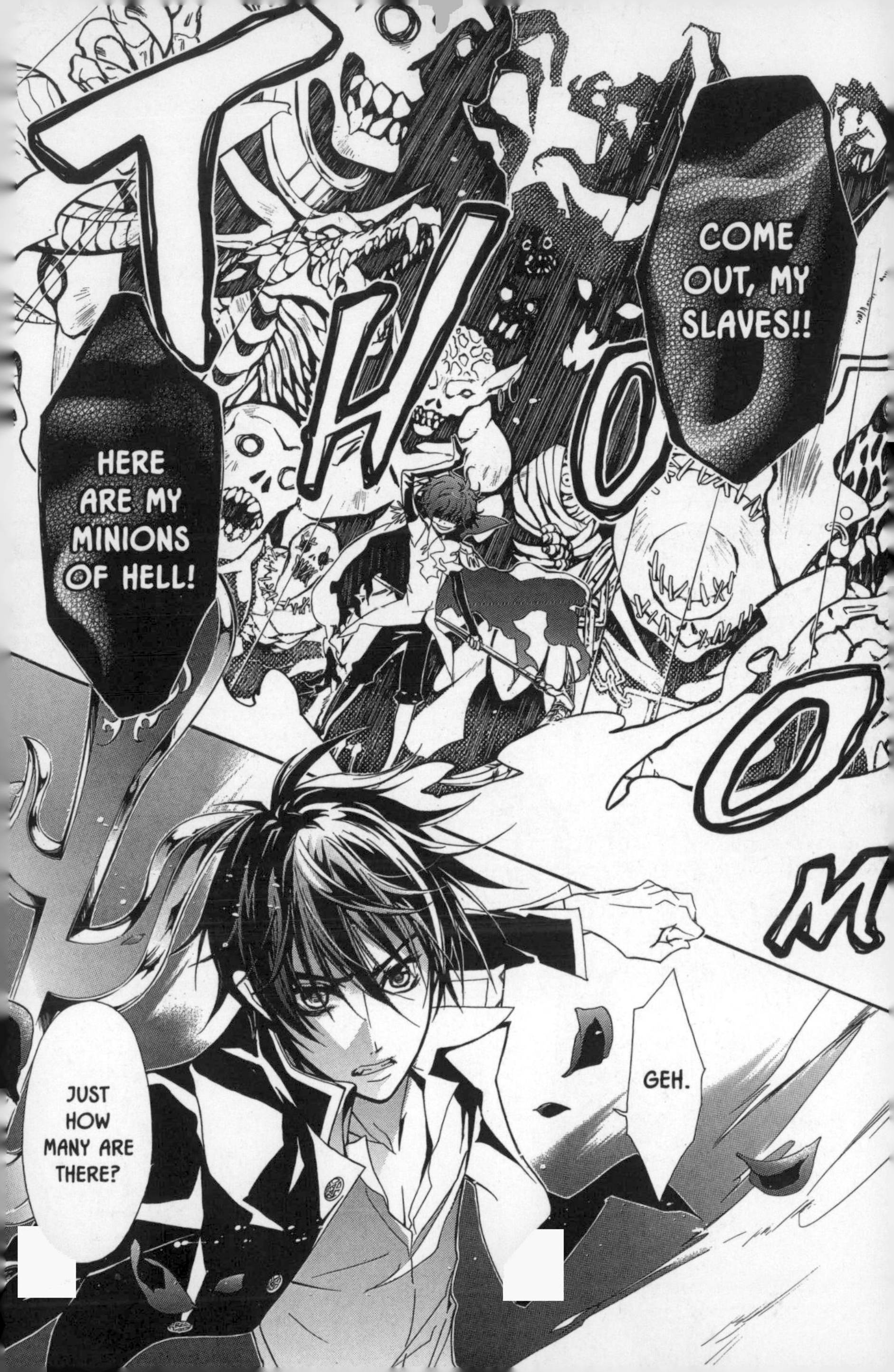
COME OUT, MY SLAVES!!
HERE ARE MY MINIONS OF HELL!
GEH.
JUST HOW MANY ARE THERE?

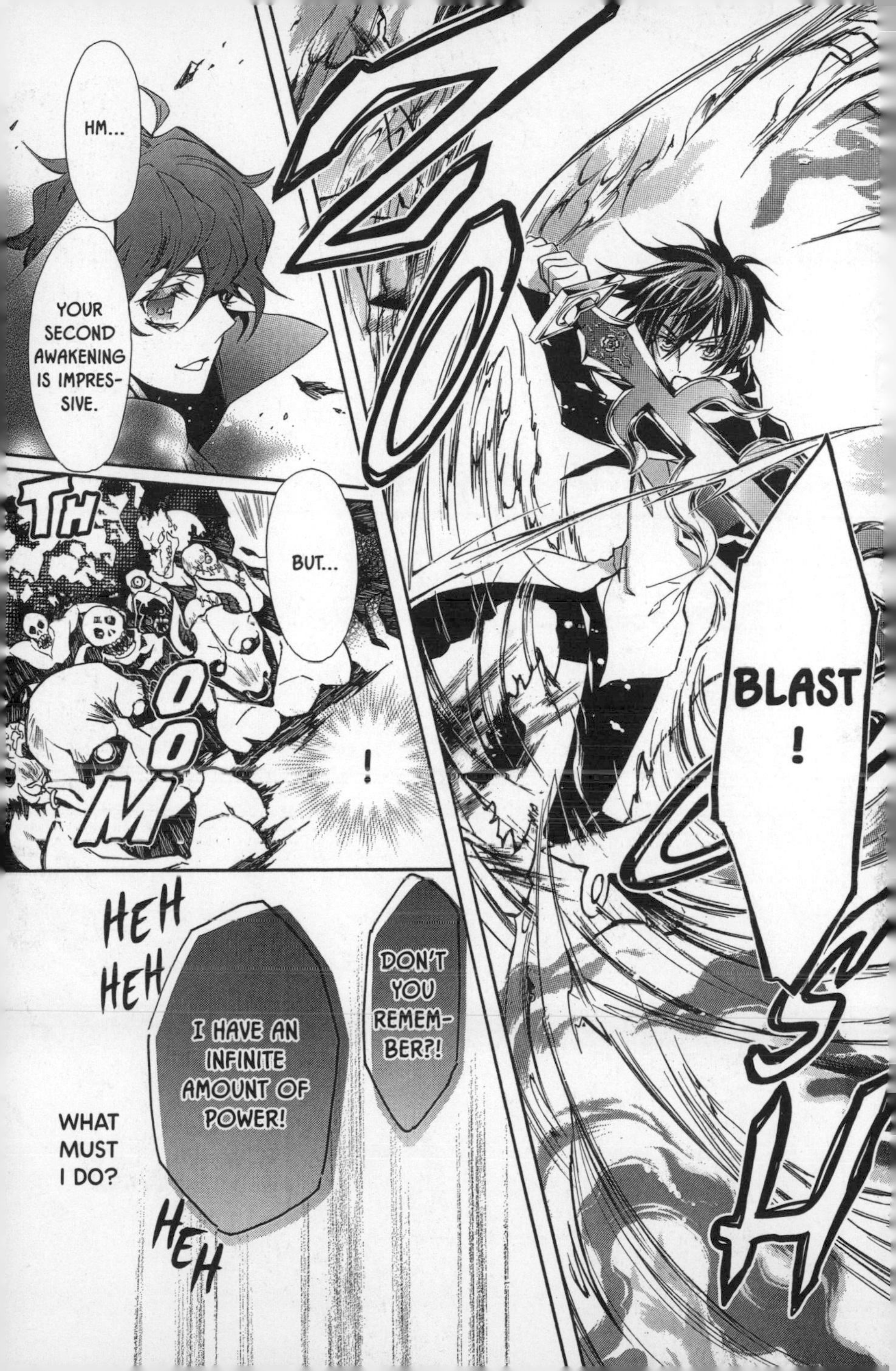
BLAST!
HM...
YOUR SECOND AWAKENING IS IMPRES-SIVE.
BUT...
THOOOM
!
DON'T YOU REMEMBER?!
I HAVE AN INFINITE AMOUNT OF POWER!
HEH HEH
HEH
WHAT MUST I DO?

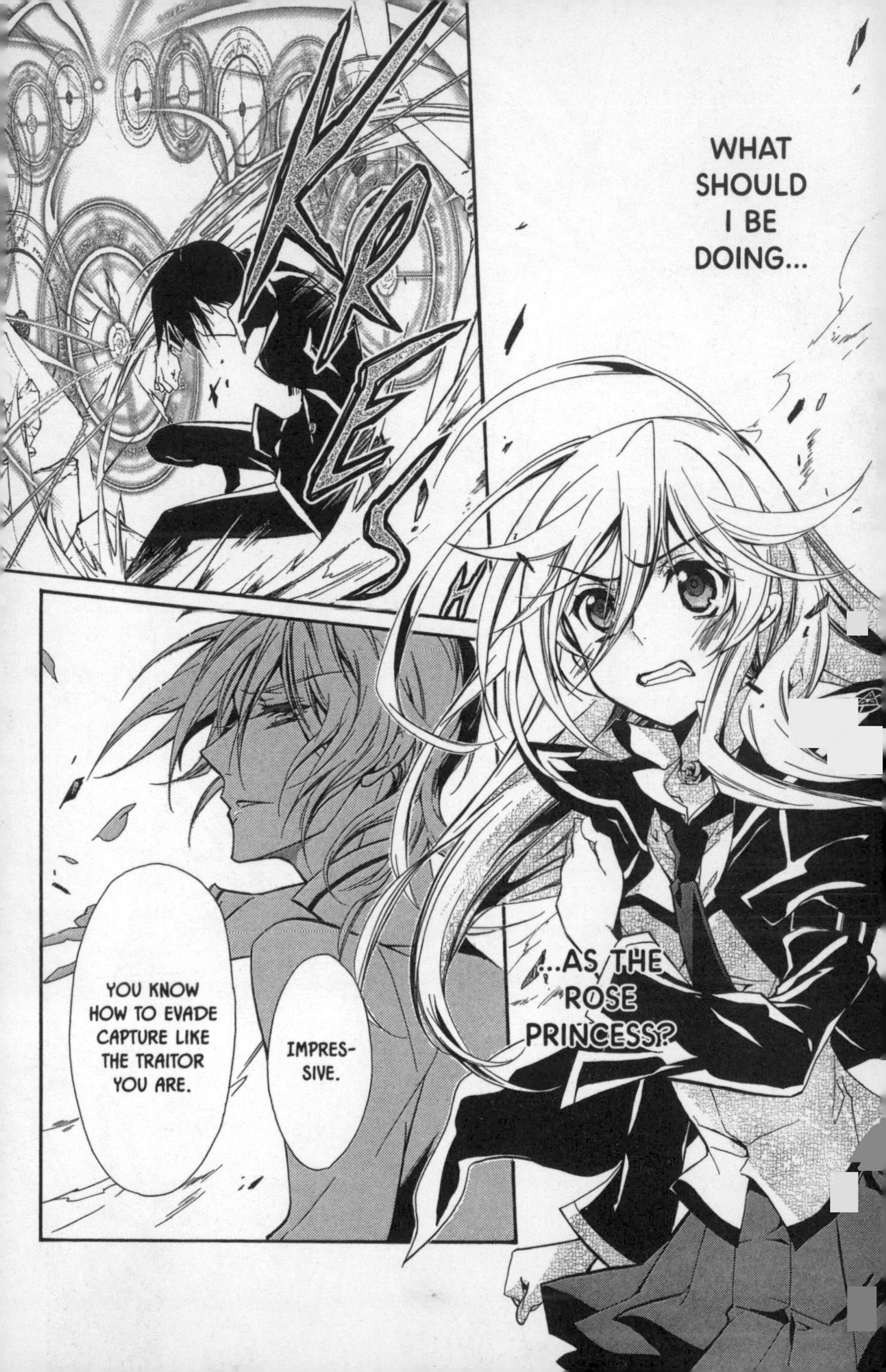
WHAT SHOULD I BE DOING...
...AS THE ROSE PRINCESS?
IMPRES-SIVE.
YOU KNOW HOW TO EVADE CAPTURE LIKE THE TRAITOR YOU ARE.

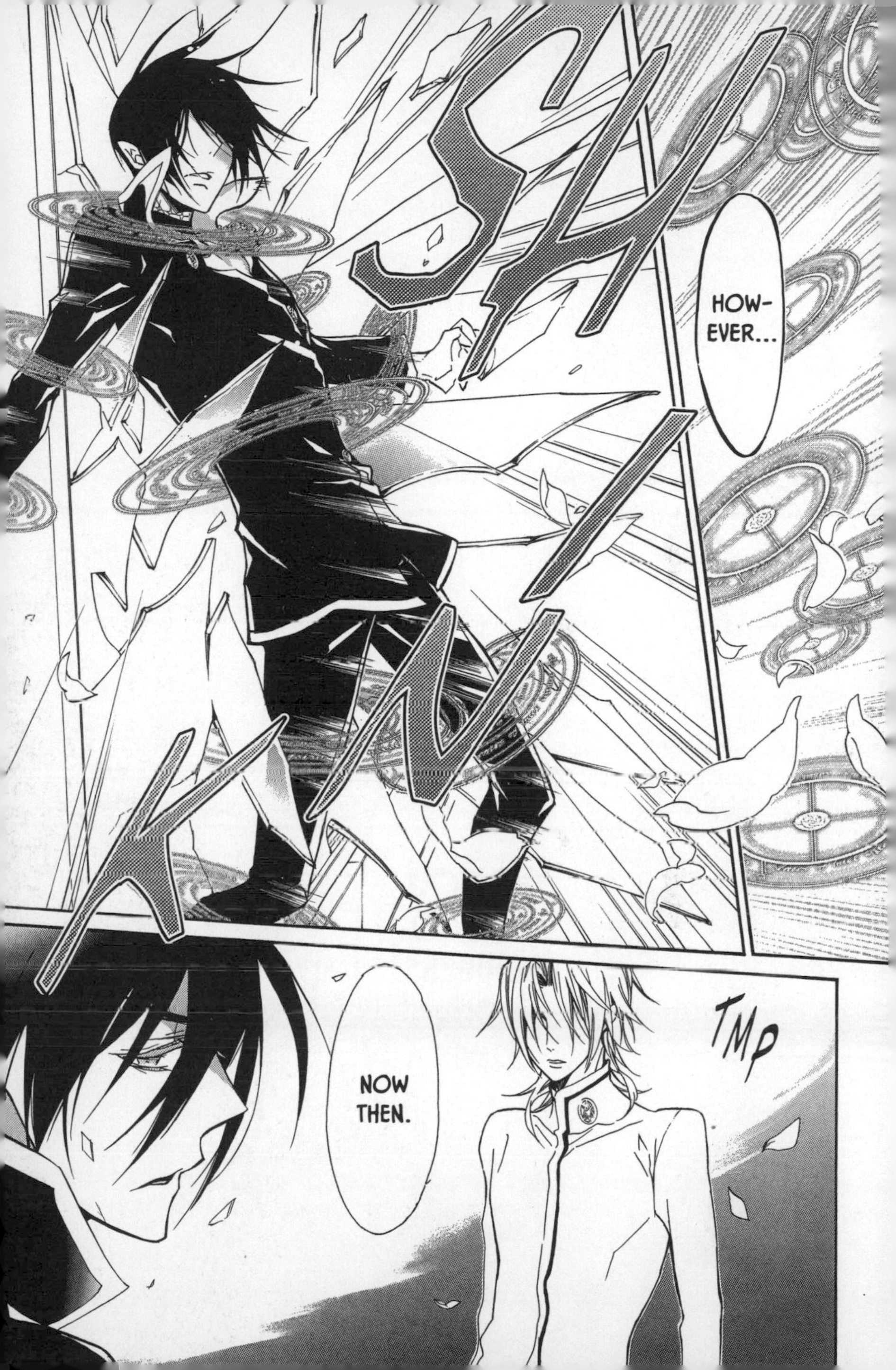
SHINK
HOW-EVER...
TMP
NOW THEN.

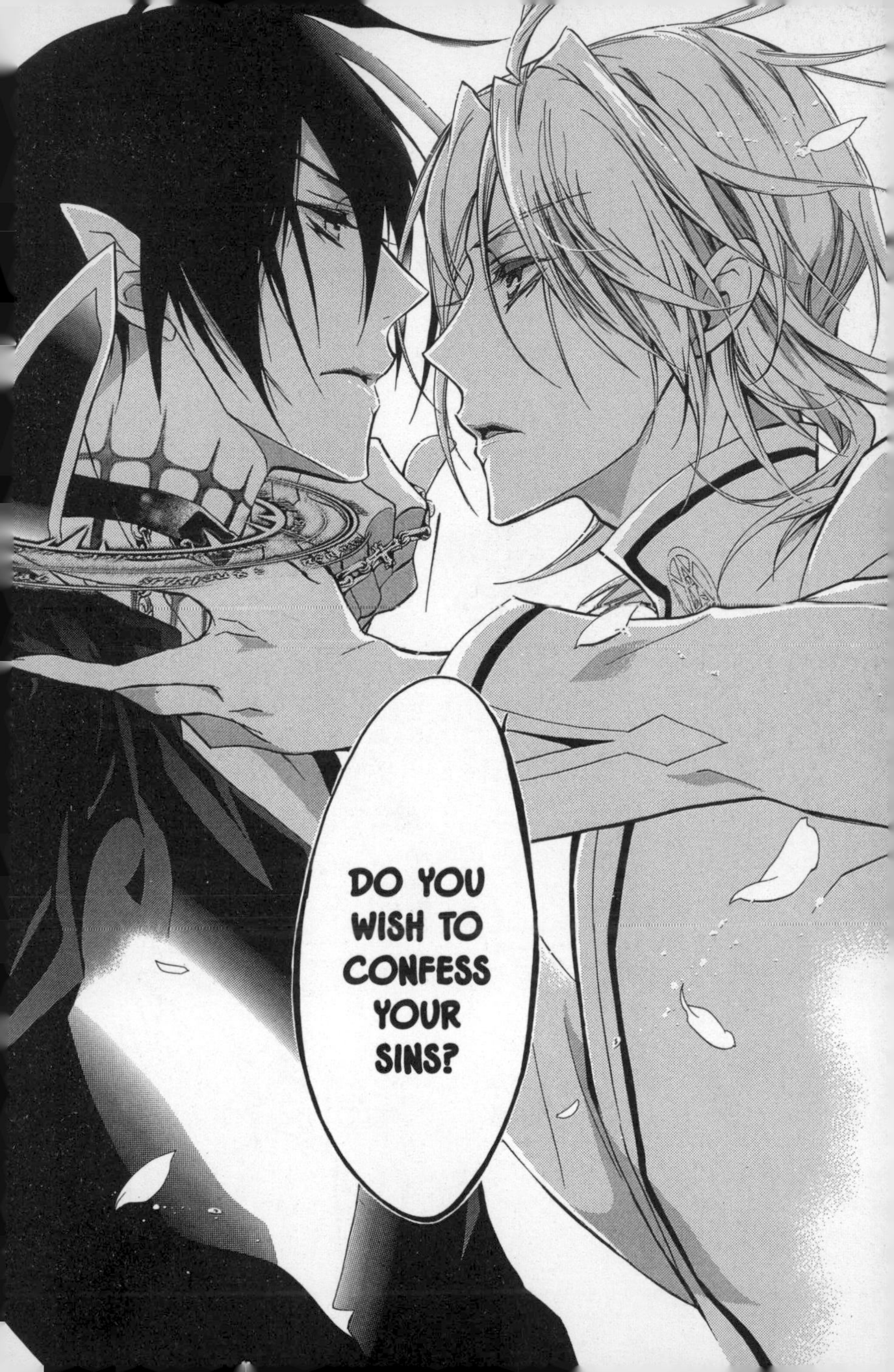
DO YOU WISH TO CONFESS YOUR SINS?

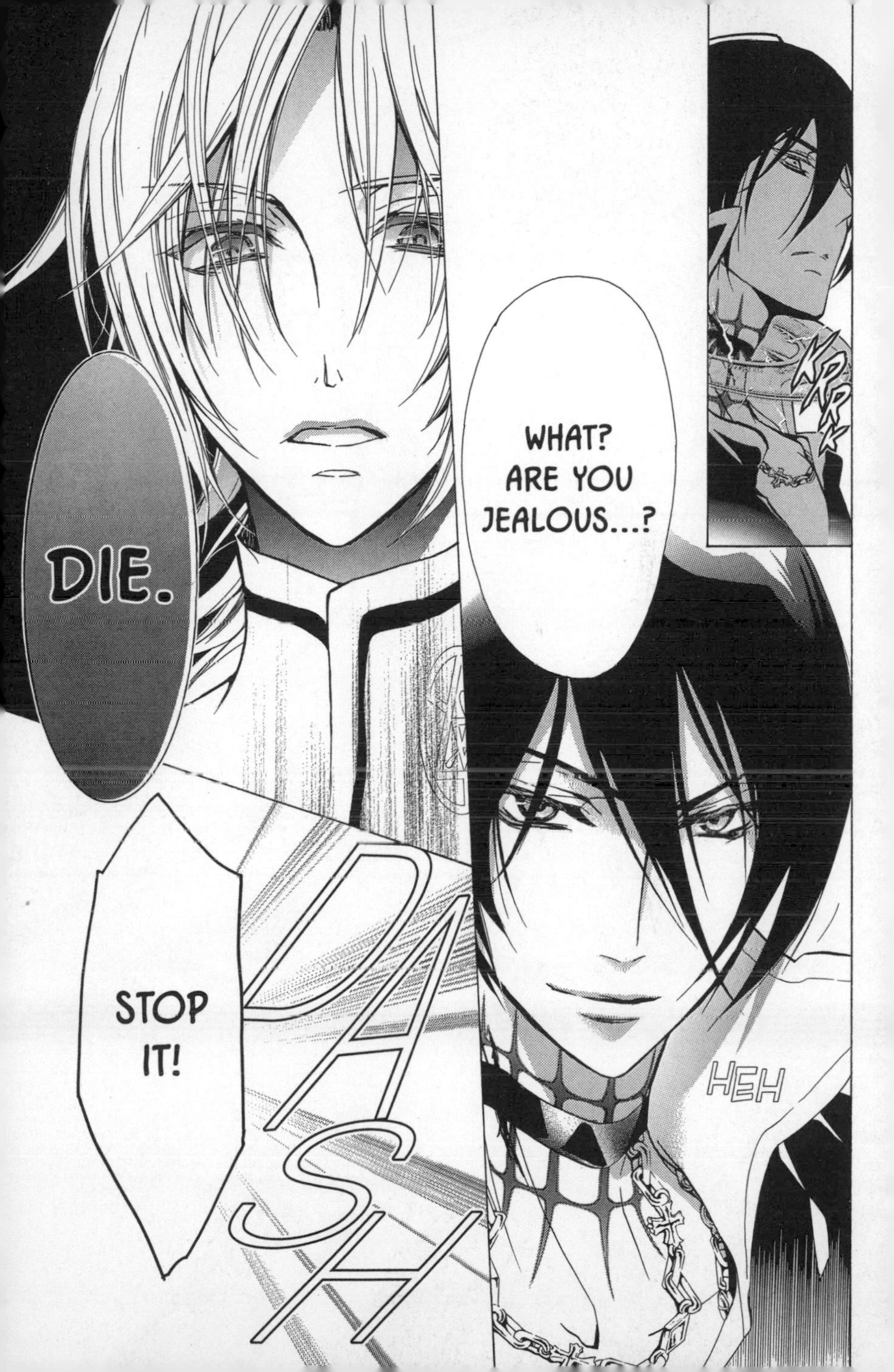
KRRK
WHAT? ARE YOU JEALOUS...?
HEH
DIE.
STOP IT!
DASH

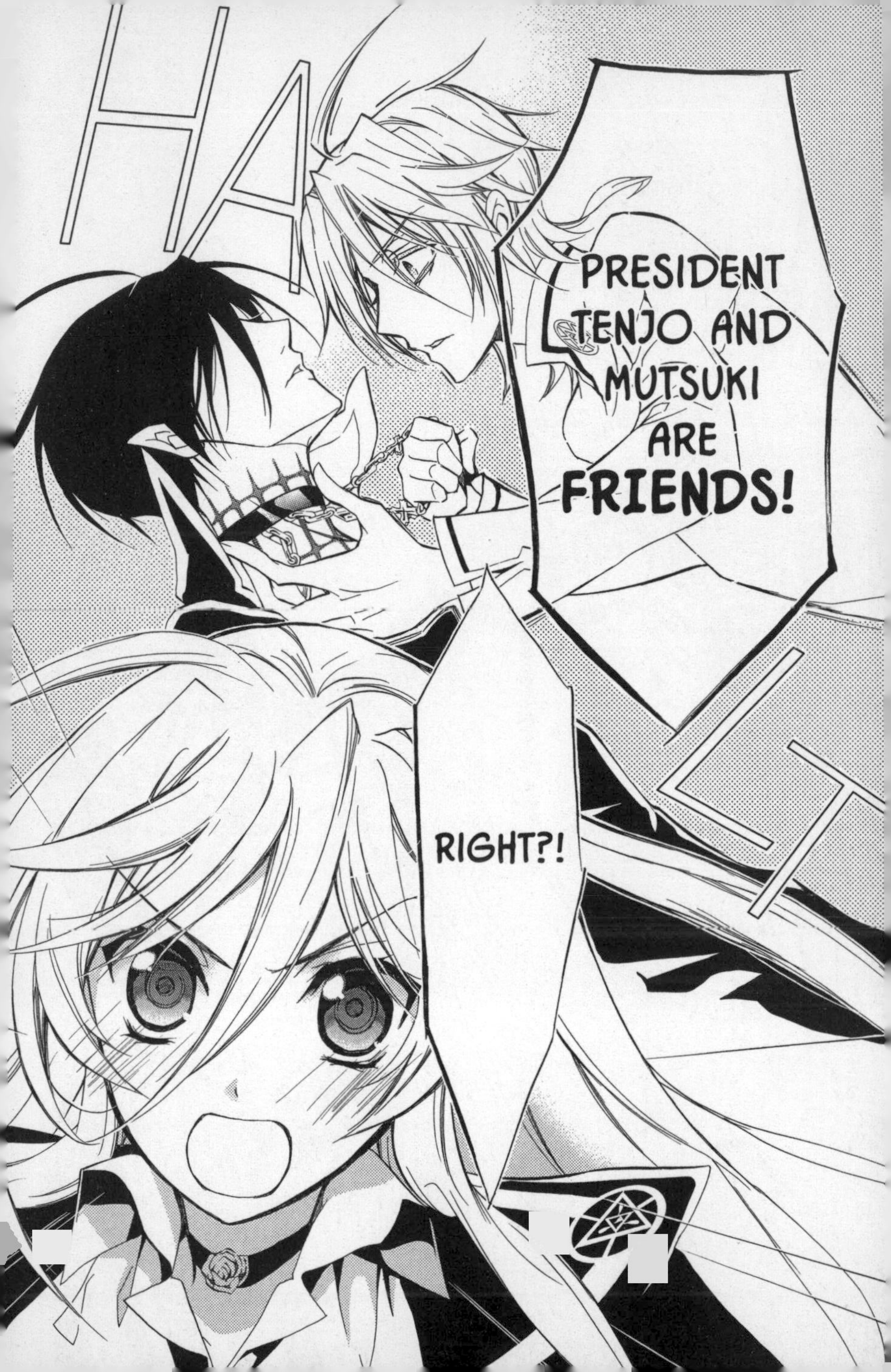
HALT
PRESIDENT TENJO AND MUTSUKI ARE FRIENDS!
RIGHT?!

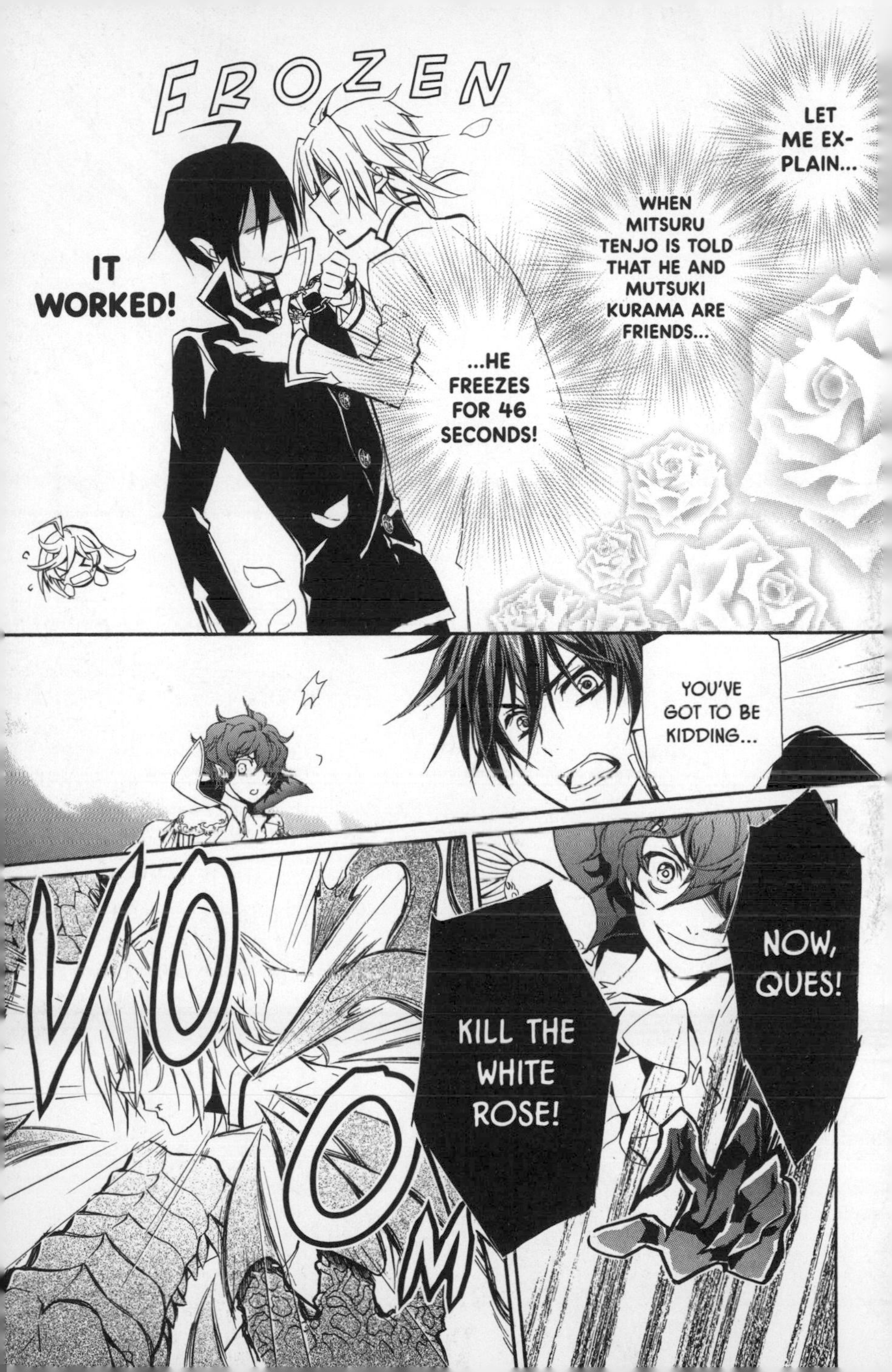
LET ME EX-PLAIN...
WHEN MITSURU TENJO IS TOLD THAT HE AND MUTSUKI KURAMA ARE FRIENDS...
...HE FREEZES FOR 46 SECONDS!
FROZEN
IT WORKED!
YOU'VE GOT TO BE KIDDING...
NOW, QUES!
KILL THE WHITE ROSE!
VOOOM

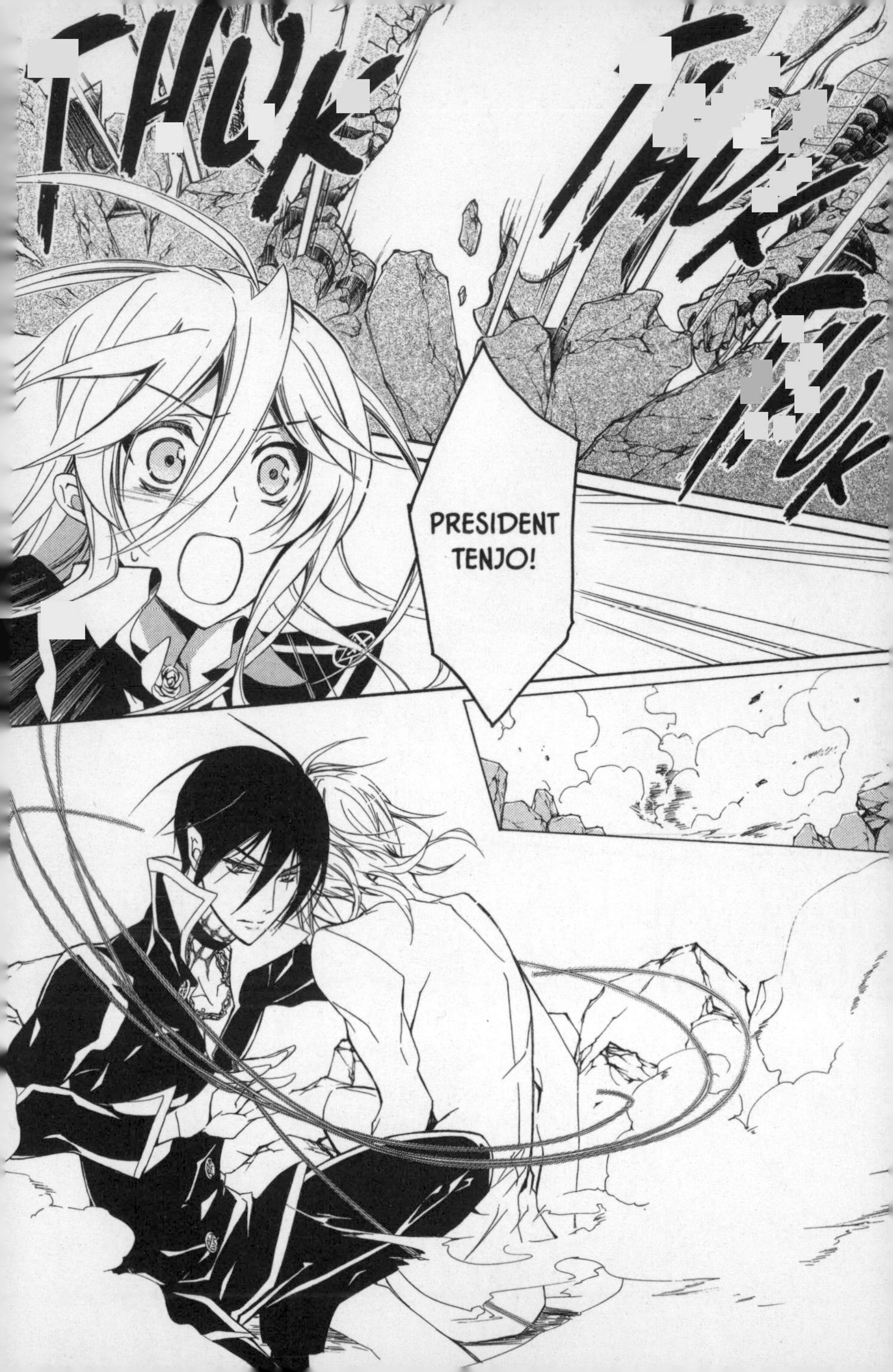
THUK
THUK
THUK
PRESIDENT TENJO!

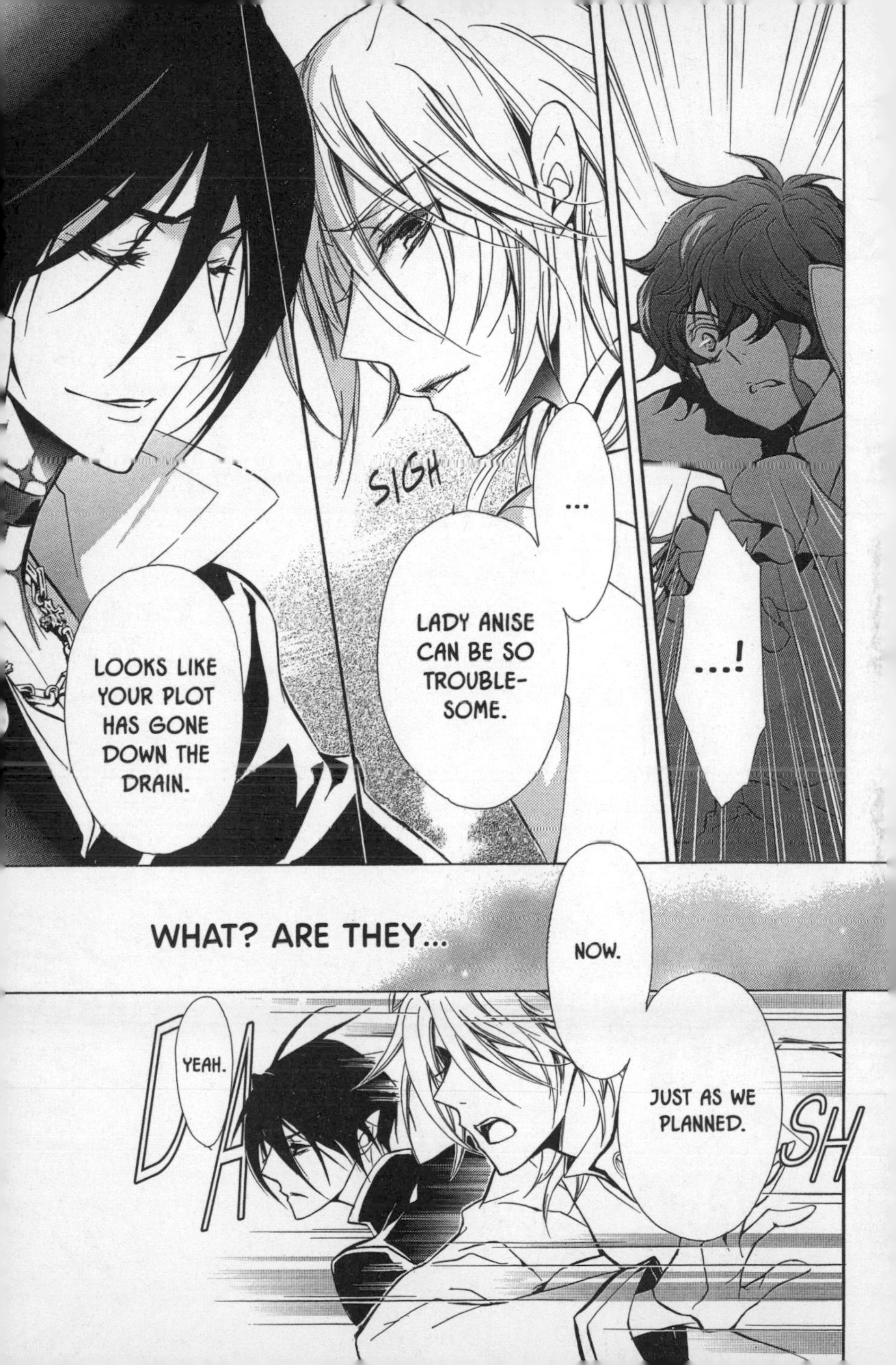
...!
SIGH
...
LADY ANISE CAN BE SO TROUBLE-SOME.
LOOKS LIKE YOUR PLOT HAS GONE DOWN THE DRAIN.
NOW.
WHAT? ARE THEY...
JUST AS WE PLANNED.
DASH
YEAH.

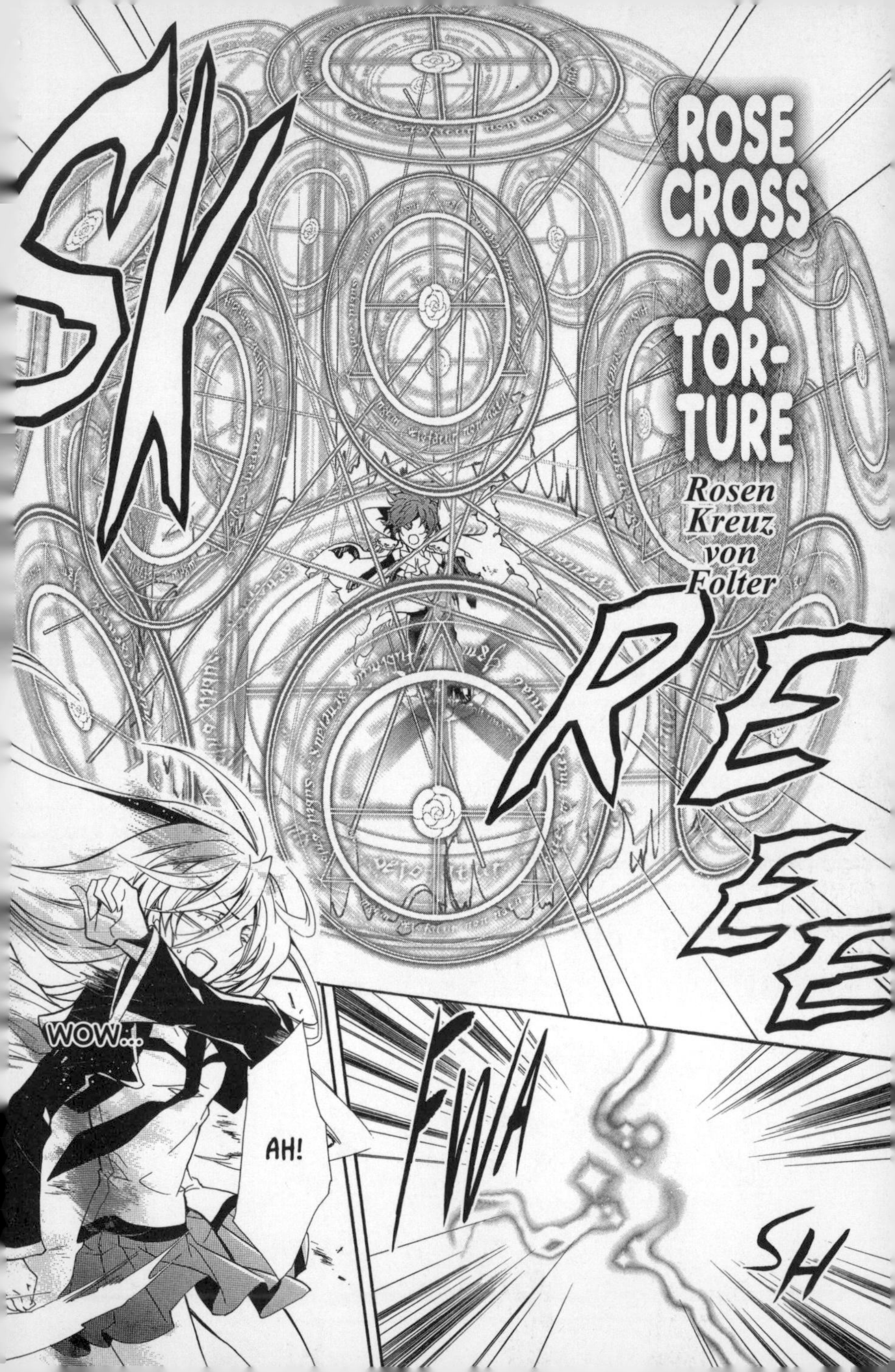
ROSE CROSS OF TOR-TURE
Rosen Kreuz von Folter
SK
REEEE
FWA
SH
WOW...
AH!

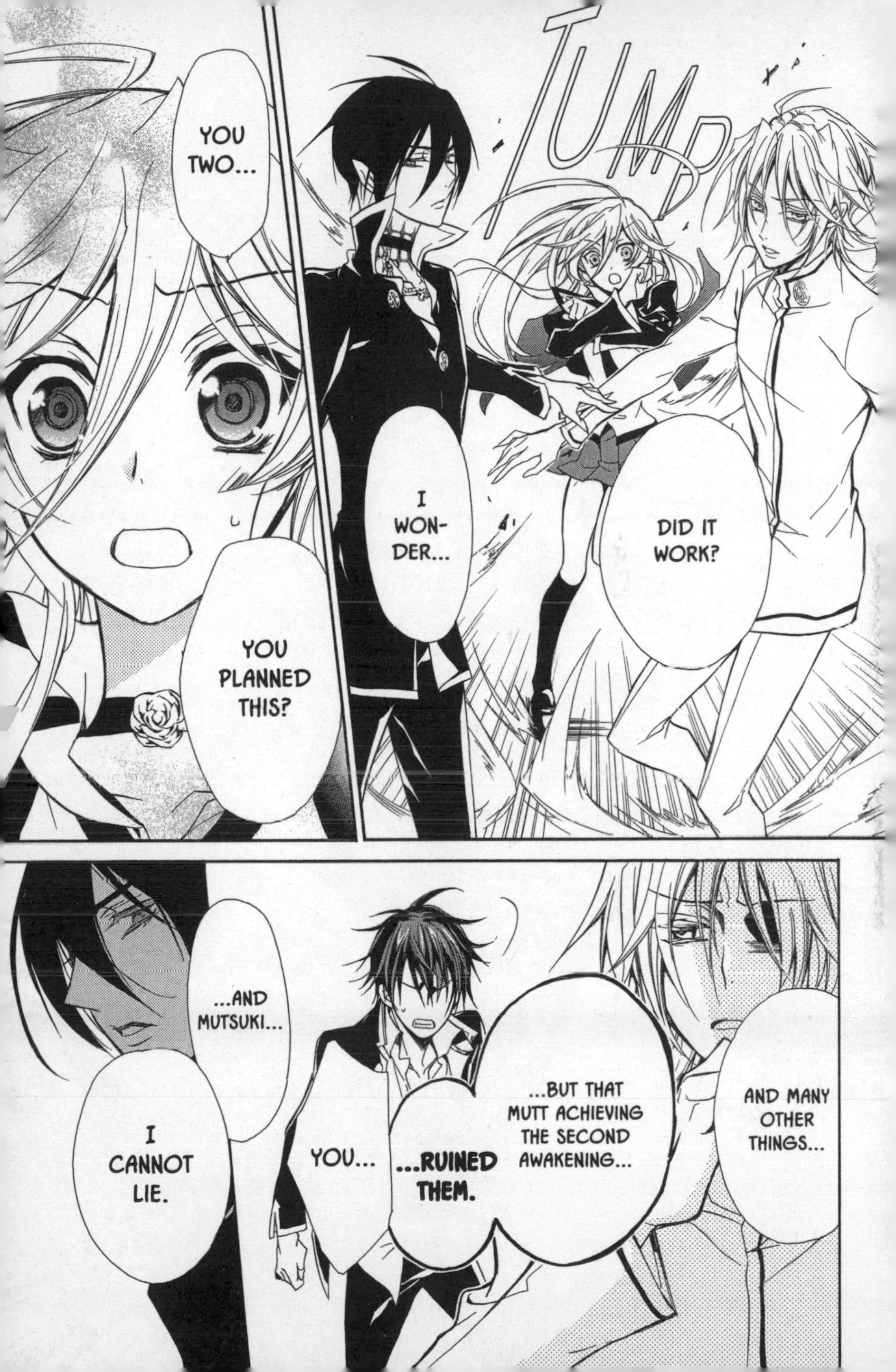
JUMP
DID IT WORK?
I WONDER...
YOU TWO...
YOU PLANNED THIS?
AND MANY OTHER THINGS...
...BUT THAT MUTT ACHIEVING THE SECOND AWAKENING...
...RUINED THEM.
YOU...
...AND MUTSUKI...
I CANNOT LIE.

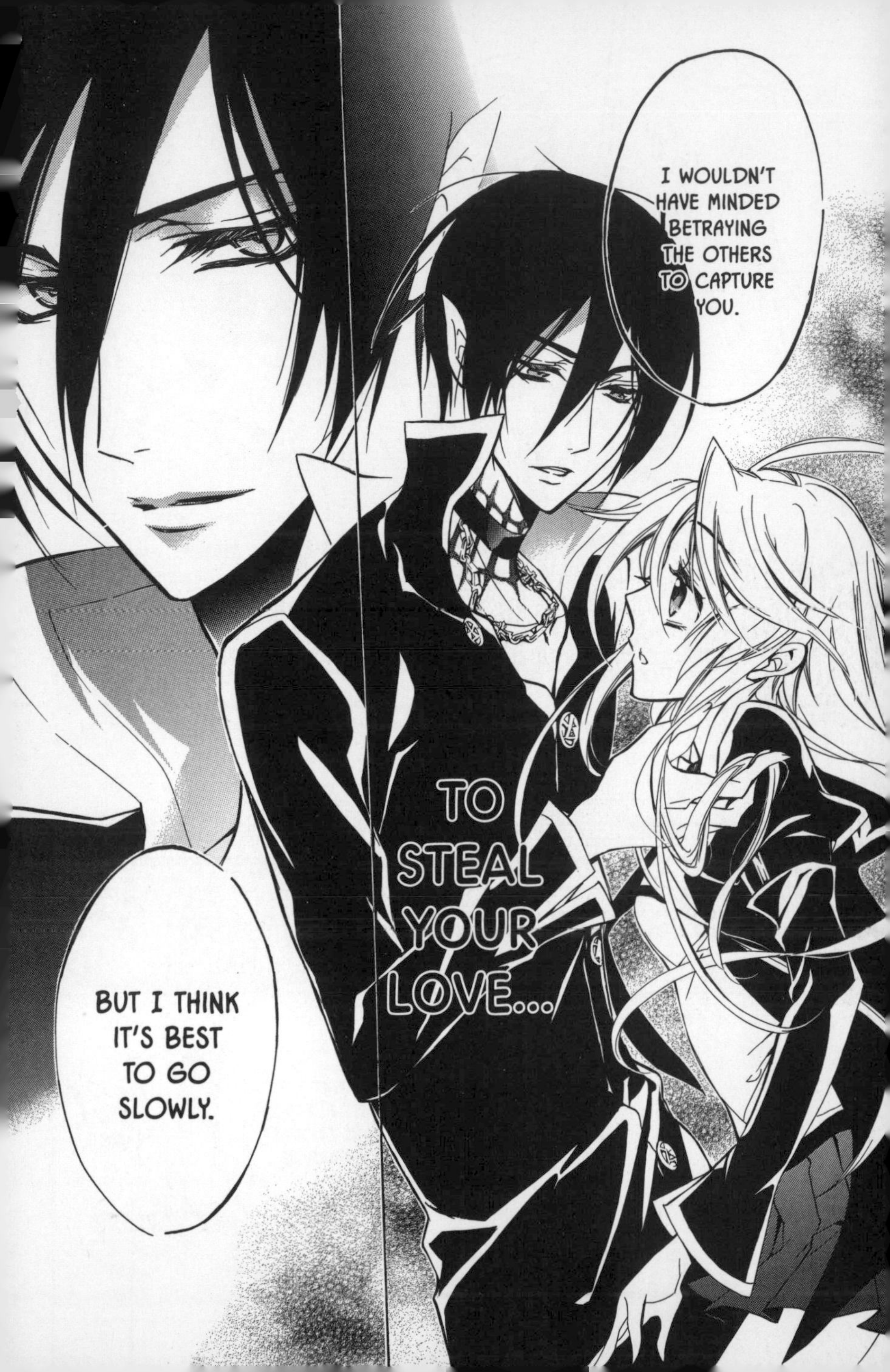
I WOULDN'T HAVE MINDED BETRAYING THE OTHERS TO CAPTURE YOU.
TO STEAL YOUR LOVE...
BUT I THINK IT'S BEST TO GO SLOWLY.

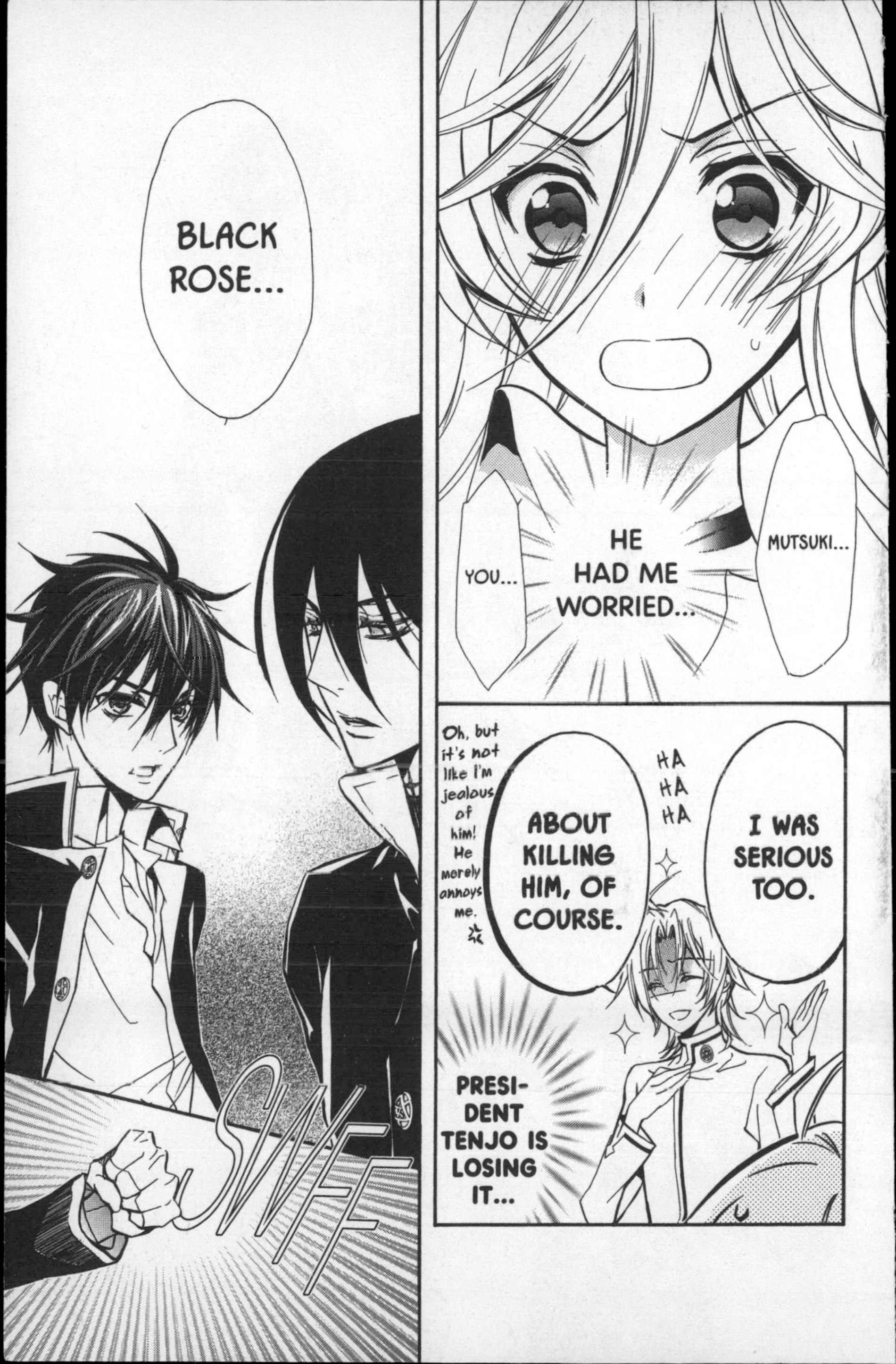
MUTSUKI...
HE HAD ME WORRIED...
YOU...
I WAS SERIOUS TOO.
HA HA HA
ABOUT KILLING HIM, OF COURSE.
Oh, but it's not like I'm jealous of him! He merely annoys me.
PRESI-DENT TENJO IS LOSING IT...
BLACK ROSE...
SNIFF

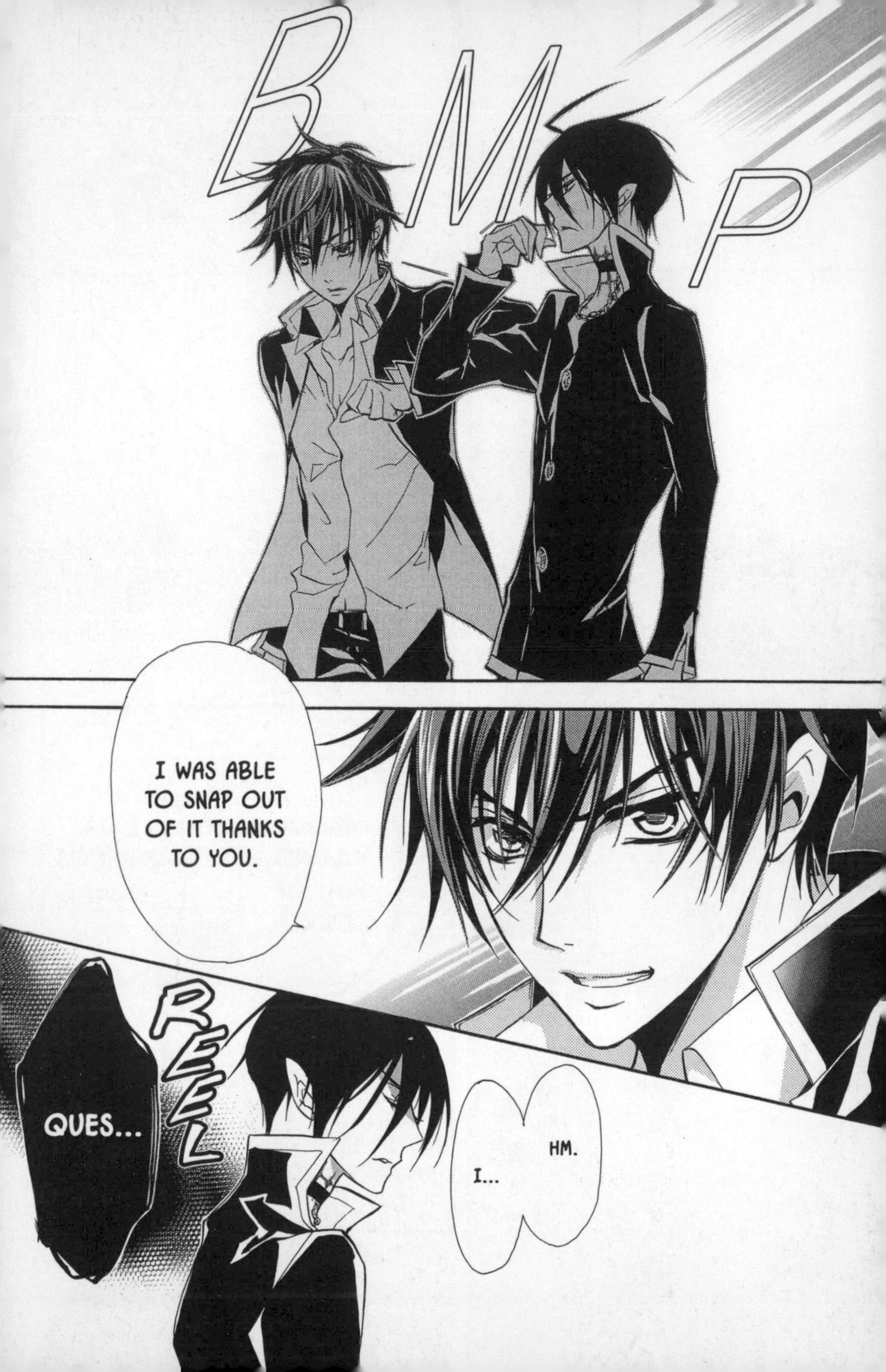
BMP
I WAS ABLE TO SNAP OUT OF IT THANKS TO YOU.
HM.
I...
REEL
QUES...

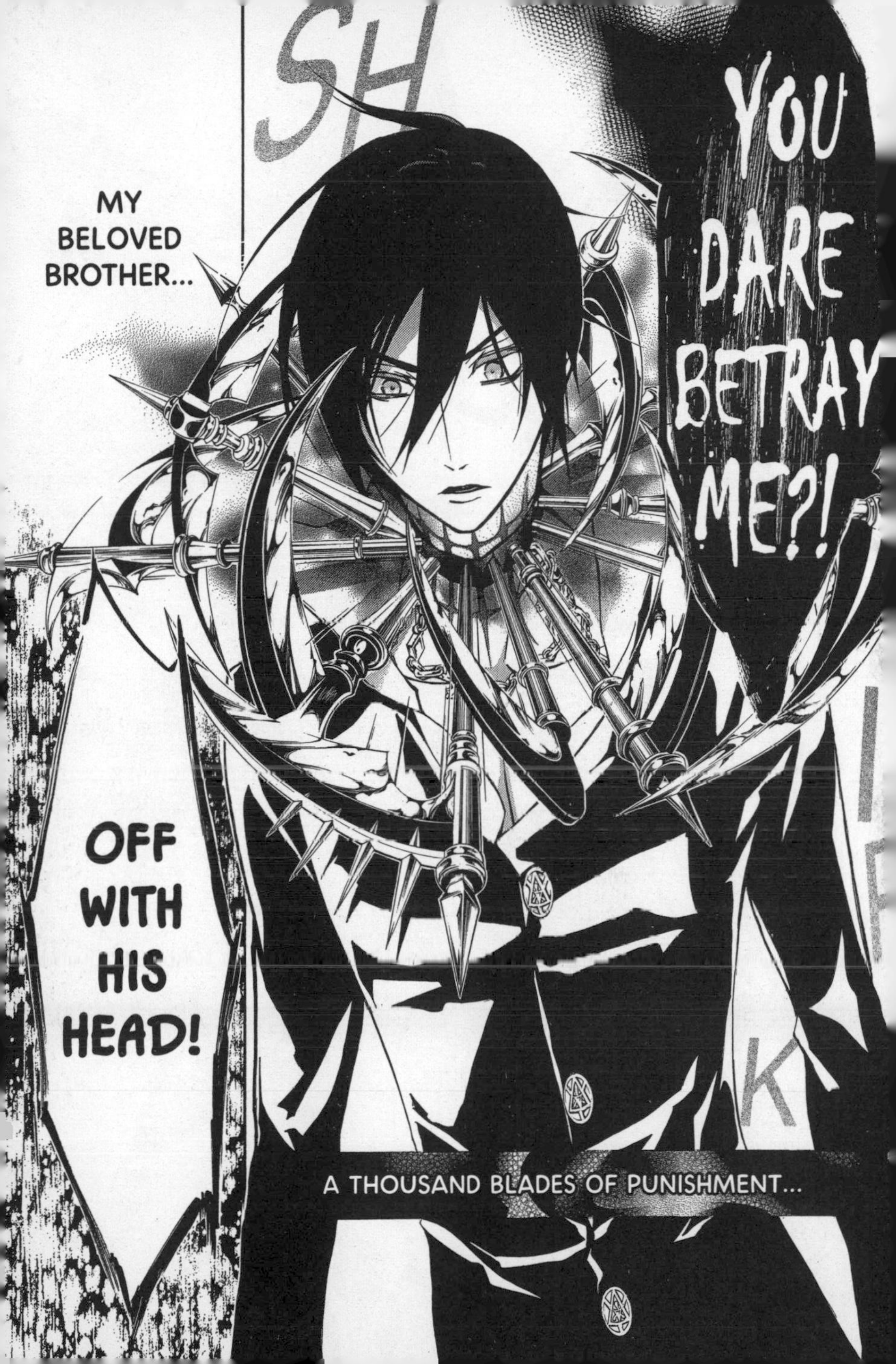
SH
YOU DARE BETRAY ME?!
MY BELOVED BROTHER...
OFF WITH HIS HEAD!
K
A THOUSAND BLADES OF PUNISHMENT...

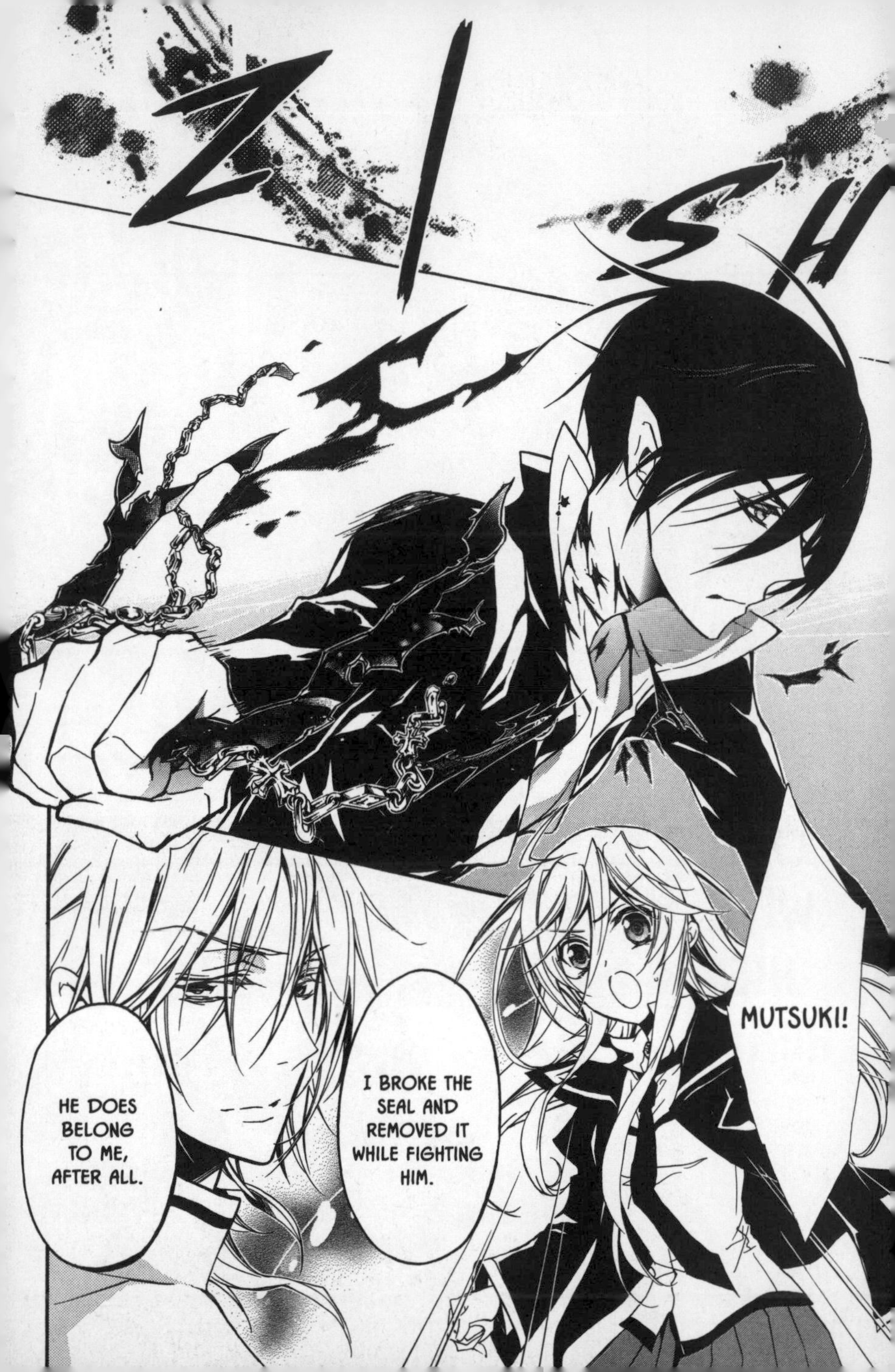
ZISH
MUTSUKI!
I BROKE THE SEAL AND REMOVED IT WHILE FIGHTING HIM.
HE DOES BELONG TO ME, AFTER ALL.

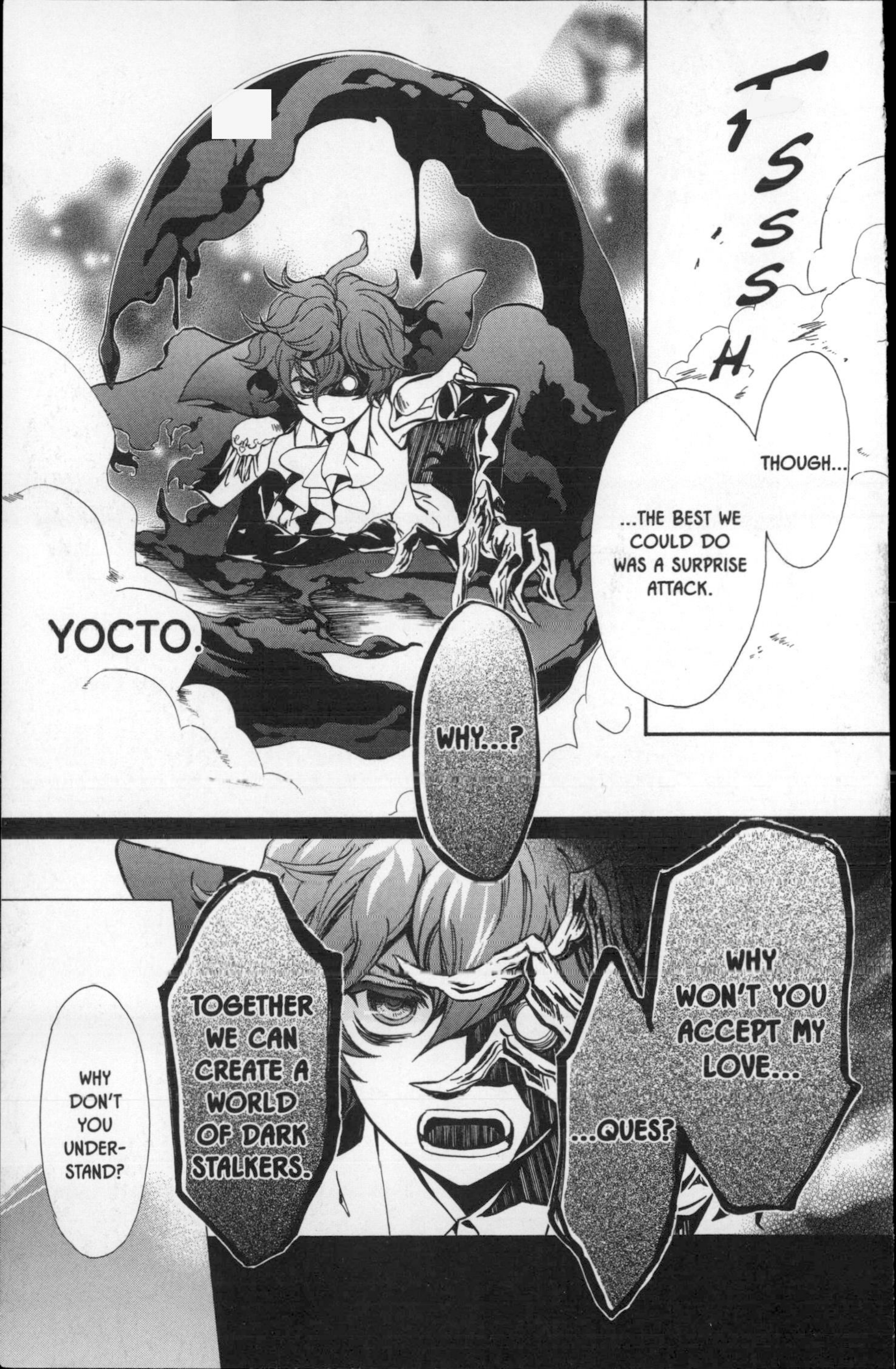
TSSSH
THOUGH...
...THE BEST WE COULD DO WAS A SURPRISE ATTACK.
YOCTO.
WHY...?
WHY WON'T YOU ACCEPT MY LOVE...
...QUES?
TOGETHER WE CAN CREATE A WORLD OF DARK STALKERS.
WHY DON'T YOU UNDER-STAND?

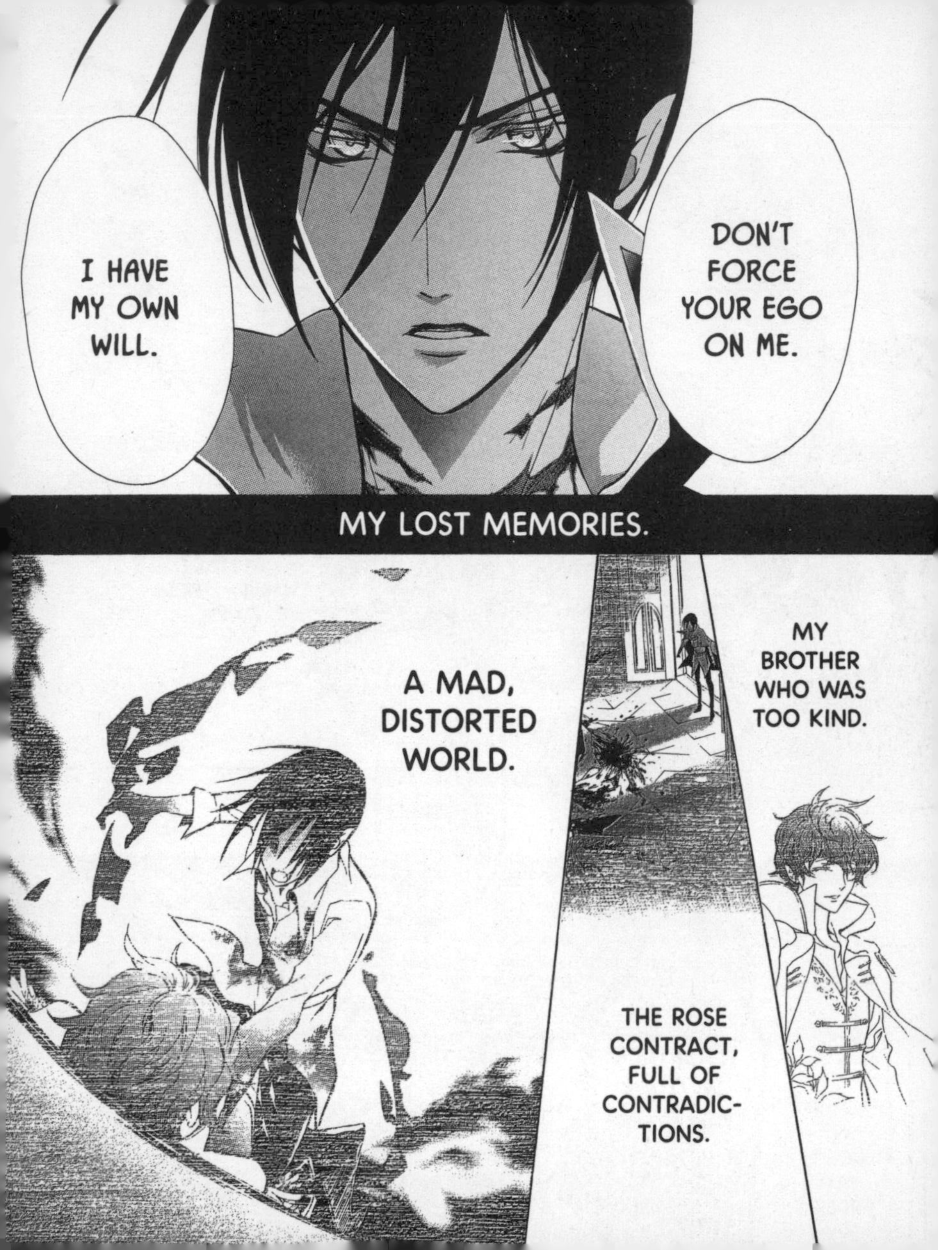
DON'T FORCE YOUR EGO ON ME.
I HAVE MY OWN WILL.
MY LOST MEMORIES.
MY BROTHER WHO WAS TOO KIND.
THE ROSE CONTRACT, FULL OF CONTRADIC-TIONS.
A MAD, DISTORTED WORLD.

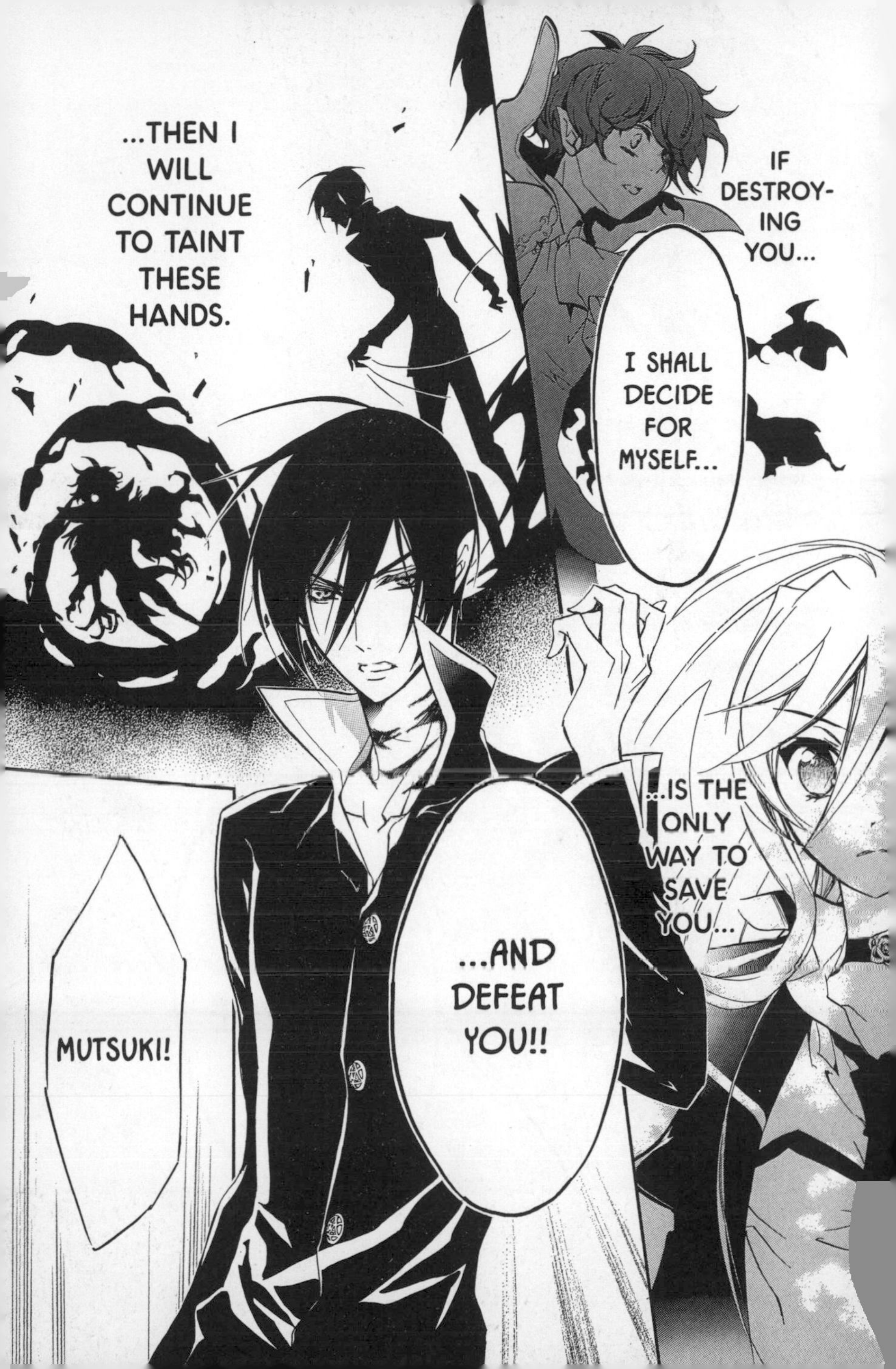
IF DESTROYING YOU...
I SHALL DECIDE FOR MYSELF...
...THEN I WILL CONTINUE TO TAINT THESE HANDS.
...IS THE ONLY WAY TO SAVE YOU...
...AND DEFEAT YOU!!
MUTSUKI!

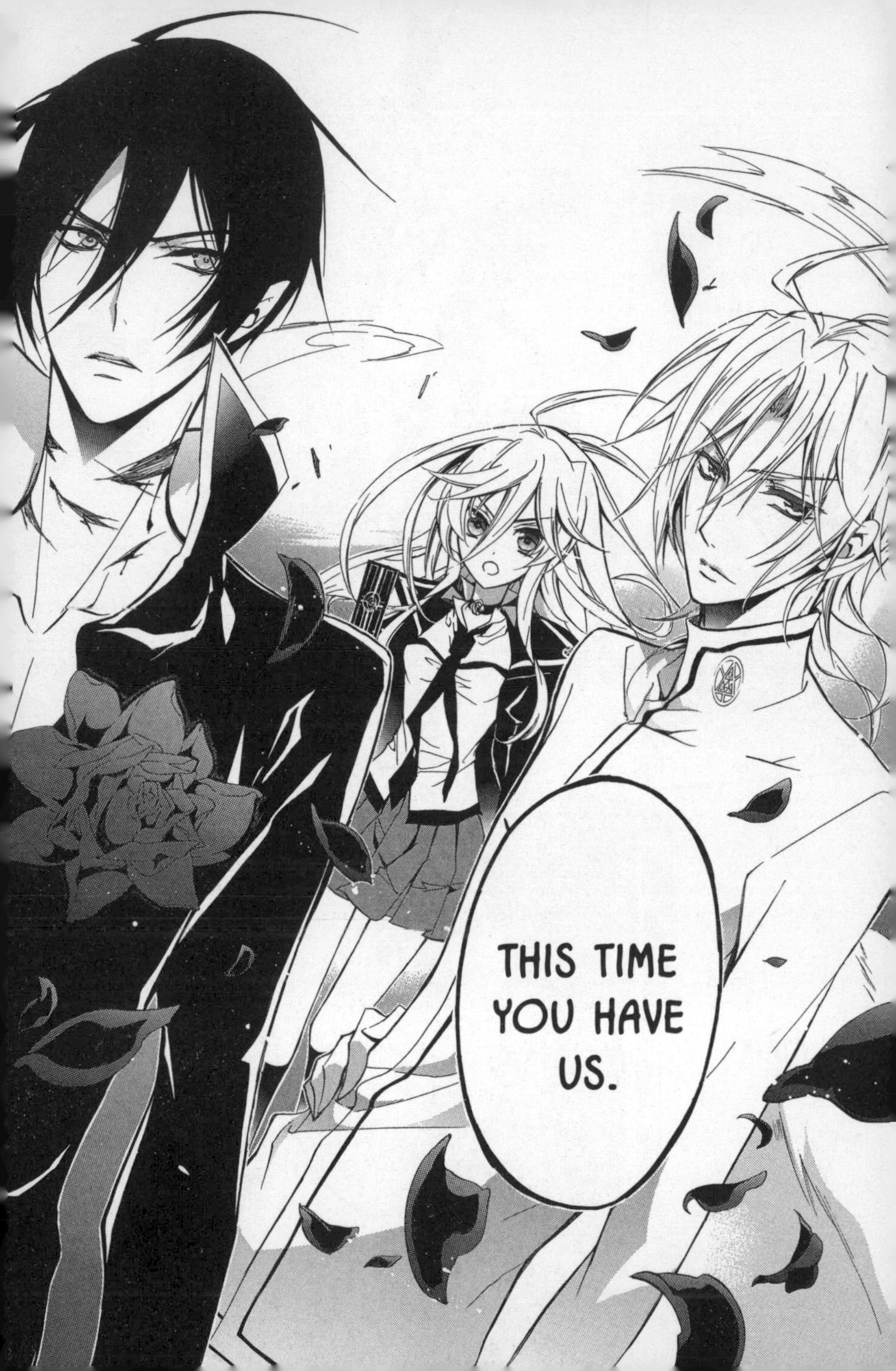
THIS TIME YOU HAVE US.

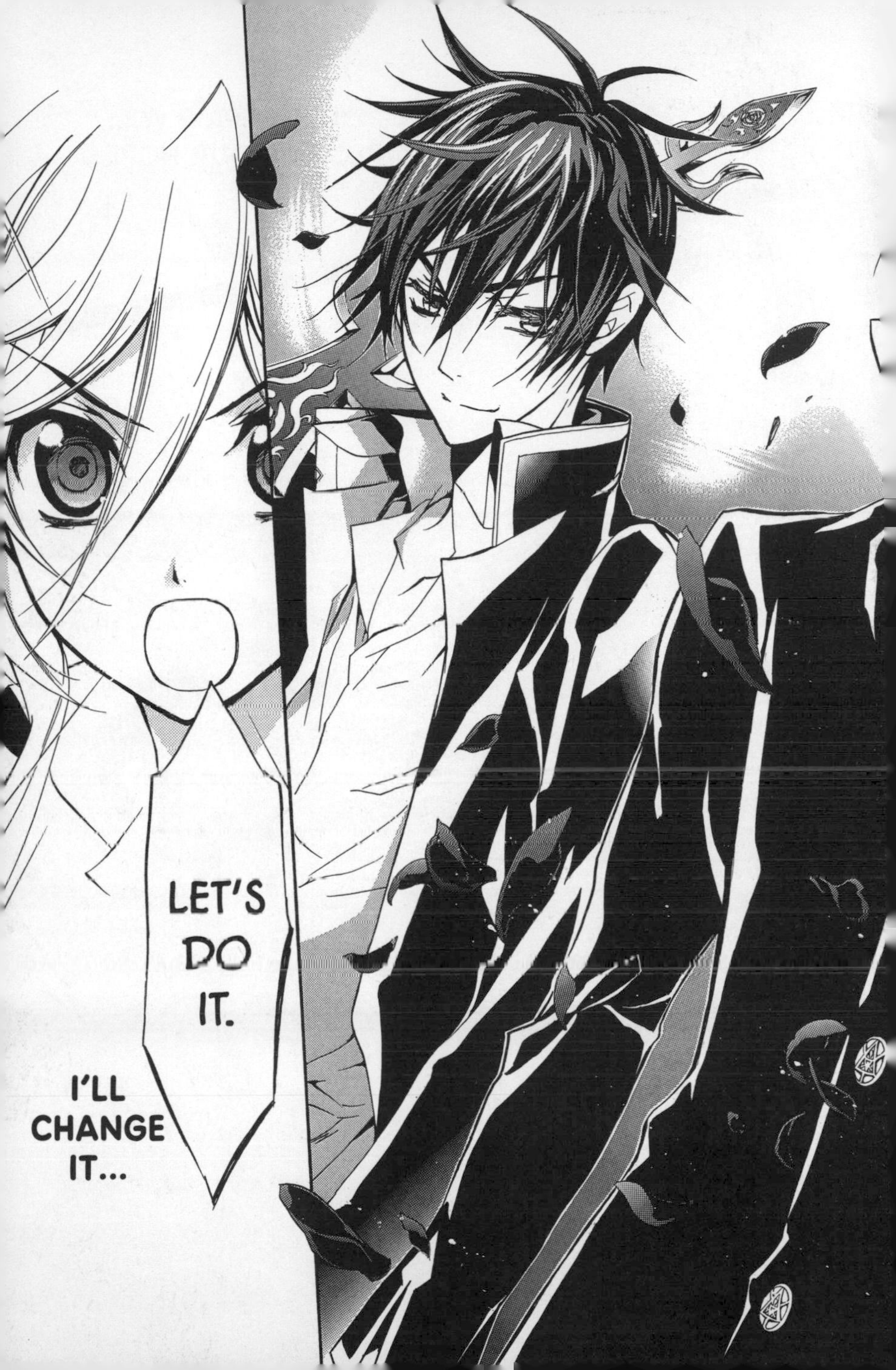
LET'S DO IT.
I'LL CHANGE IT...

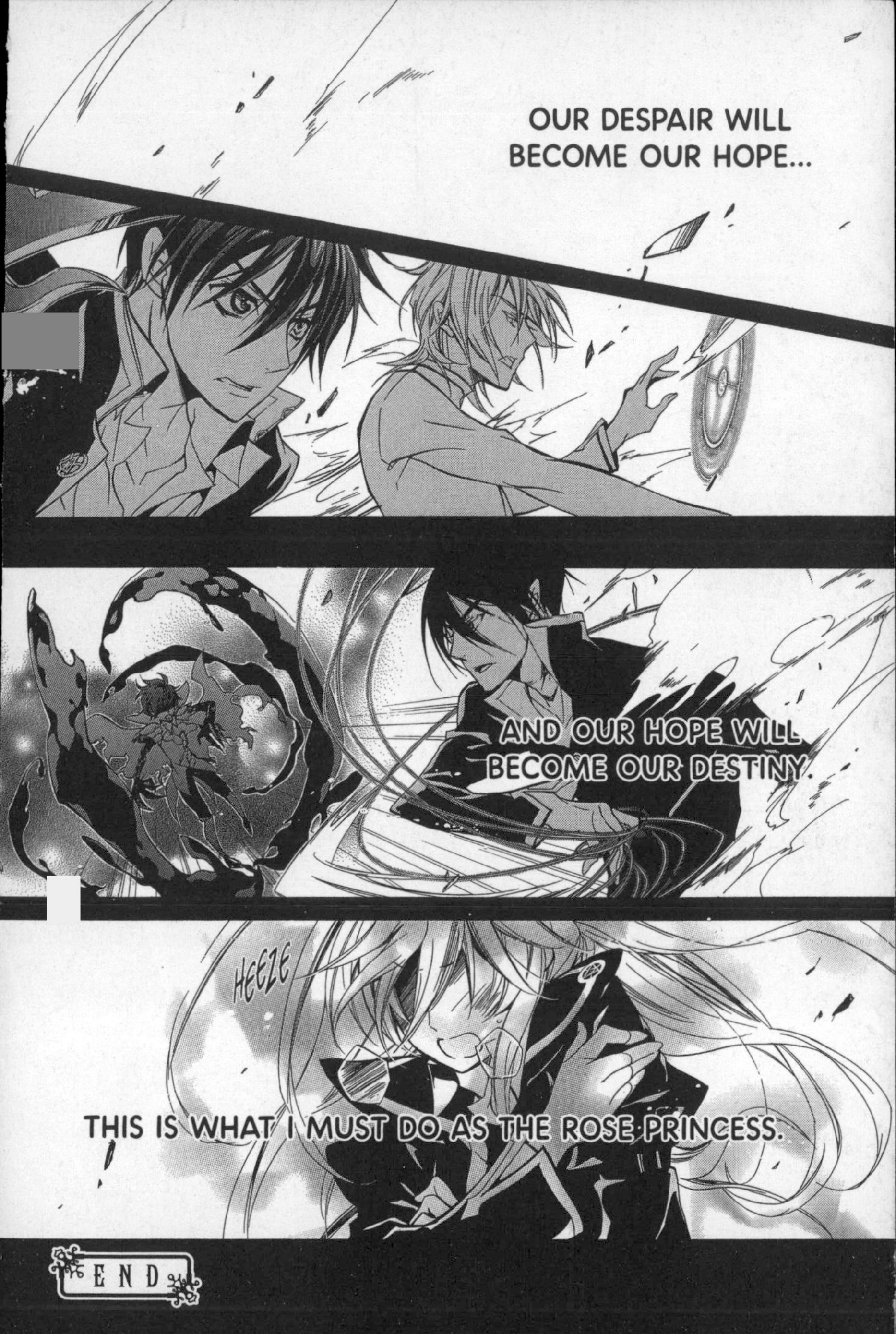
OUR DESPAIR WILL BECOME OUR HOPE...
AND OUR HOPE WILL BECOME OUR DESTINY.
HEEZE
THIS IS WHAT I MUST DO AS THE ROSE PRINCESS.
END

Kiss of the Rose Princess

Kiss of the Rose
Princess

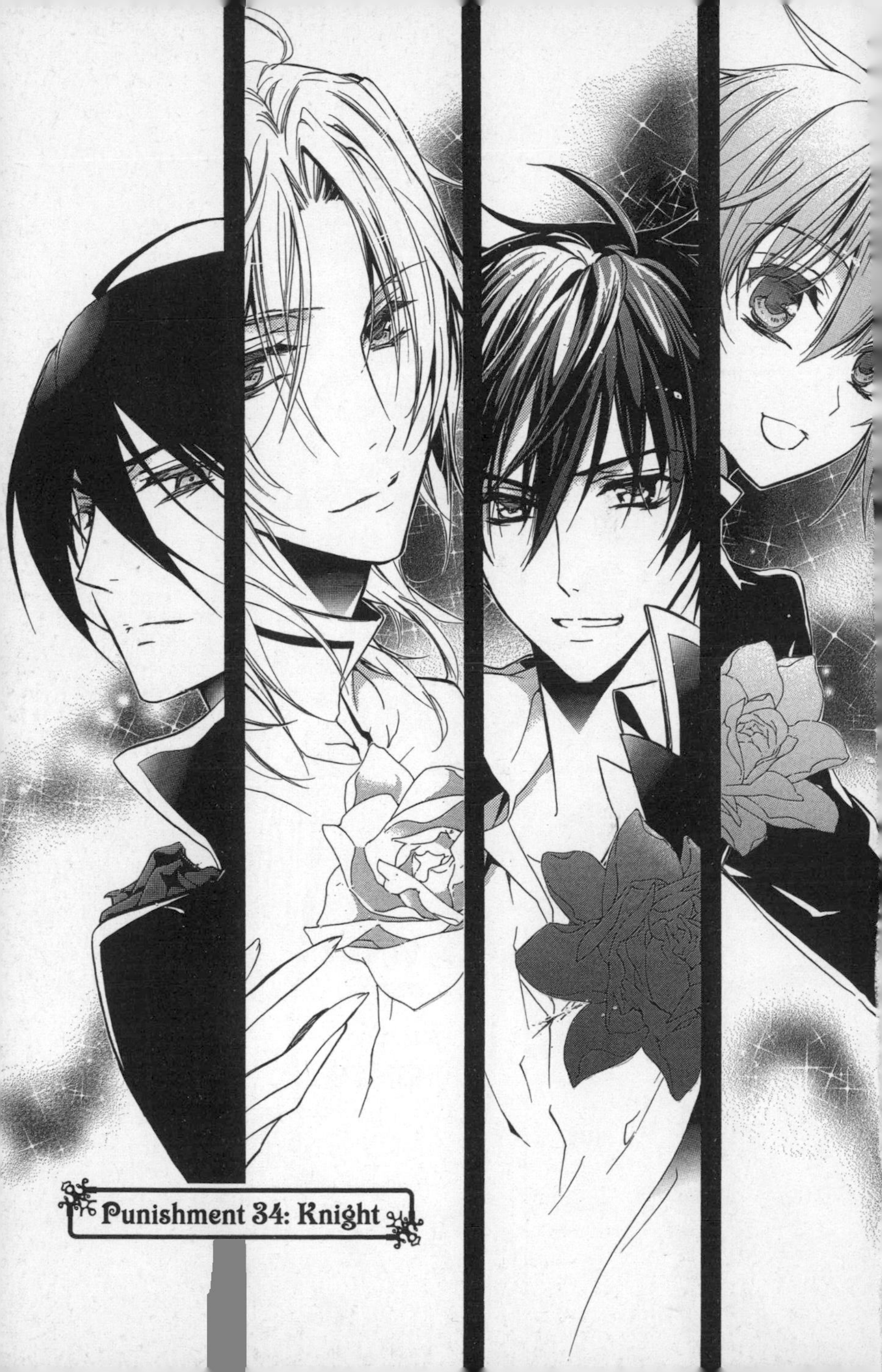

Punishment 34: Knight

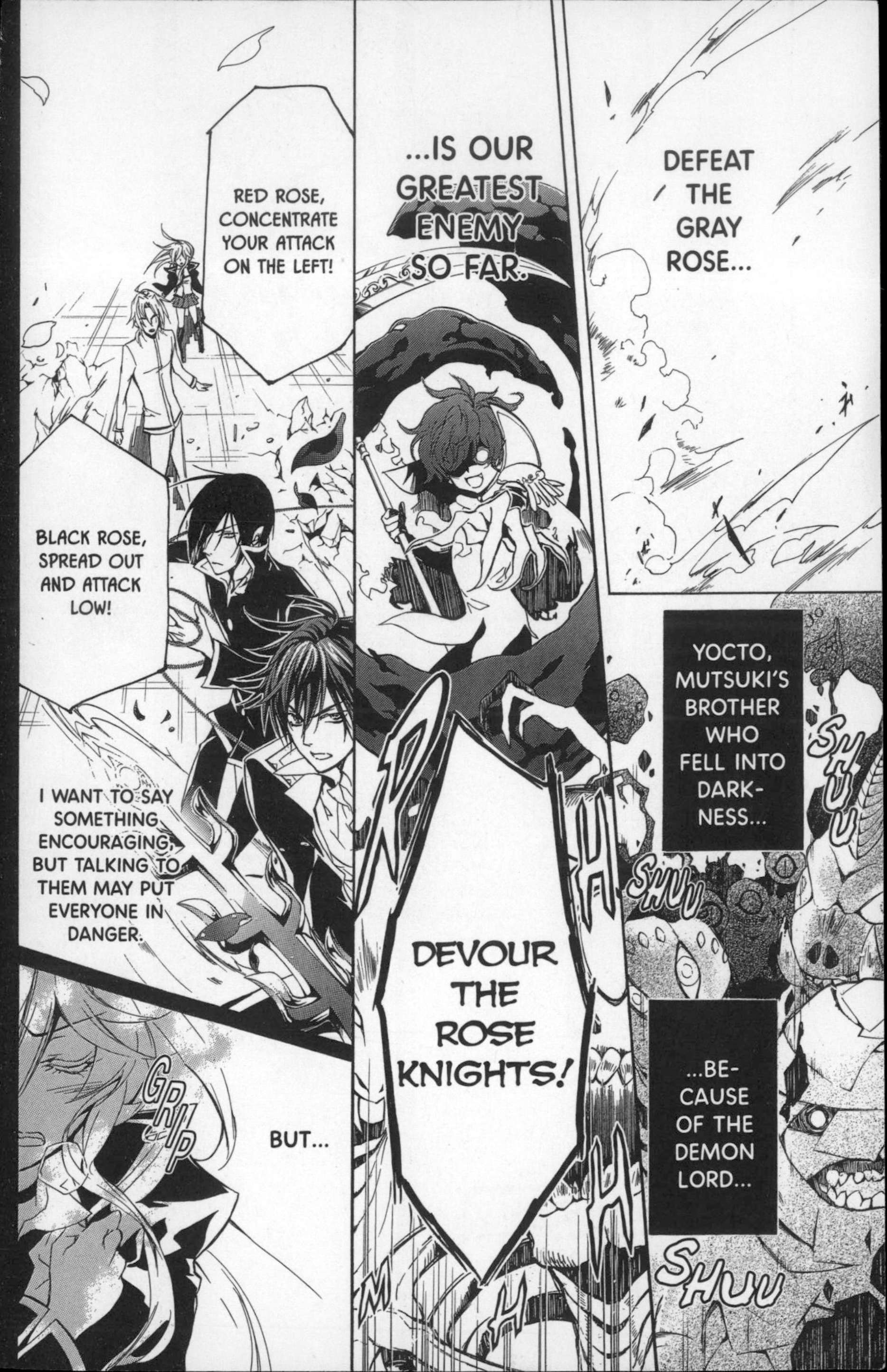

DEFEAT THE GRAY ROSE...
...IS OUR GREATEST ENEMY SO FAR.
YOCTO, MUTSUKI'S BROTHER WHO FELL INTO DARK-NESS...
SHUU
SHUU
...BE-CAUSE OF THE DEMON LORD...
SHUU
DEVOUR THE ROSE KNIGHTS!
RED ROSE, CONCENTRATE YOUR ATTACK ON THE LEFT!
BLACK ROSE, SPREAD OUT AND ATTACK LOW!
I WANT TO SAY SOMETHING ENCOURAGING, BUT TALKING TO THEM MAY PUT EVERYONE IN DANGER.
GRIP
BUT...

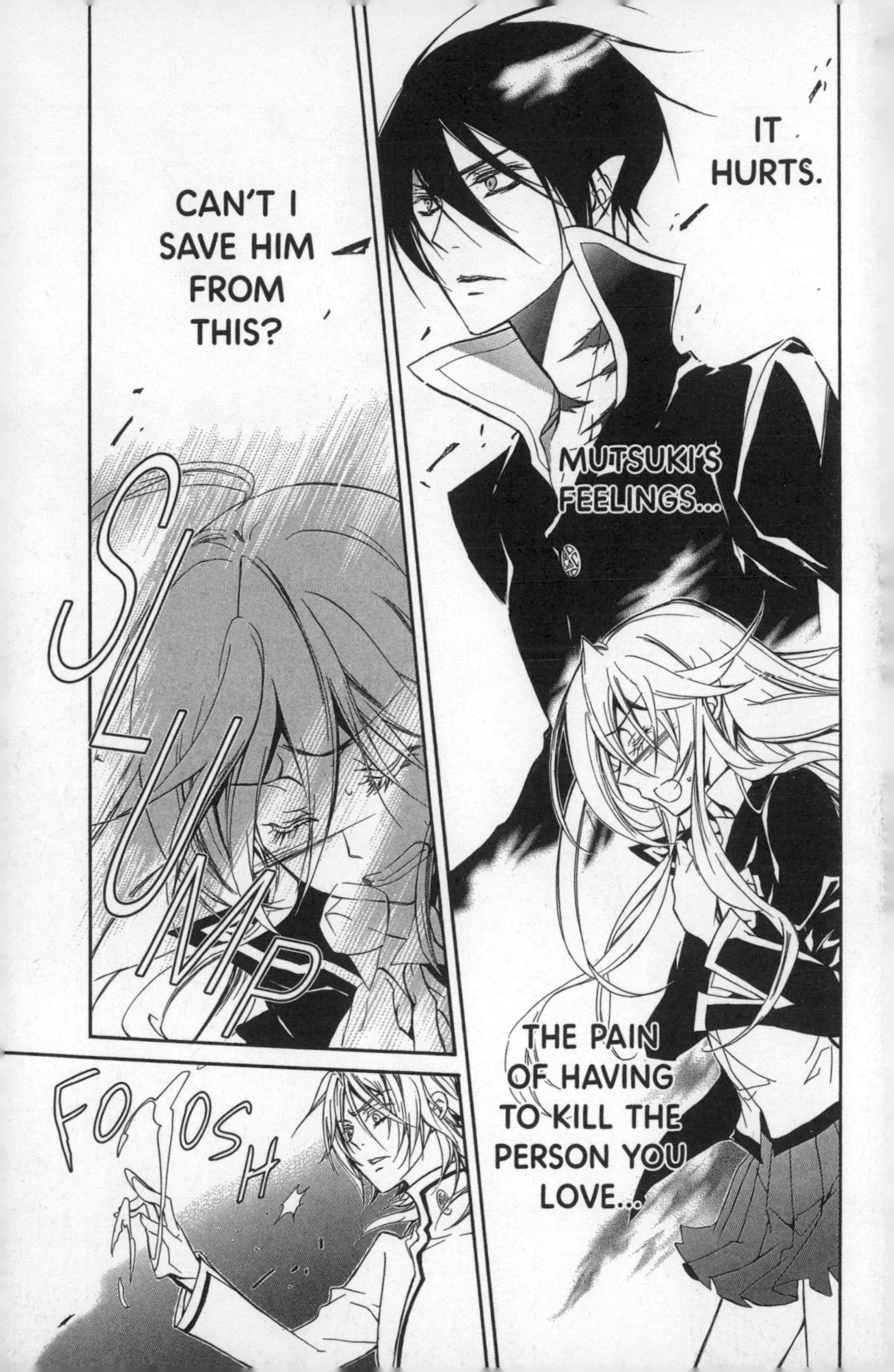
IT HURTS.
MUTSUKI'S FEELINGS...
THE PAIN OF HAVING TO KILL THE PERSON YOU LOVE...
CAN'T I SAVE HIM FROM THIS?
SLUMP
FOOSH

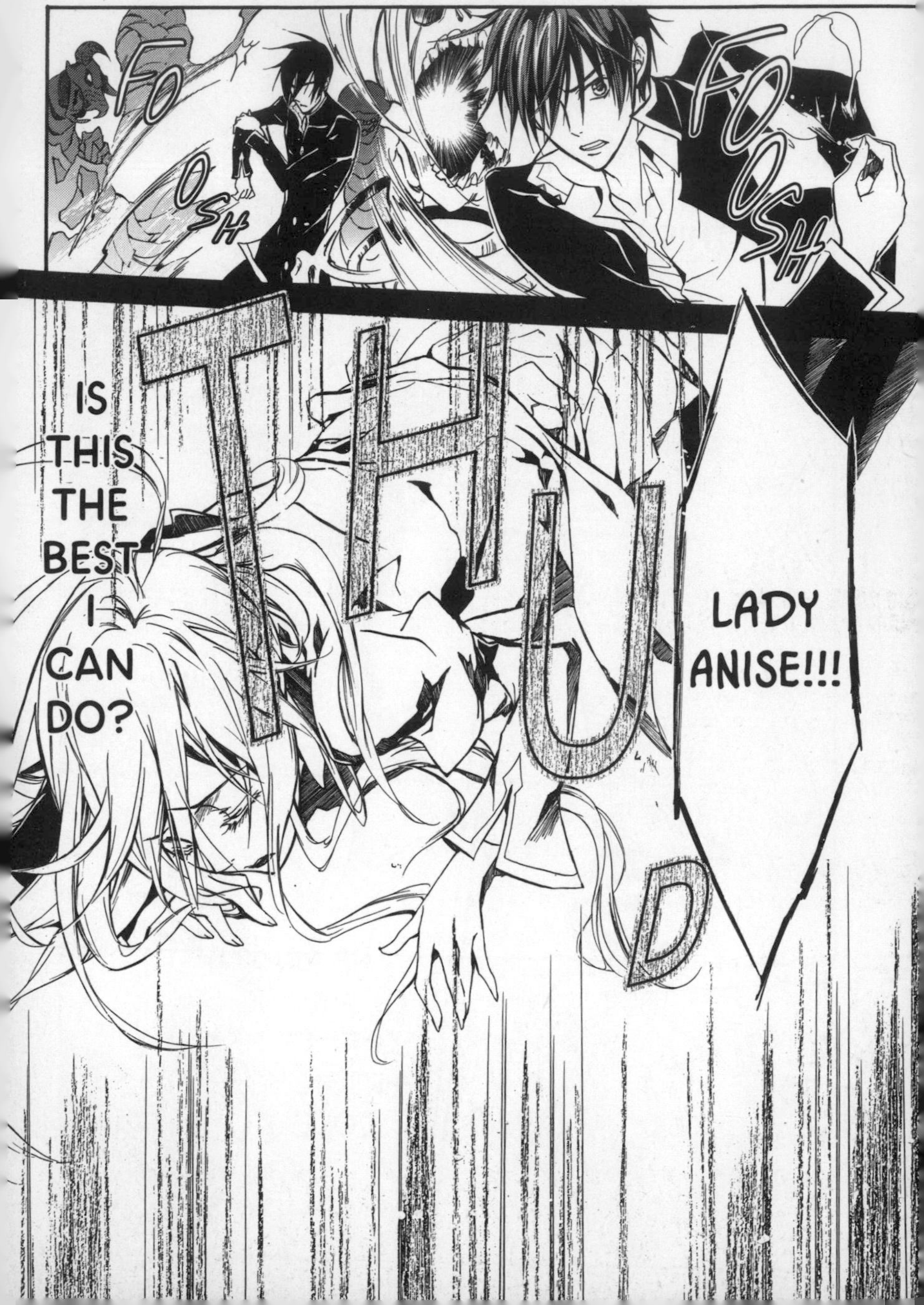
FOOSH
FOOSH
LADY ANISE!!!
THUD
IS THIS THE BEST I CAN DO?

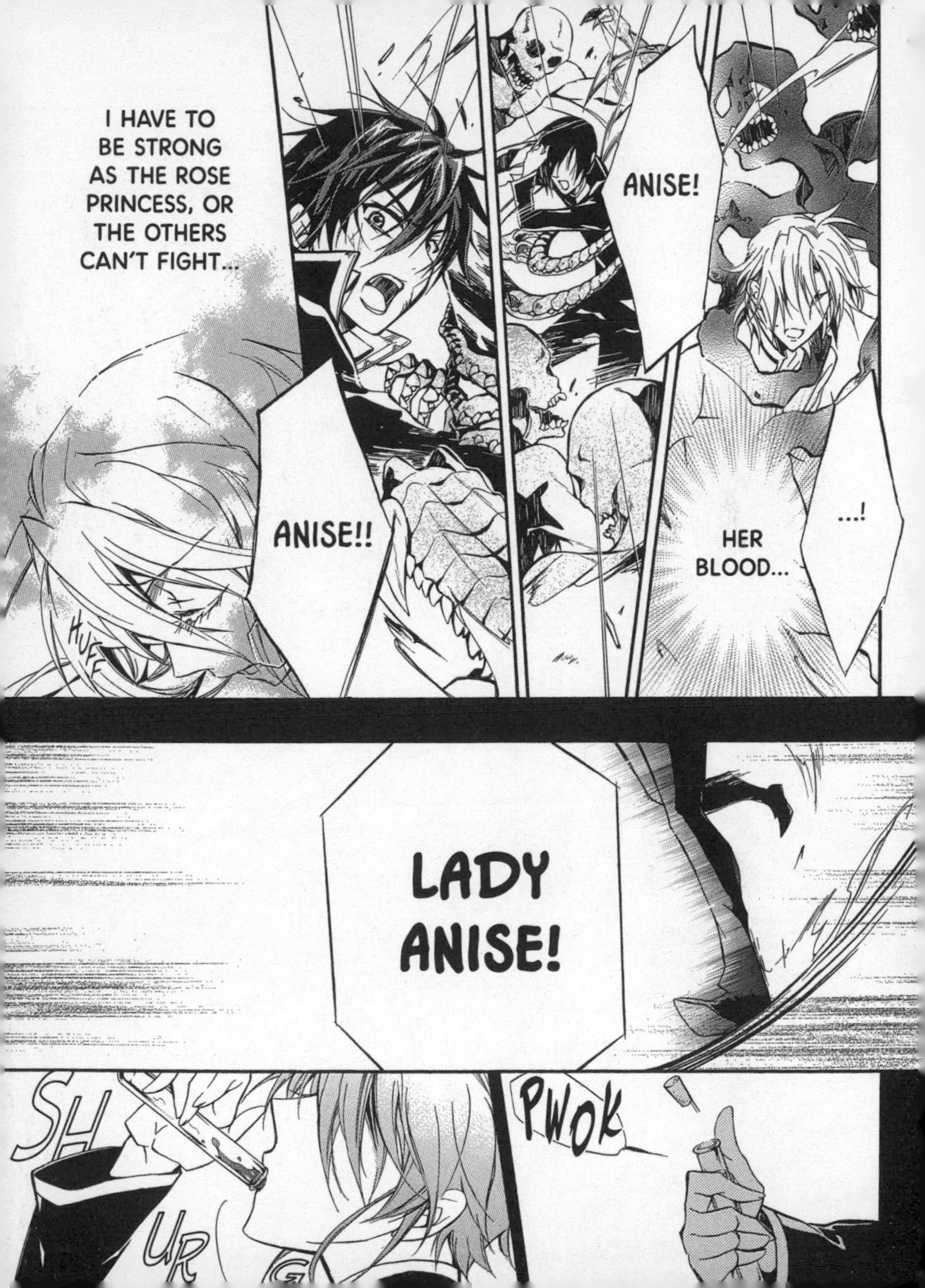
...!
HER BLOOD...
ANISE!
ANISE!!
I HAVE TO BE STRONG AS THE ROSE PRINCESS, OR THE OTHERS CAN'T FIGHT...
HUFF
LADY ANISE!
PWOK
SHURG

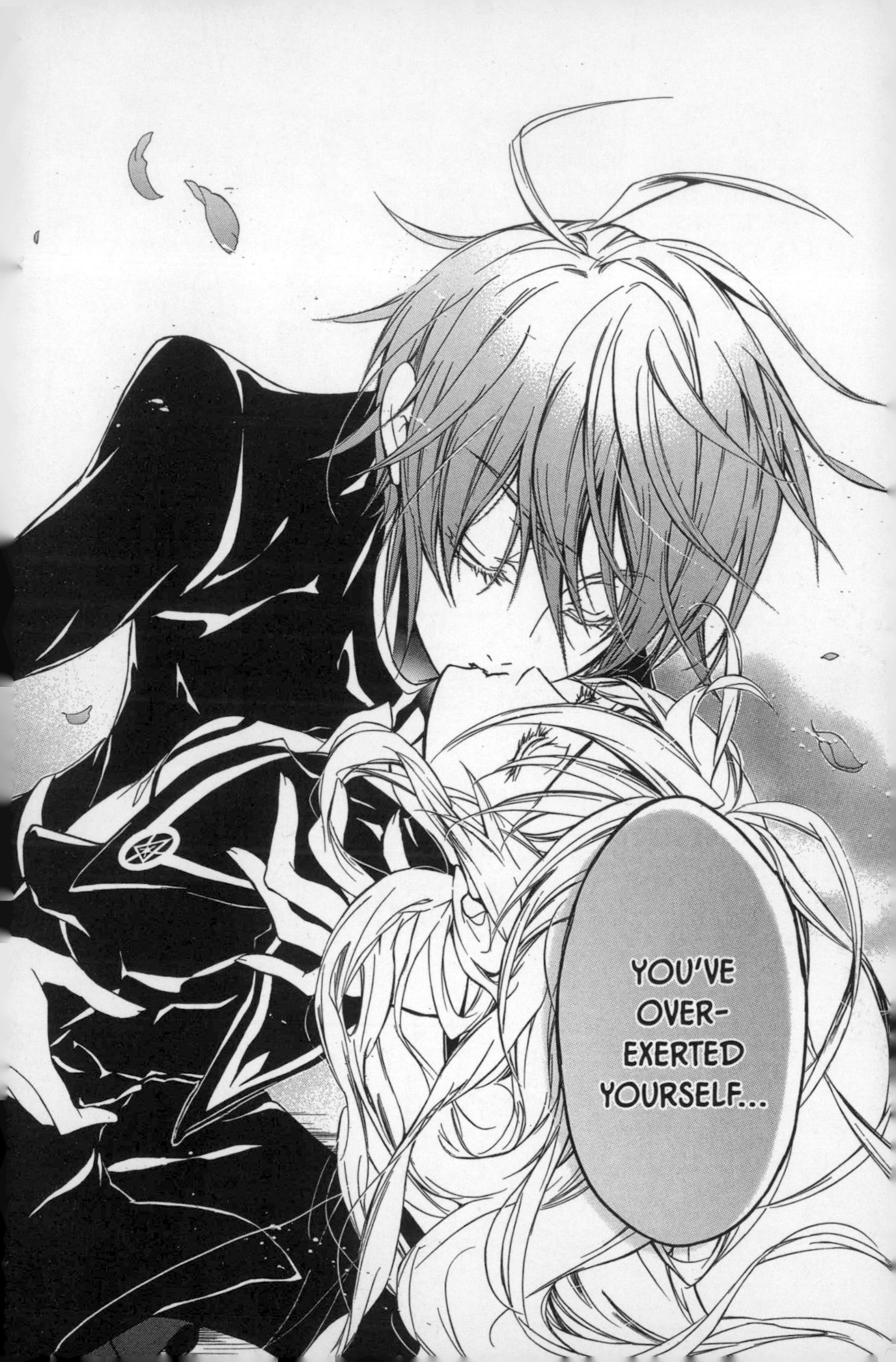
YOU'VE OVER-EXERTED YOURSELF...

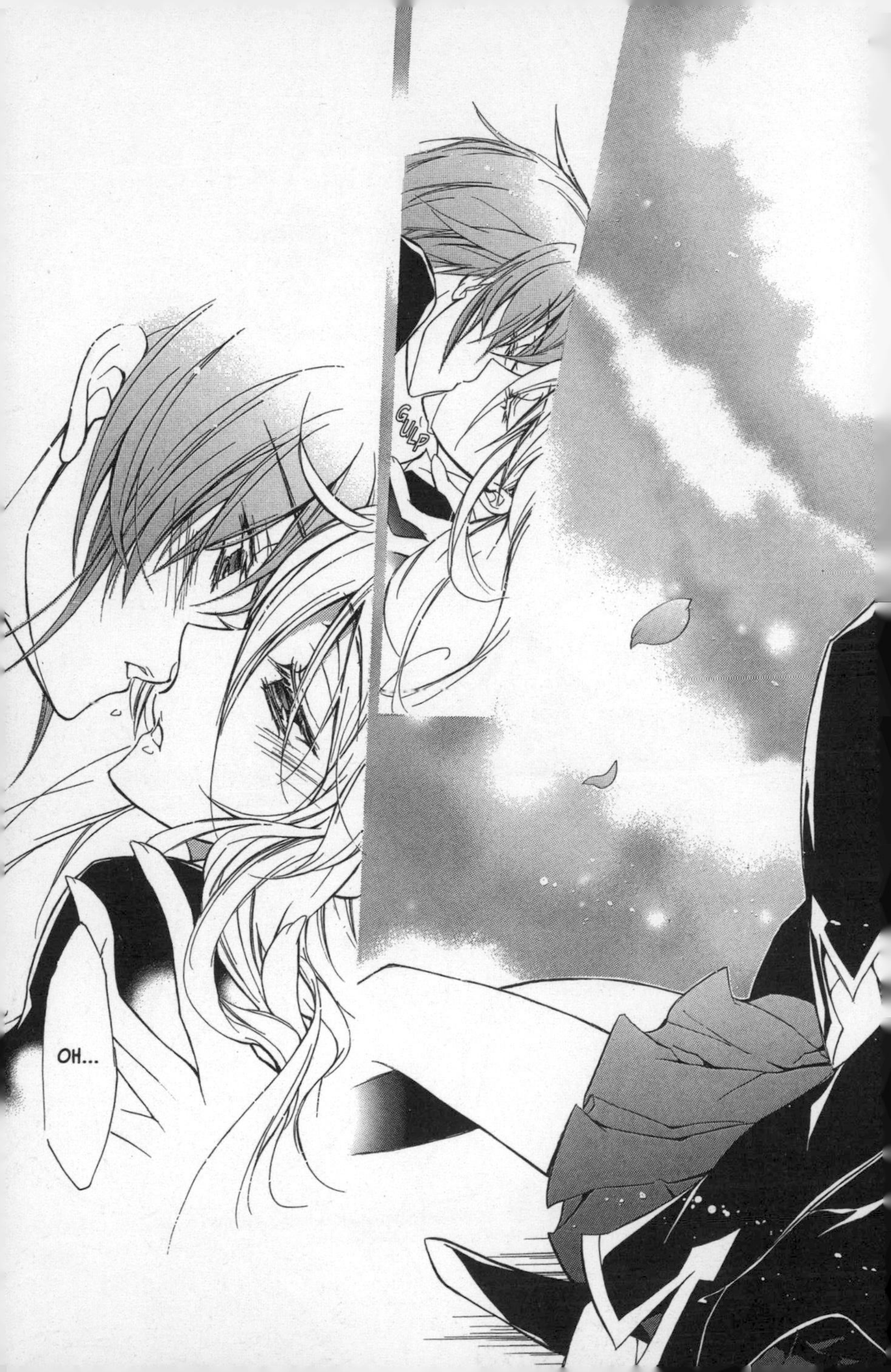
GULP
OH...

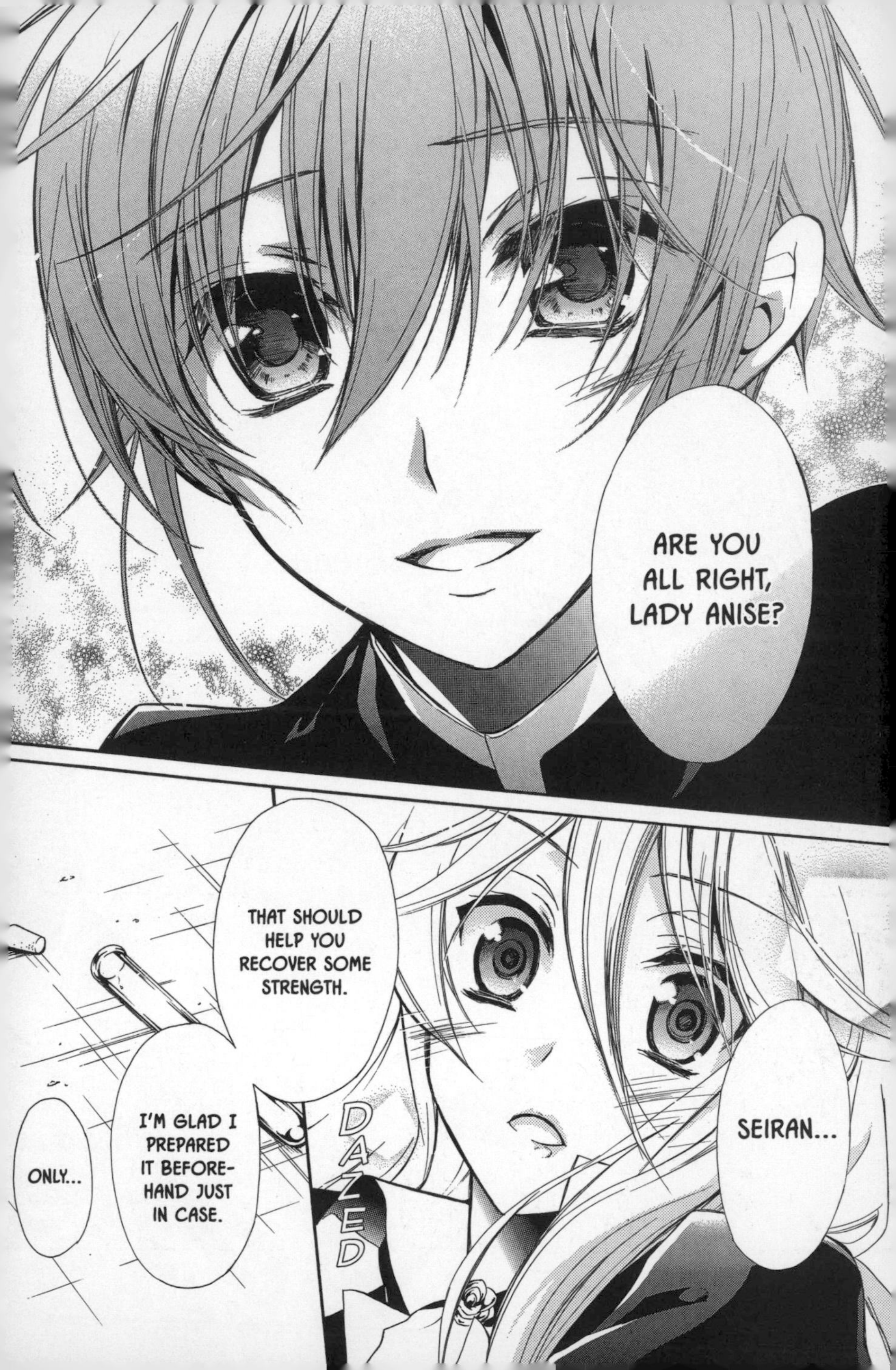
ARE YOU ALL RIGHT, LADY ANISE?
SEIRAN...
DAZED
THAT SHOULD HELP YOU RECOVER SOME STRENGTH.
I'M GLAD I PREPARED IT BEFORE-HAND JUST IN CASE.
ONLY...

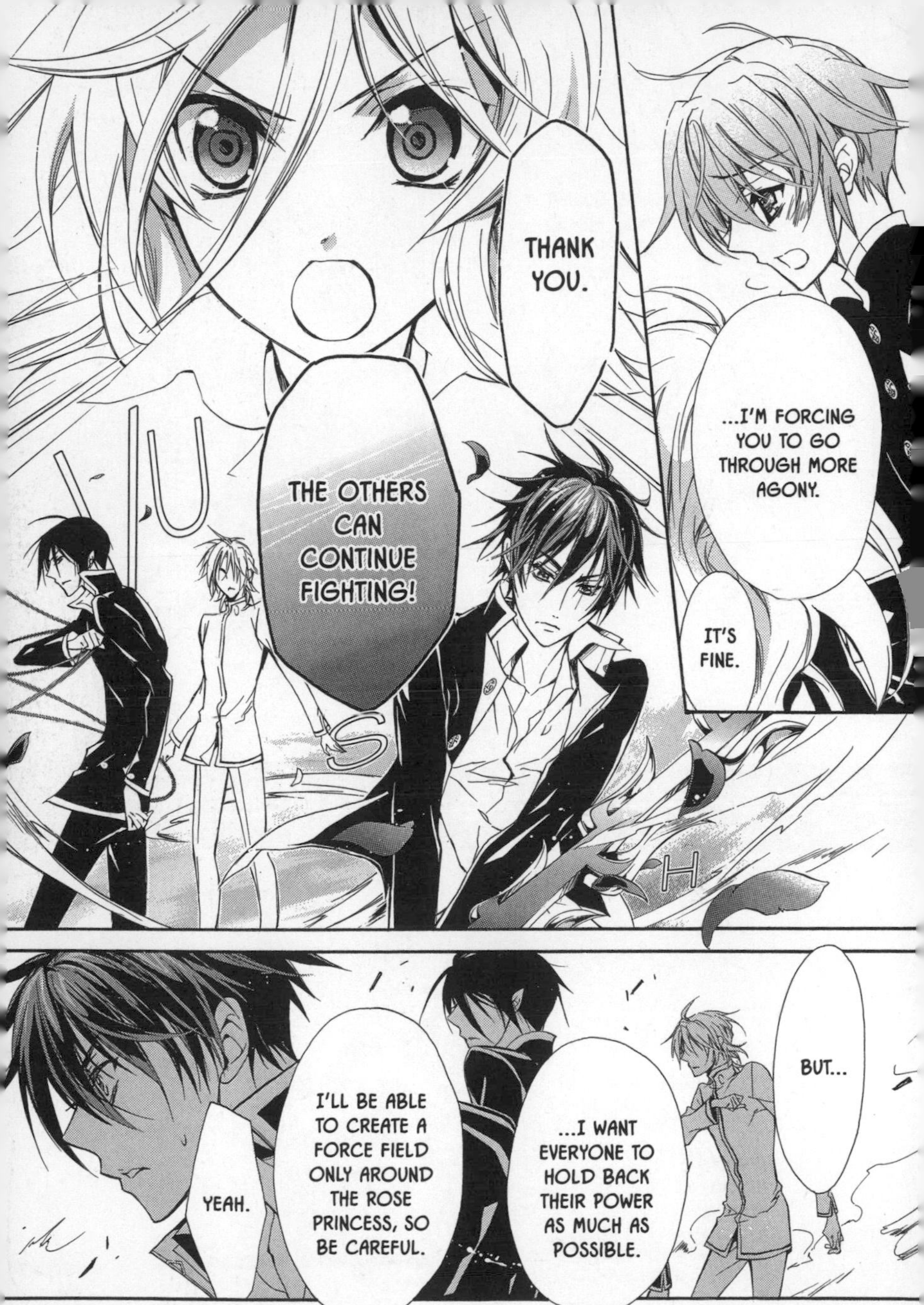

...I'M FORCING YOU TO GO THROUGH MORE AGONY.
IT'S FINE.
THANK YOU.
THE OTHERS CAN CONTINUE FIGHTING!
BUT...
...I WANT EVERYONE TO HOLD BACK THEIR POWER AS MUCH AS POSSIBLE.
I'LL BE ABLE TO CREATE A FORCE FIELD ONLY AROUND THE ROSE PRINCESS, SO BE CAREFUL.
YEAH.

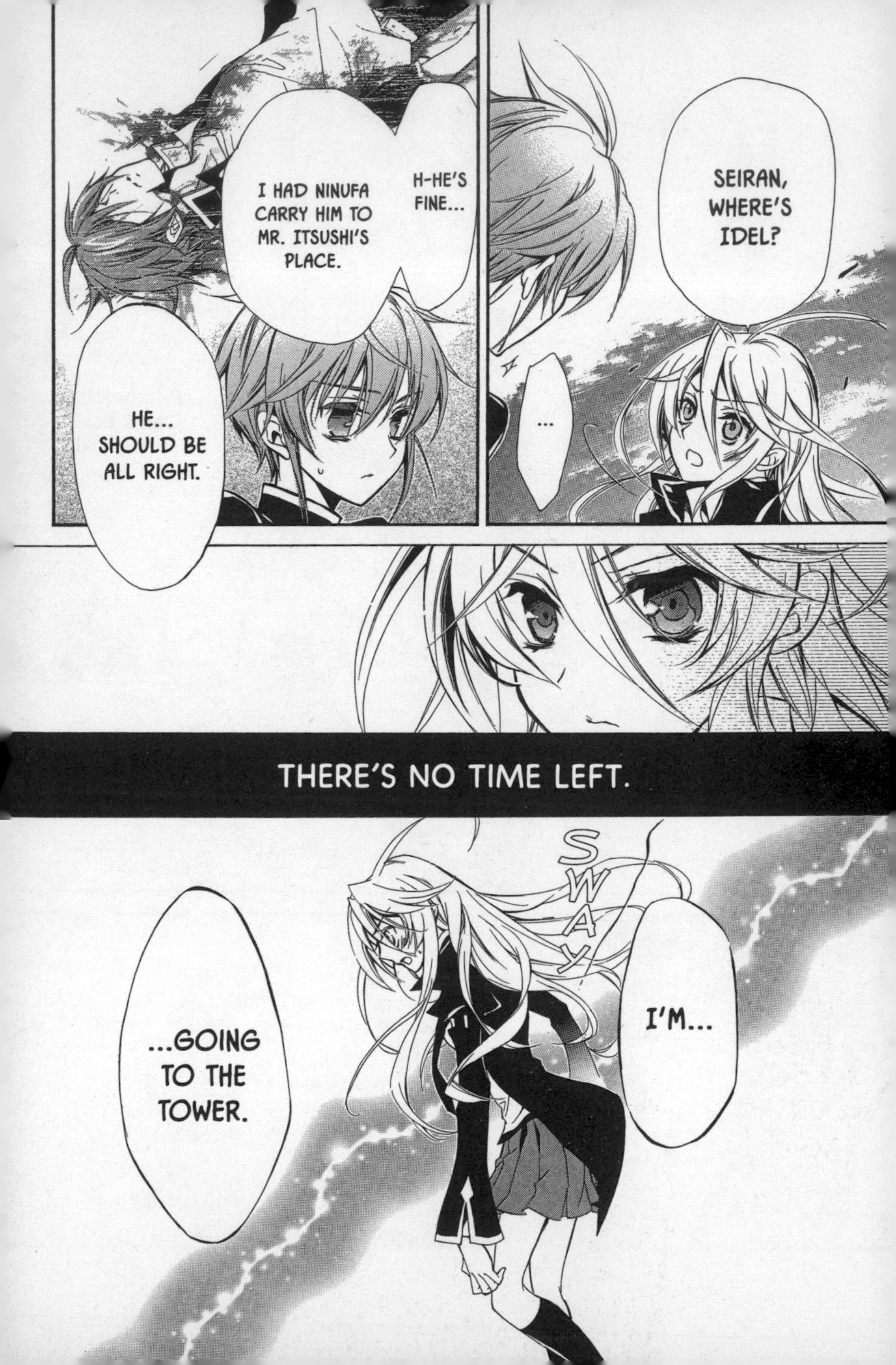
SEIRAN, WHERE'S IDEL?
...
H-HE'S FINE...
I HAD NINUFA CARRY HIM TO MR. ITSUSHI'S PLACE.
HE... SHOULD BE ALL RIGHT.
THERE'S NO TIME LEFT.
SWAY
I'M...
...GOING TO THE TOWER.

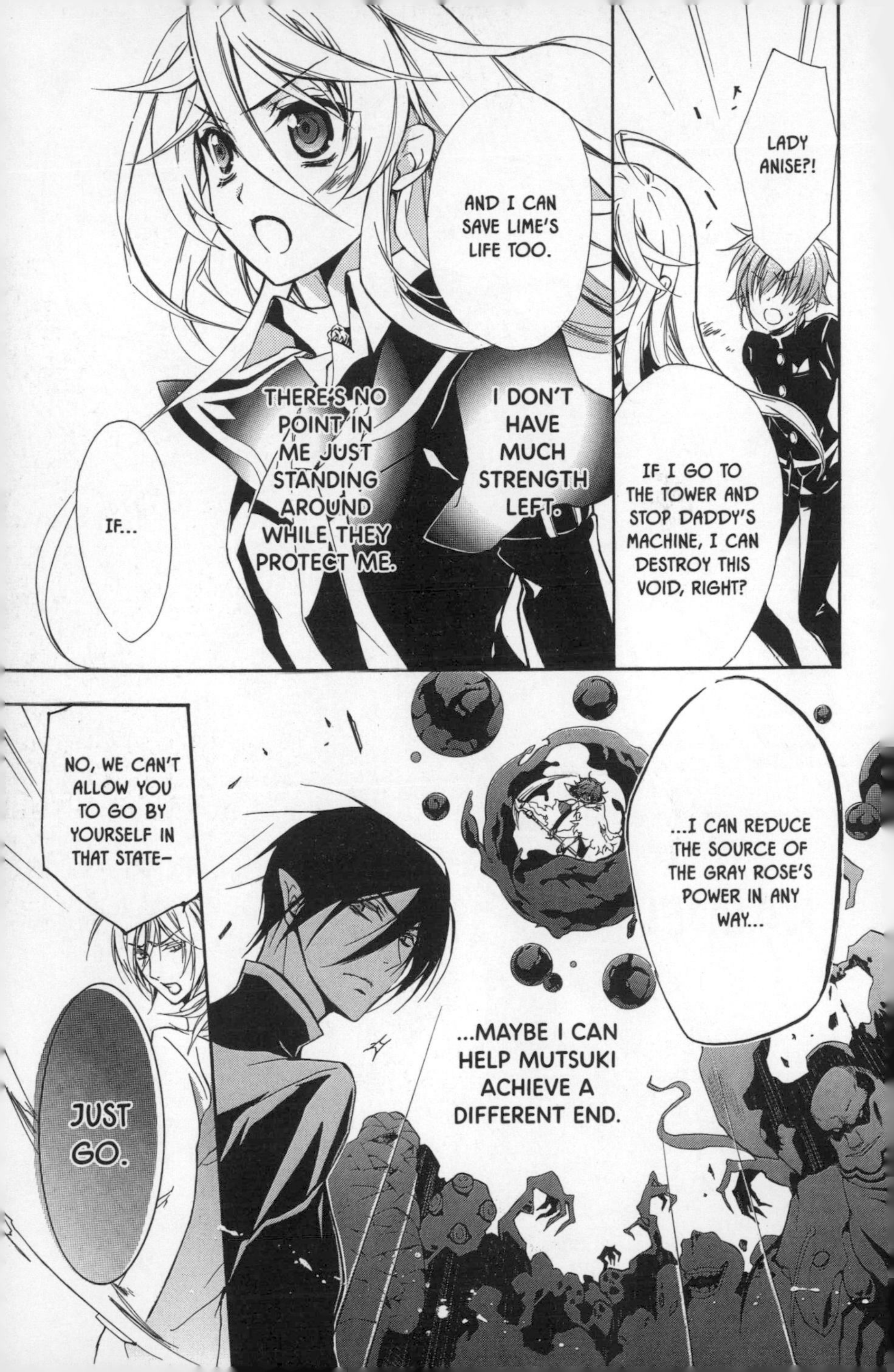
LADY ANISE?!
IF I GO TO THE TOWER AND STOP DADDY'S MACHINE, I CAN DESTROY THIS VOID, RIGHT?
AND I CAN SAVE LIME'S LIFE TOO.
I DON'T HAVE MUCH STRENGTH LEFT.
THERE'S NO POINT IN ME JUST STANDING AROUND WHILE THEY PROTECT ME.
IF...
...I CAN REDUCE THE SOURCE OF THE GRAY ROSE'S POWER IN ANY WAY...
...MAYBE I CAN HELP MUTSUKI ACHIEVE A DIFFERENT END.
NO, WE CAN'T ALLOW YOU TO GO BY YOURSELF IN THAT STATE–
JUST GO.

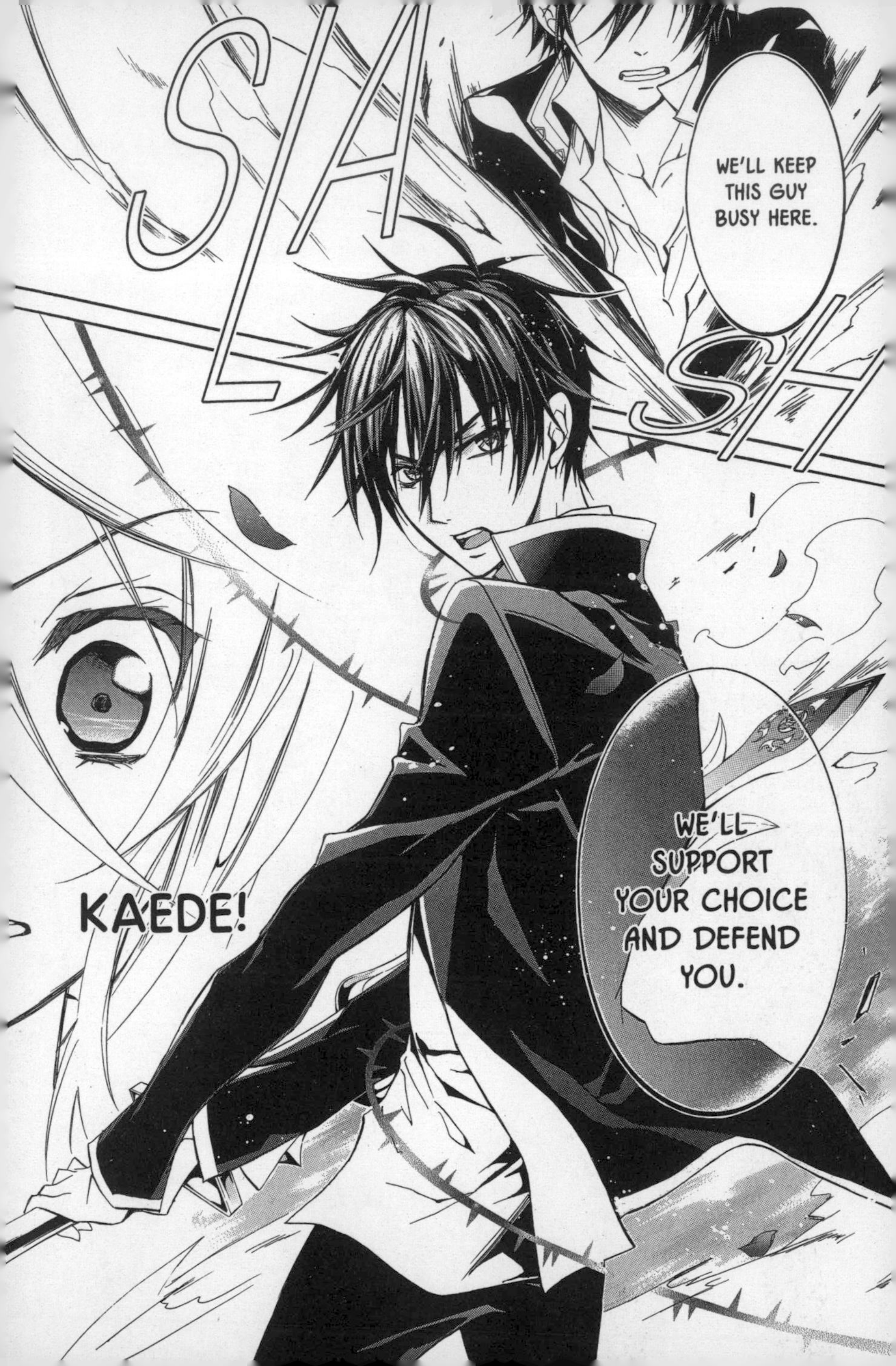
WE'LL KEEP THIS GUY BUSY HERE.
SLASH
WE'LL SUPPORT YOUR CHOICE AND DEFEND YOU.
KAEDE!

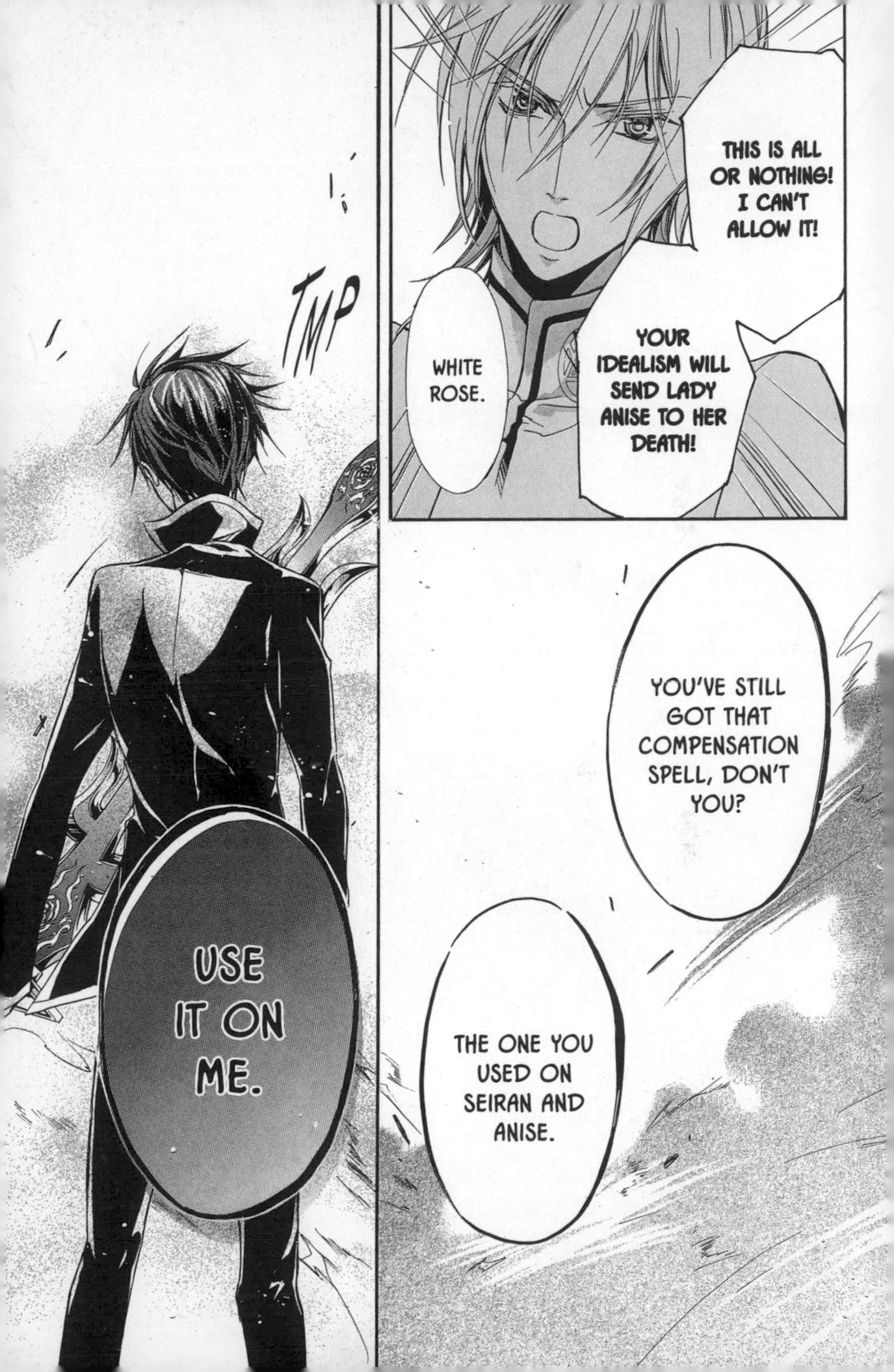
THIS IS ALL OR NOTHING! I CAN'T ALLOW IT!
YOUR IDEALISM WILL SEND LADY ANISE TO HER DEATH!
WHITE ROSE.
YOU'VE STILL GOT THAT COMPENSATION SPELL, DON'T YOU?
THE ONE YOU USED ON SEIRAN AND ANISE.
TMP
USE IT ON ME.

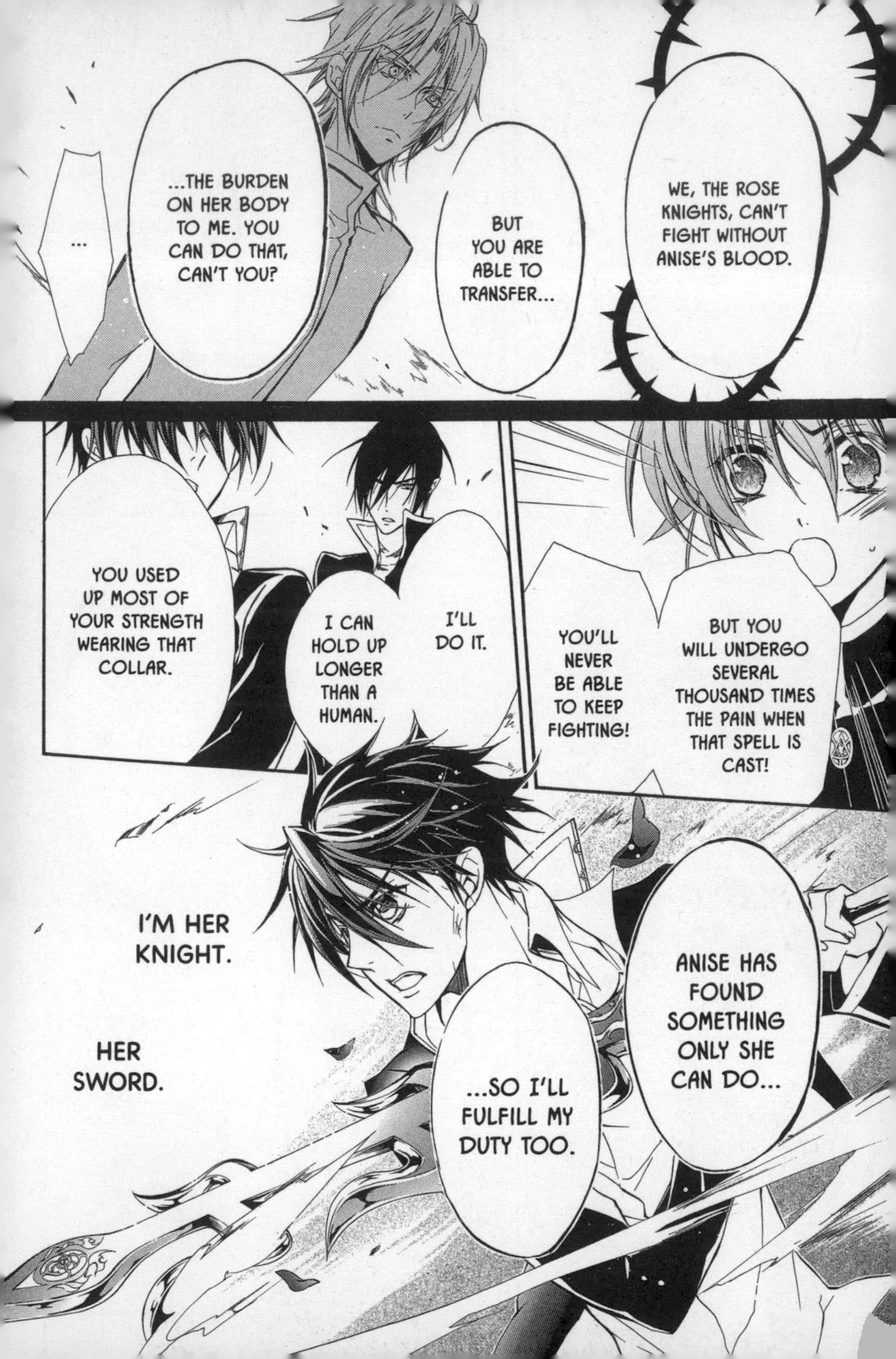
WE, THE ROSE KNIGHTS, CAN'T FIGHT WITHOUT ANISE'S BLOOD.
BUT YOU ARE ABLE TO TRANSFER...
...THE BURDEN ON HER BODY TO ME. YOU CAN DO THAT, CAN'T YOU?
...
BUT YOU WILL UNDERGO SEVERAL THOUSAND TIMES THE PAIN WHEN THAT SPELL IS CAST!
YOU'LL NEVER BE ABLE TO KEEP FIGHTING!
I'LL DO IT.
I CAN HOLD UP LONGER THAN A HUMAN.
YOU USED UP MOST OF YOUR STRENGTH WEARING THAT COLLAR.
ANISE HAS FOUND SOMETHING ONLY SHE CAN DO...
...SO I'LL FULFILL MY DUTY TOO.
I'M HER KNIGHT.
HER SWORD.

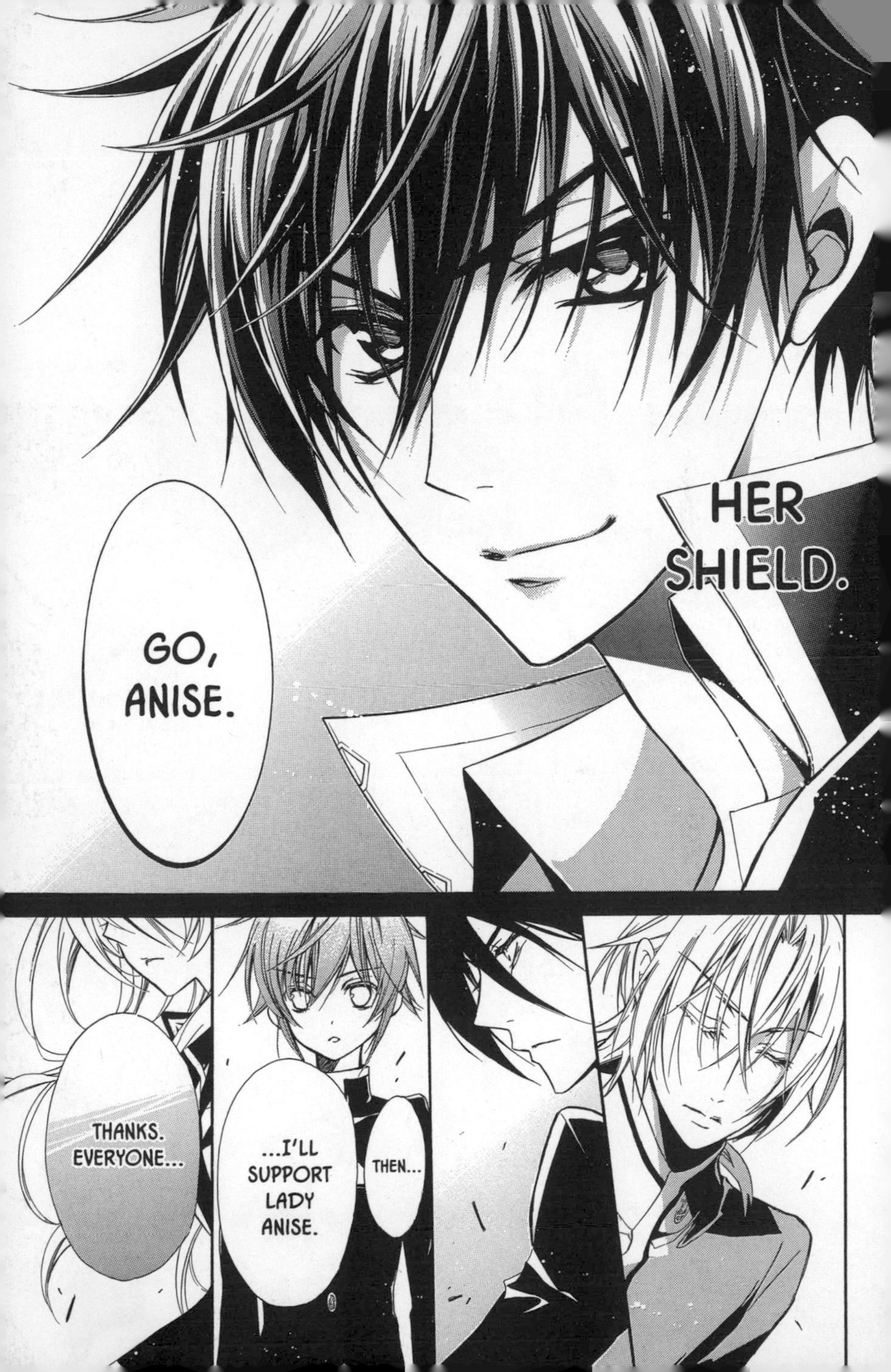
HER SHIELD.
GO, ANISE.
THEN...
...I'LL SUPPORT LADY ANISE.
THANKS. EVERYONE...

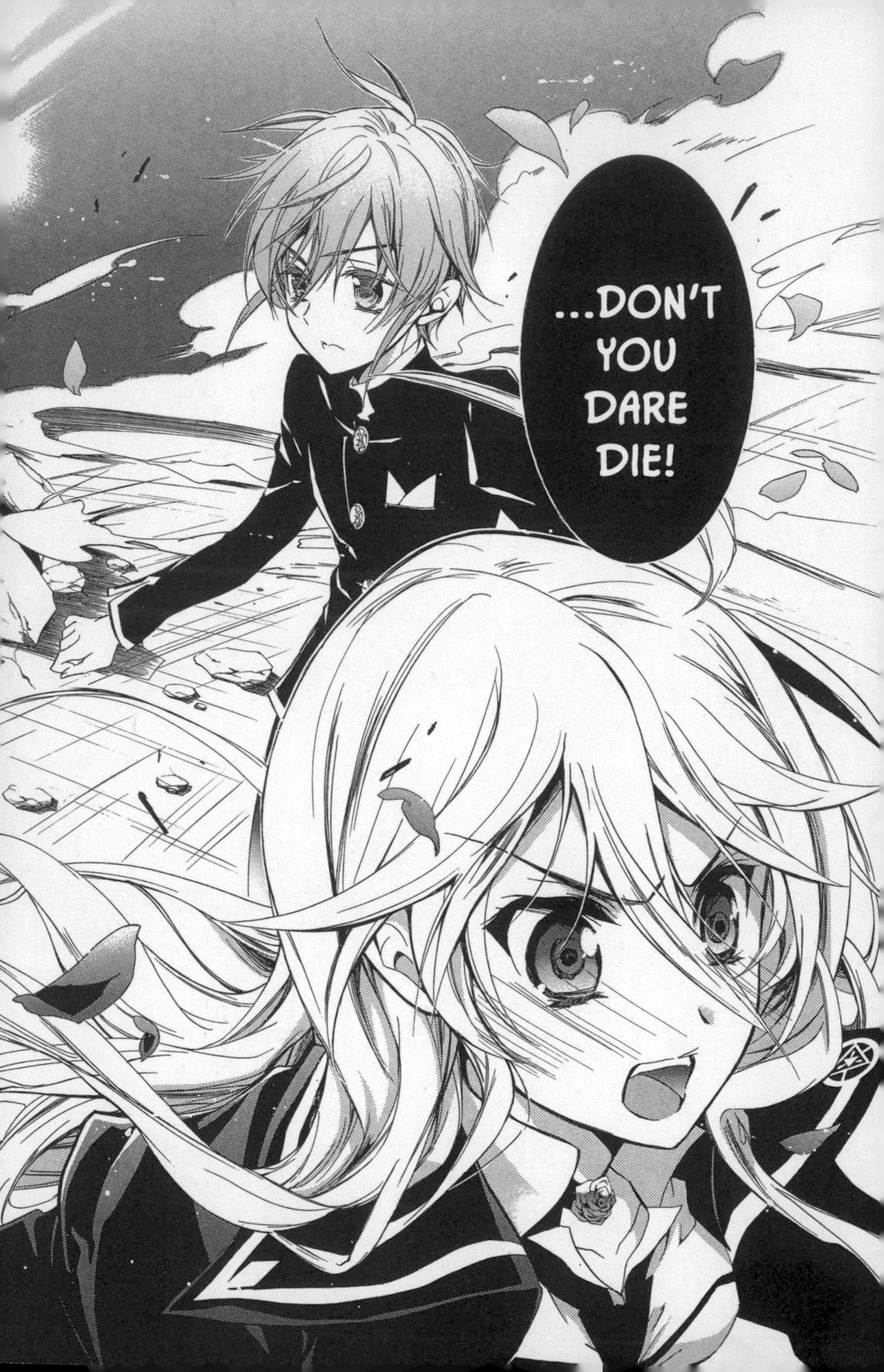
...DON'T YOU DARE DIE!

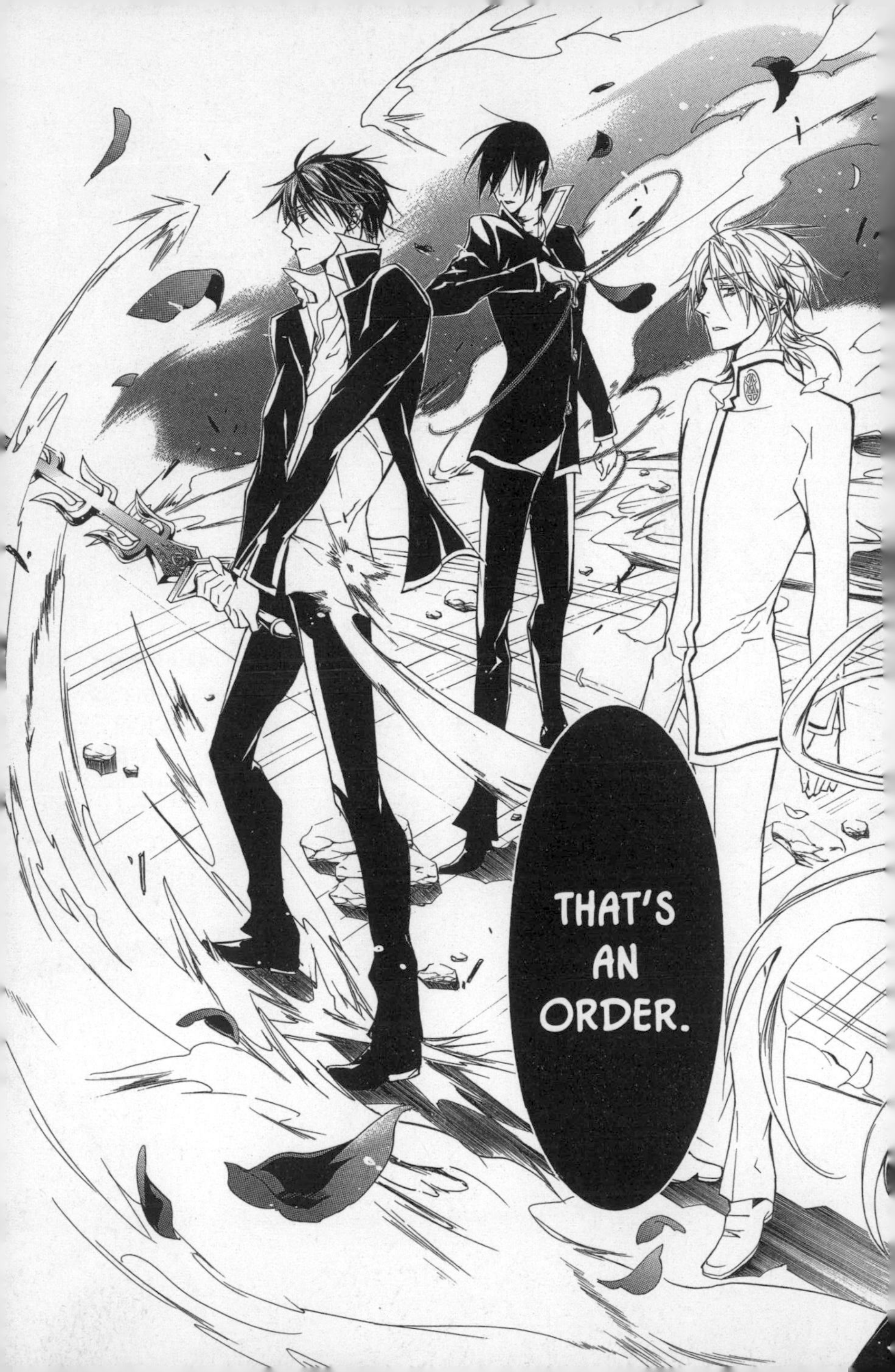
THAT'S AN ORDER.

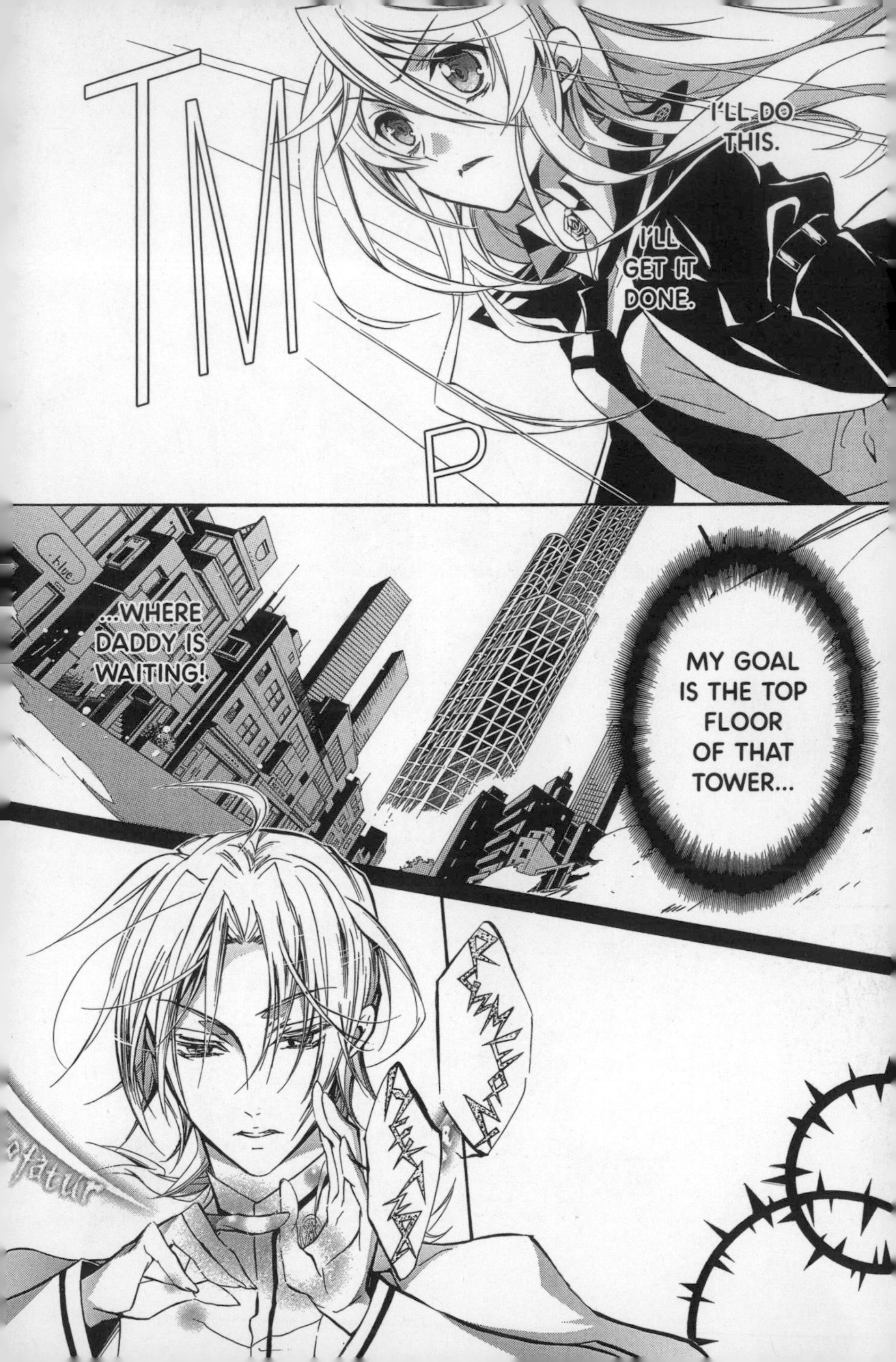
I'LL DO THIS.
I'LL GET IT DONE.
TMP
MY GOAL IS THE TOP FLOOR OF THAT TOWER...
...WHERE DADDY IS WAITING!
blue

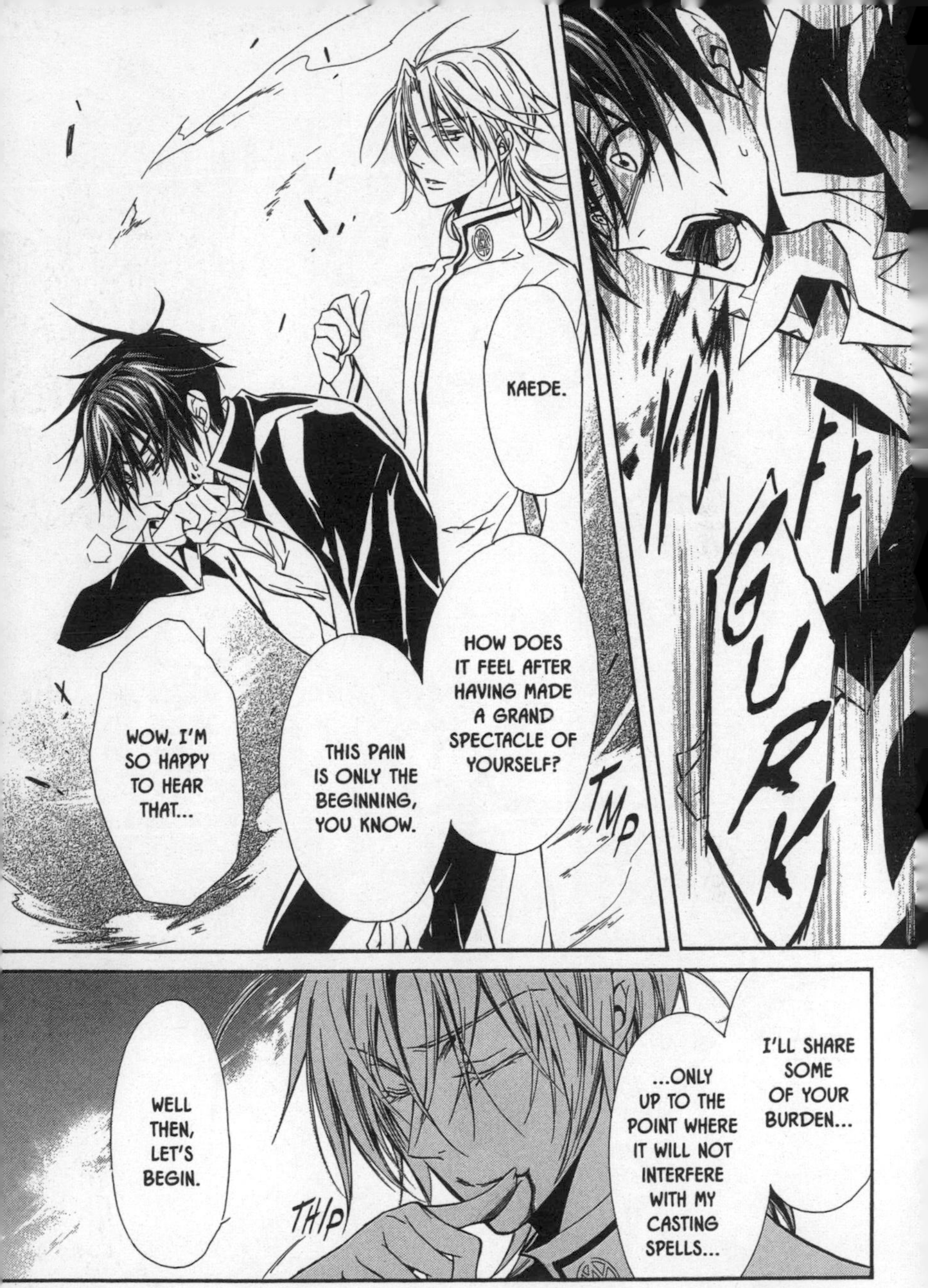
KOFF
GURK
KAEDE.
HOW DOES IT FEEL AFTER HAVING MADE A GRAND SPECTACLE OF YOURSELF?
THIS PAIN IS ONLY THE BEGINNING, YOU KNOW.
TMP
WOW, I'M SO HAPPY TO HEAR THAT...
I'LL SHARE SOME OF YOUR BURDEN...
...ONLY UP TO THE POINT WHERE IT WILL NOT INTERFERE WITH MY CASTING SPELLS...
THIP
WELL THEN, LET'S BEGIN.

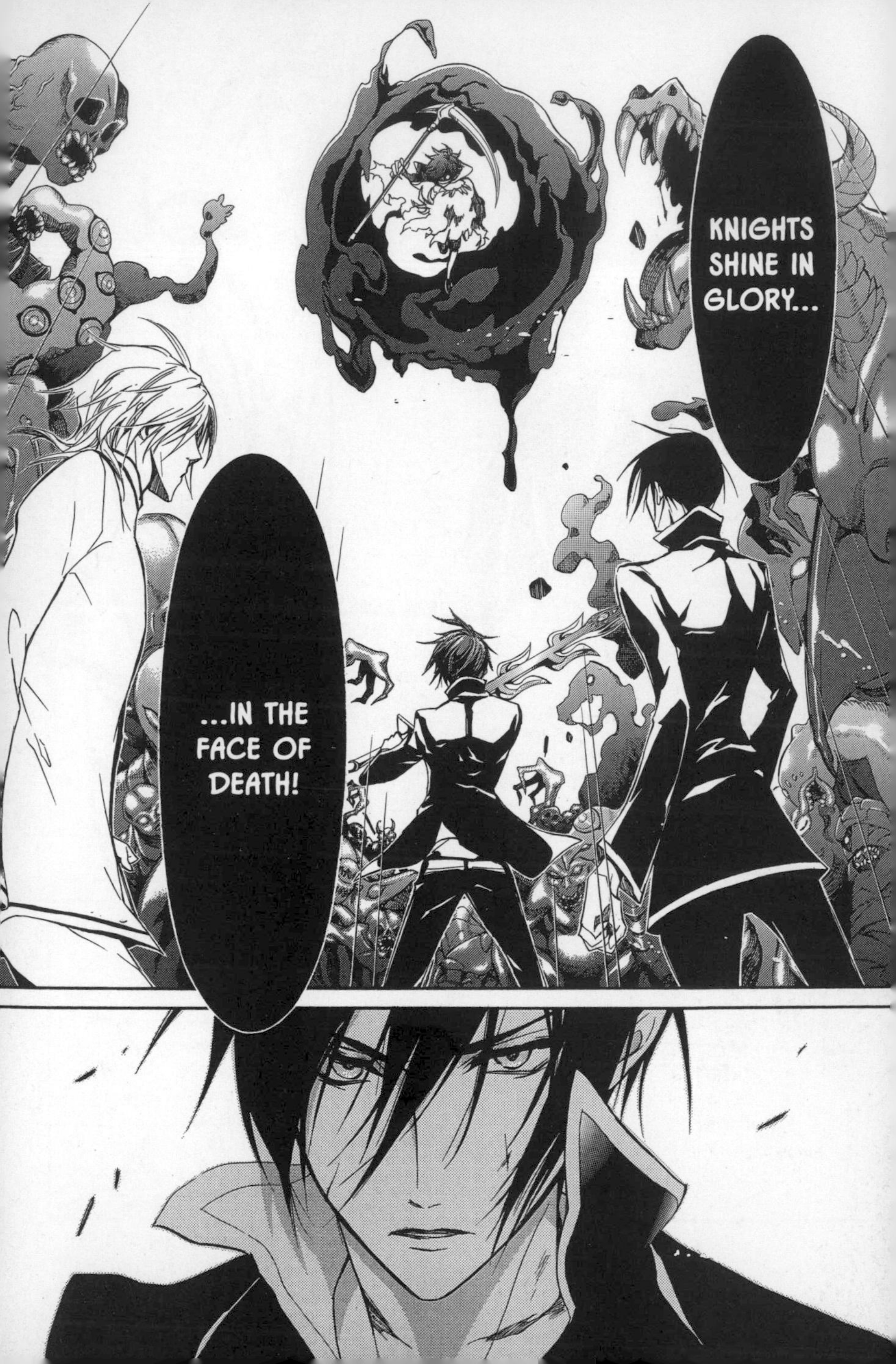
KNIGHTS SHINE IN GLORY...
...IN THE FACE OF DEATH!

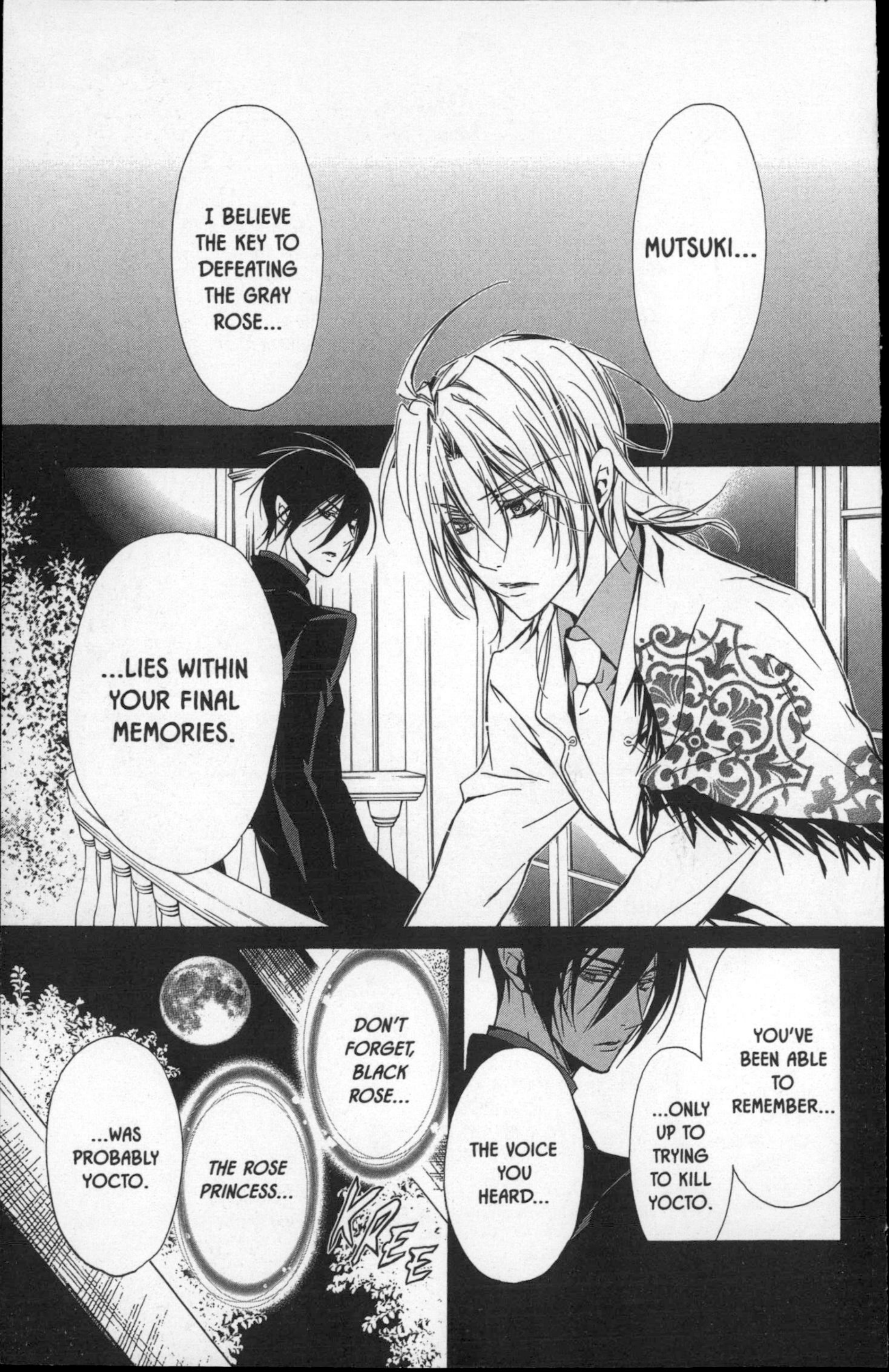
MUTSUKI...
I BELIEVE THE KEY TO DEFEATING THE GRAY ROSE...
...LIES WITHIN YOUR FINAL MEMORIES.
YOU'VE BEEN ABLE TO REMEMBER...
...ONLY UP TO TRYING TO KILL YOCTO.
THE VOICE YOU HEARD...
DON'T FORGET, BLACK ROSE...
THE ROSE PRINCESS...
KSHREE
...WAS PROBABLY YOCTO.

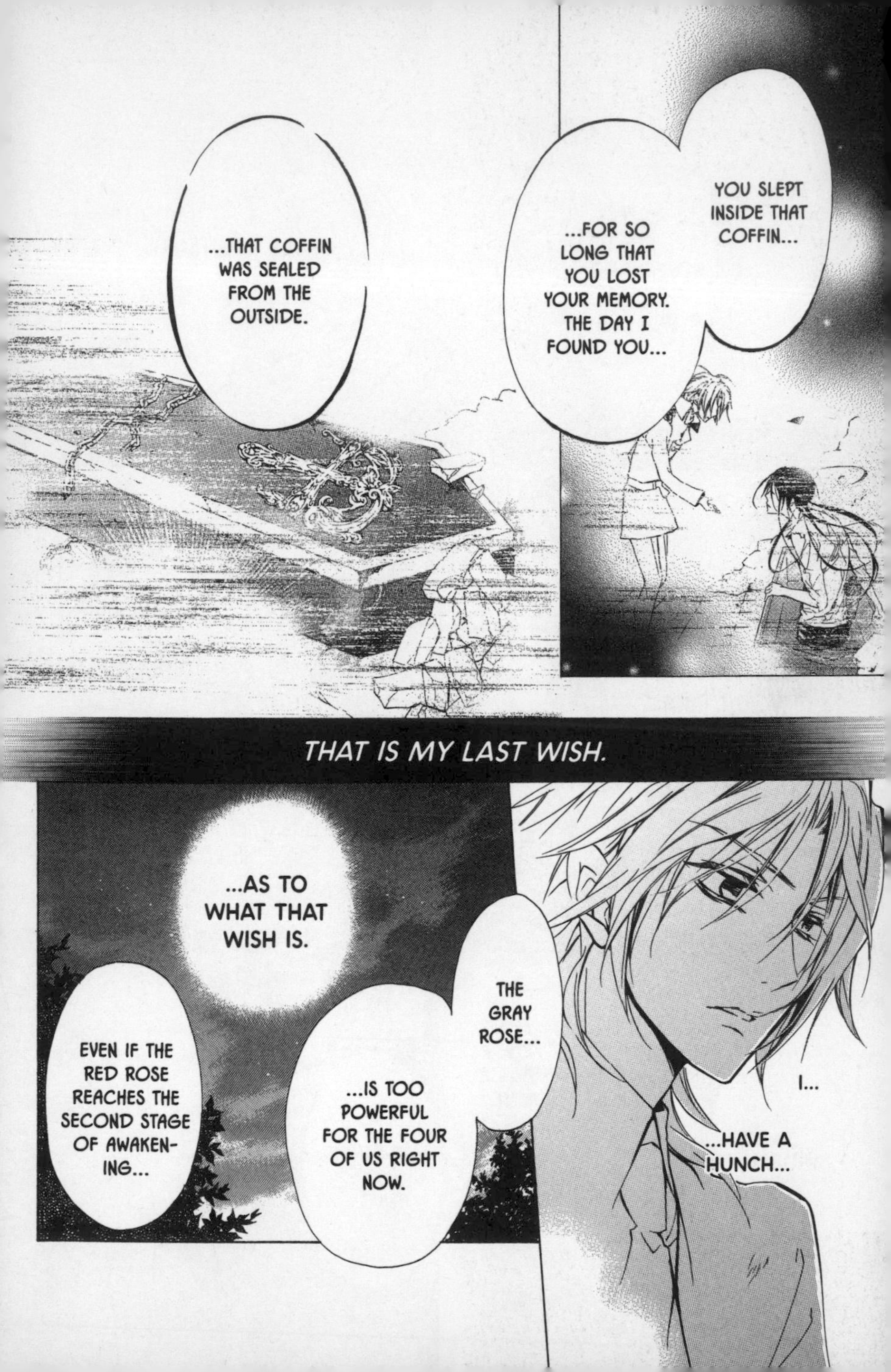
YOU SLEPT INSIDE THAT COFFIN...
...FOR SO LONG THAT YOU LOST YOUR MEMORY. THE DAY I FOUND YOU...
...THAT COFFIN WAS SEALED FROM THE OUTSIDE.
THAT IS MY LAST WISH.
I...
...HAVE A HUNCH...
...AS TO WHAT THAT WISH IS.
THE GRAY ROSE...
...IS TOO POWERFUL FOR THE FOUR OF US RIGHT NOW.
EVEN IF THE RED ROSE REACHES THE SECOND STAGE OF AWAKEN-ING...

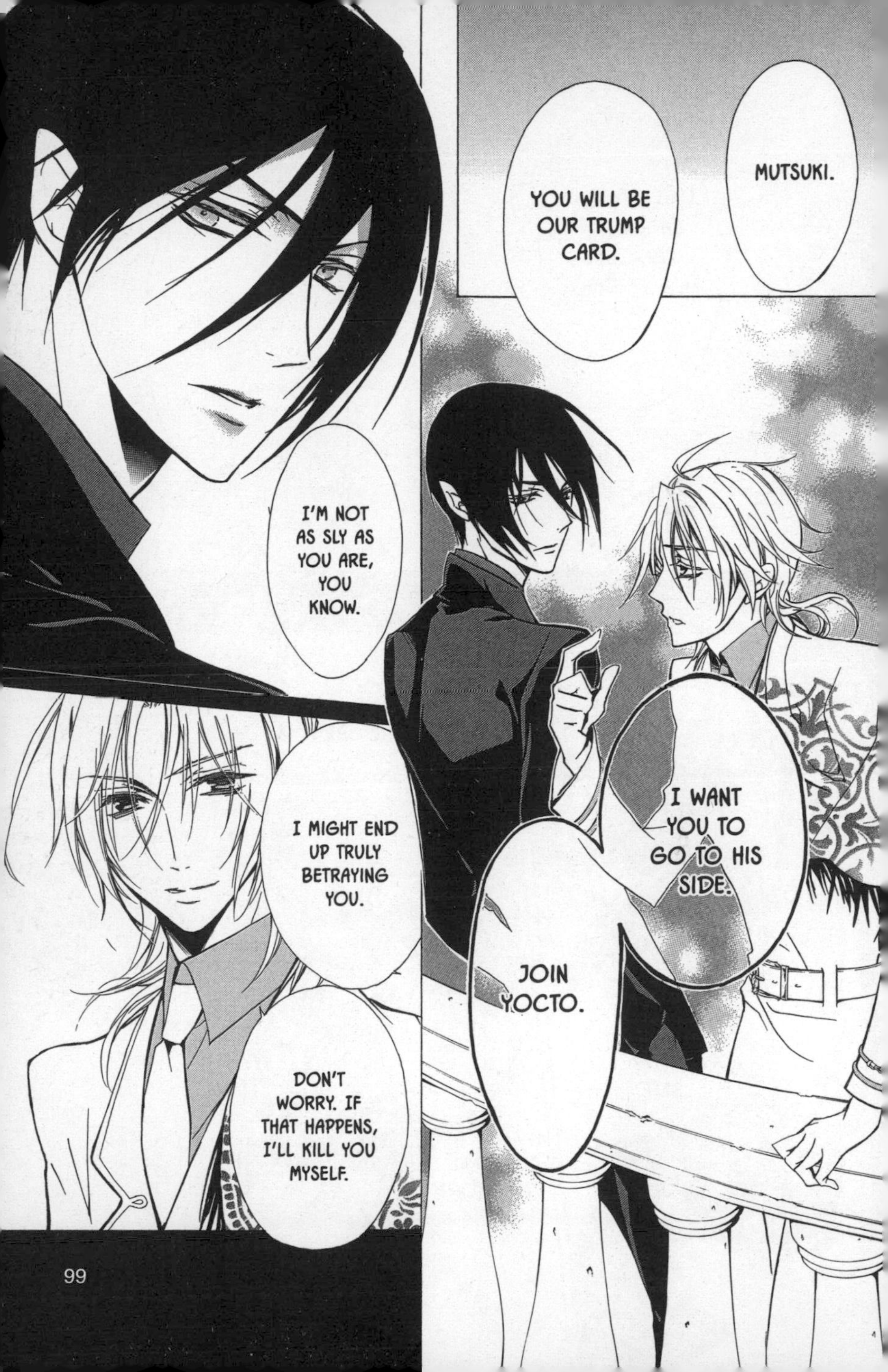
MUTSUKI.
YOU WILL BE OUR TRUMP CARD.
I WANT YOU TO GO TO HIS SIDE.
JOIN YOCTO.
I'M NOT AS SLY AS YOU ARE, YOU KNOW.
I MIGHT END UP TRULY BETRAYING YOU.
DON'T WORRY. IF THAT HAPPENS, I'LL KILL YOU MYSELF.

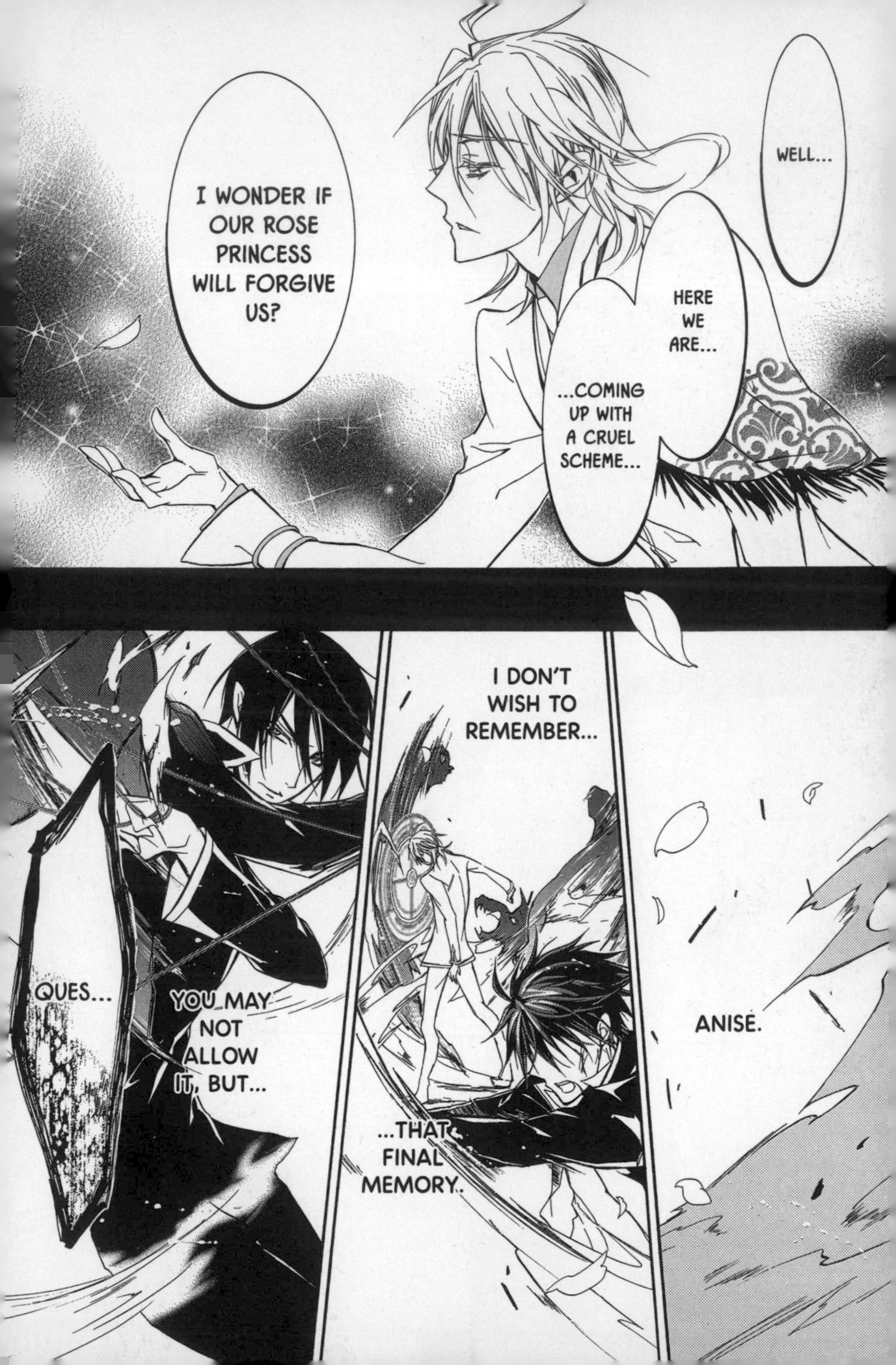
WELL...
HERE WE ARE...
...COMING UP WITH A CRUEL SCHEME...
I WONDER IF OUR ROSE PRINCESS WILL FORGIVE US?
ANISE.
I DON'T WISH TO REMEMBER...
...THAT FINAL MEMORY.
YOU MAY NOT ALLOW IT, BUT...
QUES...

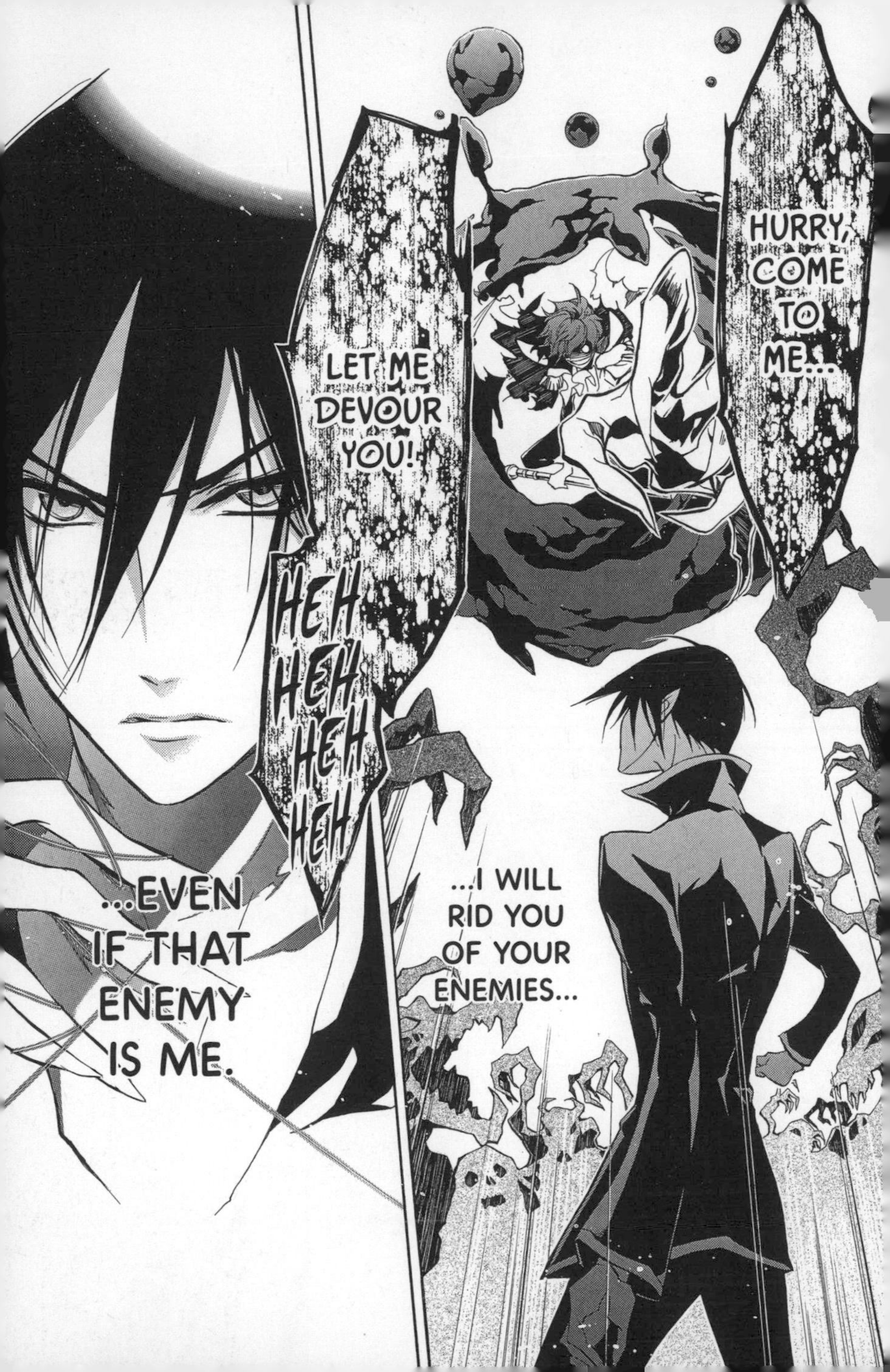
HURRY, COME TO ME...
LET ME DEVOUR YOU!
HEH HEH HEH HEH
...I WILL RID YOU OF YOUR ENEMIES...
...EVEN IF THAT ENEMY IS ME.

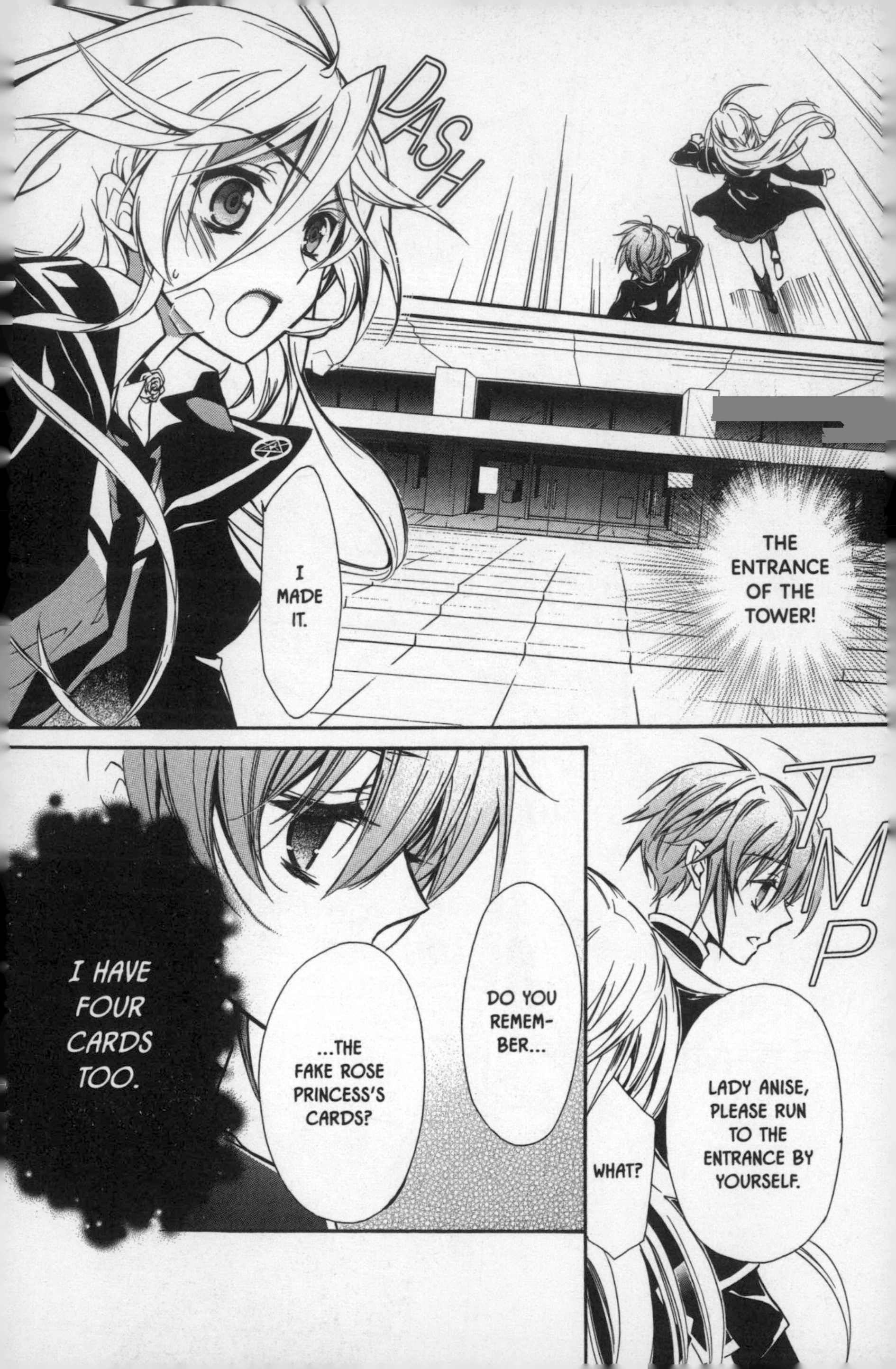
DASH
THE ENTRANCE OF THE TOWER!
I MADE IT.
TMP
LADY ANISE, PLEASE RUN TO THE ENTRANCE BY YOURSELF.
WHAT?
DO YOU REMEMBER...
...THE FAKE ROSE PRINCESS'S CARDS?
I HAVE FOUR CARDS TOO.

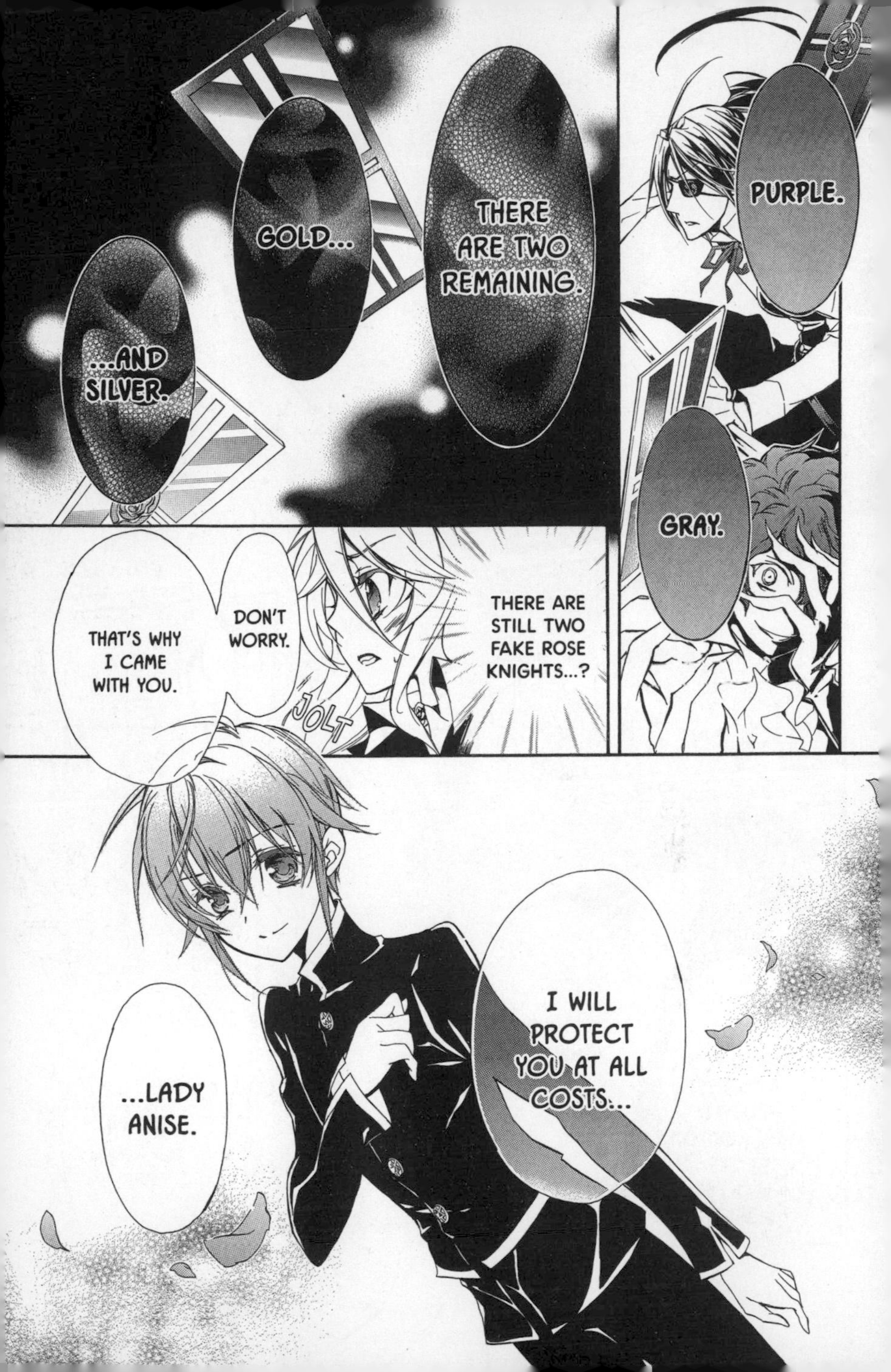
PURPLE.
GRAY.
THERE ARE TWO REMAINING.
GOLD...
...AND SILVER.
THERE ARE STILL TWO FAKE ROSE KNIGHTS...?
JOLT
DON'T WORRY.
THAT'S WHY I CAME WITH YOU.
I WILL PROTECT YOU AT ALL COSTS...
...LADY ANISE.

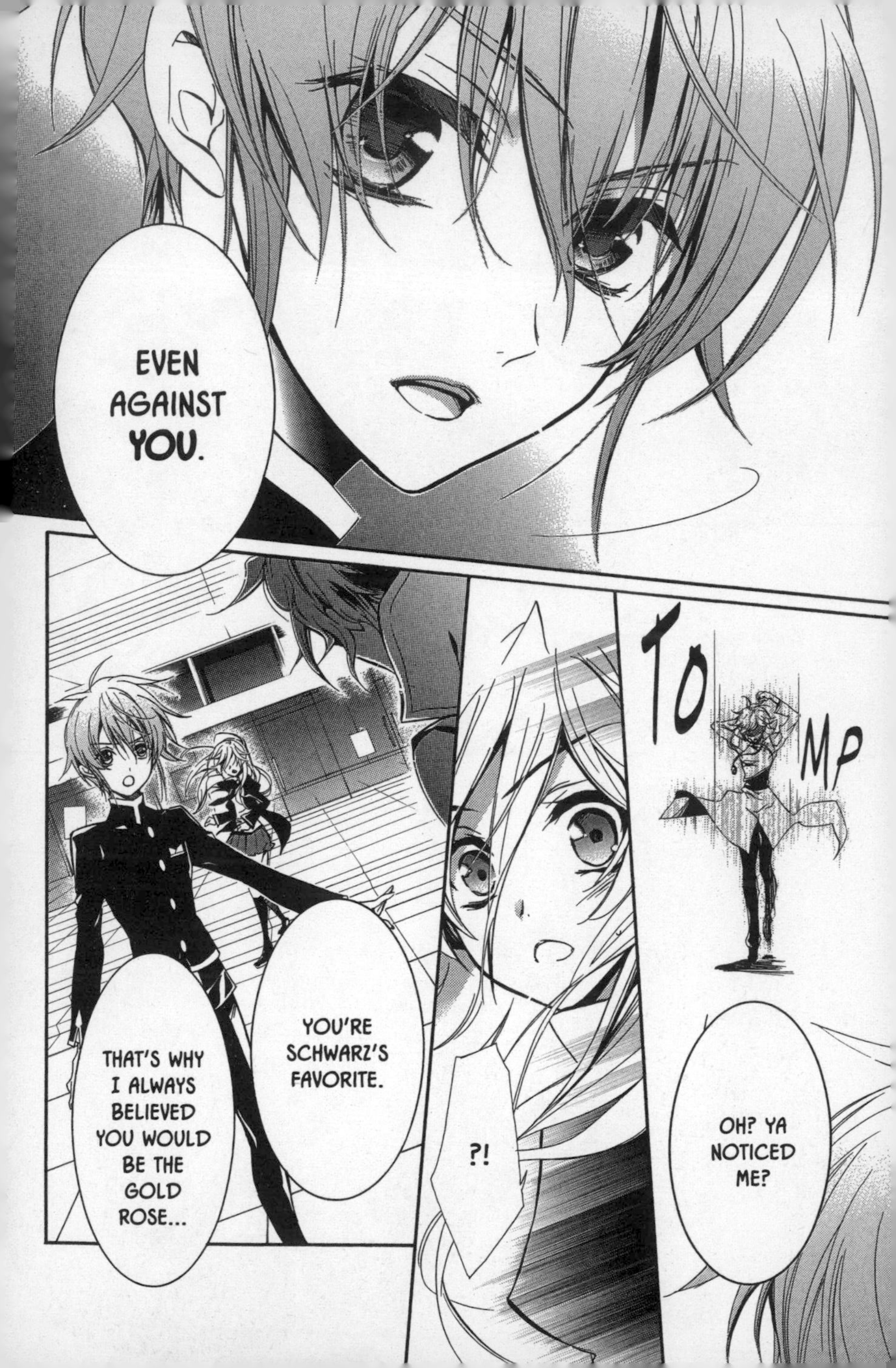
EVEN AGAINST YOU.
TOMP
OH? YA NOTICED ME?
?!
YOU'RE SCHWARZ'S FAVORITE.
THAT'S WHY I ALWAYS BELIEVED YOU WOULD BE THE GOLD ROSE...

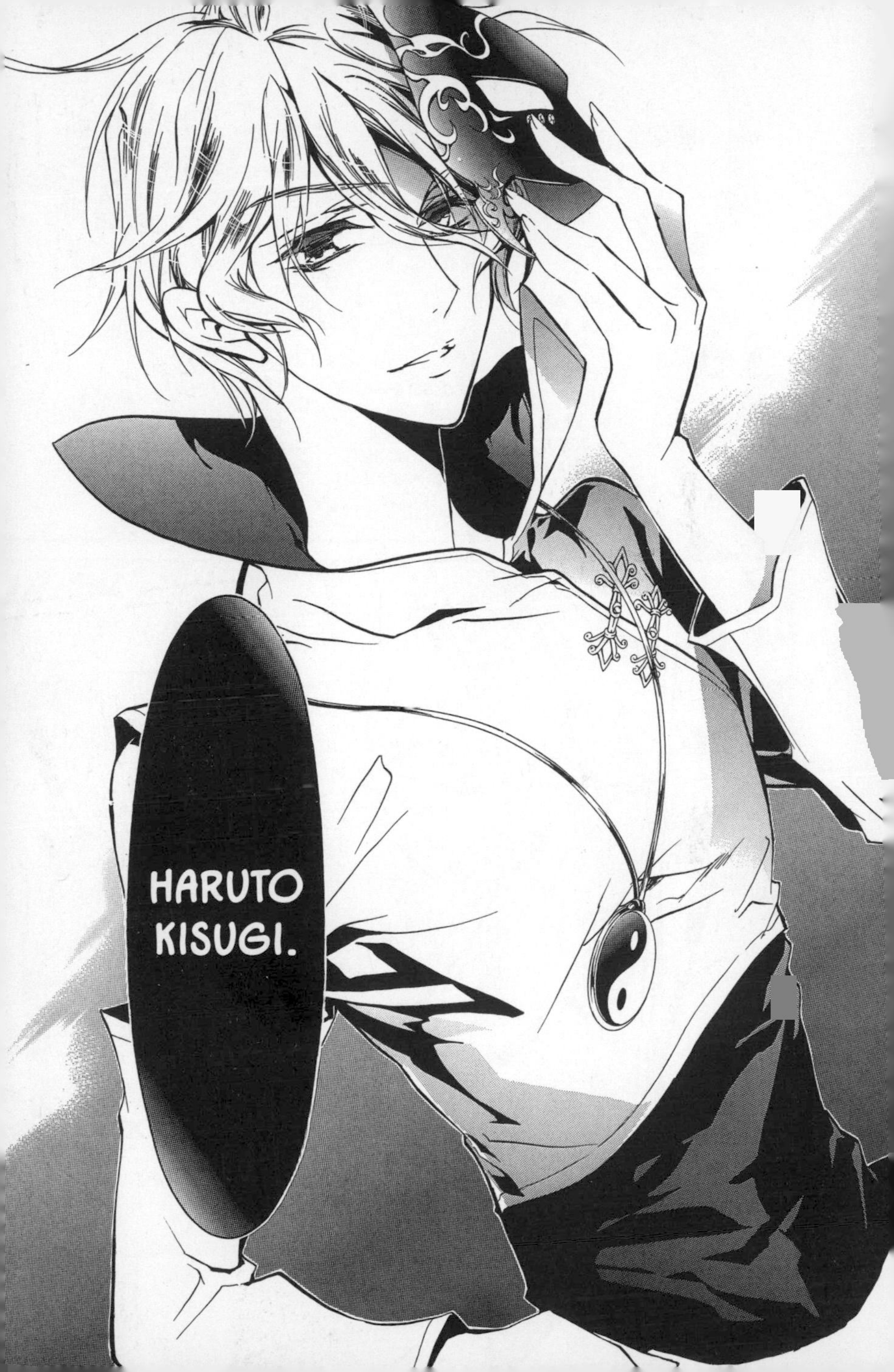
HARUTO KISUGI.

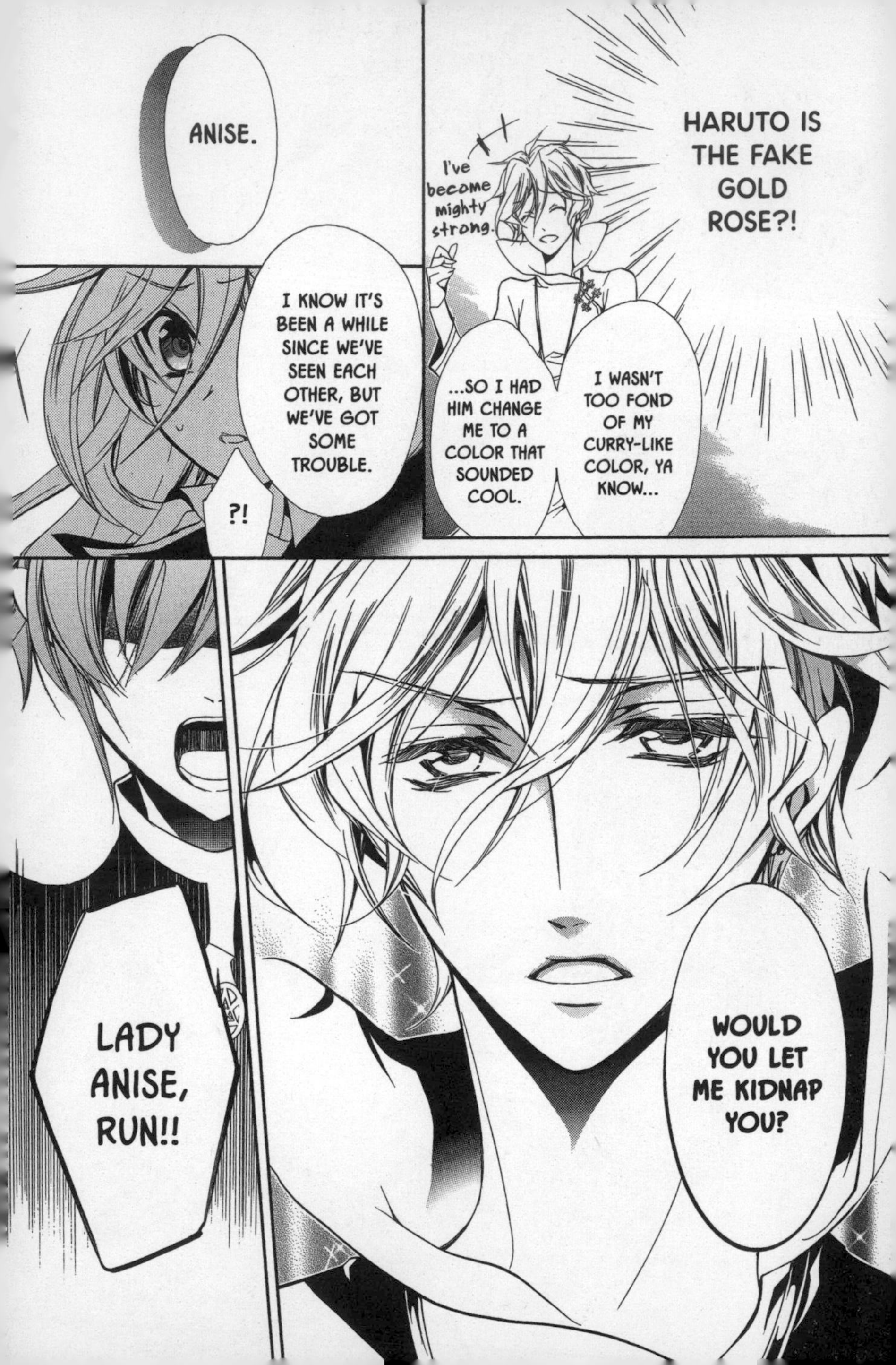
HARUTO IS THE FAKE GOLD ROSE?!
I've become mighty strong.
I WASN'T TOO FOND OF MY CURRY-LIKE COLOR, YA KNOW...
...SO I HAD HIM CHANGE ME TO A COLOR THAT SOUNDED COOL.
ANISE.
I KNOW IT'S BEEN A WHILE SINCE WE'VE SEEN EACH OTHER, BUT WE'VE GOT SOME TROUBLE.
?!
WOULD YOU LET ME KIDNAP YOU?
LADY ANISE, RUN!!

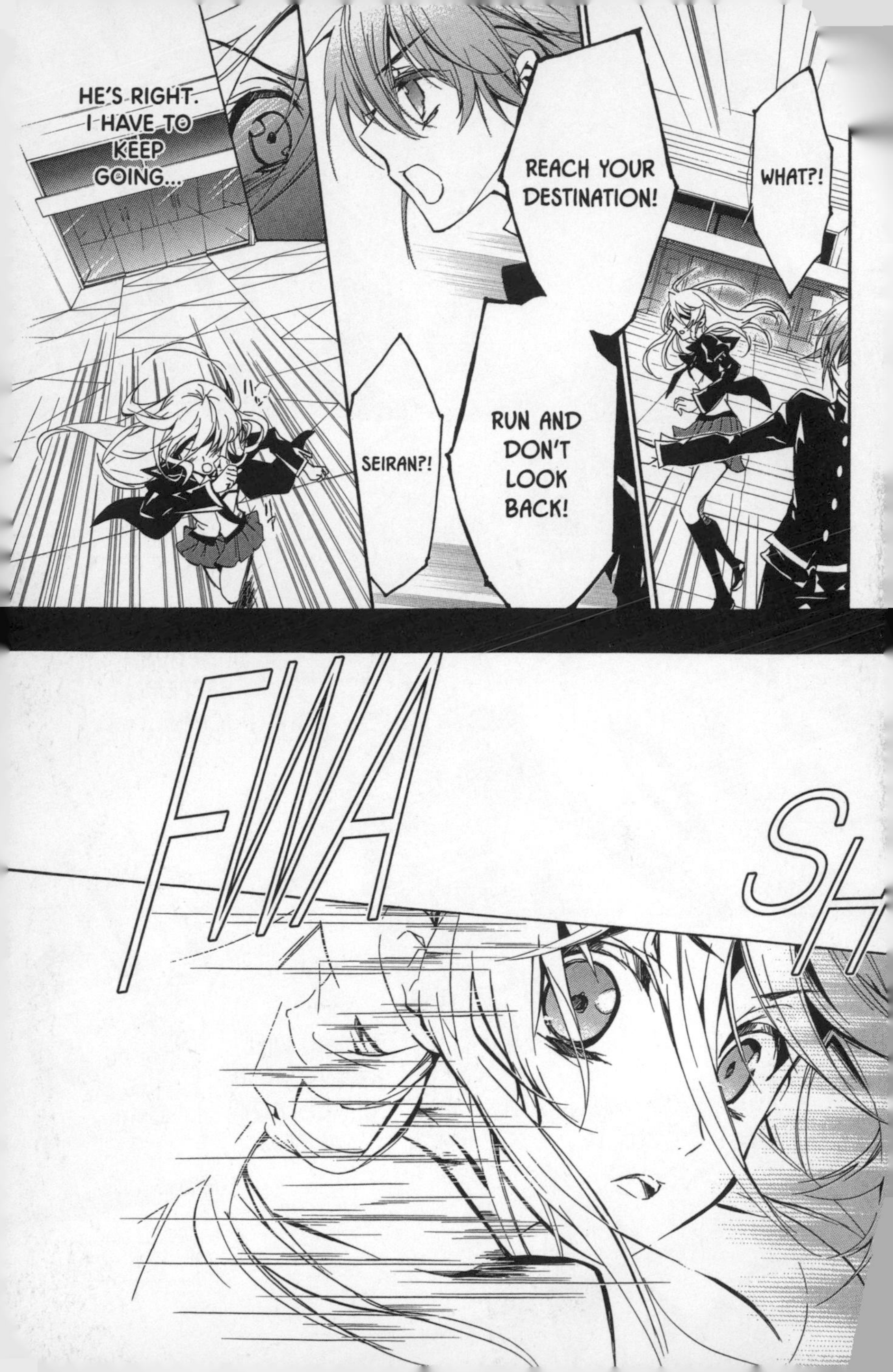
WHAT?!
REACH YOUR DESTINATION!
RUN AND DON'T LOOK BACK!
SEIRAN?!
HE'S RIGHT. I HAVE TO KEEP GOING...
FWA SH

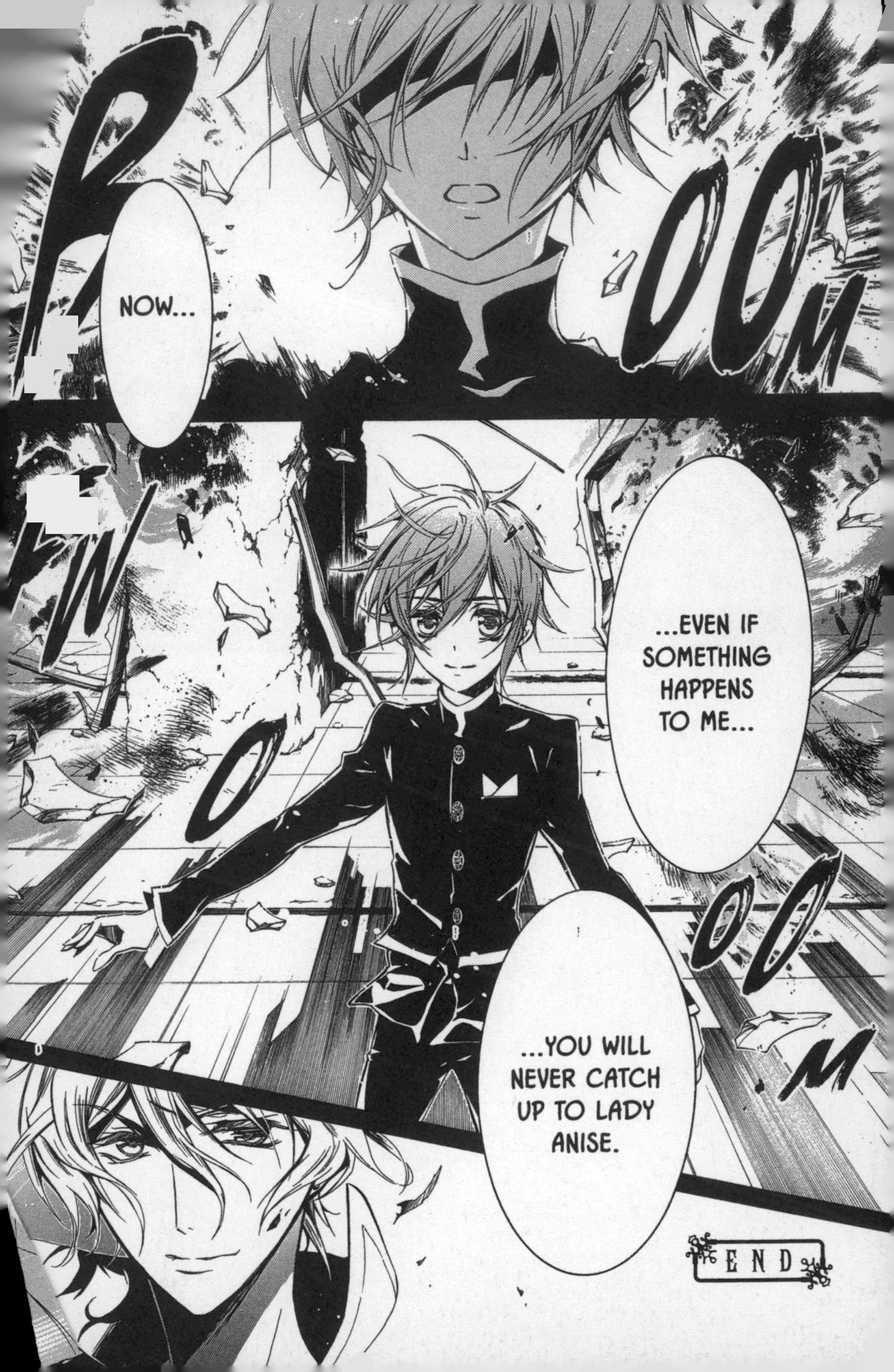
NOW...
...EVEN IF SOMETHING HAPPENS TO ME...
...YOU WILL NEVER CATCH UP TO LADY ANISE.
END

Kiss of the Rose Princess

Kiss of the Rose
Princess

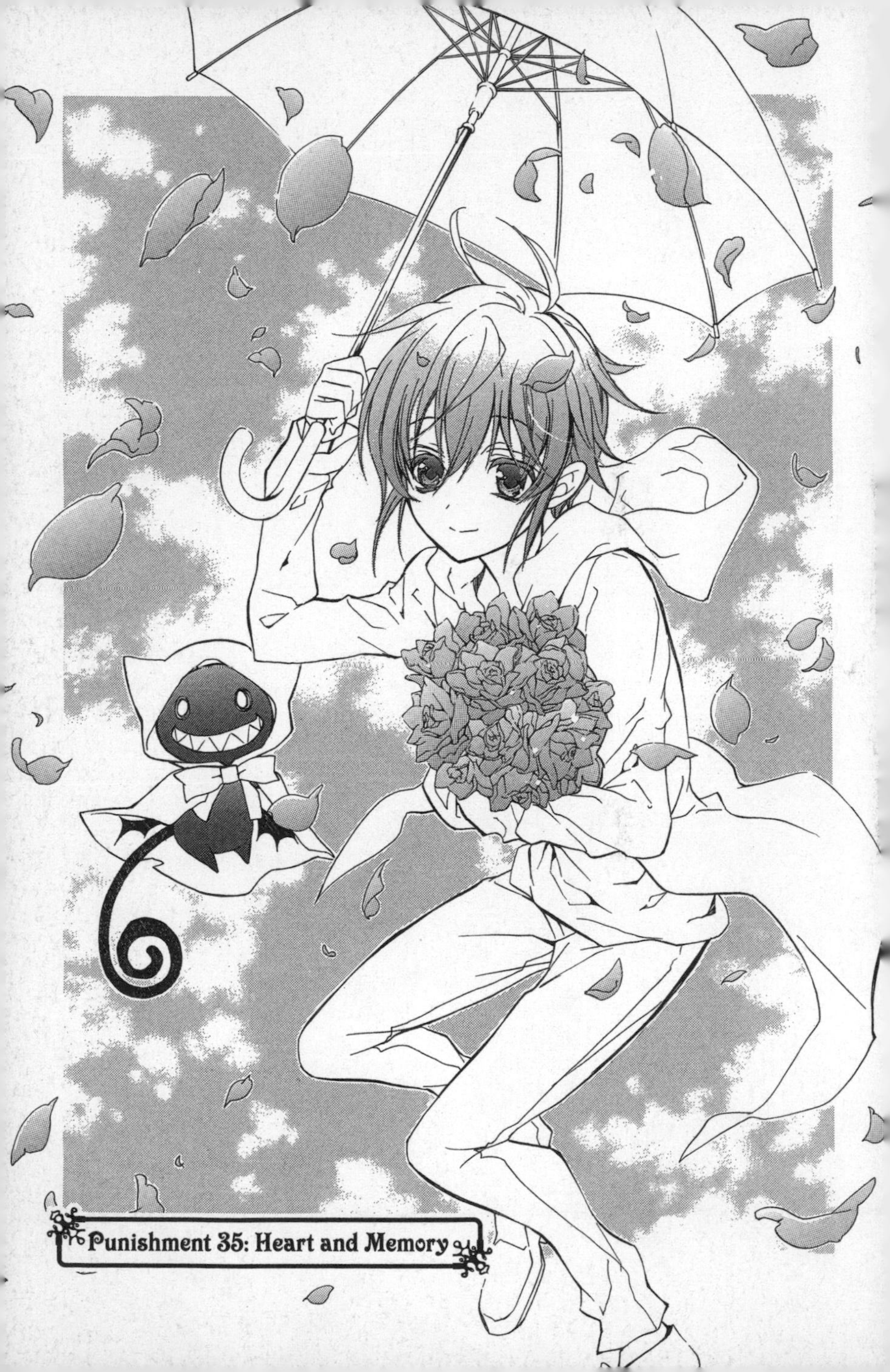
Punishment 35: Heart and Memory

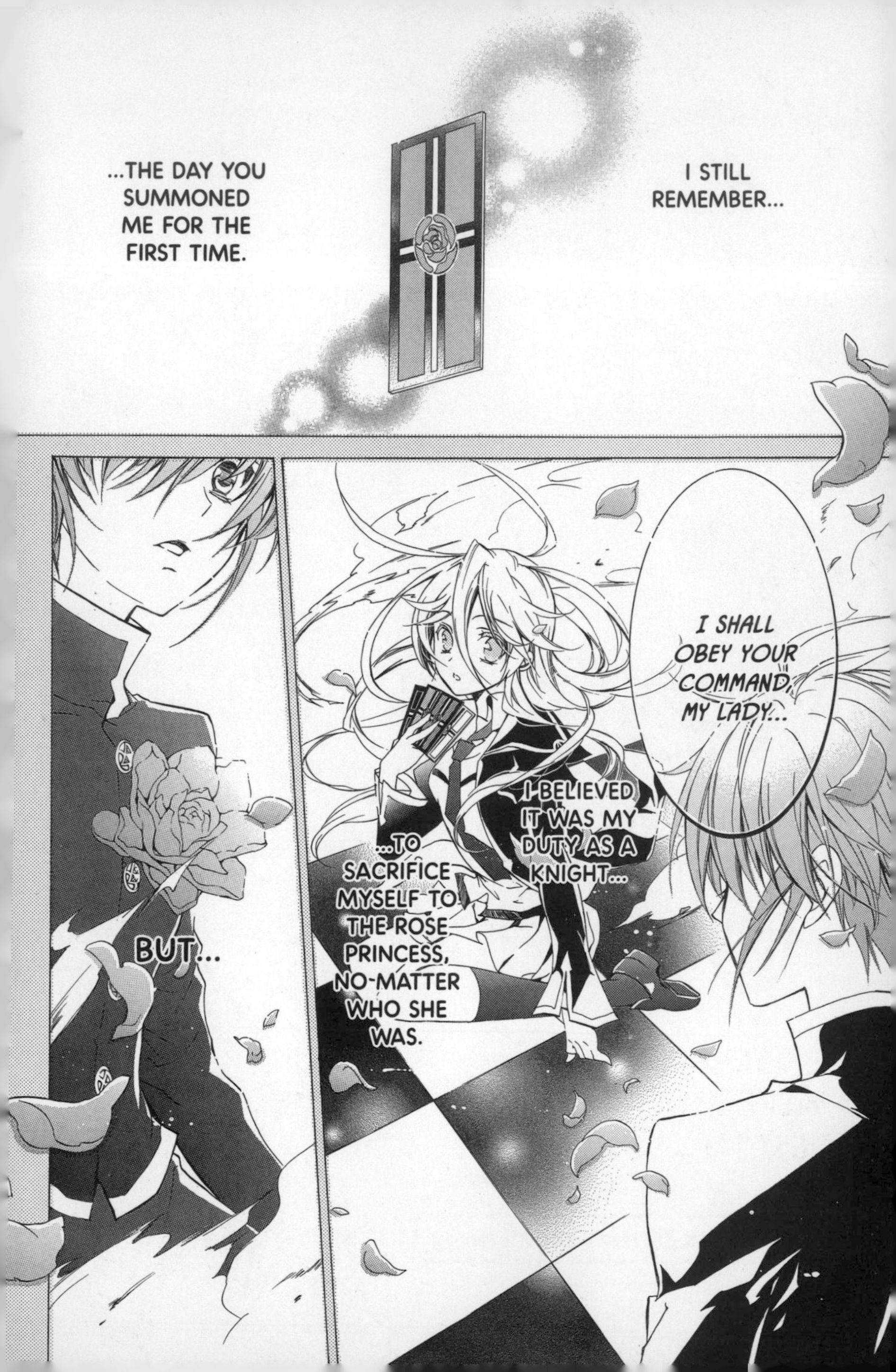
I STILL REMEMBER...
...THE DAY YOU SUMMONED ME FOR THE FIRST TIME.
I SHALL OBEY YOUR COMMAND, MY LADY...
I BELIEVED IT WAS MY DUTY AS A KNIGHT...
...TO SACRIFICE MYSELF TO THE ROSE PRINCESS, NO MATTER WHO SHE WAS.
BUT...

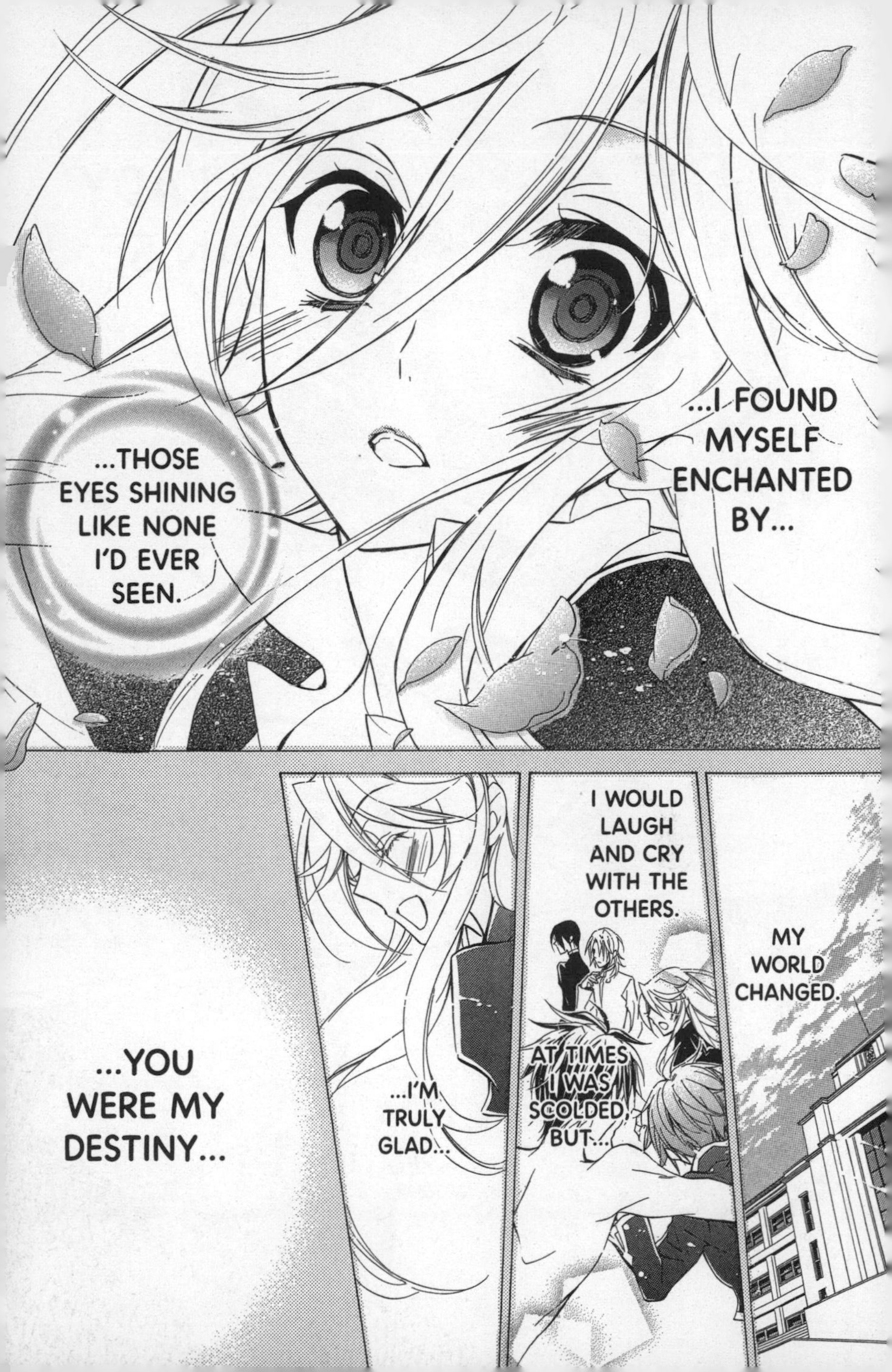
...I FOUND MYSELF ENCHANTED BY...
...THOSE EYES SHINING LIKE NONE I'D EVER SEEN.
MY WORLD CHANGED.
I WOULD LAUGH AND CRY WITH THE OTHERS.
AT TIMES I WAS SCOLDED, BUT...
...I'M TRULY GLAD...
...YOU WERE MY DESTINY...

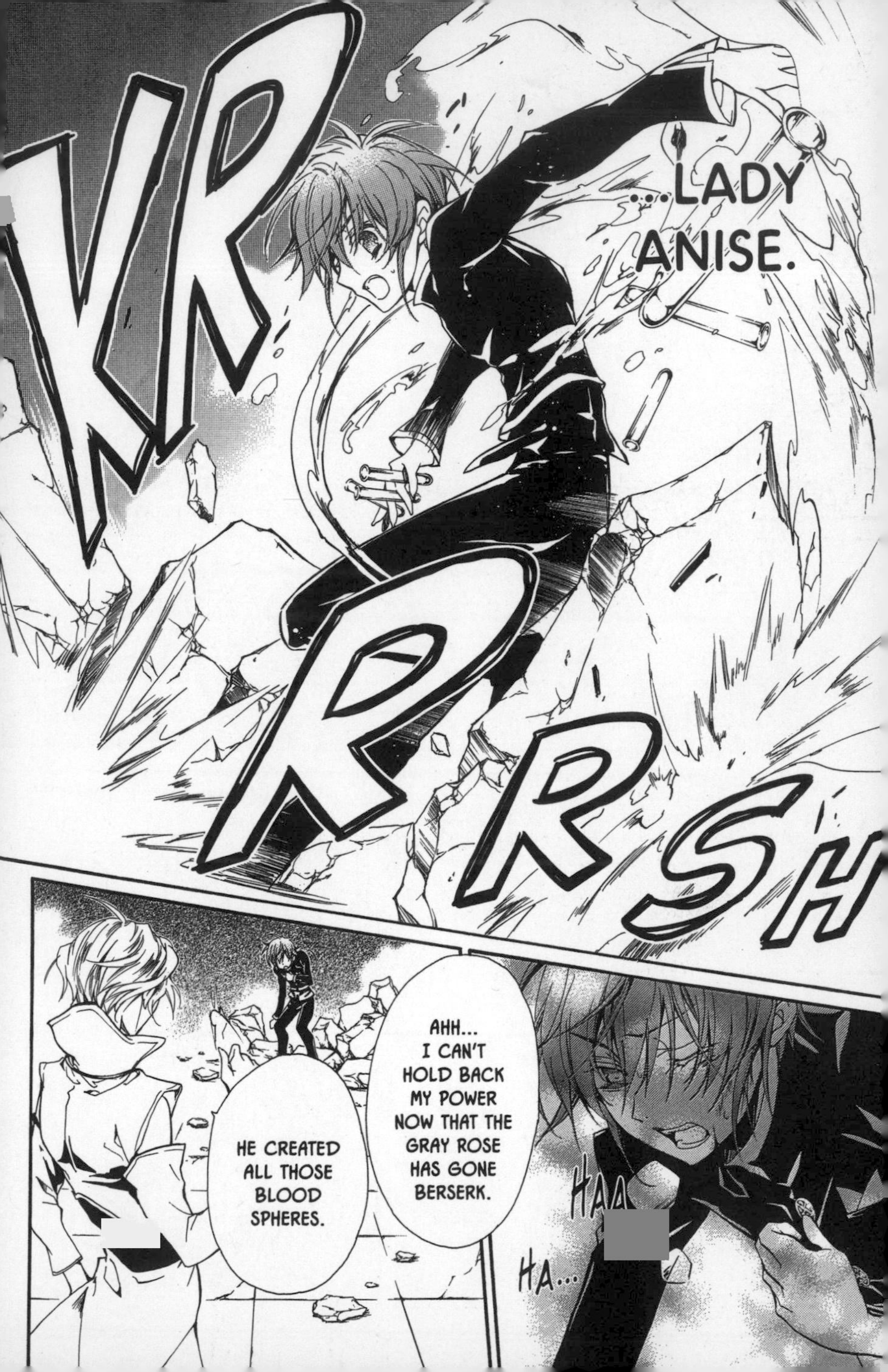
...LADY ANISE.
KRRRSH
HAA
HA...
AHH... I CAN'T HOLD BACK MY POWER NOW THAT THE GRAY ROSE HAS GONE BERSERK.
HE CREATED ALL THOSE BLOOD SPHERES.

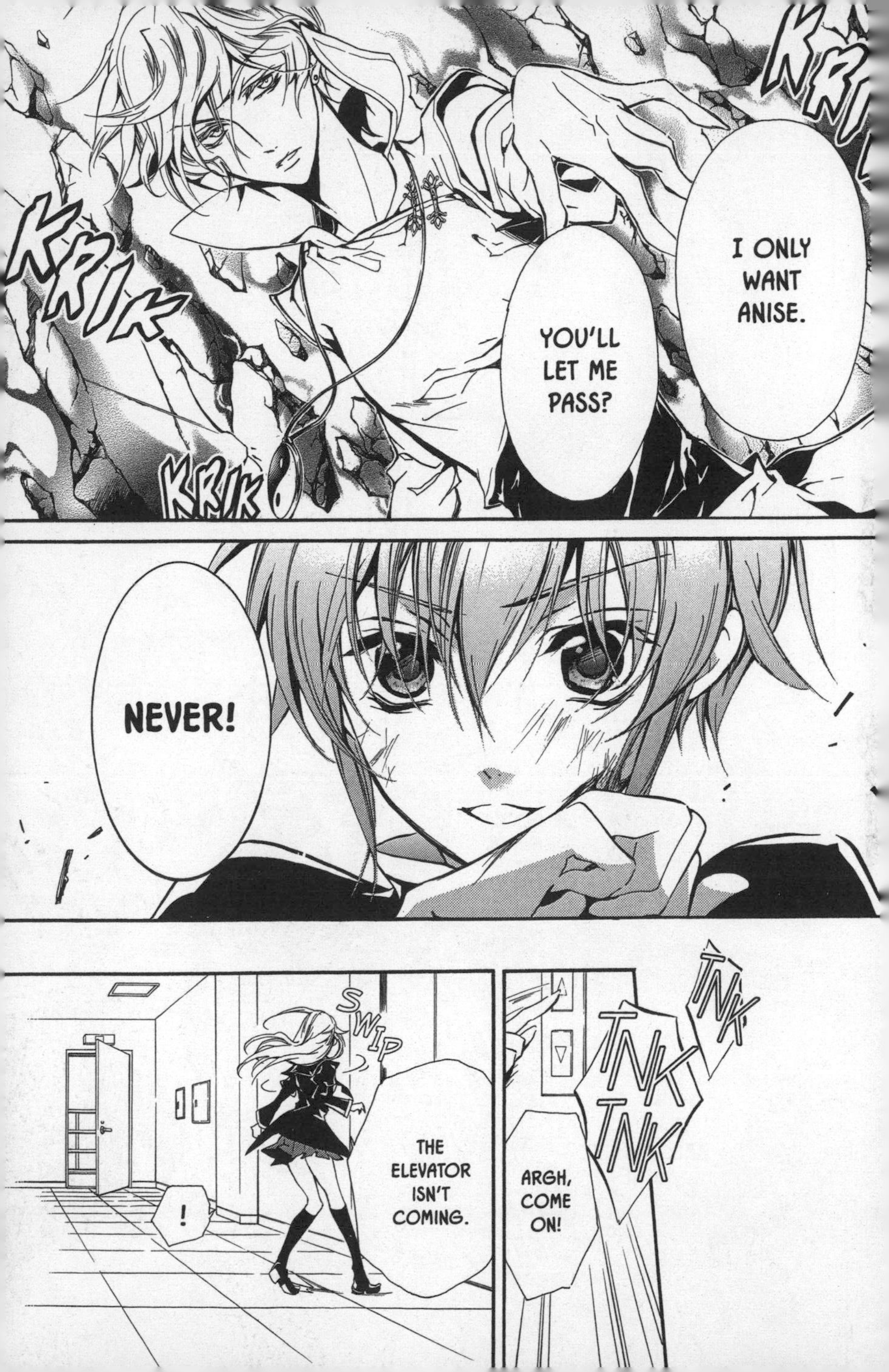
I ONLY WANT ANISE.
YOU'LL LET ME PASS?
KRIK
KRIK
NEVER!
TNK,
TNK TNK
ARGH, COME ON!
SWIP
THE ELEVATOR ISN'T COMING.
!

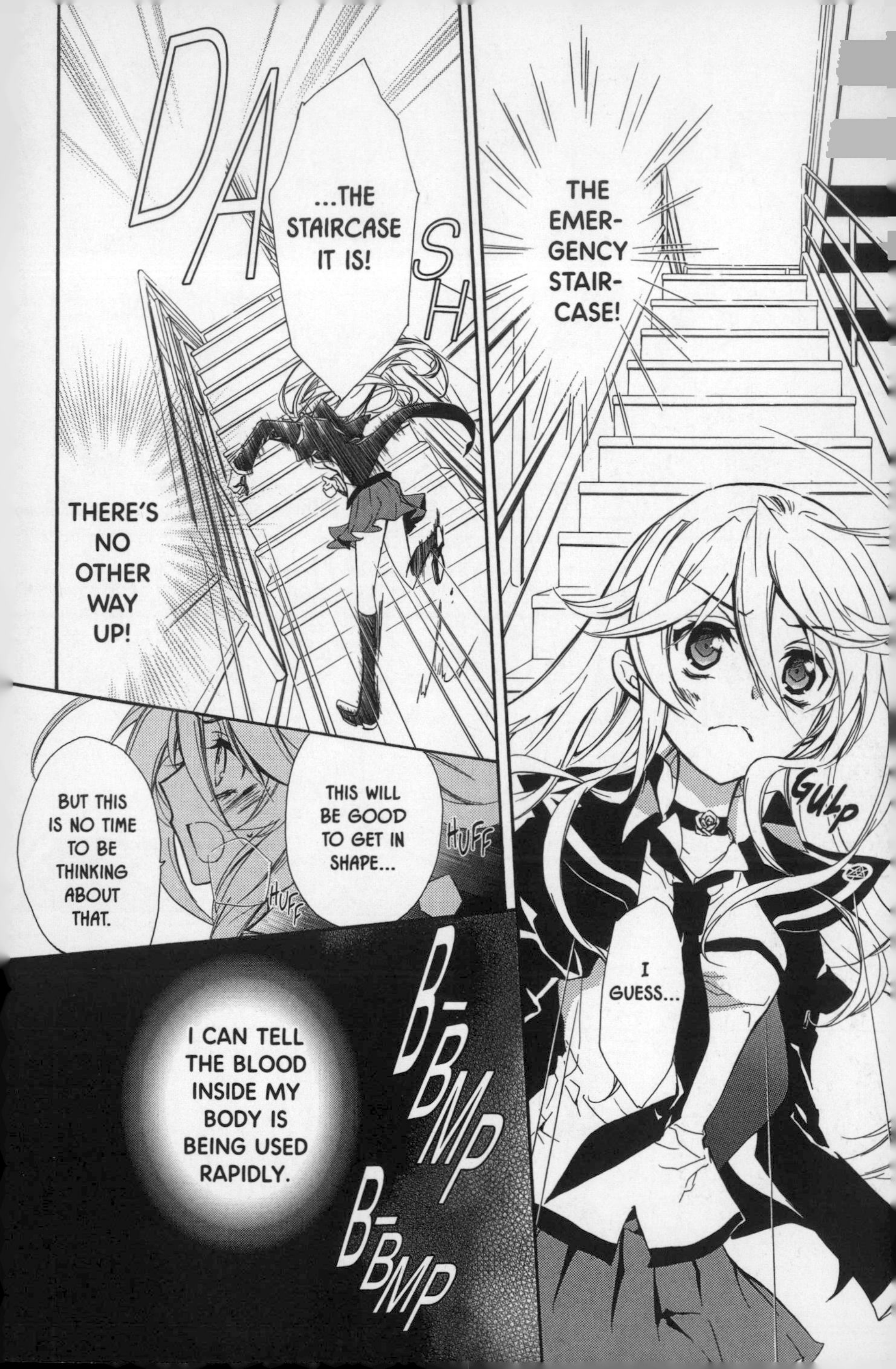
THE EMERGENCY STAIRCASE!
GULP
I GUESS...
...THE STAIRCASE IT IS!
DASH
THERE'S NO OTHER WAY UP!
THIS WILL BE GOOD TO GET IN SHAPE...
HUFF
HUFF
BUT THIS IS NO TIME TO BE THINKING ABOUT THAT.
B-BMP
B-BMP
I CAN TELL THE BLOOD INSIDE MY BODY IS BEING USED RAPIDLY.

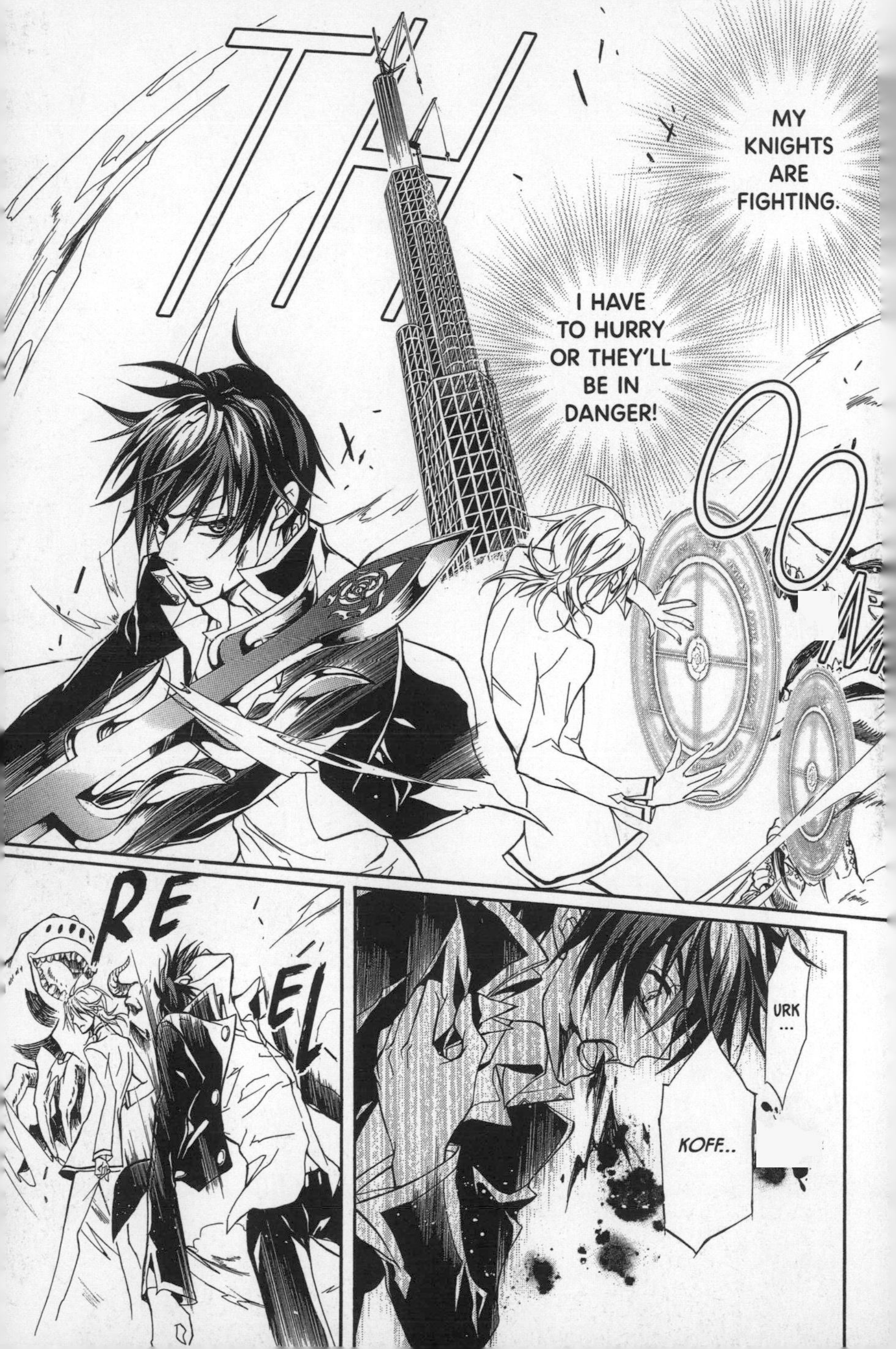
MY KNIGHTS ARE FIGHTING.
I HAVE TO HURRY OR THEY'LL BE IN DANGER!
TH
OOM
URK...
KOFF...
RE
EL

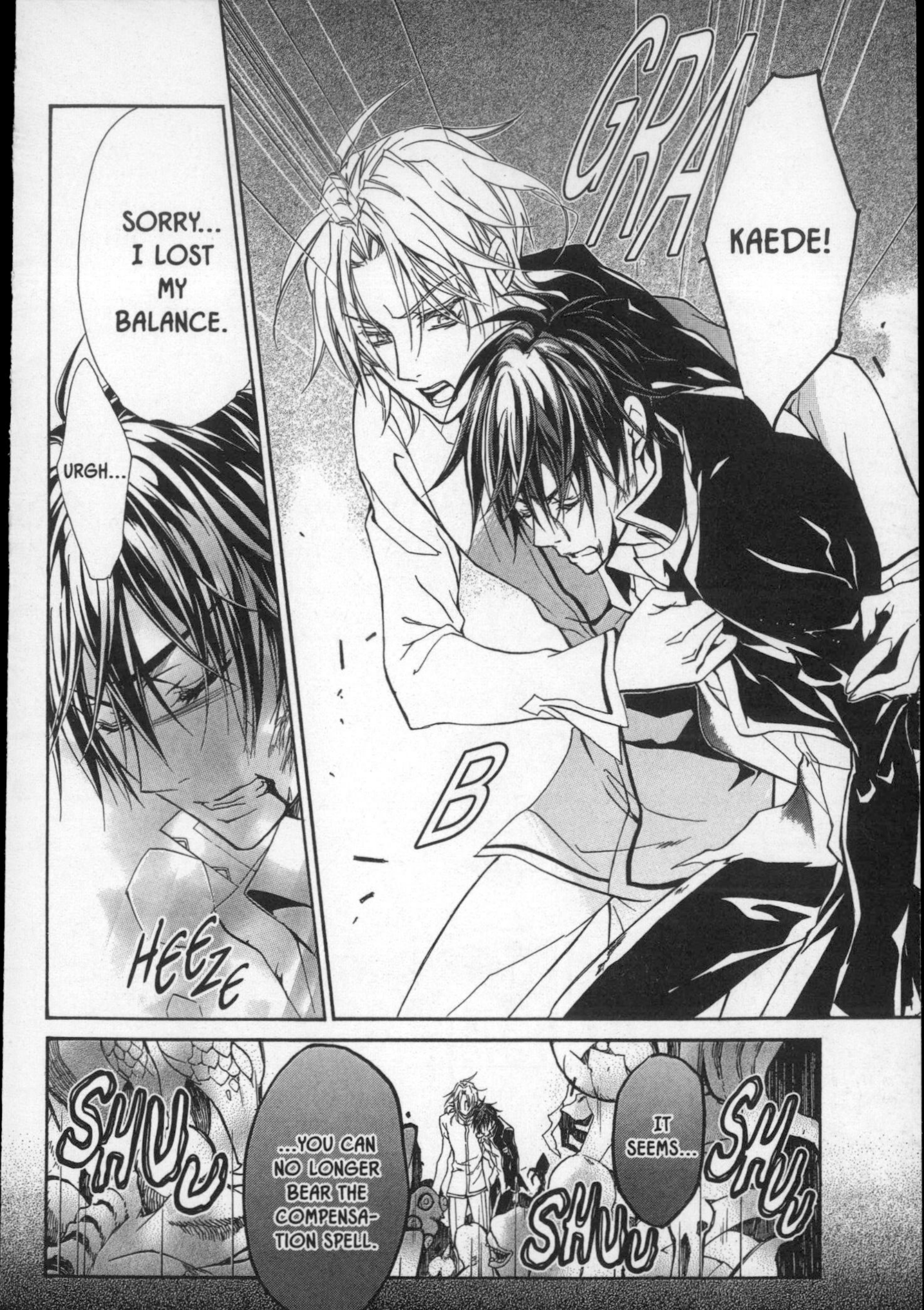
GRA
KAEDE!
B
SORRY... I LOST MY BALANCE.
URGH...
HEEZE
SHU
IT SEEMS...
SHU
...YOU CAN NO LONGER BEAR THE COMPENSA-TION SPELL.
SHU

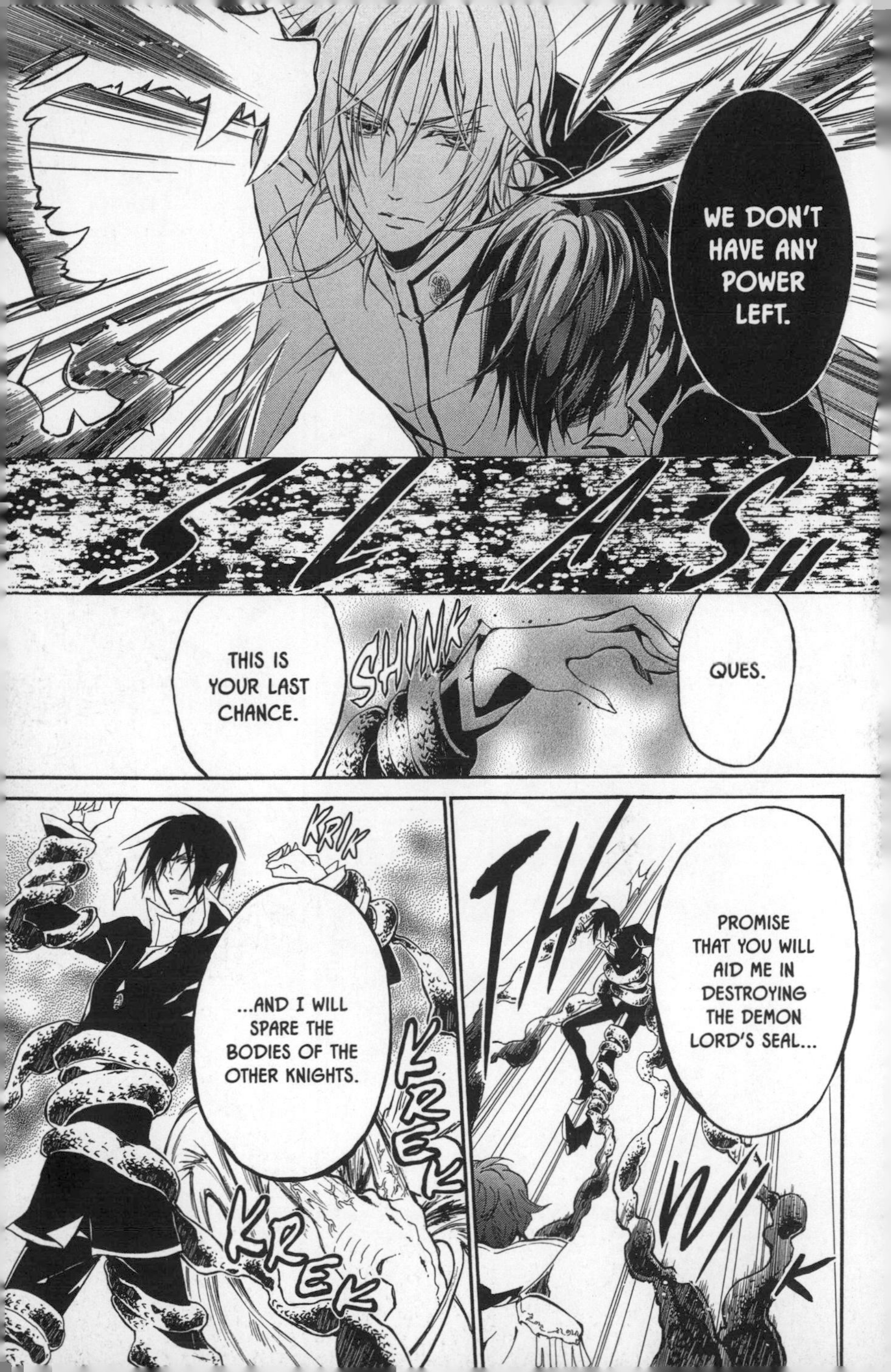
WE DON'T HAVE ANY POWER LEFT.
SLASH
QUES.
SHINK
THIS IS YOUR LAST CHANCE.
THWK
PROMISE THAT YOU WILL AID ME IN DESTROYING THE DEMON LORD'S SEAL...
KRIK
...AND I WILL SPARE THE BODIES OF THE OTHER KNIGHTS.
KREK
KREK

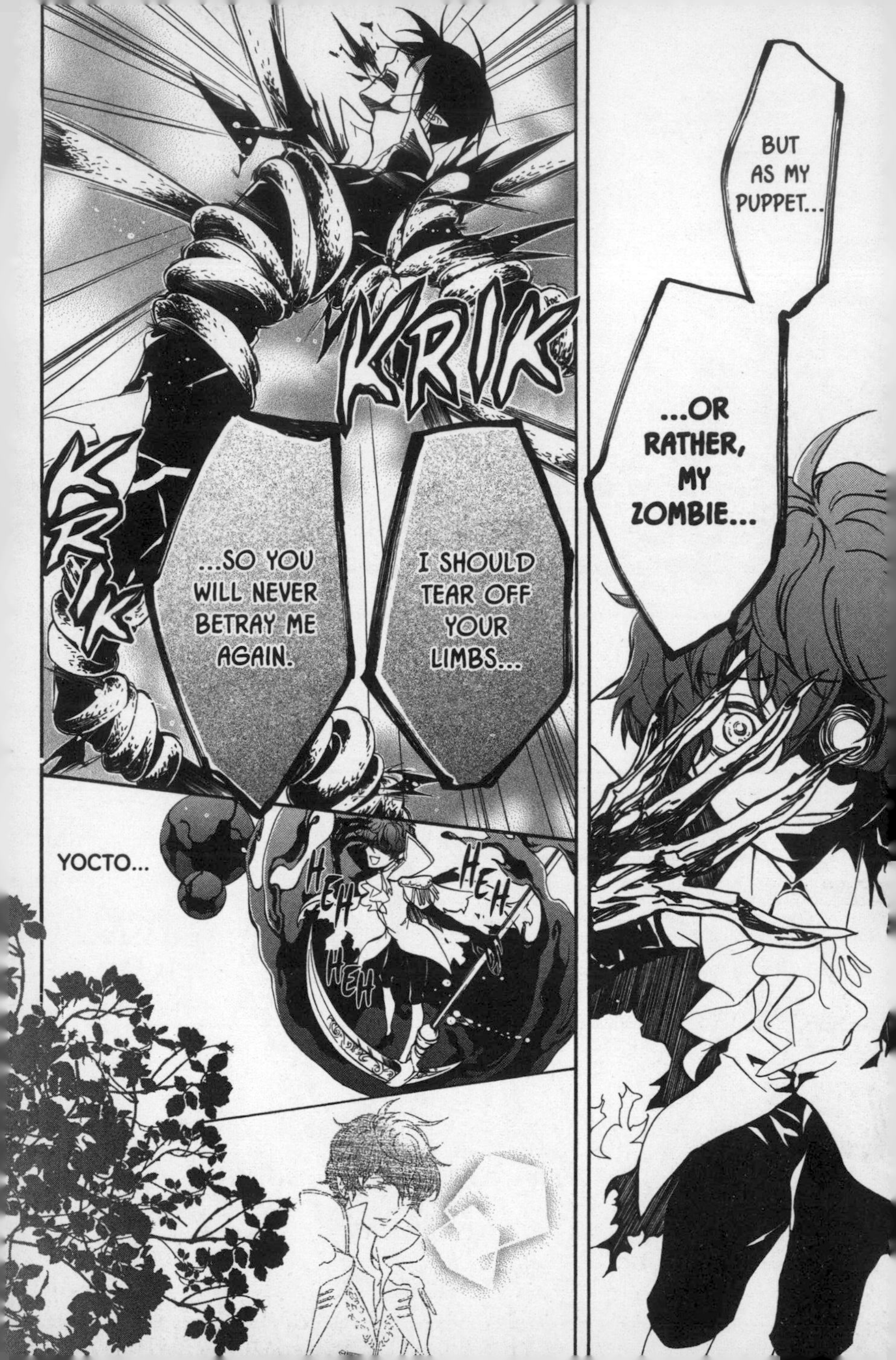
BUT AS MY PUPPET...
...OR RATHER, MY ZOMBIE...
KRIK
I SHOULD TEAR OFF YOUR LIMBS...
...SO YOU WILL NEVER BETRAY ME AGAIN.
KRIK KRIK
HEH HEH
HEH HEH
HEH HEH
YOCTO...

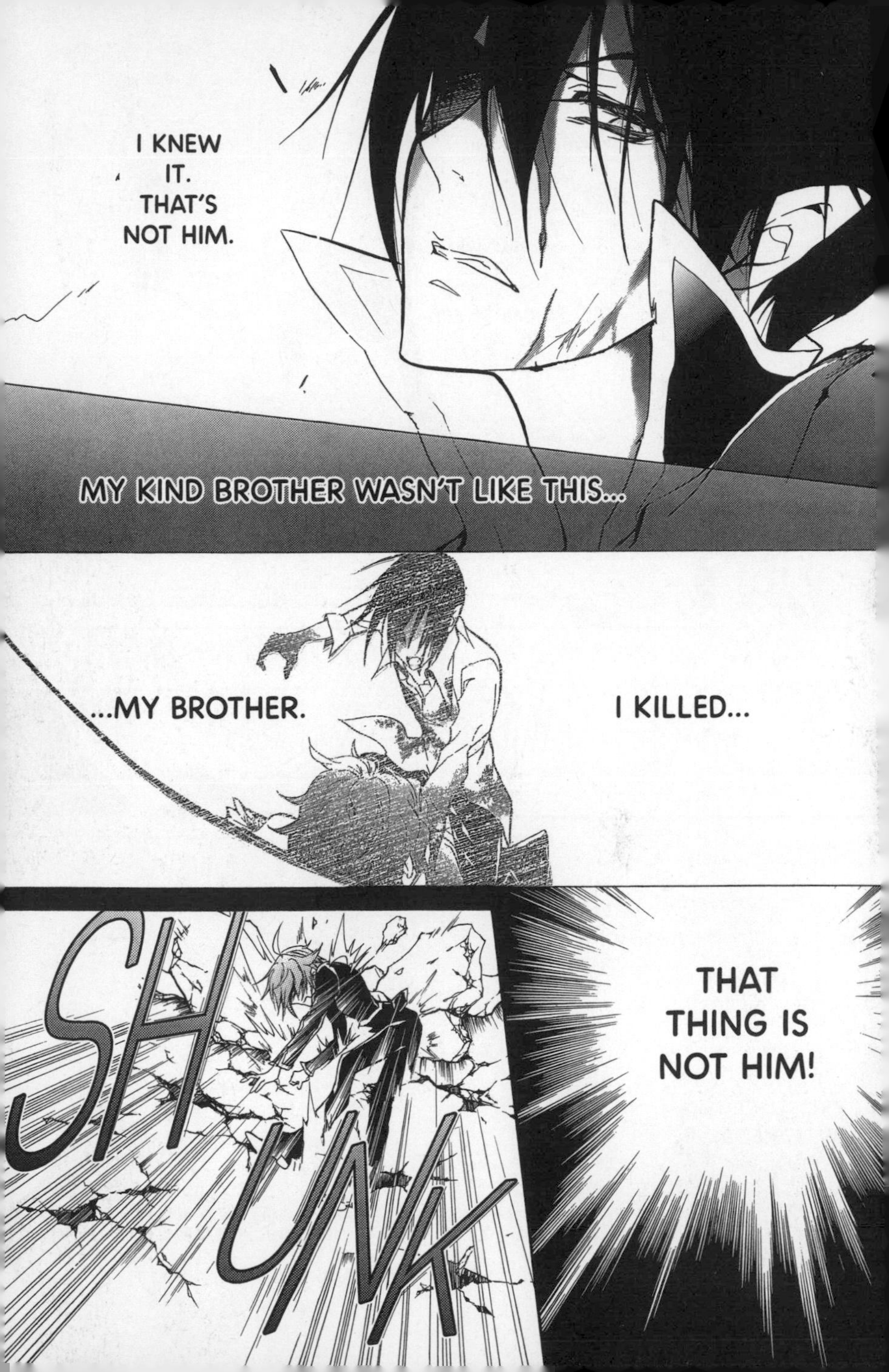
I KNEW IT. THAT'S NOT HIM.
MY KIND BROTHER WASN'T LIKE THIS...
I KILLED...
...MY BROTHER.
THAT THING IS NOT HIM!
SHUNK

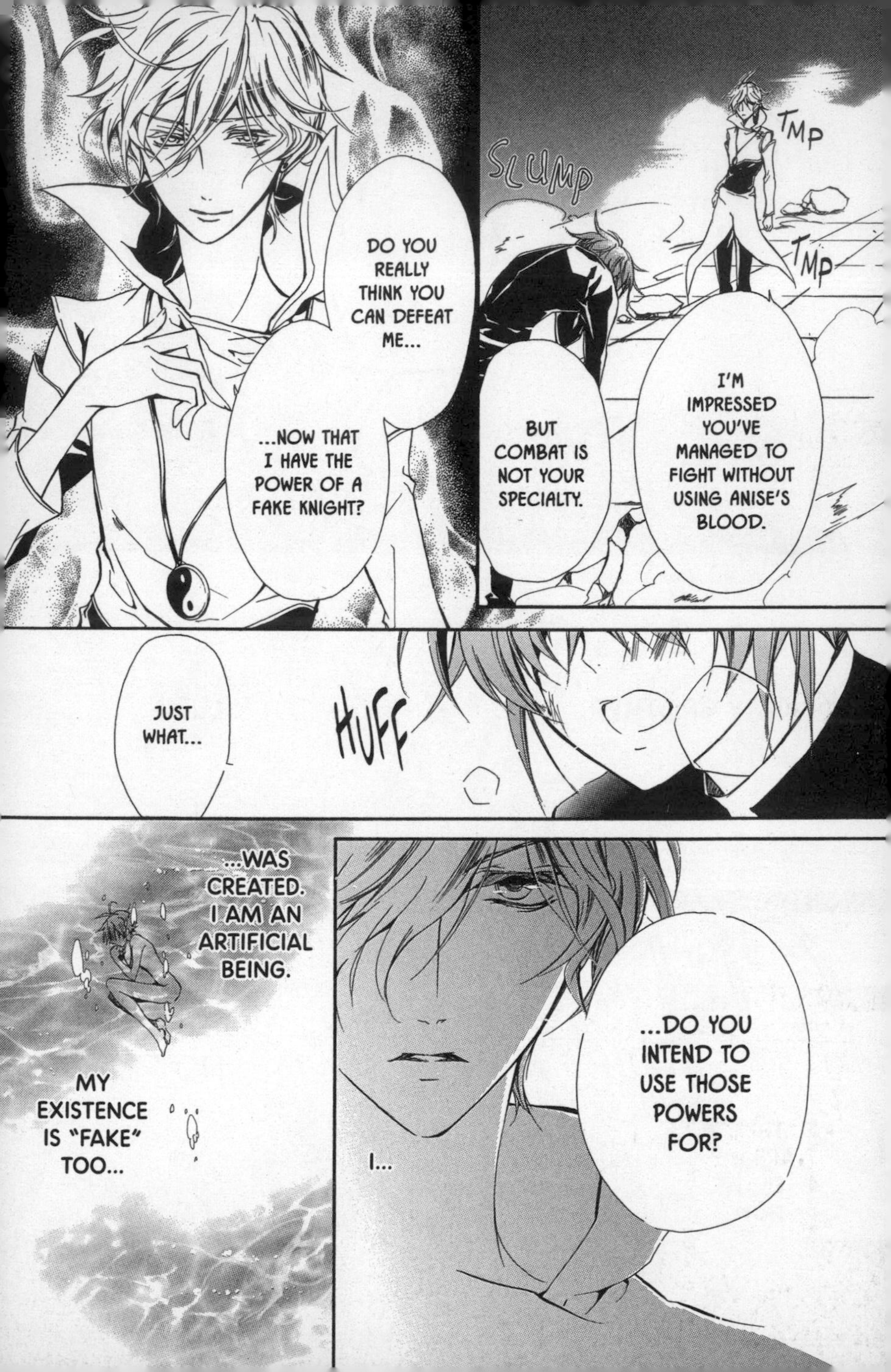
TMP
SLUMP
TMP
I'M IMPRESSED YOU'VE MANAGED TO FIGHT WITHOUT USING ANISE'S BLOOD.
BUT COMBAT IS NOT YOUR SPECIALTY.
DO YOU REALLY THINK YOU CAN DEFEAT ME...
...NOW THAT I HAVE THE POWER OF A FAKE KNIGHT?
HUFF
JUST WHAT...
...DO YOU INTEND TO USE THOSE POWERS FOR?
I...
...WAS CREATED. I AM AN ARTIFICIAL BEING.
MY EXISTENCE IS "FAKE" TOO...

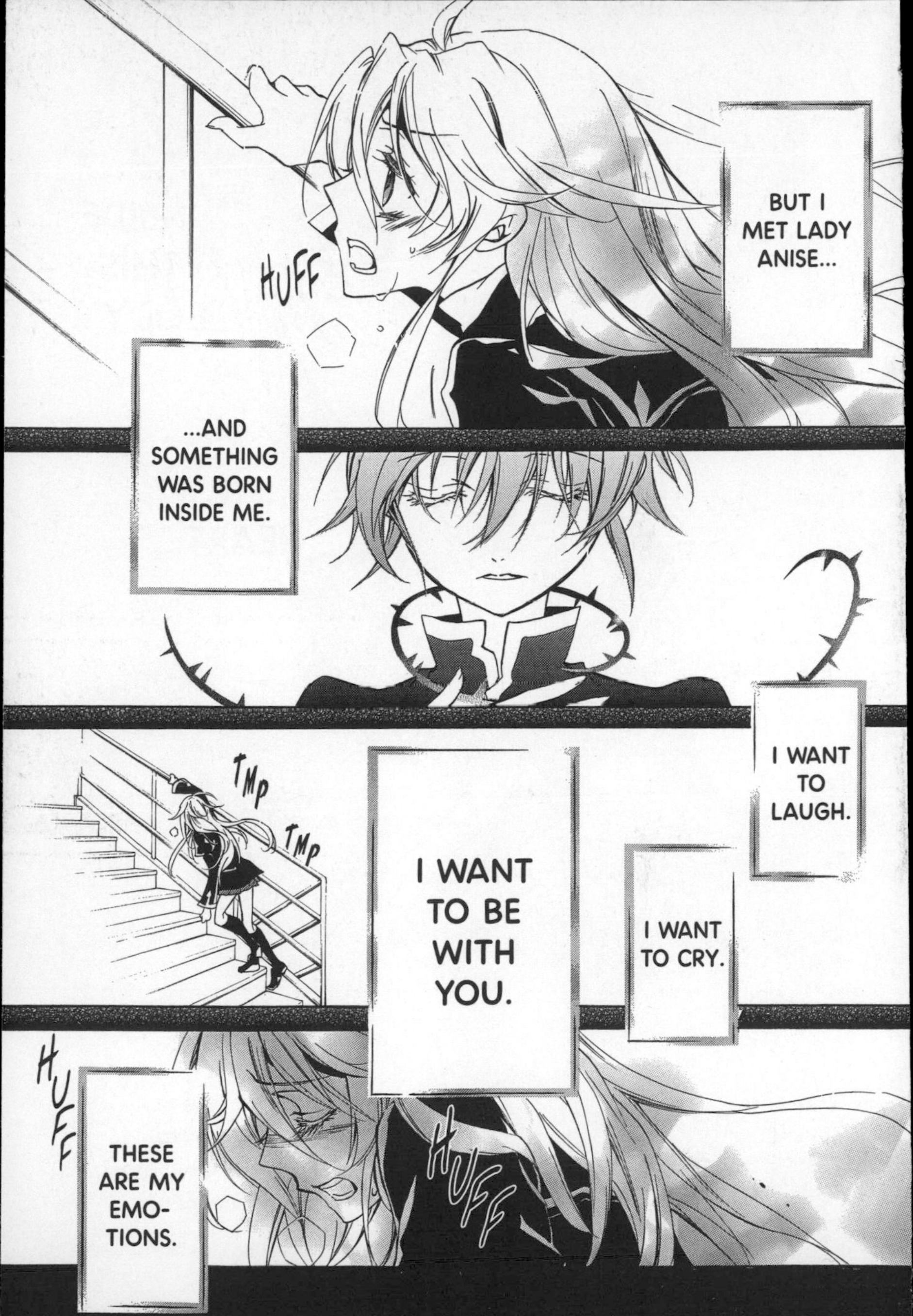
BUT I MET LADY ANISE...
HUFF
...AND SOMETHING WAS BORN INSIDE ME.
I WANT TO LAUGH.
I WANT TO CRY.
I WANT TO BE WITH YOU.
TMP
TMP
HUFF
HUFF
THESE ARE MY EMO-TIONS.

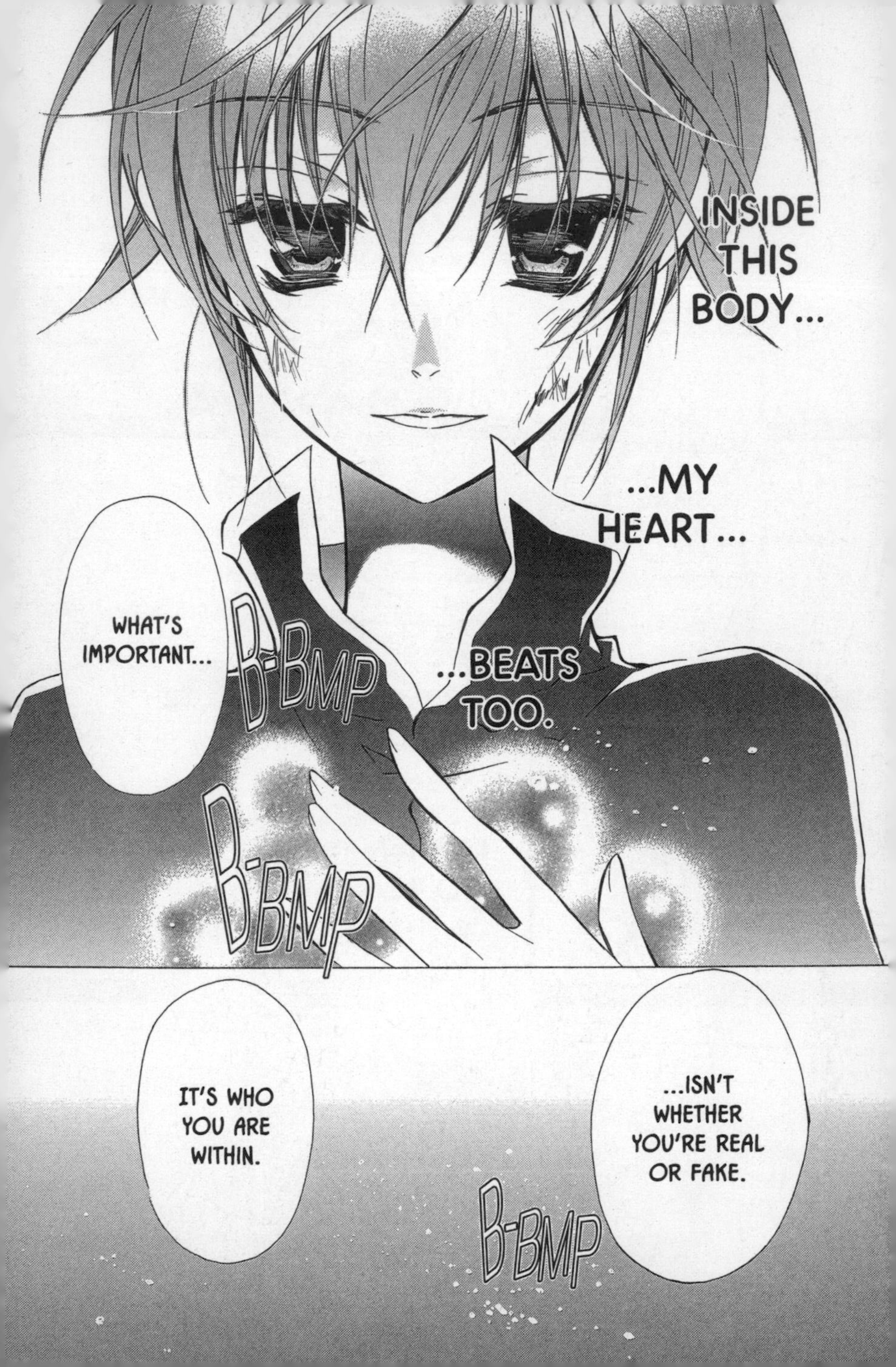
INSIDE THIS BODY...
...MY HEART...
...BEATS TOO.
B-BMP
WHAT'S IMPORTANT...
B-BMP
...ISN'T WHETHER YOU'RE REAL OR FAKE.
B-BMP
IT'S WHO YOU ARE WITHIN.

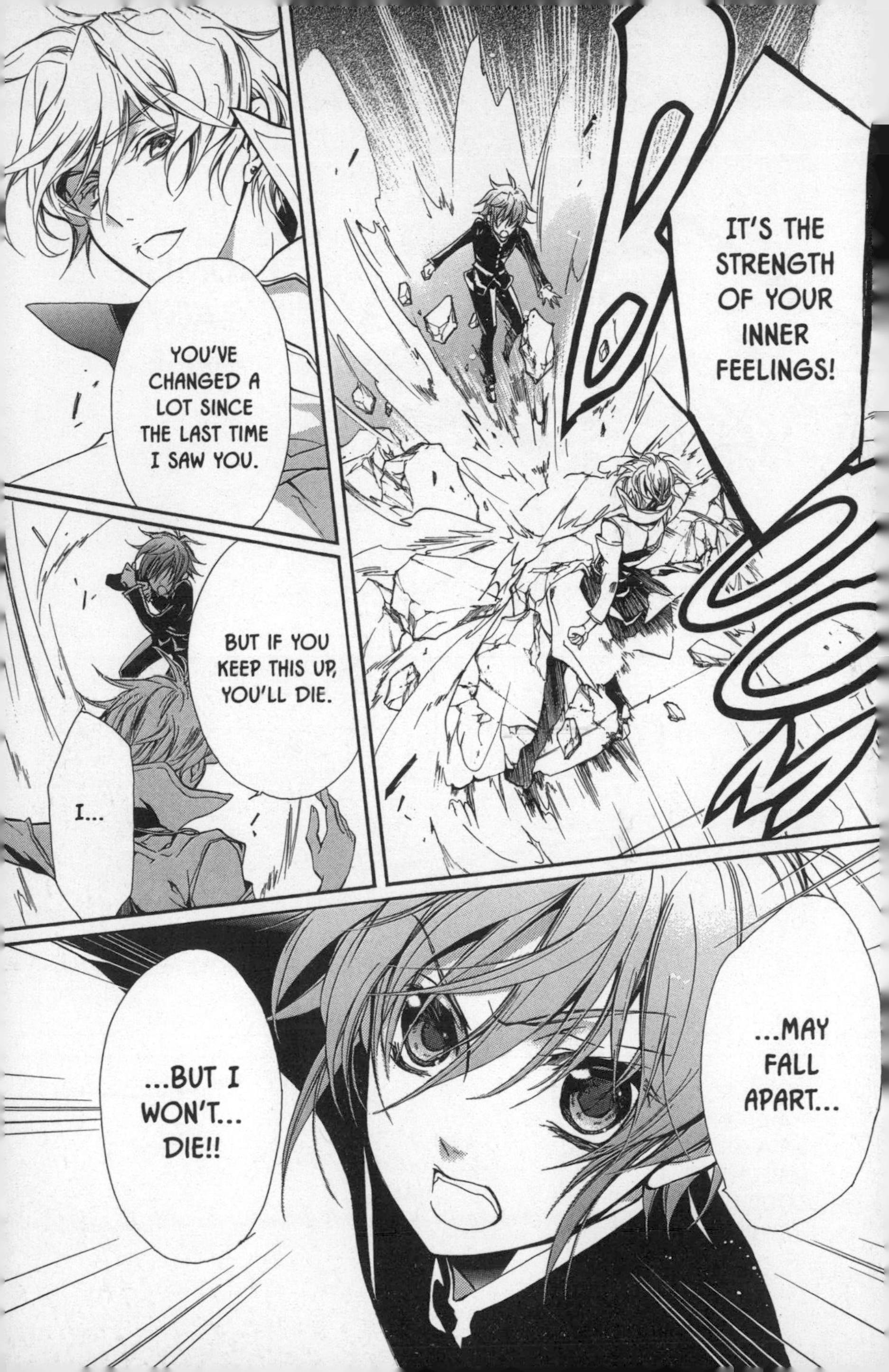
IT'S THE STRENGTH OF YOUR INNER FEELINGS!
YOU'VE CHANGED A LOT SINCE THE LAST TIME I SAW YOU.
BUT IF YOU KEEP THIS UP, YOU'LL DIE.
I...
...MAY FALL APART...
...BUT I WON'T... DIE!!

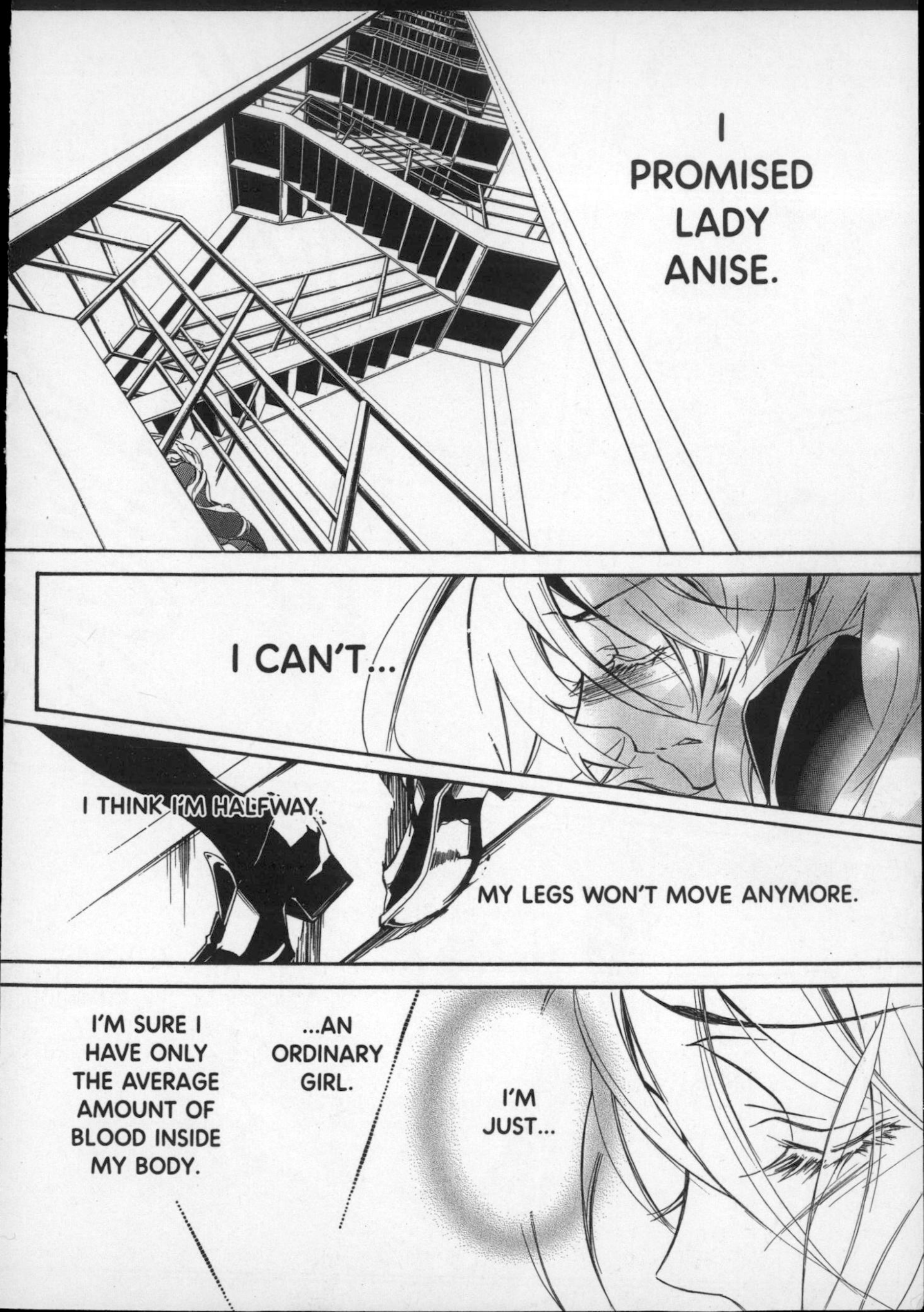
I PROMISED LADY ANISE.
I CAN'T...
I THINK I'M HALFWAY.
MY LEGS WON'T MOVE ANYMORE.
I'M JUST...
...AN ORDINARY GIRL.
I'M SURE I HAVE ONLY THE AVERAGE AMOUNT OF BLOOD INSIDE MY BODY.

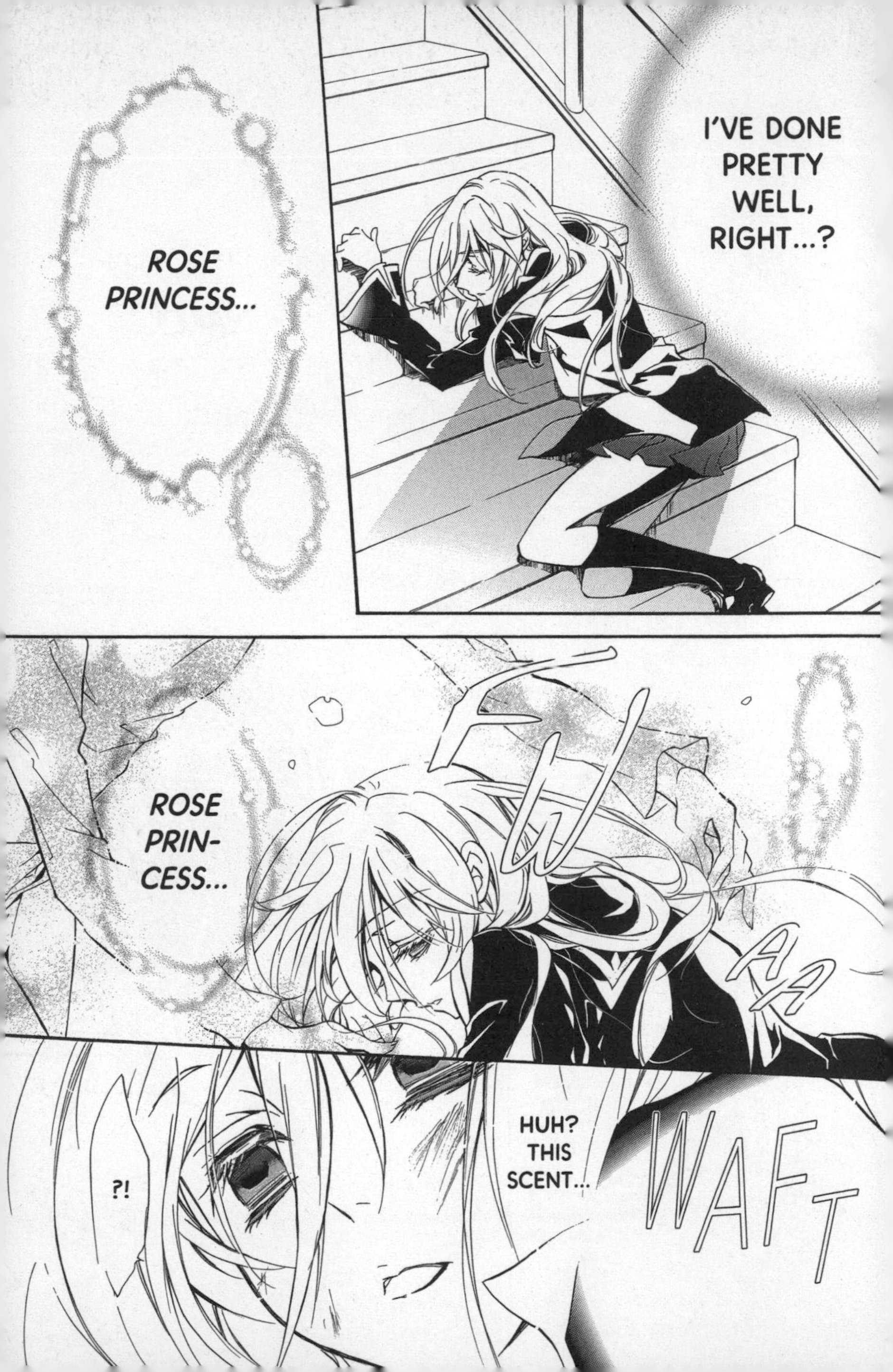
I'VE DONE PRETTY WELL, RIGHT...?
ROSE PRINCESS...
FWAA
ROSE PRIN-CESS...
WAFT
HUH? THIS SCENT...
?!

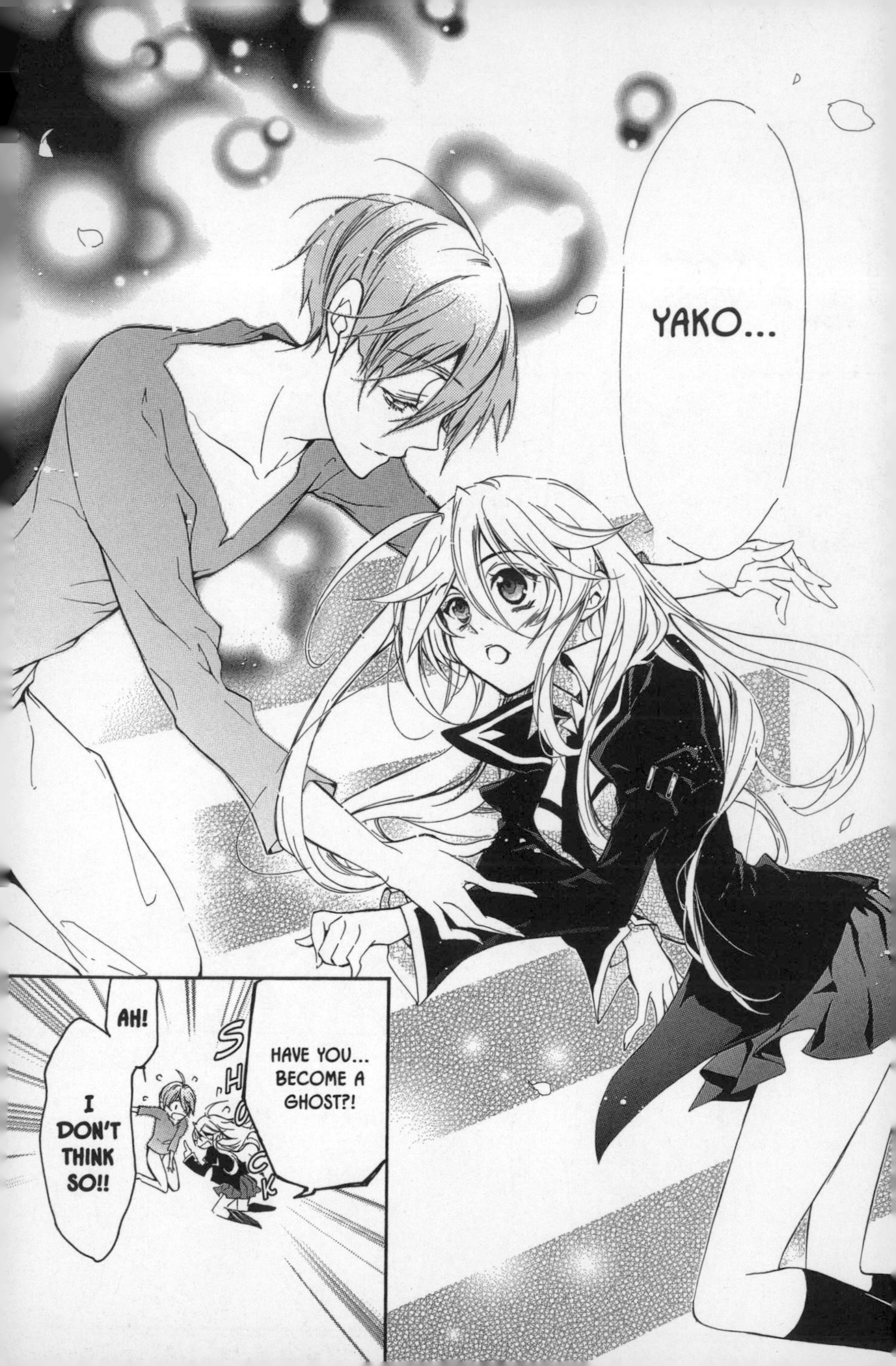
YAKO...
HAVE YOU... BECOME A GHOST?!
SHOCK
AH!
I DON'T THINK SO!!

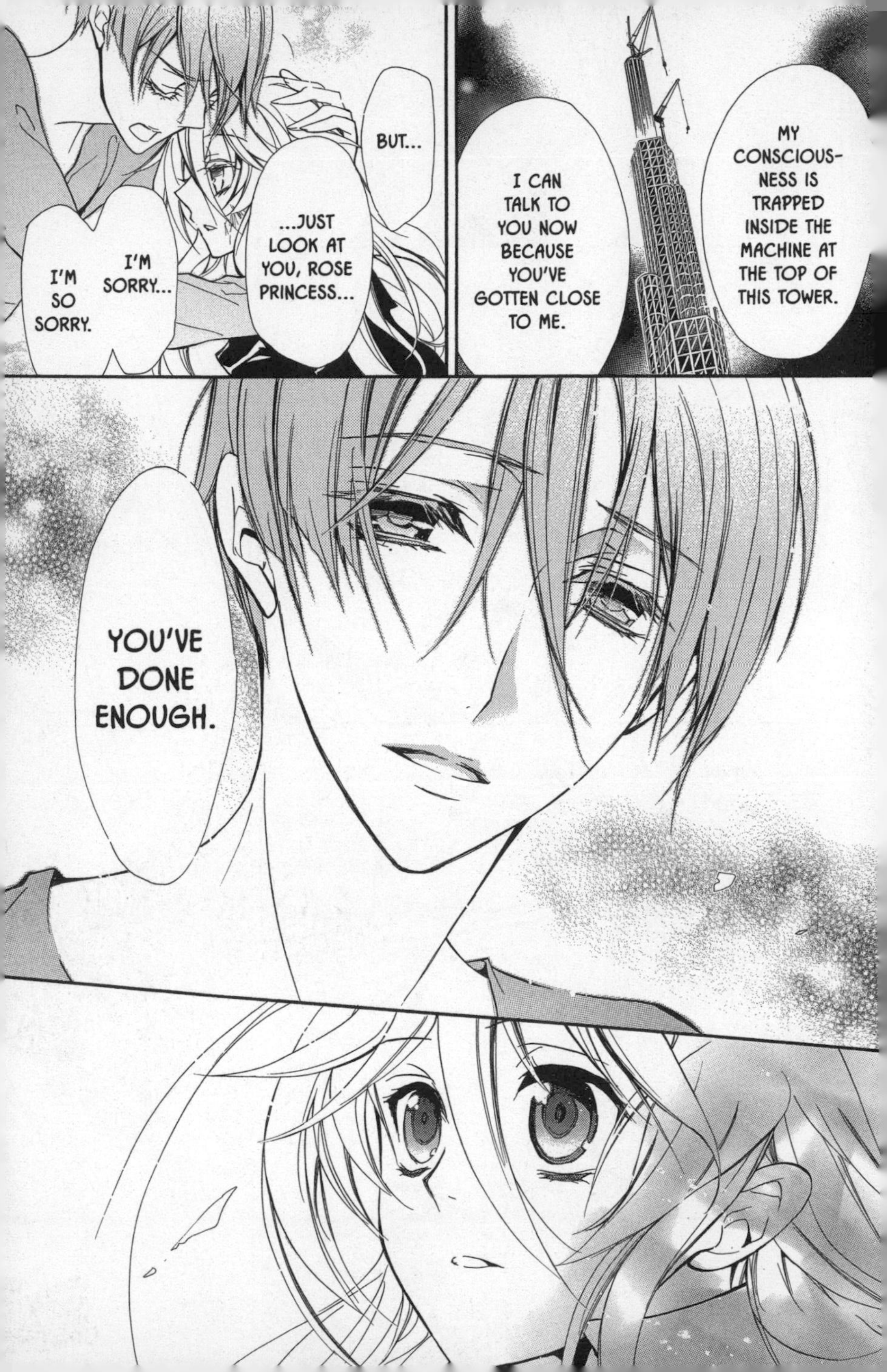
MY CONSCIOUS-NESS IS TRAPPED INSIDE THE MACHINE AT THE TOP OF THIS TOWER.
I CAN TALK TO YOU NOW BECAUSE YOU'VE GOTTEN CLOSE TO ME.
BUT...
...JUST LOOK AT YOU, ROSE PRINCESS...
I'M SORRY...
I'M SO SORRY.
YOU'VE DONE ENOUGH.

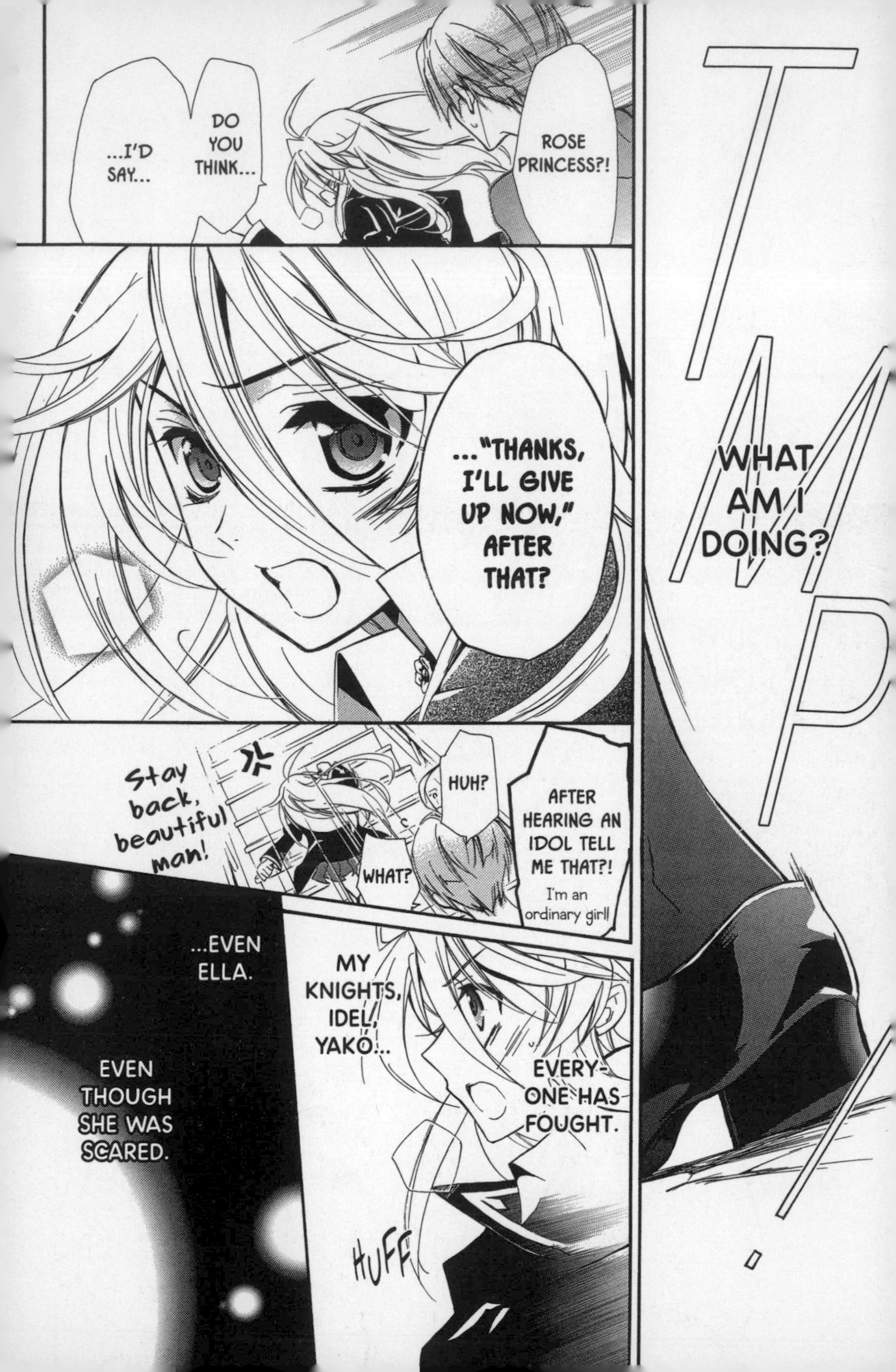
TMP
WHAT AM I DOING?
ROSE PRINCESS?!
DO YOU THINK...
...I'D SAY...
..."THANKS, I'LL GIVE UP NOW," AFTER THAT?
AFTER HEARING AN IDOL TELL ME THAT?!
I'm an ordinary girl!
HUH?
WHAT?
Stay back, beautiful man!
MY KNIGHTS, IDEL, YAKO...
EVERY-ONE HAS FOUGHT.
HUFF
...EVEN ELLA.
EVEN THOUGH SHE WAS SCARED.

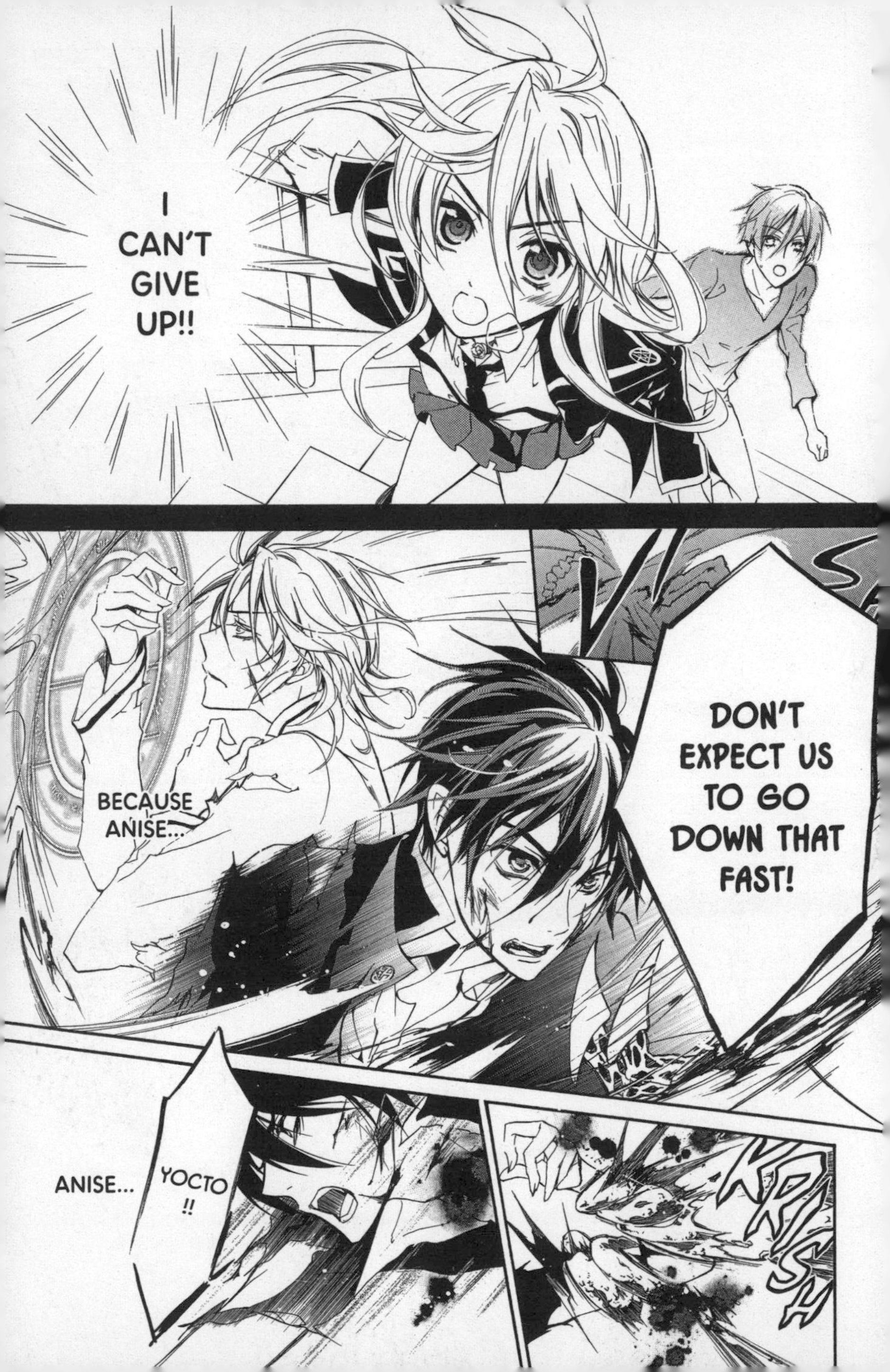
I CAN'T GIVE UP!!
DON'T EXPECT US TO GO DOWN THAT FAST!
BECAUSE ANISE...
KRSH
YOCTO !!
ANISE...

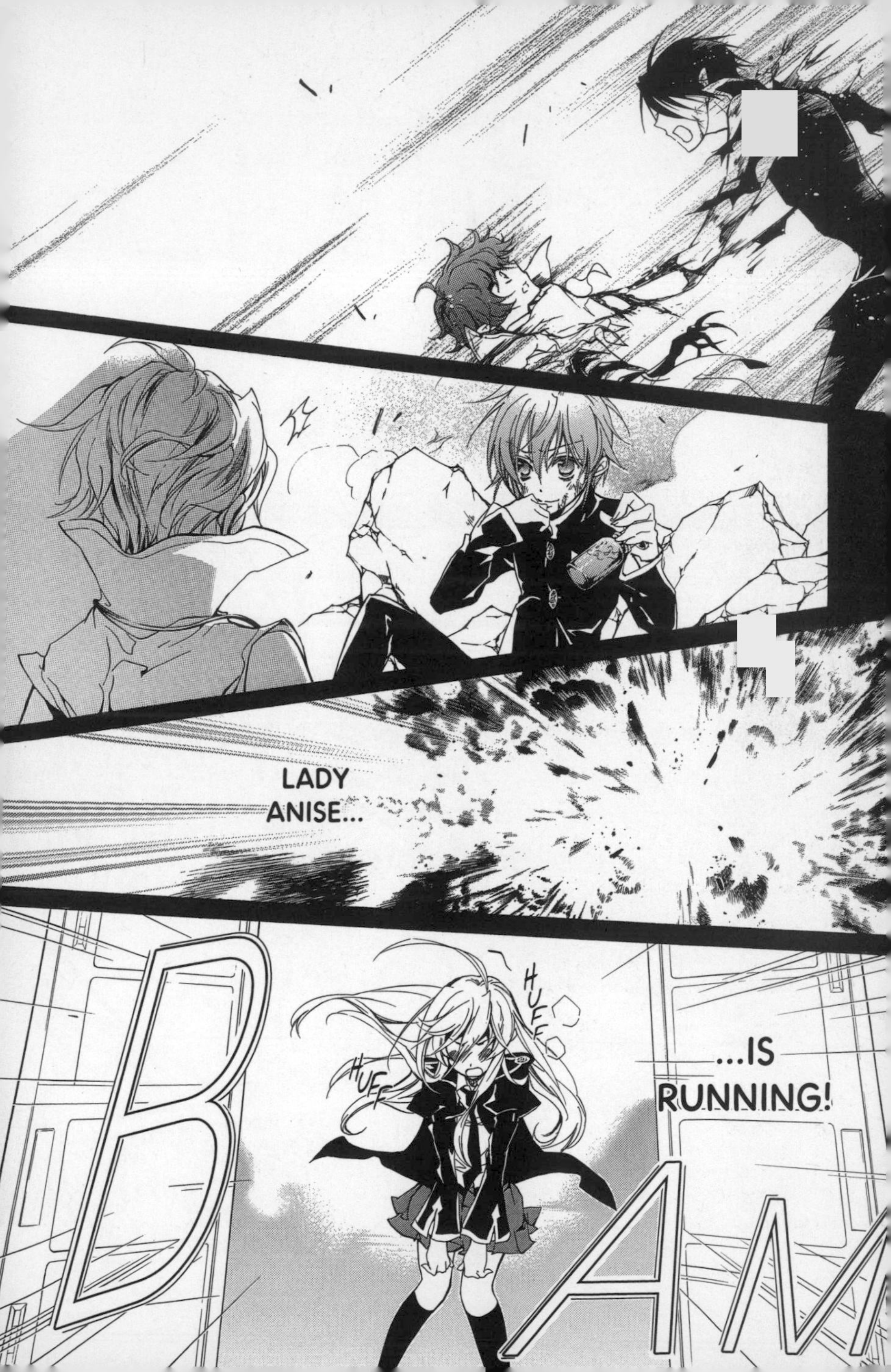
LADY ANISE...
HUFF
...IS RUNNING!
HUFF
BAM

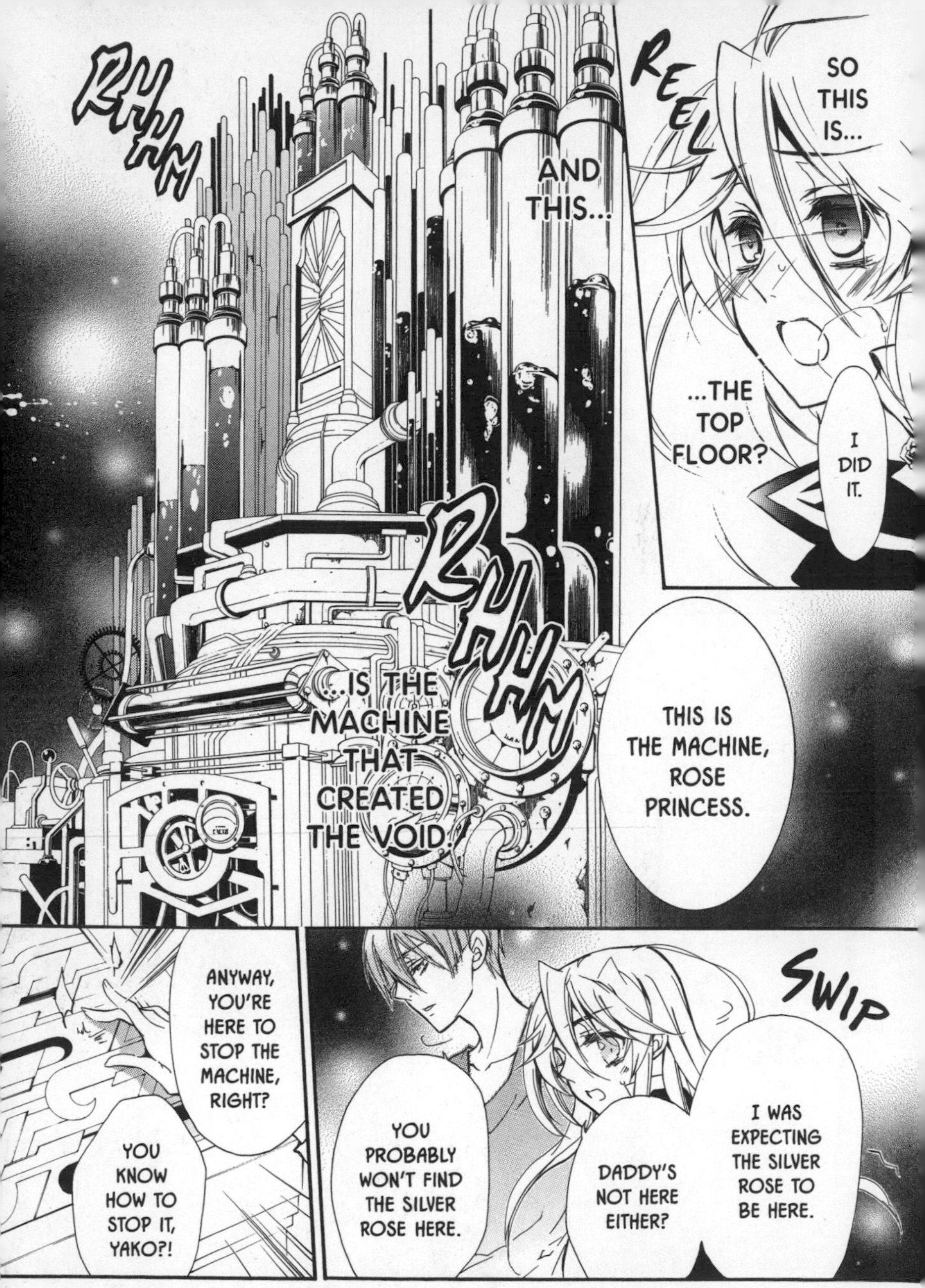

SO THIS IS...
REEL
...THE TOP FLOOR?
I DID IT.
AND THIS...
RHHM
THIS IS THE MACHINE, ROSE PRINCESS.
RHHM
...IS THE MACHINE THAT CREATED THE VOID!
SWIP
I WAS EXPECTING THE SILVER ROSE TO BE HERE.
DADDY'S NOT HERE EITHER?
YOU PROBABLY WON'T FIND THE SILVER ROSE HERE.
ANYWAY, YOU'RE HERE TO STOP THE MACHINE, RIGHT?
YOU KNOW HOW TO STOP IT, YAKO?!

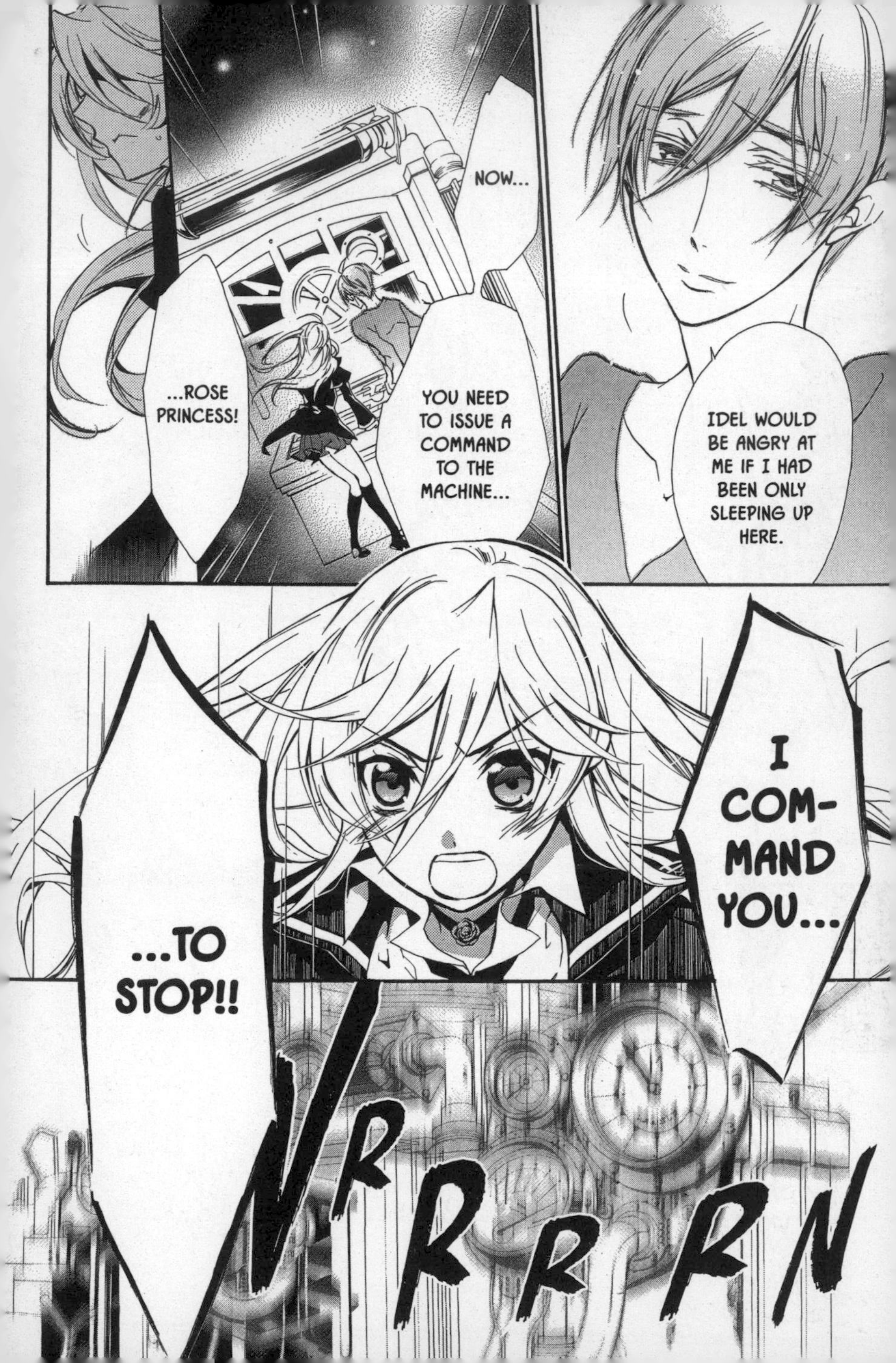
IDEL WOULD BE ANGRY AT ME IF I HAD BEEN ONLY SLEEPING UP HERE.
NOW...
YOU NEED TO ISSUE A COMMAND TO THE MACHINE...
...ROSE PRINCESS!
I COM-MAND YOU...
...TO STOP!!
VRRRRN

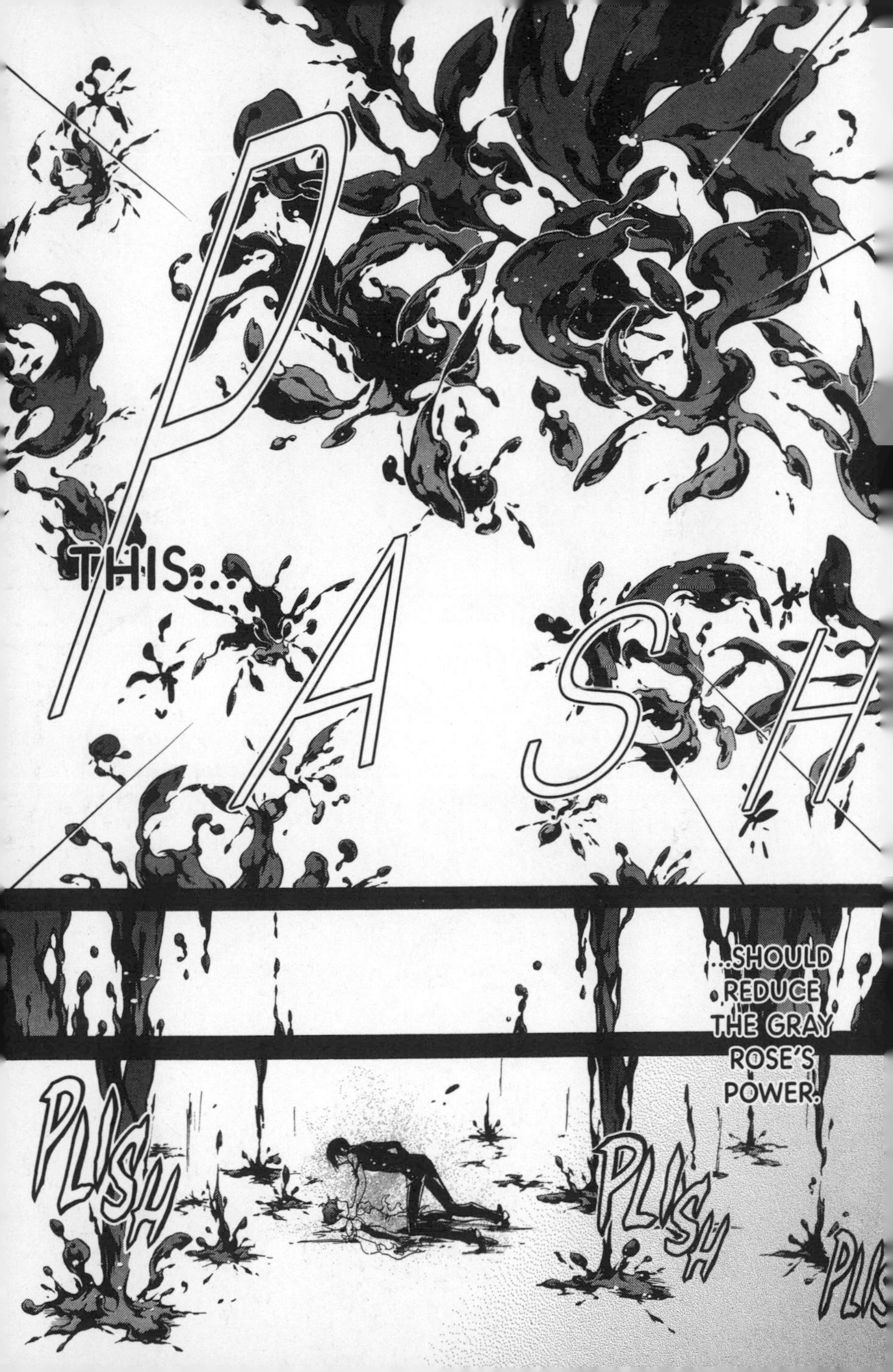

THIS...
PASH
...SHOULD REDUCE THE GRAY ROSE'S POWER.
PLIS
PLISH
PLISH

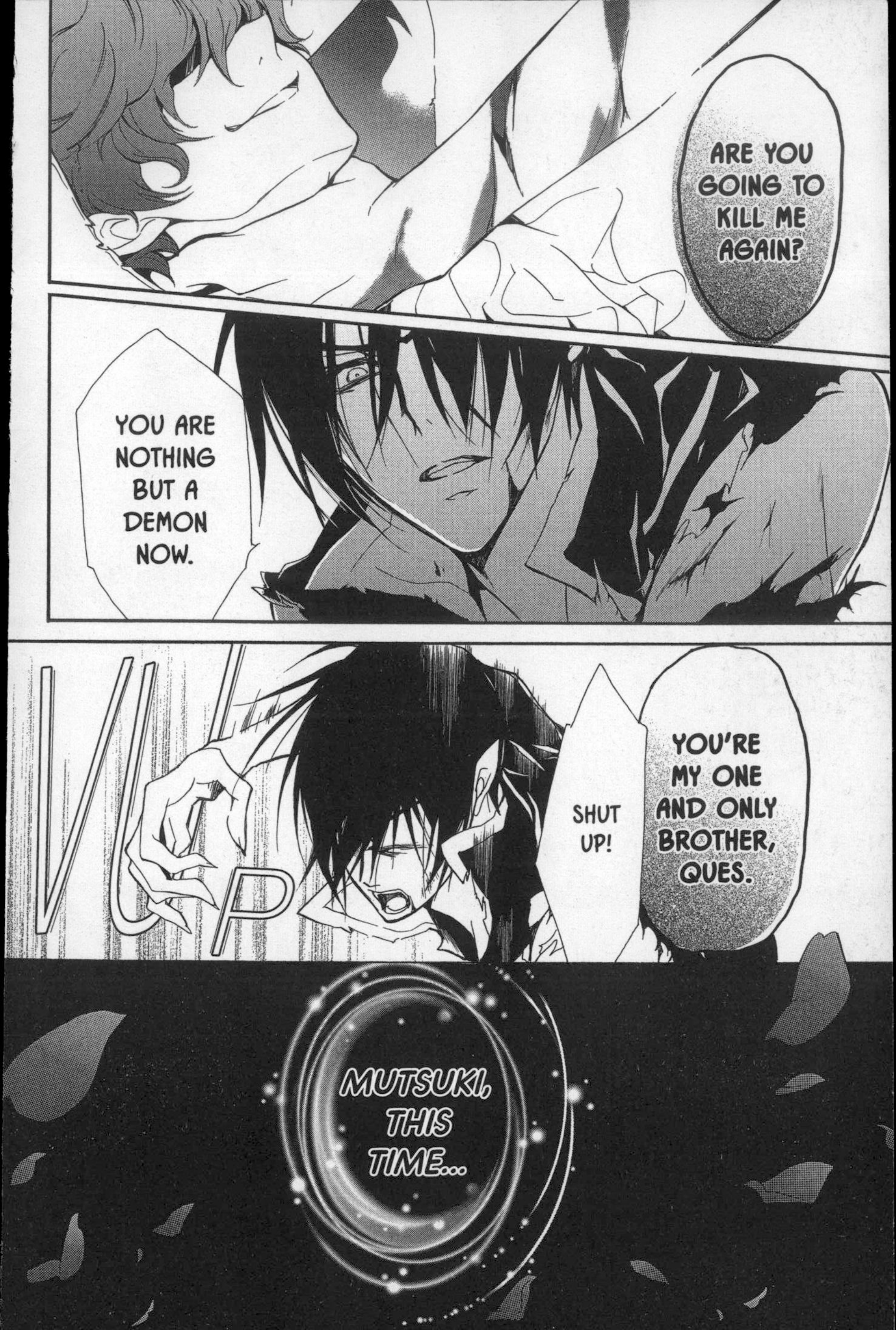
ARE YOU GOING TO KILL ME AGAIN?
YOU ARE NOTHING BUT A DEMON NOW.
YOU'RE MY ONE AND ONLY BROTHER, QUES.
SHUT UP!
VUP
MUTSUKI, THIS TIME...

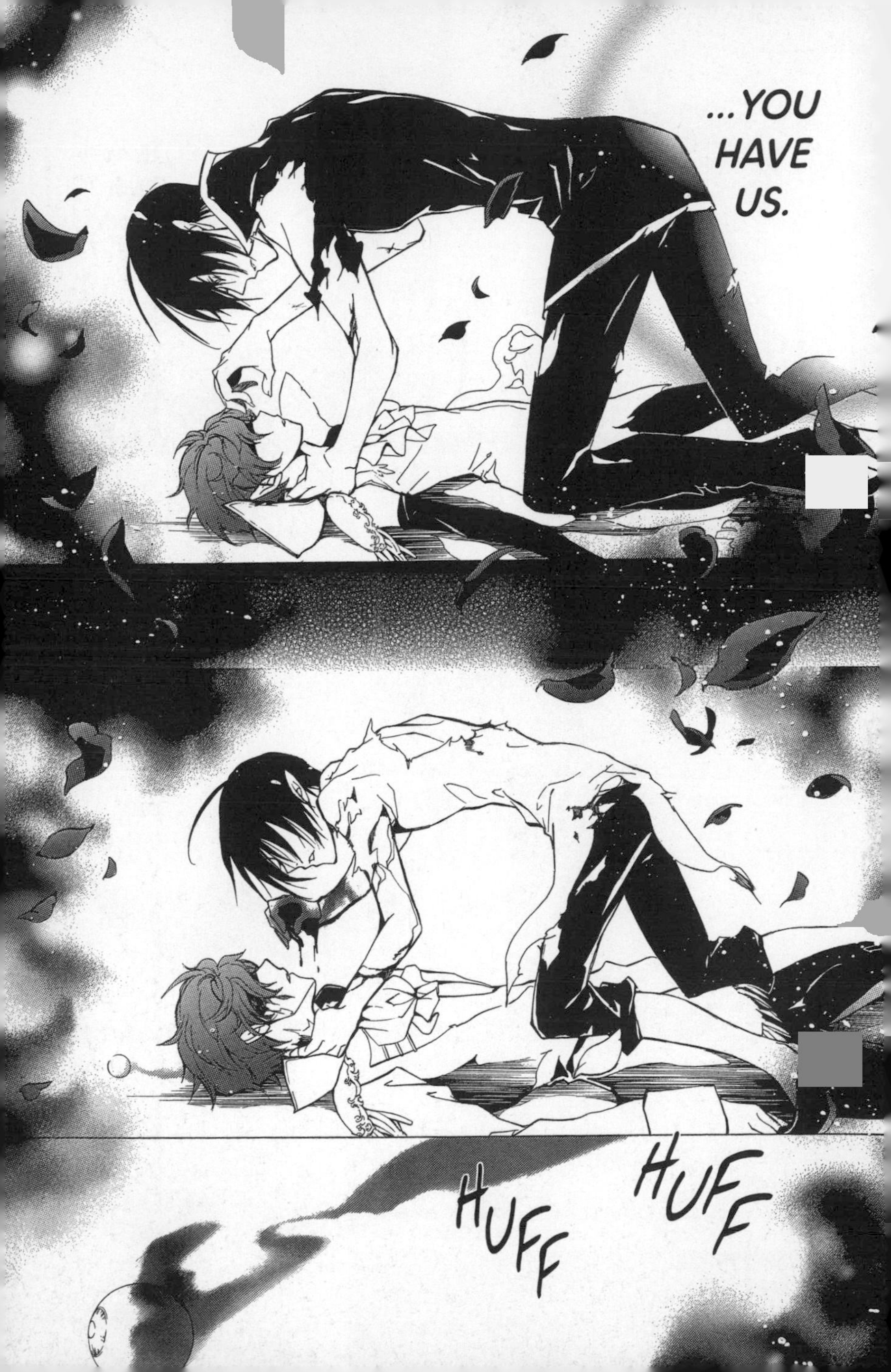
...YOU HAVE US.
HUFF
HUFF

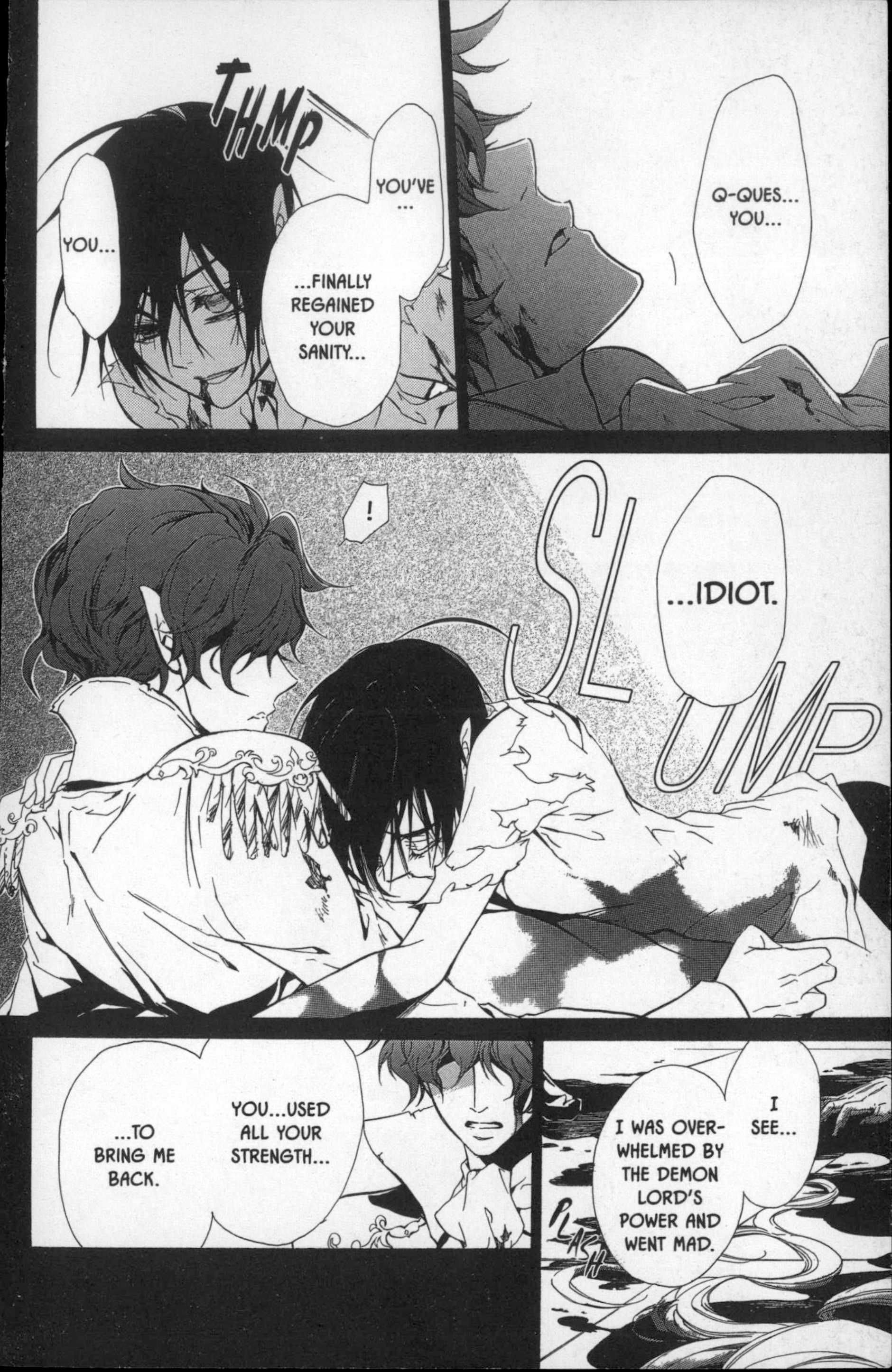
Q-QUES... YOU...
THMP
YOU'VE ...
...FINALLY REGAINED YOUR SANITY...
YOU...
SLUMP
...IDIOT.
!
I SEE...
I WAS OVER-WHELMED BY THE DEMON LORD'S POWER AND WENT MAD.
PLASH
YOU...USED ALL YOUR STRENGTH...
...TO BRING ME BACK.

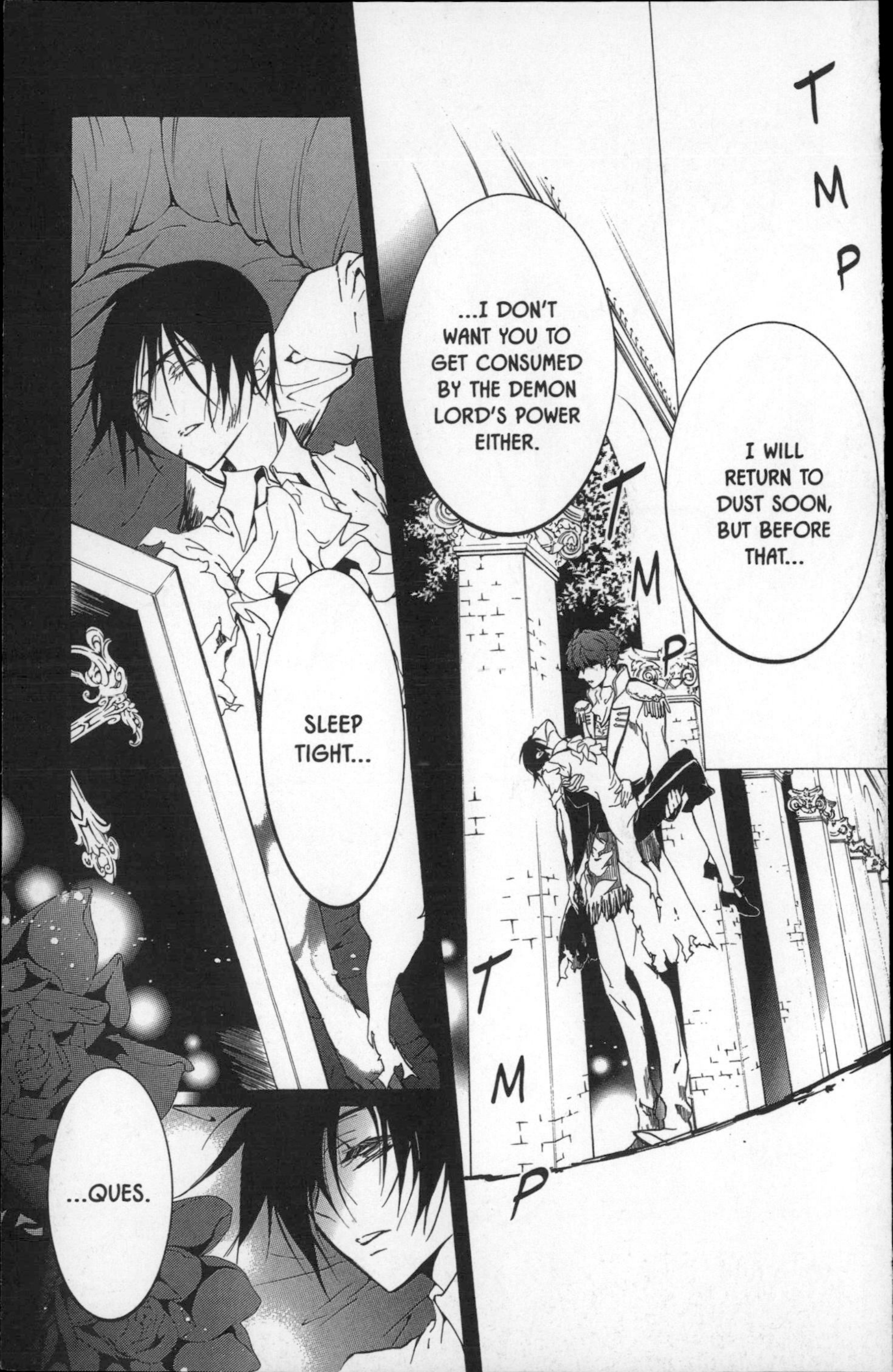
TMP
I WILL RETURN TO DUST SOON, BUT BEFORE THAT...
...I DON'T WANT YOU TO GET CONSUMED BY THE DEMON LORD'S POWER EITHER.
TMP
TMP
SLEEP TIGHT...
...QUES.

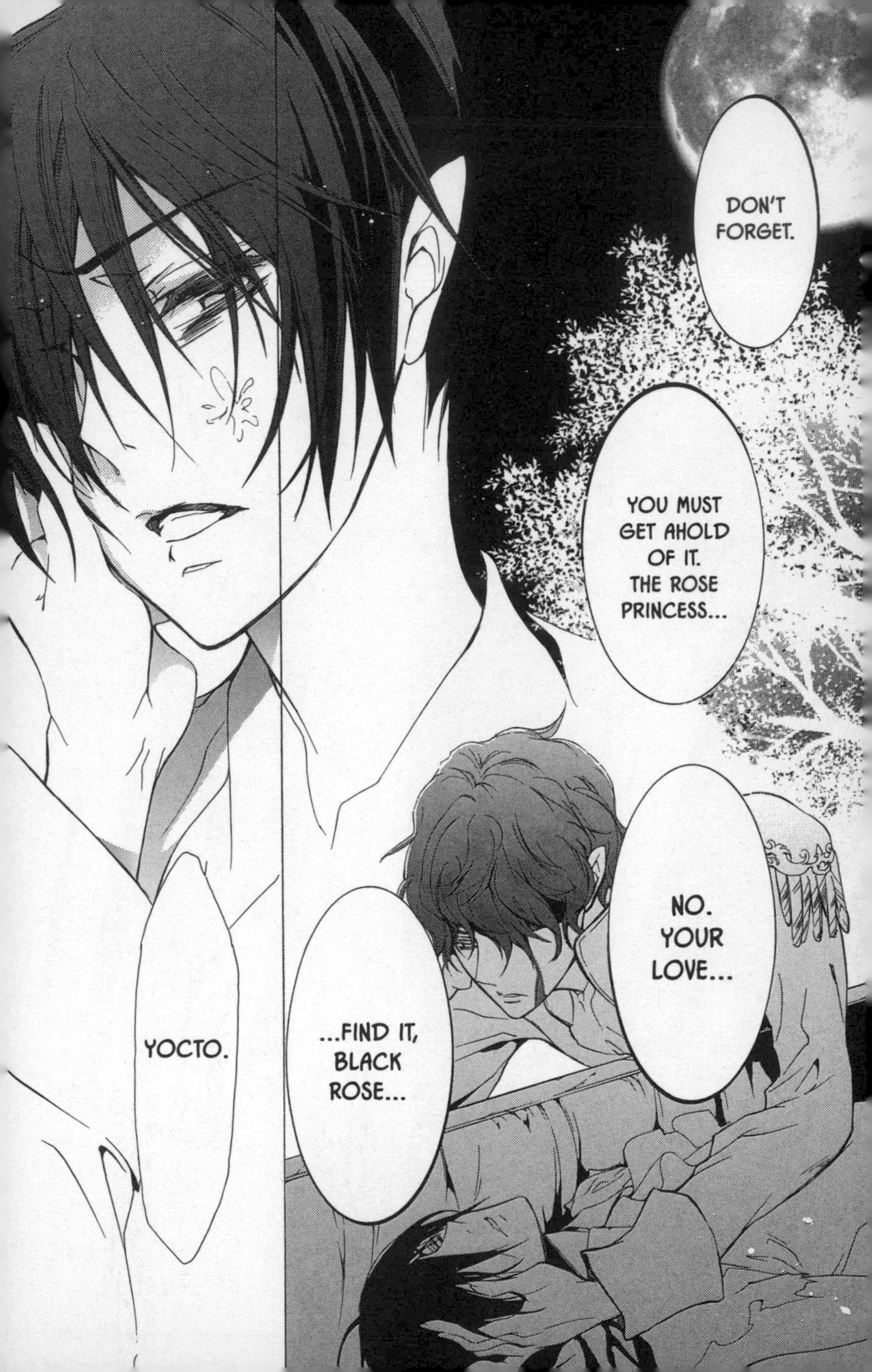
DON'T FORGET.
YOU MUST GET AHOLD OF IT. THE ROSE PRINCESS...
NO. YOUR LOVE...
...FIND IT, BLACK ROSE...
YOCTO.

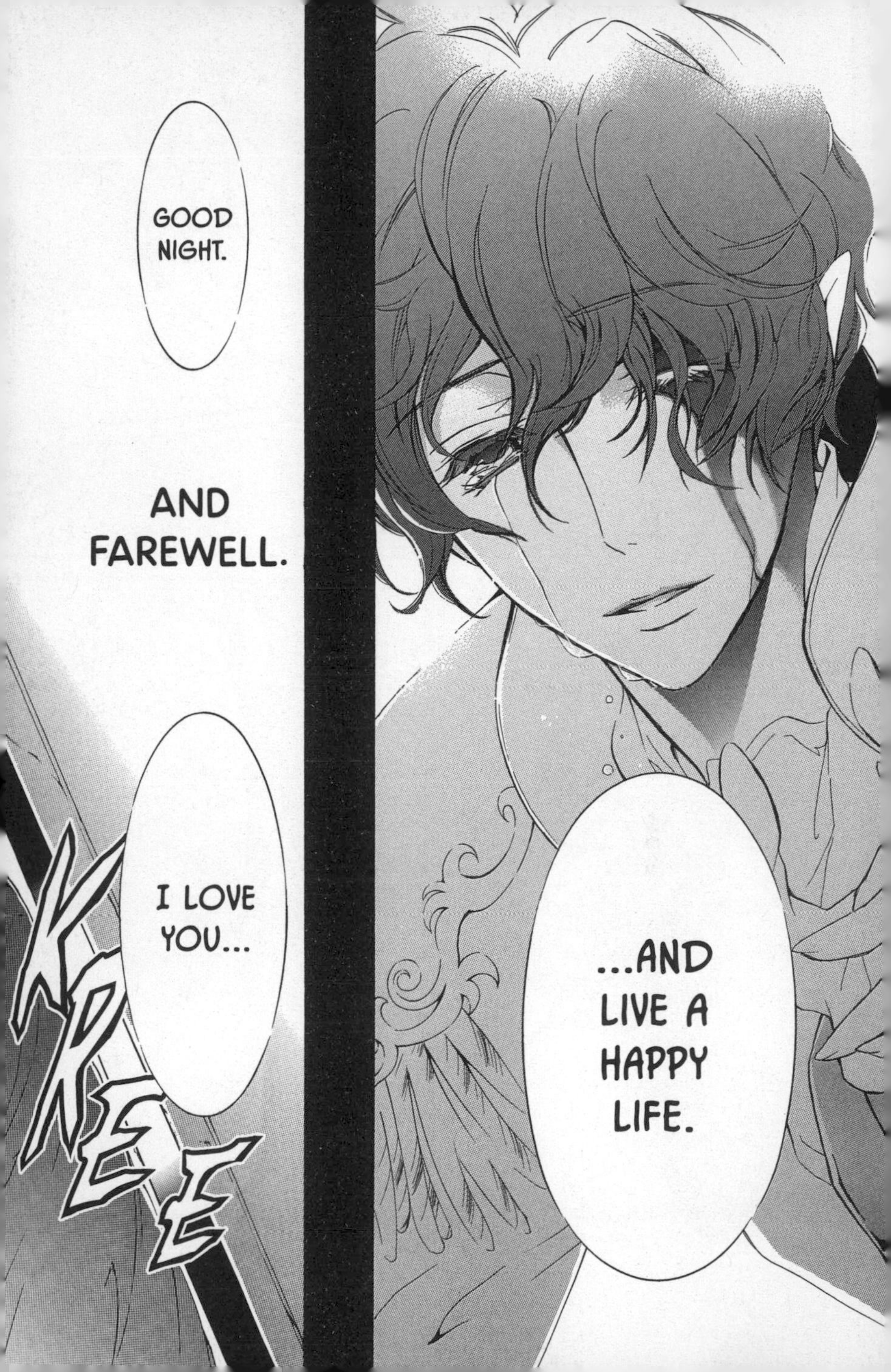
...AND LIVE A HAPPY LIFE.
GOOD NIGHT.
AND FAREWELL.
I LOVE YOU...
KREE

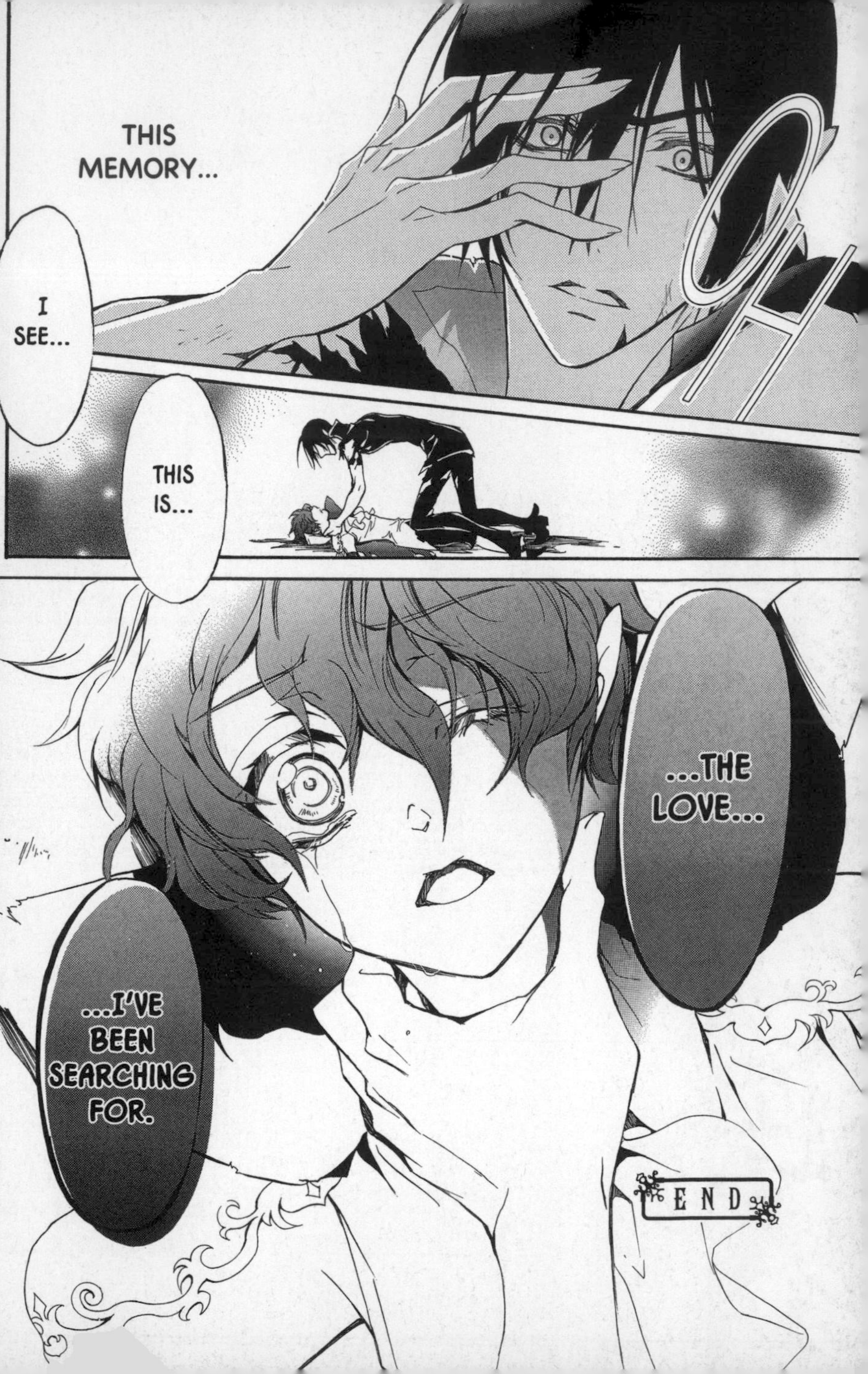
THIS MEMORY...
I SEE...
THIS IS...
...THE LOVE...
...I'VE BEEN SEARCHING FOR.
END

Kiss of the Rose Princess

Kiss of the Rose Princess

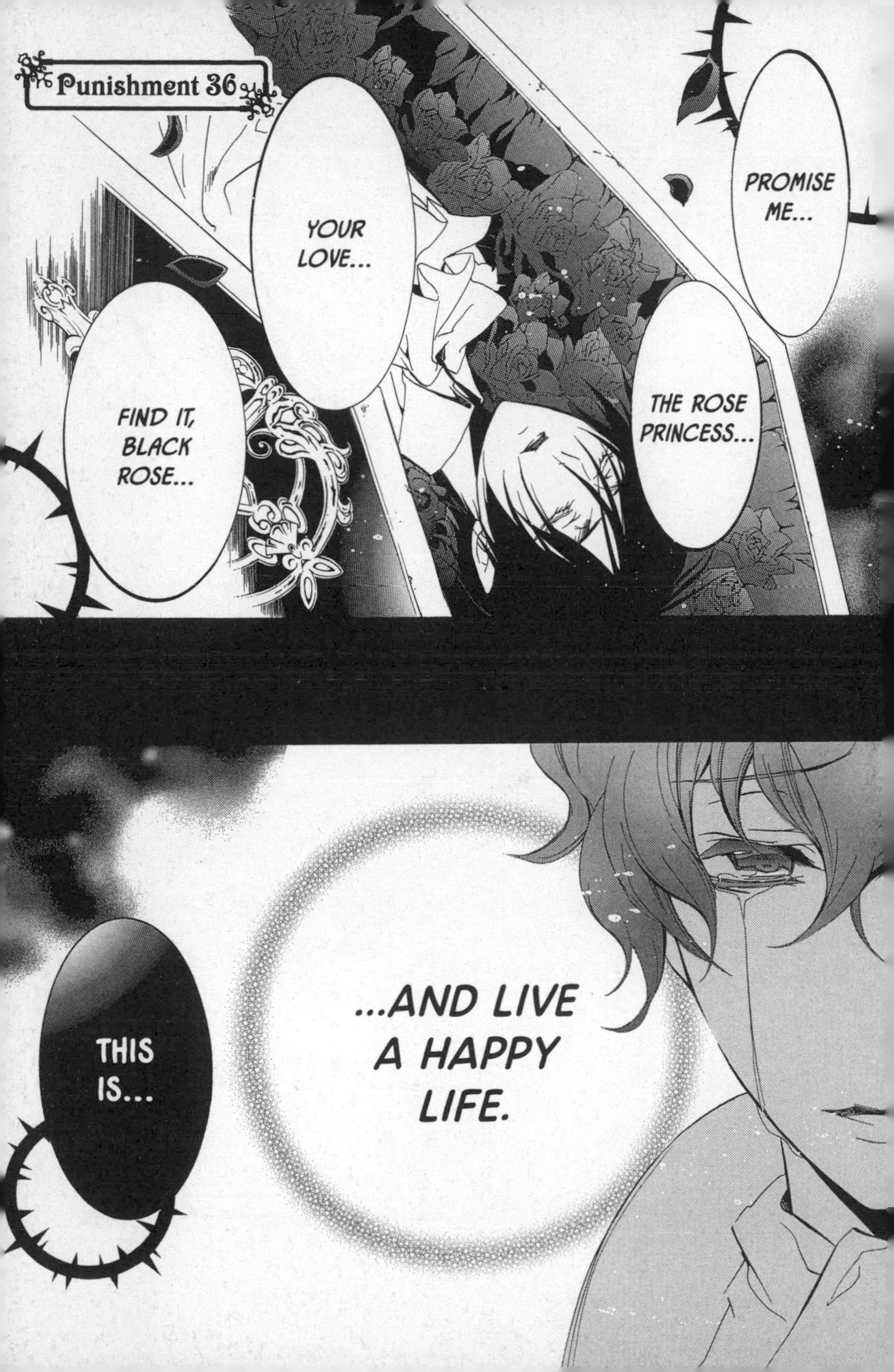
Punishment 36
PROMISE ME...
THE ROSE PRINCESS...
YOUR LOVE...
FIND IT, BLACK ROSE...
...AND LIVE A HAPPY LIFE.
THIS IS...

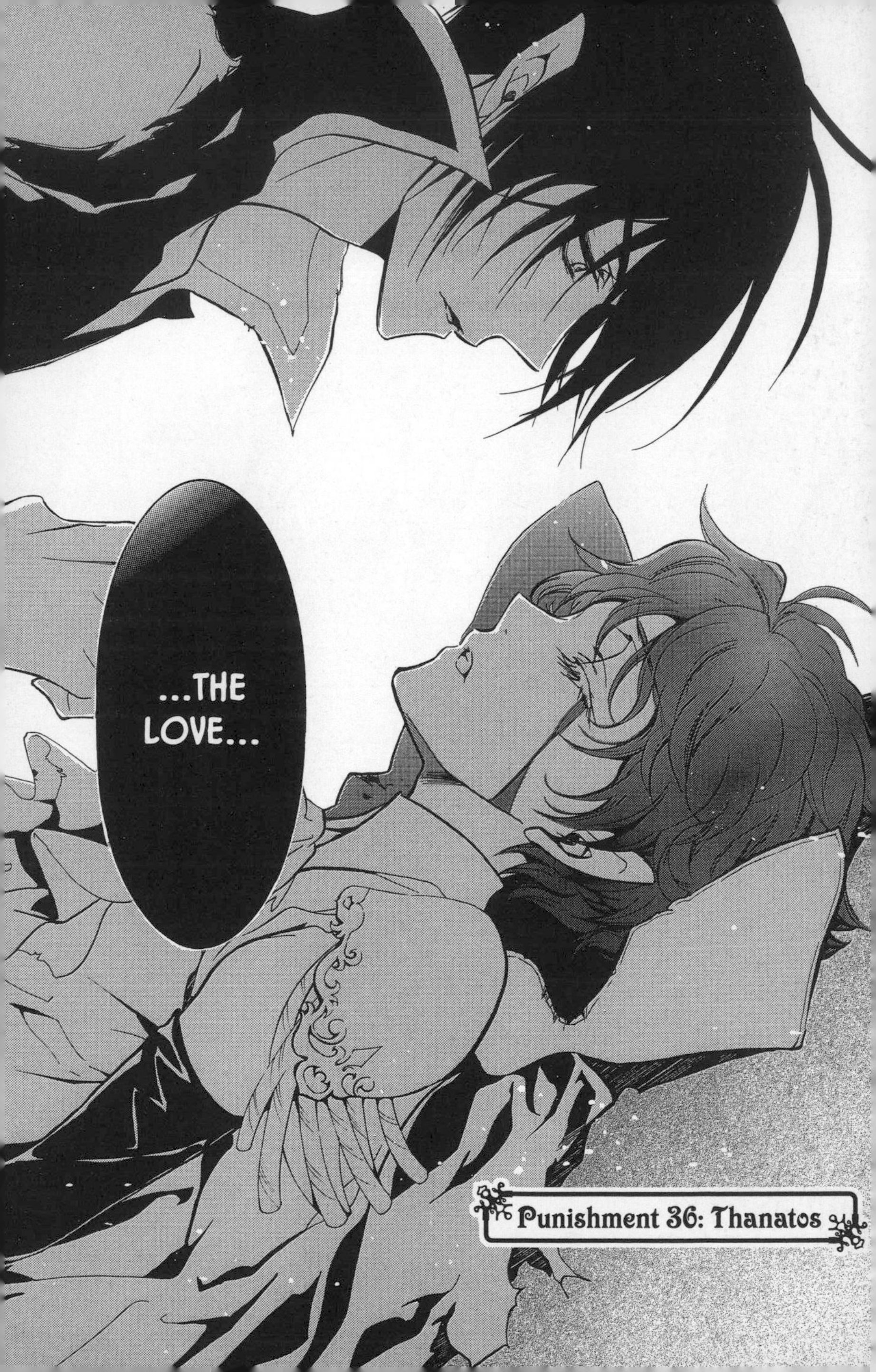
...THE LOVE...
Punishment 36: Thanatos

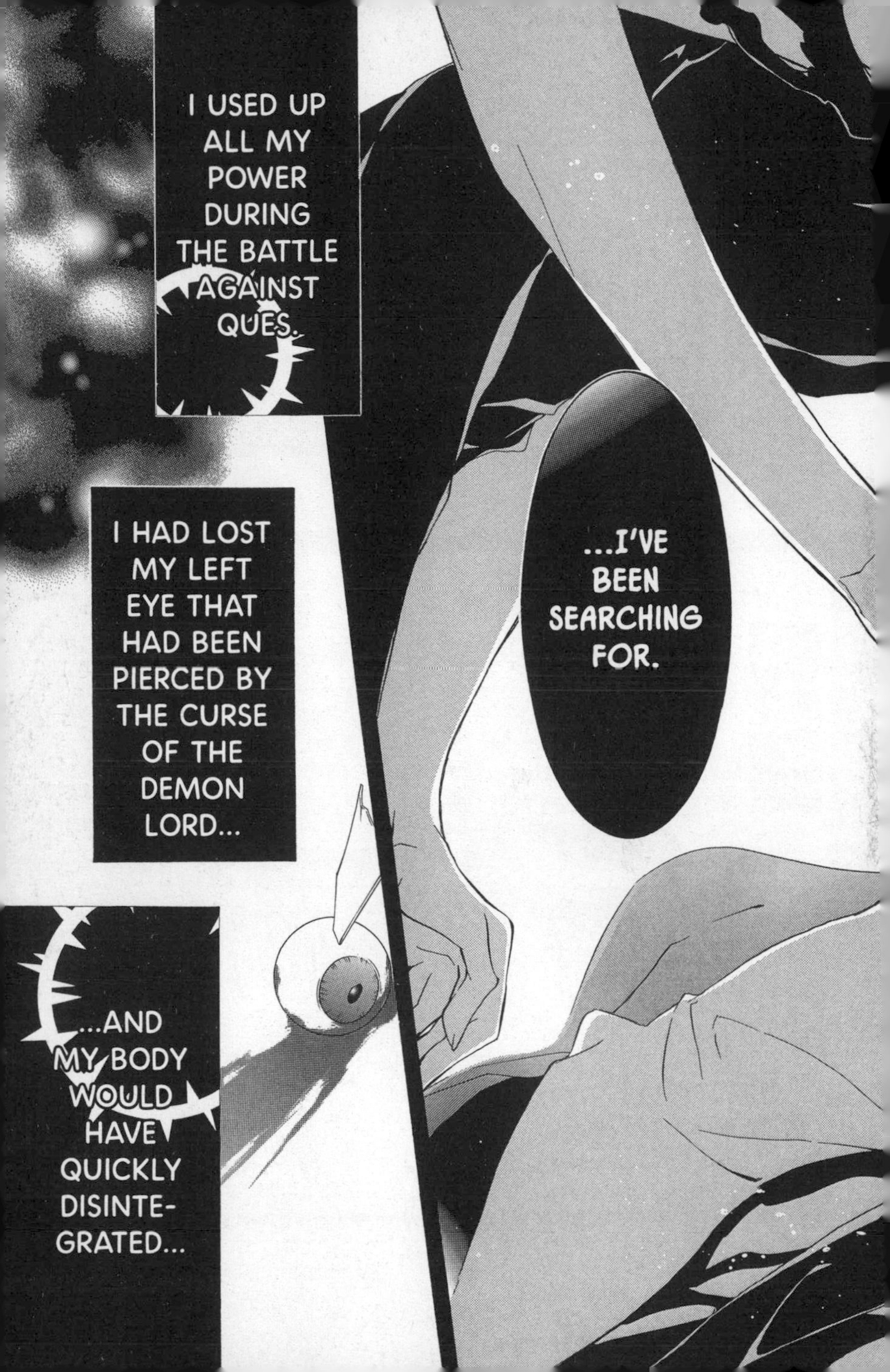
...I'VE BEEN SEARCHING FOR.
I USED UP ALL MY POWER DURING THE BATTLE AGAINST QUES.
I HAD LOST MY LEFT EYE THAT HAD BEEN PIERCED BY THE CURSE OF THE DEMON LORD...
...AND MY BODY WOULD HAVE QUICKLY DISINTE-GRATED...

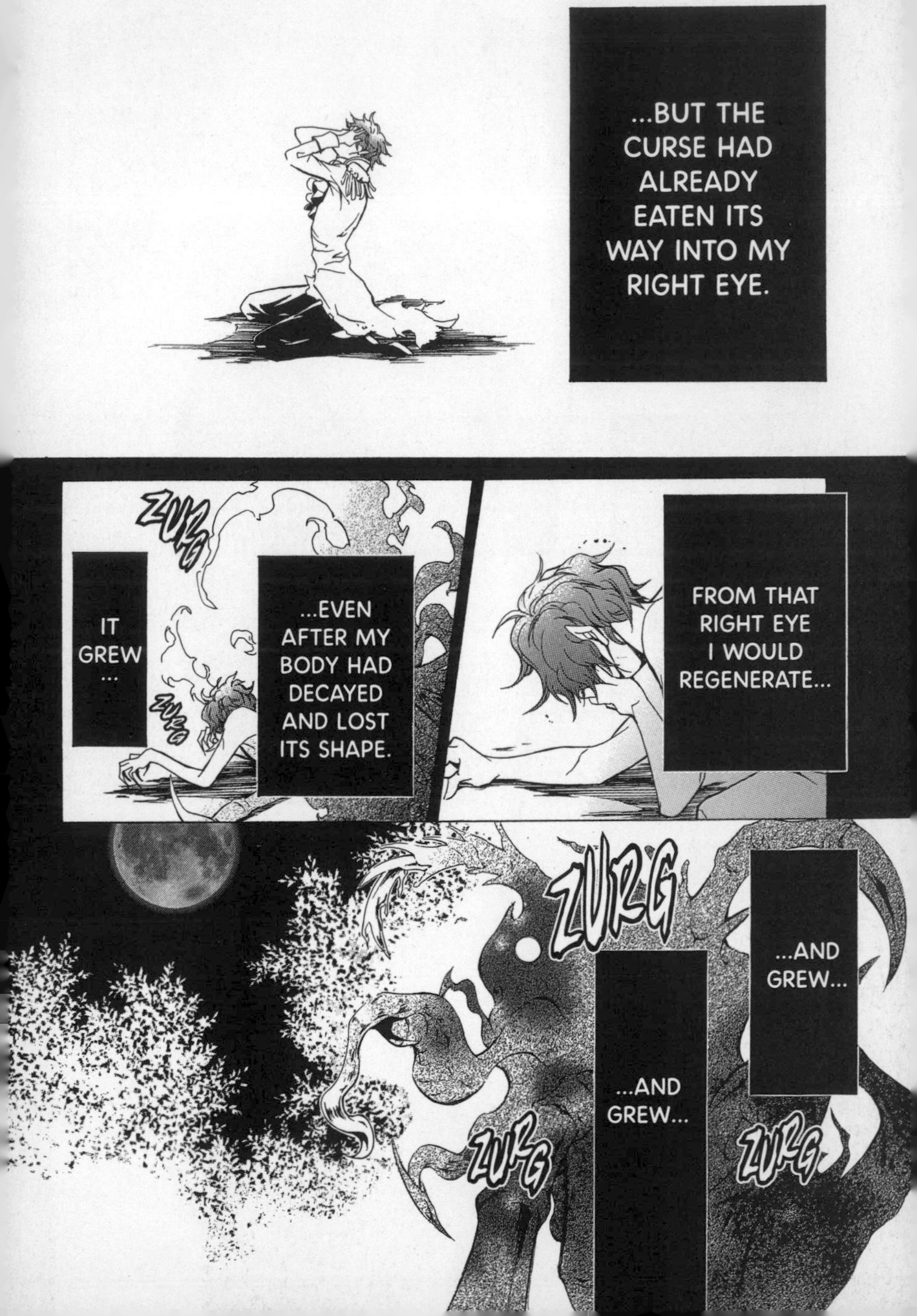
...BUT THE CURSE HAD ALREADY EATEN ITS WAY INTO MY RIGHT EYE.
FROM THAT RIGHT EYE I WOULD REGENERATE...
...EVEN AFTER MY BODY HAD DECAYED AND LOST ITS SHAPE.
ZURG
IT GREW...
ZURG
ZURG
...AND GREW...
...AND GREW...
ZURG
ZURG

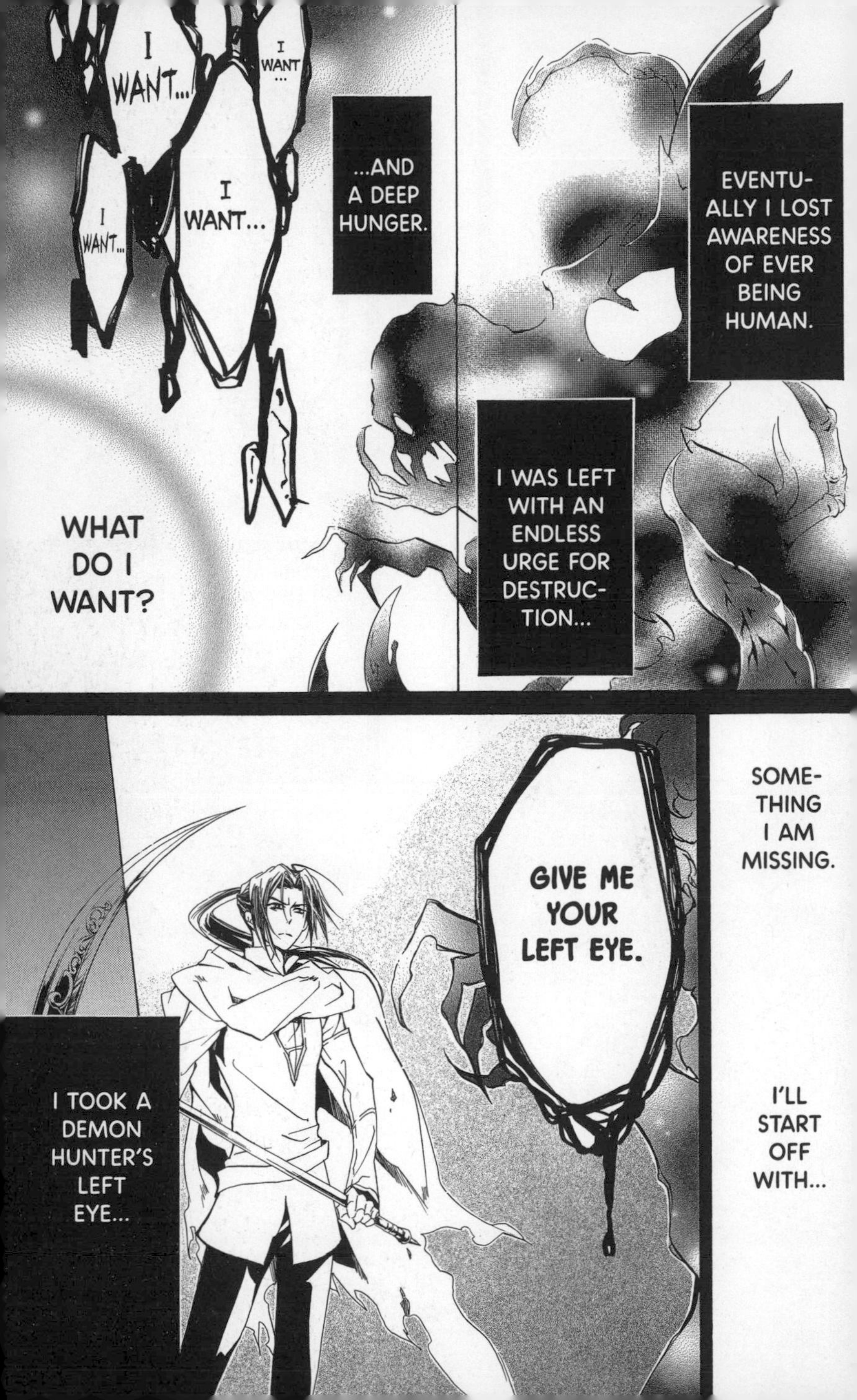
EVENTU-ALLY I LOST AWARENESS OF EVER BEING HUMAN.
I WAS LEFT WITH AN ENDLESS URGE FOR DESTRUC-TION...
...AND A DEEP HUNGER.
I WANT...
I WANT...
I WANT...
I WANT...
WHAT DO I WANT?
SOME-THING I AM MISSING.
I'LL START OFF WITH...
GIVE ME YOUR LEFT EYE.
I TOOK A DEMON HUNTER'S LEFT EYE...

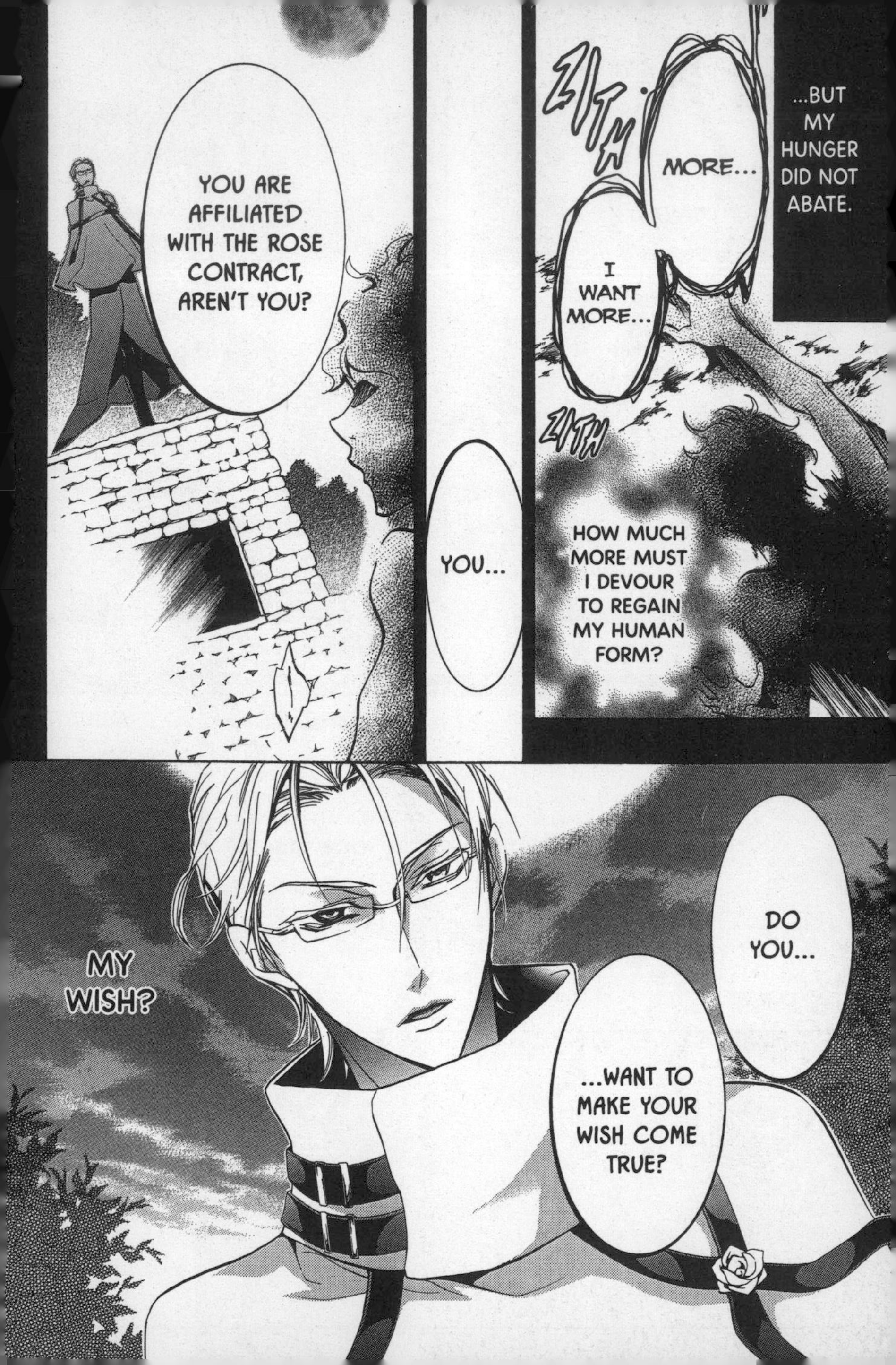
...BUT MY HUNGER DID NOT ABATE.
ZITH
MORE...
I WANT MORE...
ZITH
HOW MUCH MORE MUST I DEVOUR TO REGAIN MY HUMAN FORM?
YOU...
YOU ARE AFFILIATED WITH THE ROSE CONTRACT, AREN'T YOU?
DO YOU...
...WANT TO MAKE YOUR WISH COME TRUE?
MY WISH?

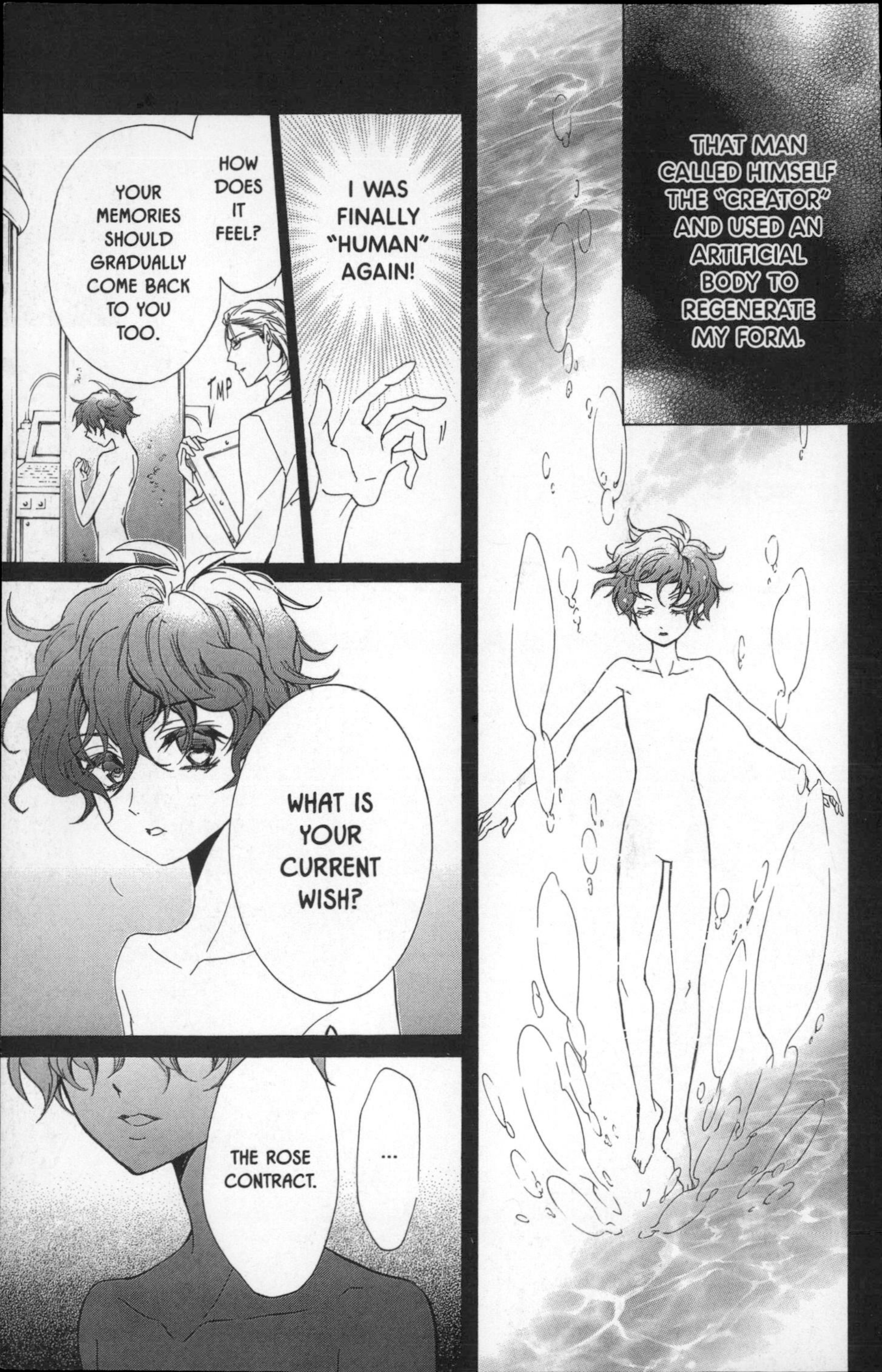
THAT MAN CALLED HIMSELF THE "CREATOR" AND USED AN ARTIFICIAL BODY TO REGENERATE MY FORM.
I WAS FINALLY "HUMAN" AGAIN!
HOW DOES IT FEEL?
TMP
YOUR MEMORIES SHOULD GRADUALLY COME BACK TO YOU TOO.
WHAT IS YOUR CURRENT WISH?
...
THE ROSE CONTRACT.

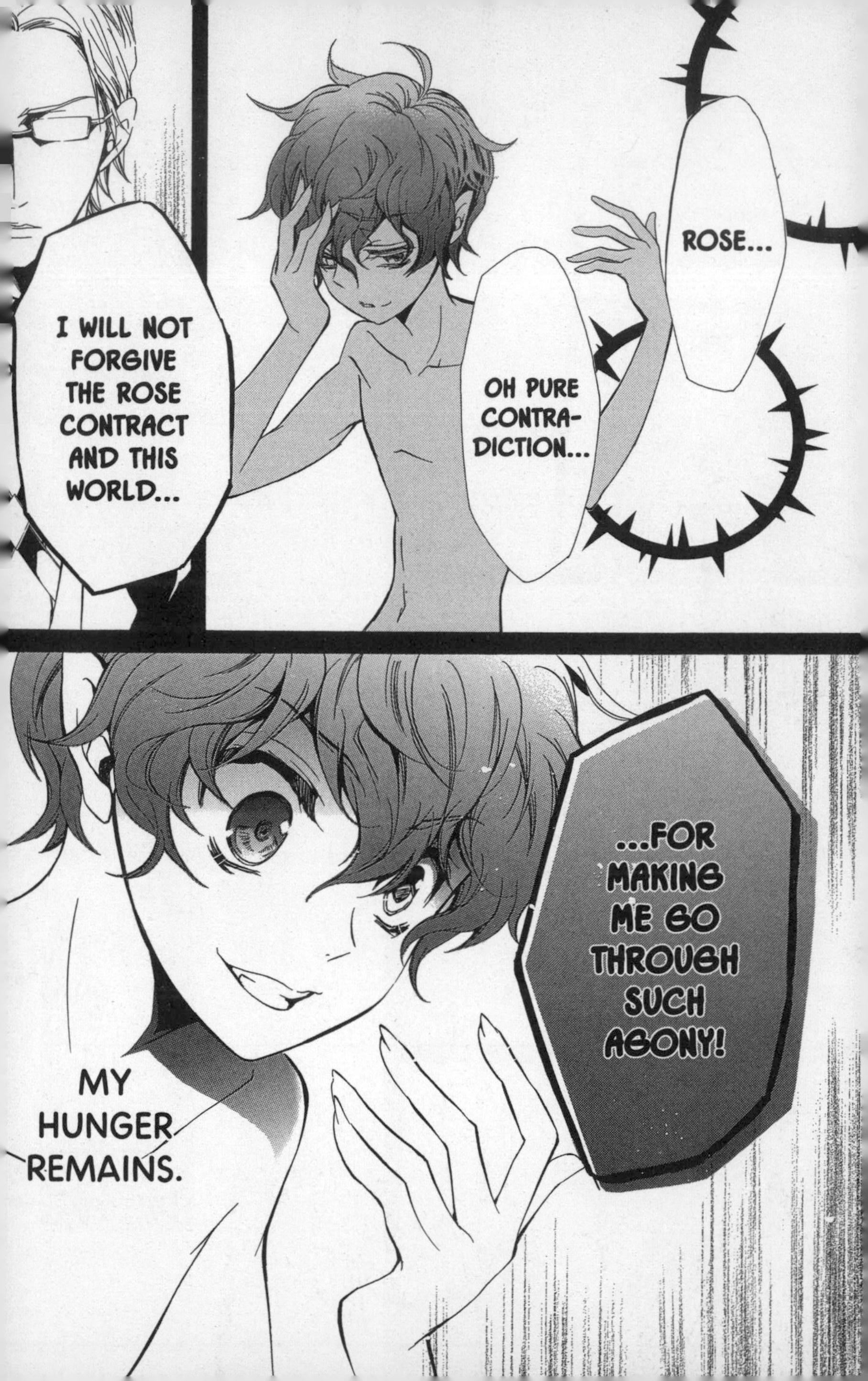
ROSE...
OH PURE CONTRA-DICTION...
I WILL NOT FORGIVE THE ROSE CONTRACT AND THIS WORLD...
...FOR MAKING ME GO THROUGH SUCH AGONY!
MY HUNGER REMAINS.

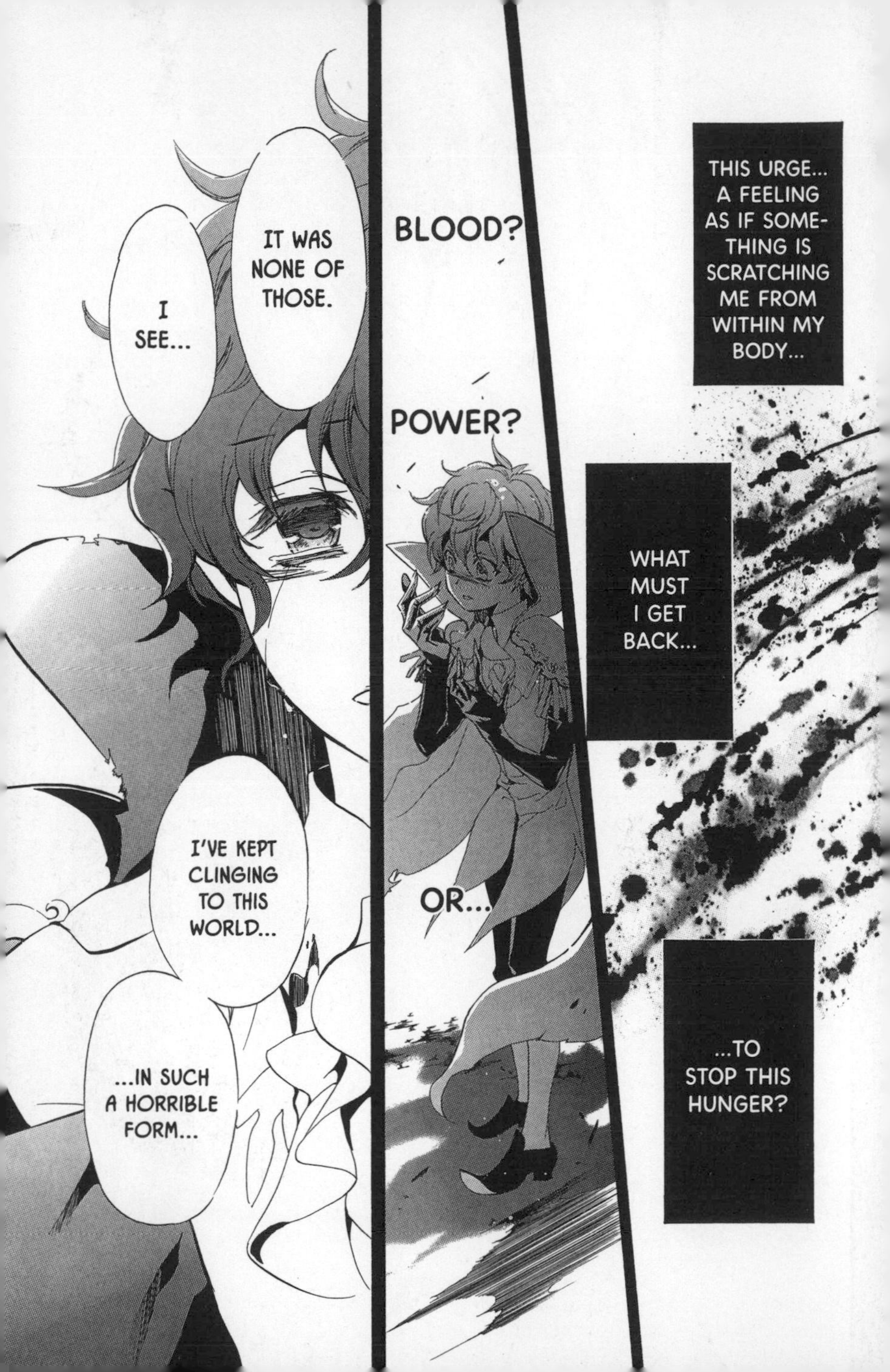
THIS URGE... A FEELING AS IF SOME-THING IS SCRATCHING ME FROM WITHIN MY BODY...
WHAT MUST I GET BACK...
...TO STOP THIS HUNGER?
BLOOD?
POWER?
OR...
IT WAS NONE OF THOSE.
I SEE...
I'VE KEPT CLINGING TO THIS WORLD...
...IN SUCH A HORRIBLE FORM...

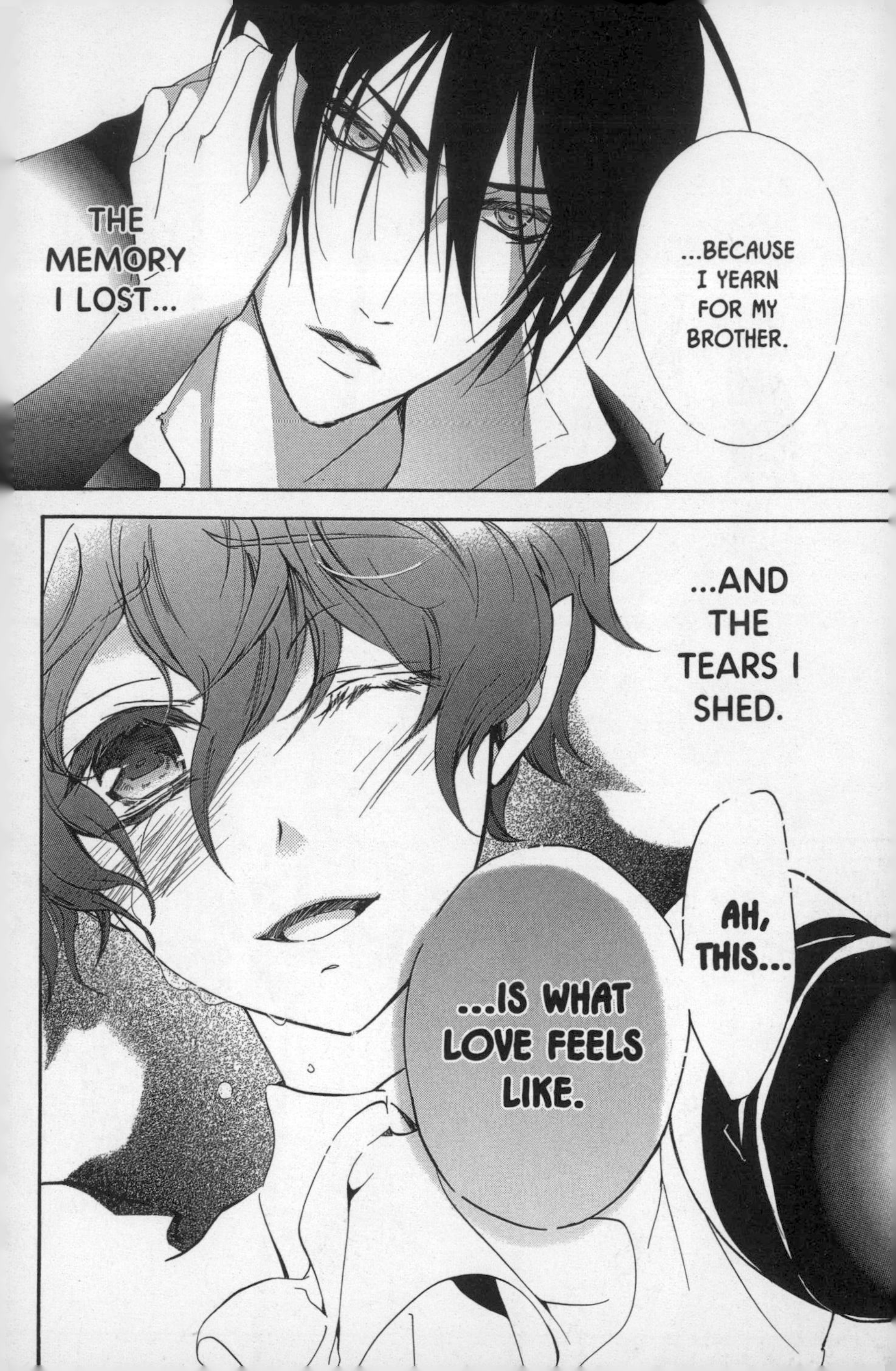
...BECAUSE I YEARN FOR MY BROTHER.
THE MEMORY I LOST...
...AND THE TEARS I SHED.
AH, THIS...
...IS WHAT LOVE FEELS LIKE.

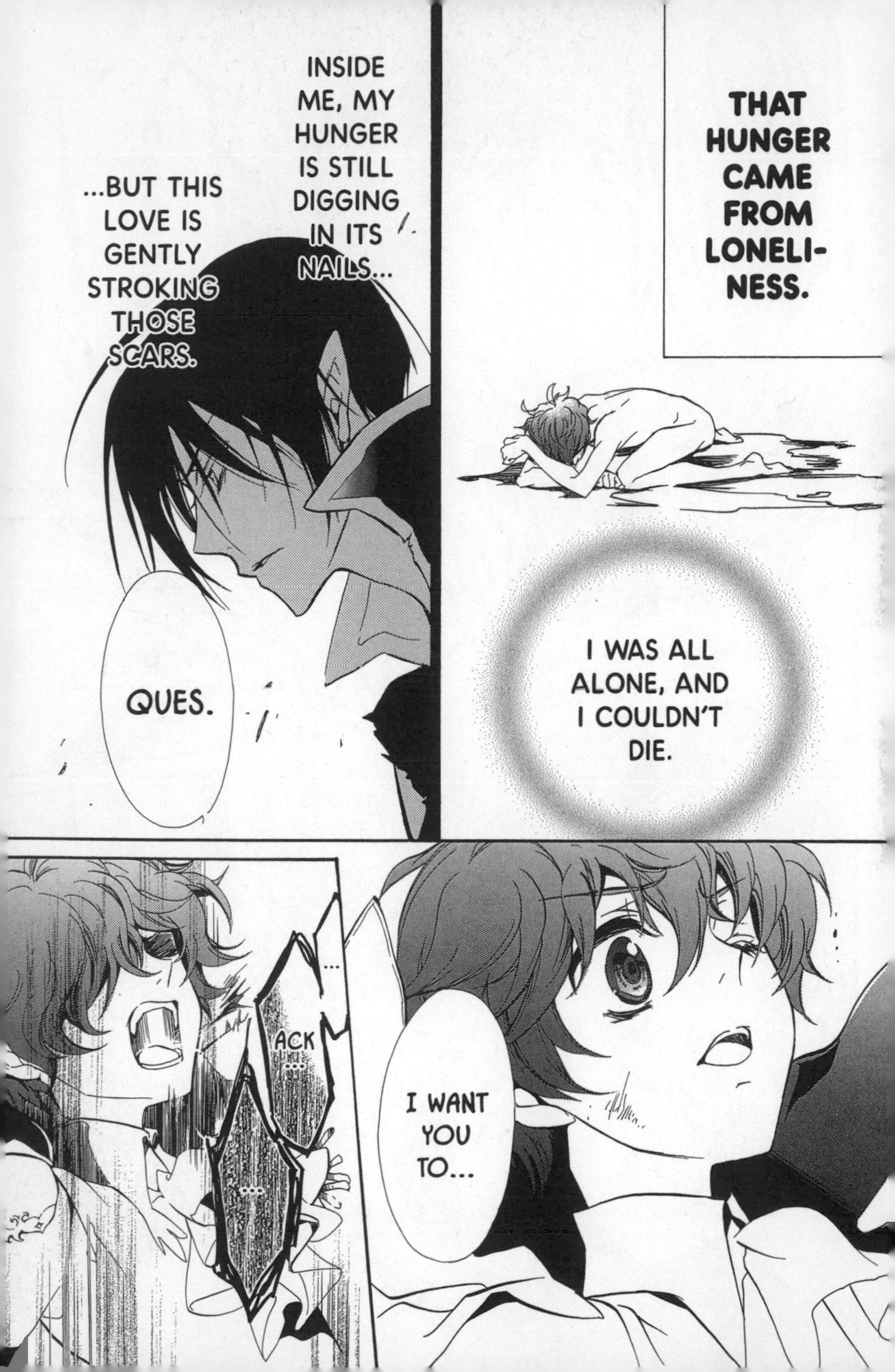
THAT HUNGER CAME FROM LONELI-NESS.
I WAS ALL ALONE, AND I COULDN'T DIE.
INSIDE ME, MY HUNGER IS STILL DIGGING IN ITS NAILS...
...BUT THIS LOVE IS GENTLY STROKING THOSE SCARS.
QUES.
I WANT YOU TO...
...
ACK ...
...

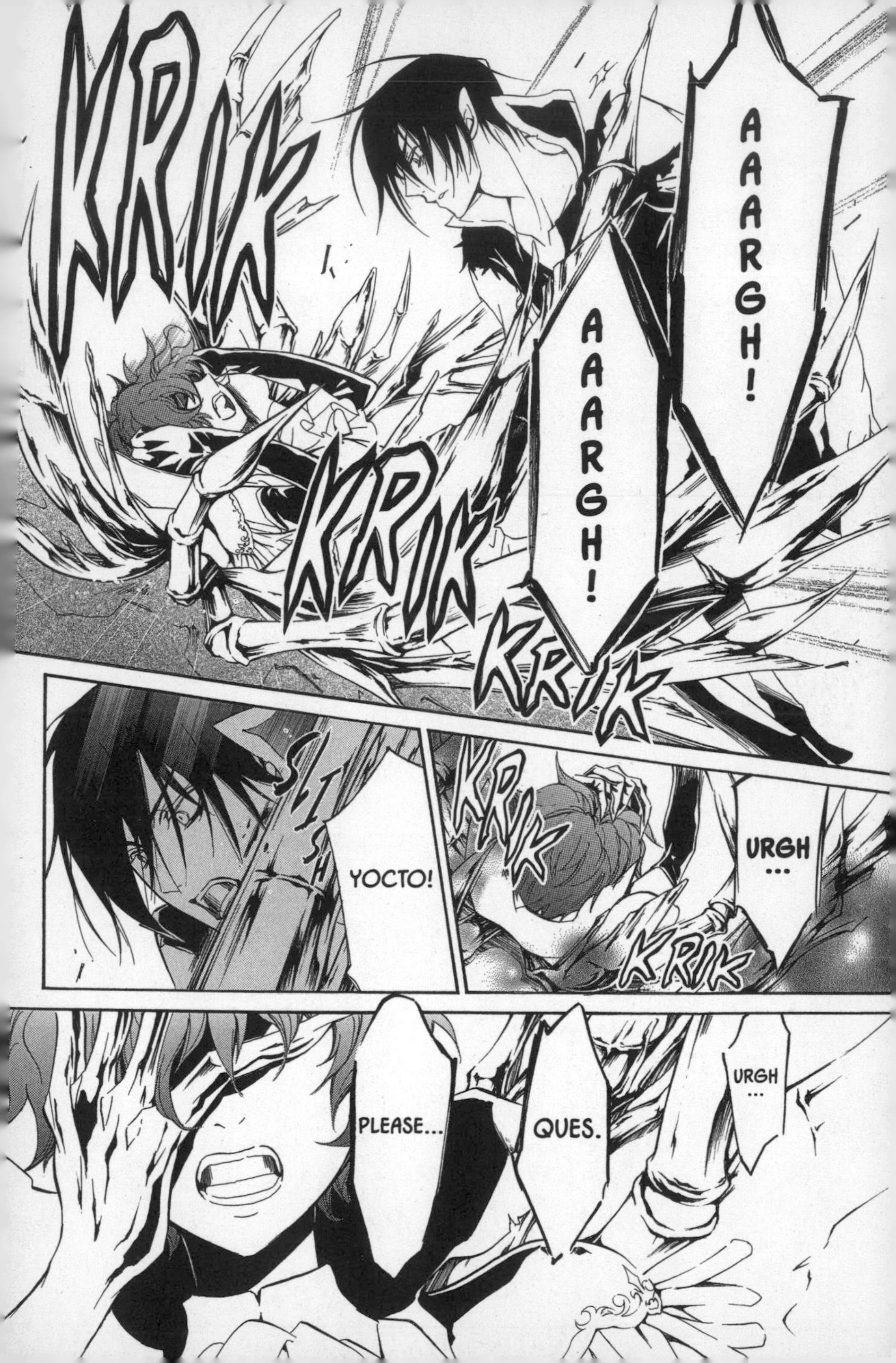
AAARGH!
KRIK
AAAARGH!
KRIK
KRIK
URGH...
KRIK
KRIK
SLISH
YOCTO!
URGH...
QUES.
PLEASE...

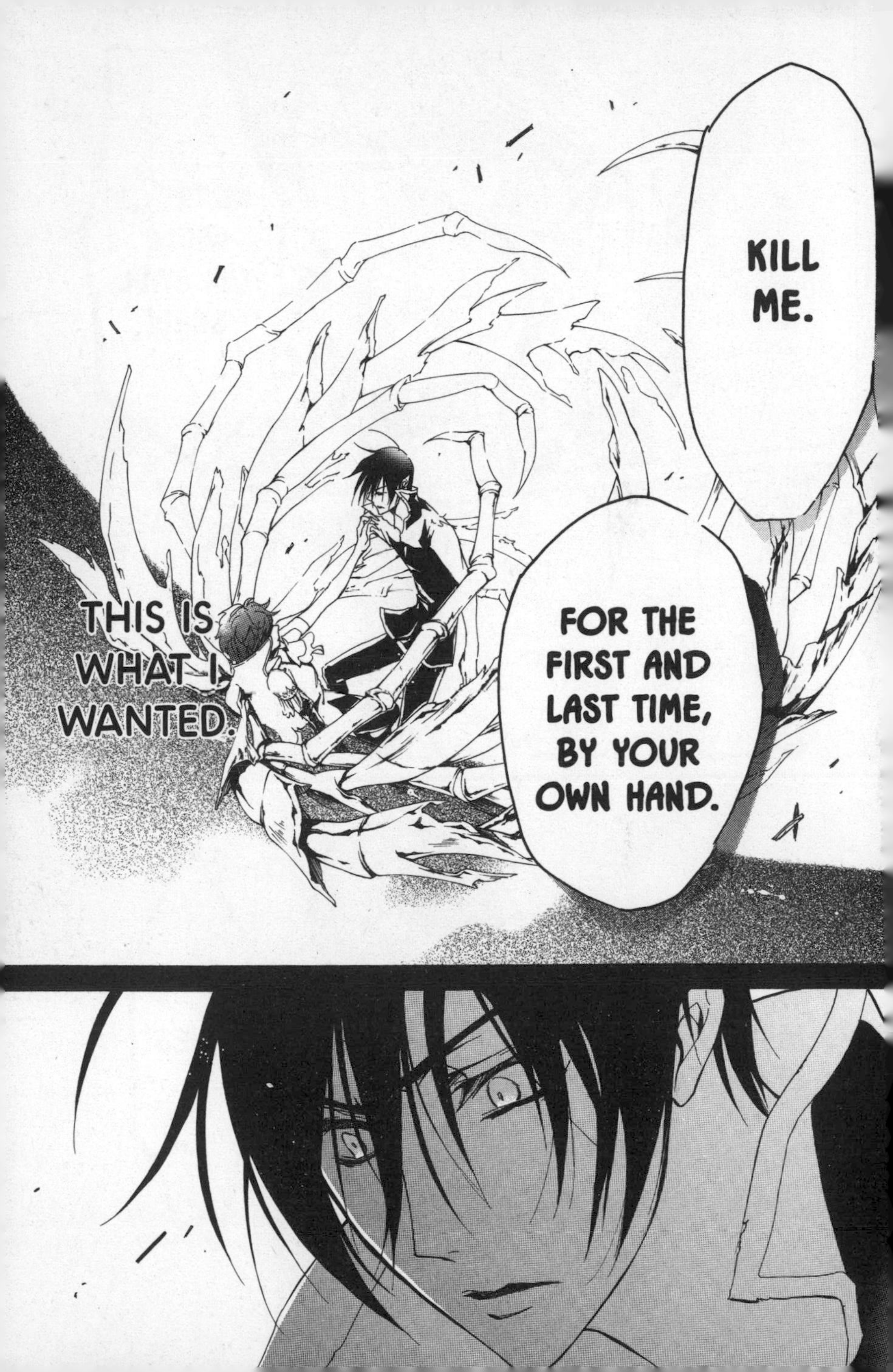
KILL ME.
FOR THE FIRST AND LAST TIME, BY YOUR OWN HAND.
THIS IS WHAT I WANTED.

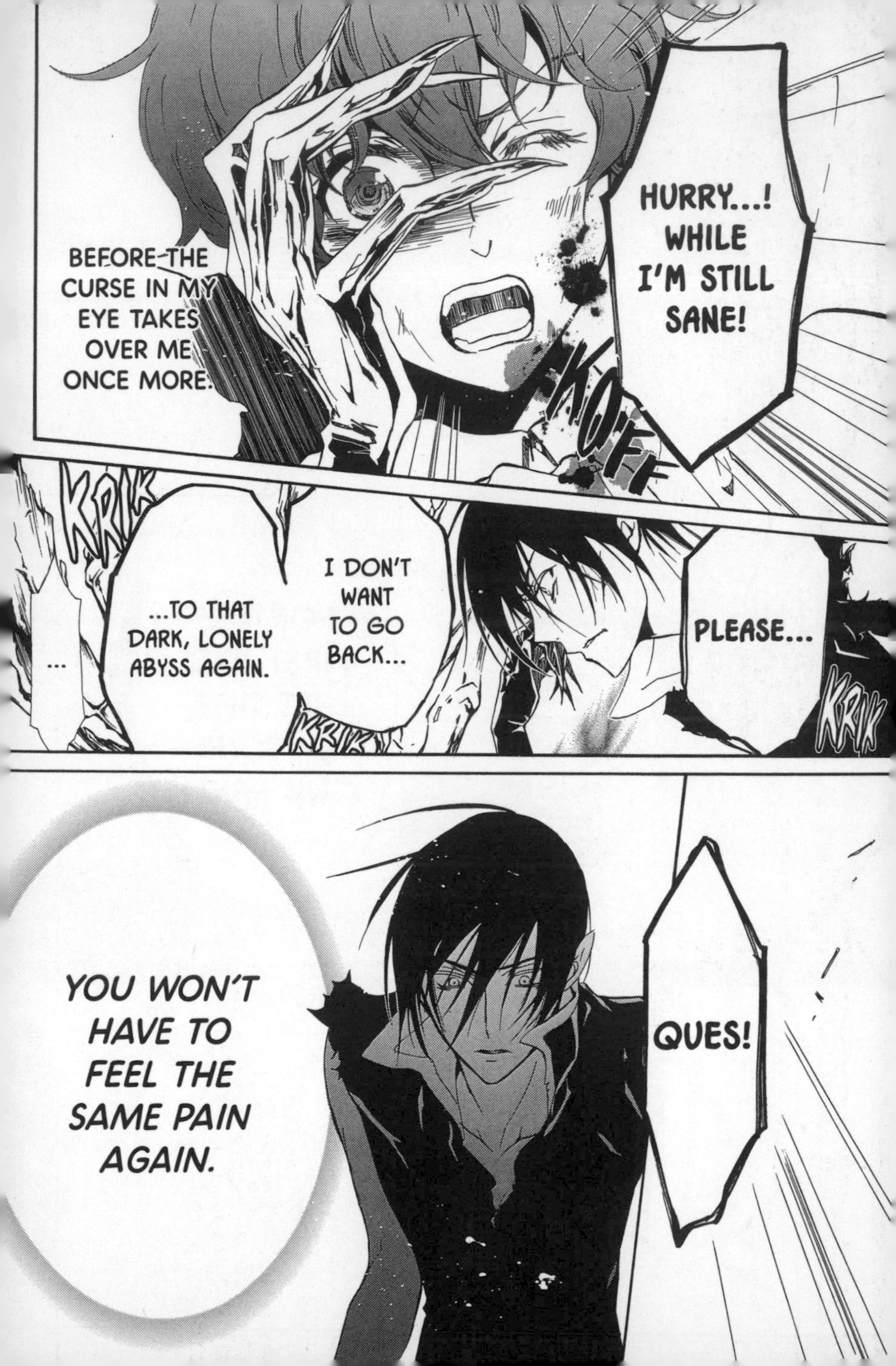
HURRY...! WHILE I'M STILL SANE!
BEFORE THE CURSE IN MY EYE TAKES OVER ME ONCE MORE...
KOFF
KRIK
PLEASE...
I DON'T WANT TO GO BACK...
...TO THAT DARK, LONELY ABYSS AGAIN.
...
KRIK
KRIK
QUES!
YOU WON'T HAVE TO FEEL THE SAME PAIN AGAIN.

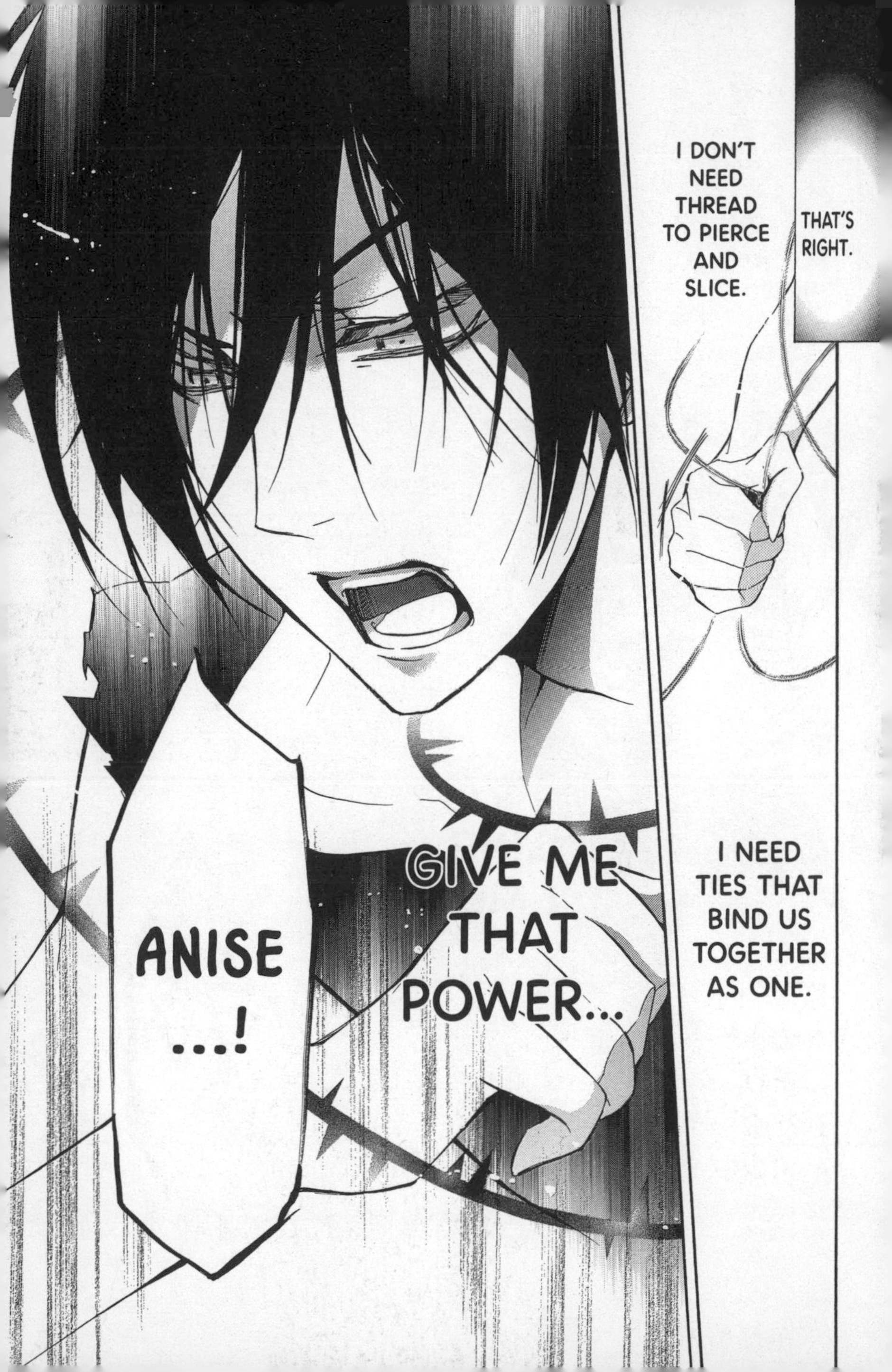
THAT'S RIGHT.
I DON'T NEED THREAD TO PIERCE AND SLICE.
I NEED TIES THAT BIND US TOGETHER AS ONE.
GIVE ME THAT POWER...
ANISE ...!

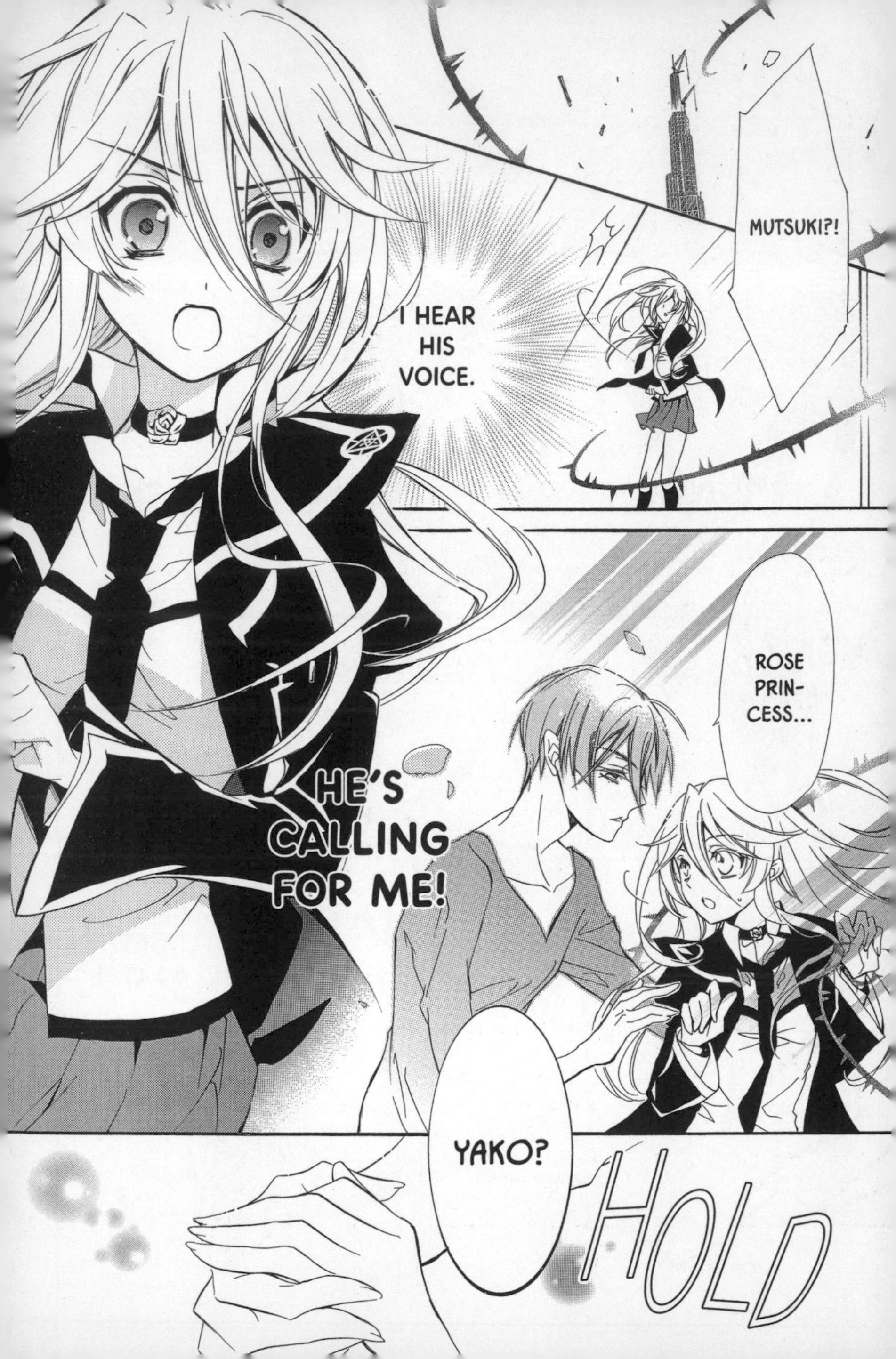
MUTSUKI?!
I HEAR HIS VOICE.
ROSE PRINCESS...
YAKO?
HE'S CALLING FOR ME!
HOLD

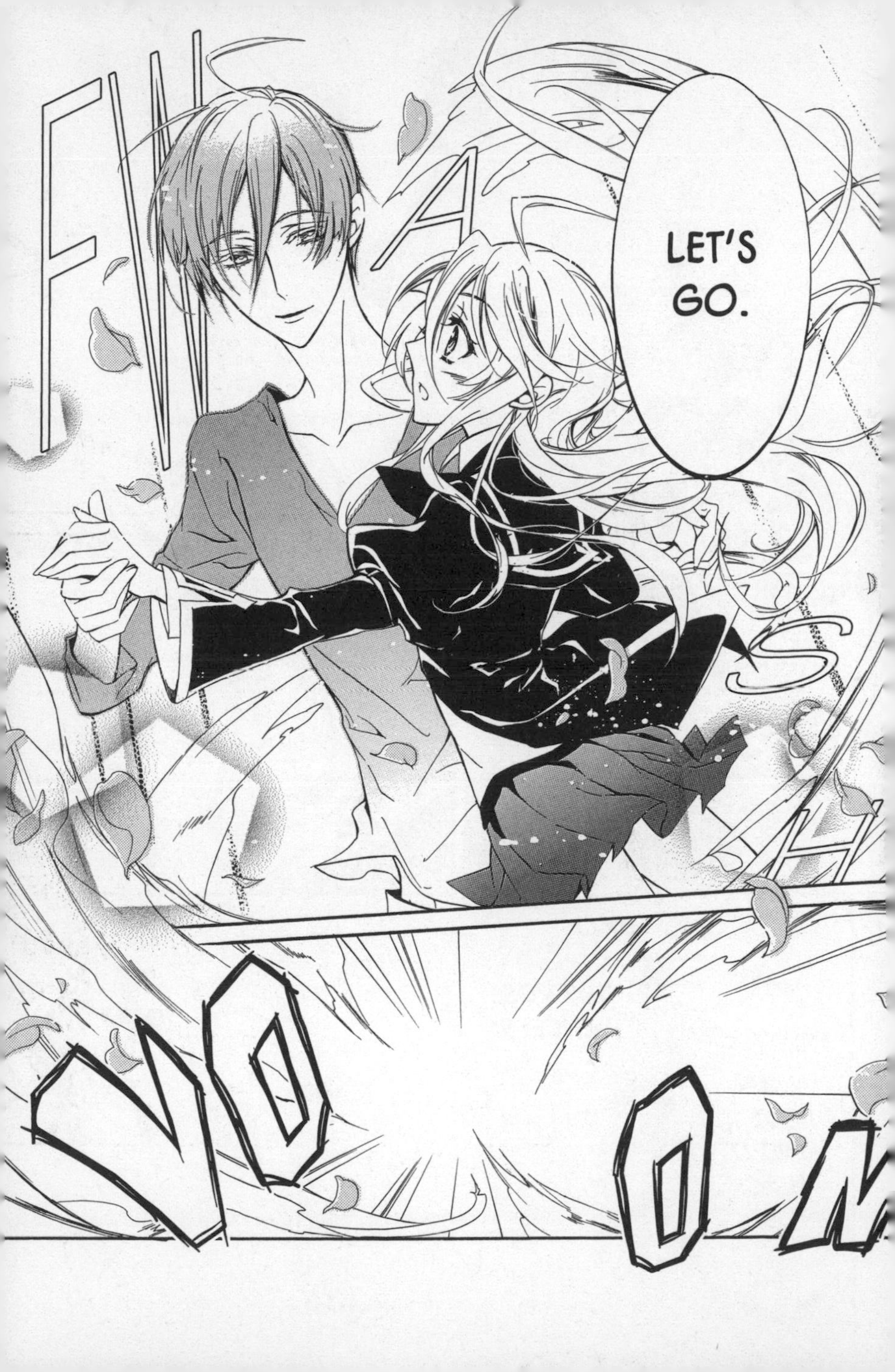
LET'S GO.
FWASH
DOON

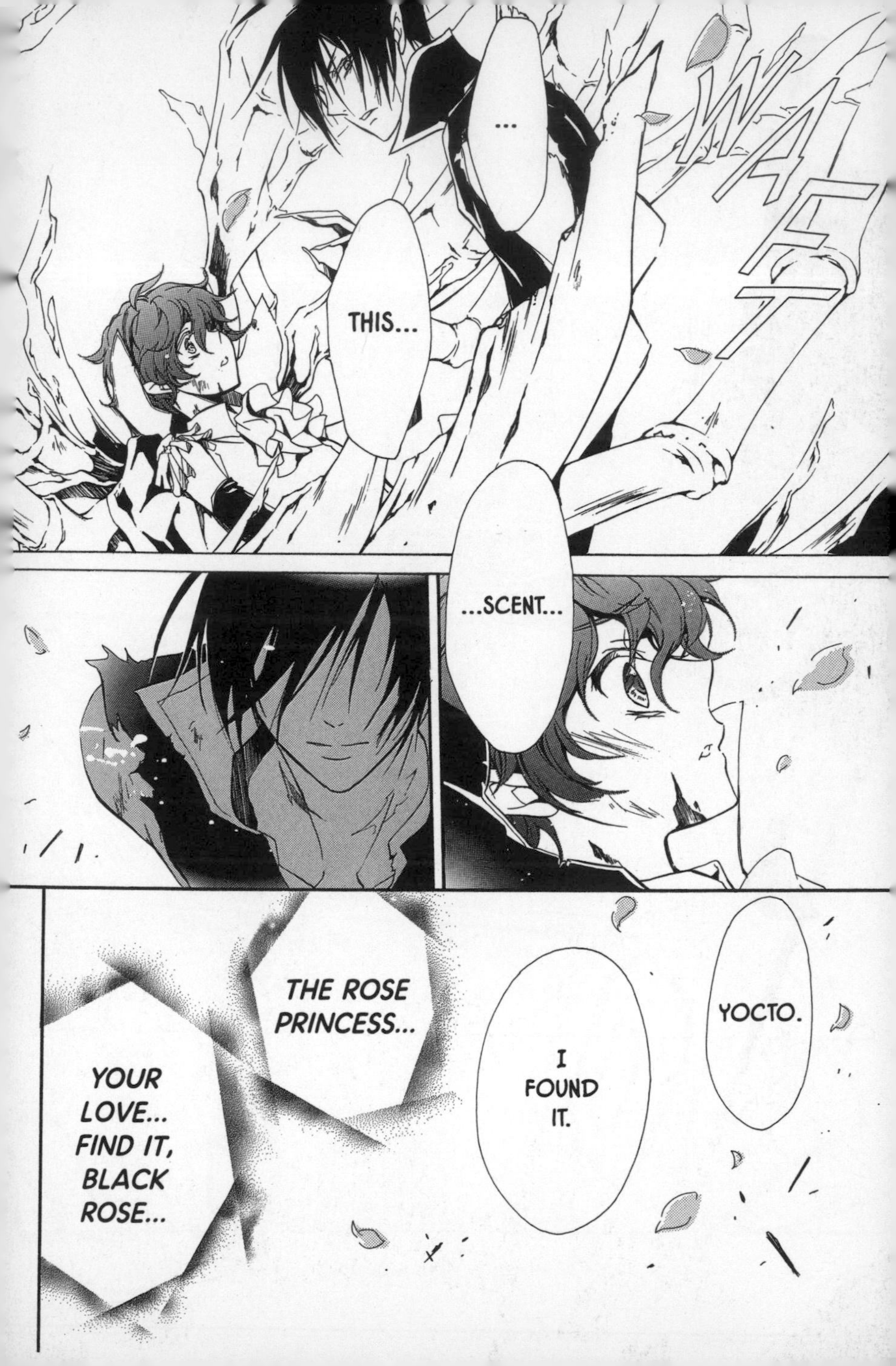
WAFT
...
THIS...
...SCENT...
YOCTO.
I FOUND IT.
THE ROSE PRINCESS...
YOUR LOVE... FIND IT, BLACK ROSE...

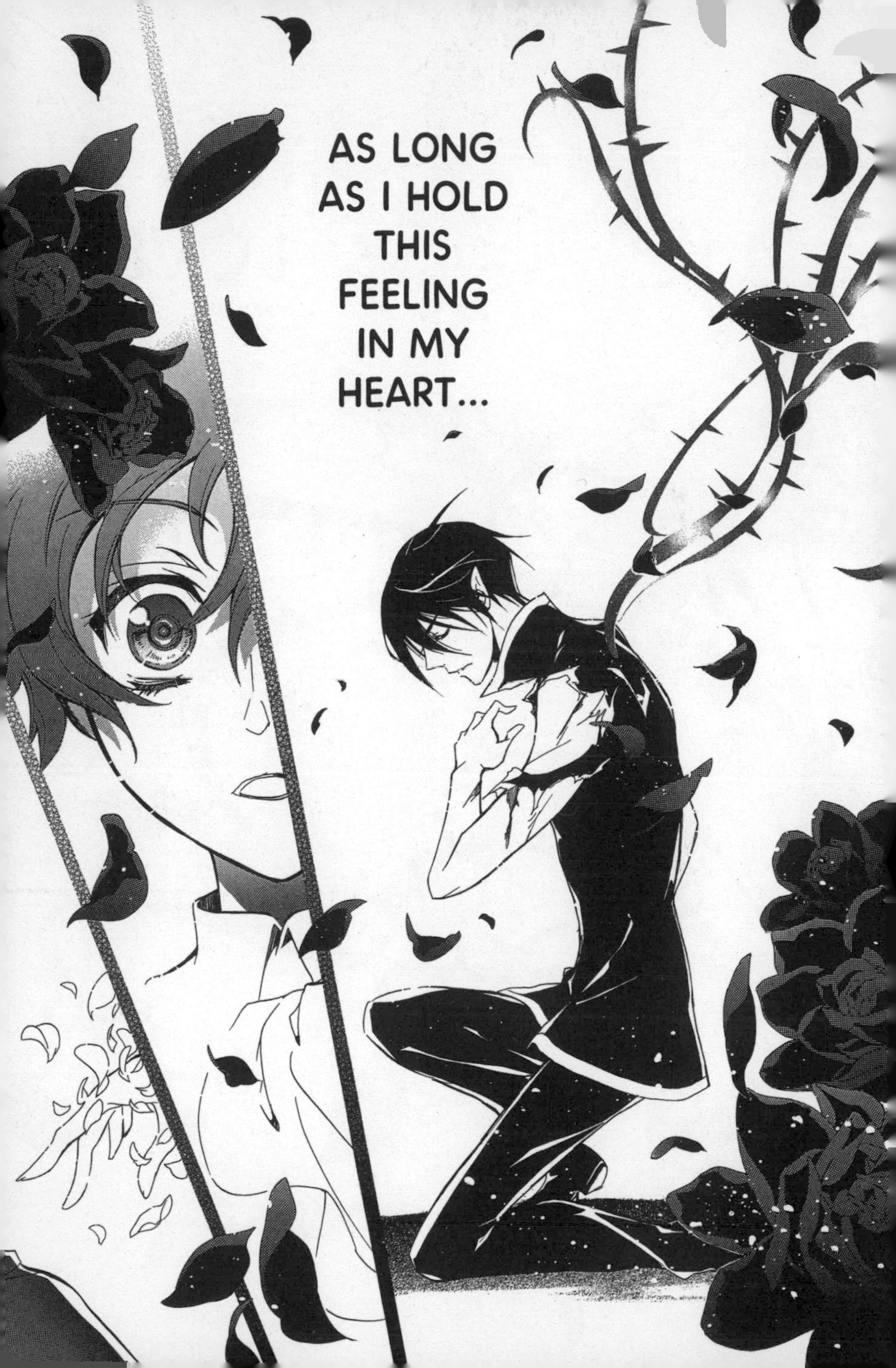
AS LONG AS I HOLD THIS FEELING IN MY HEART...

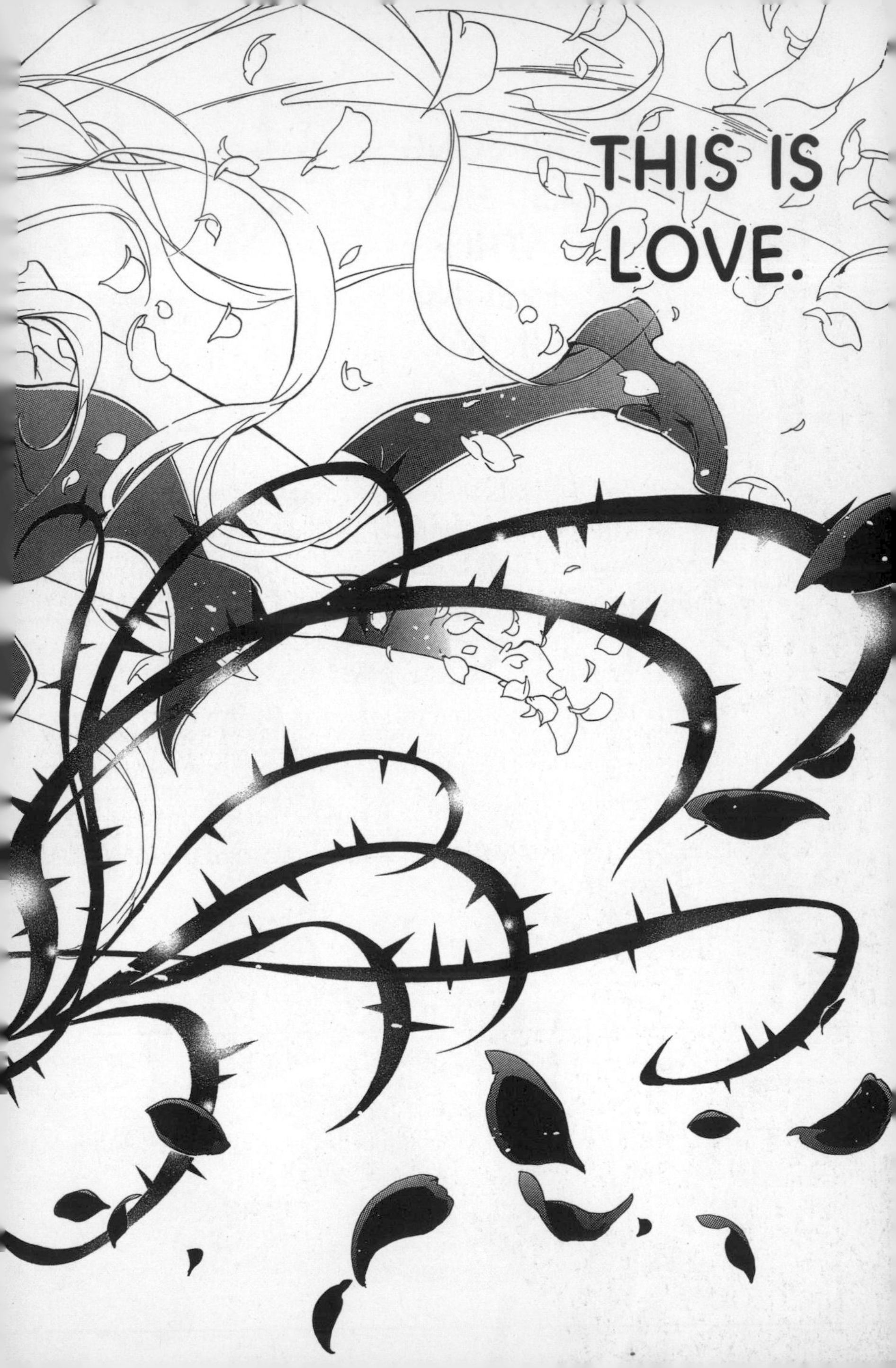

THIS IS LOVE.

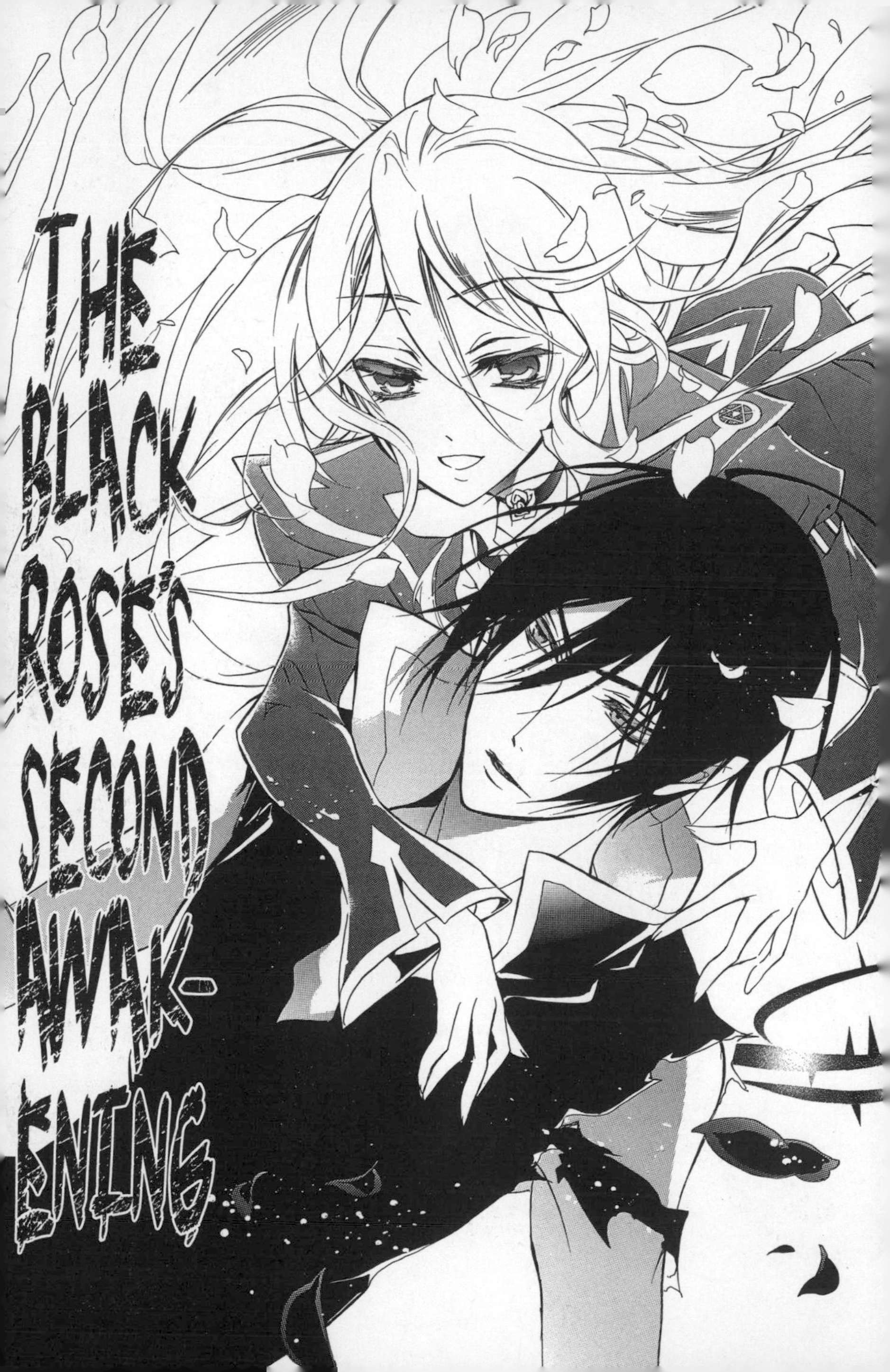
THE BLACK ROSE'S SECOND AWAK-ENING

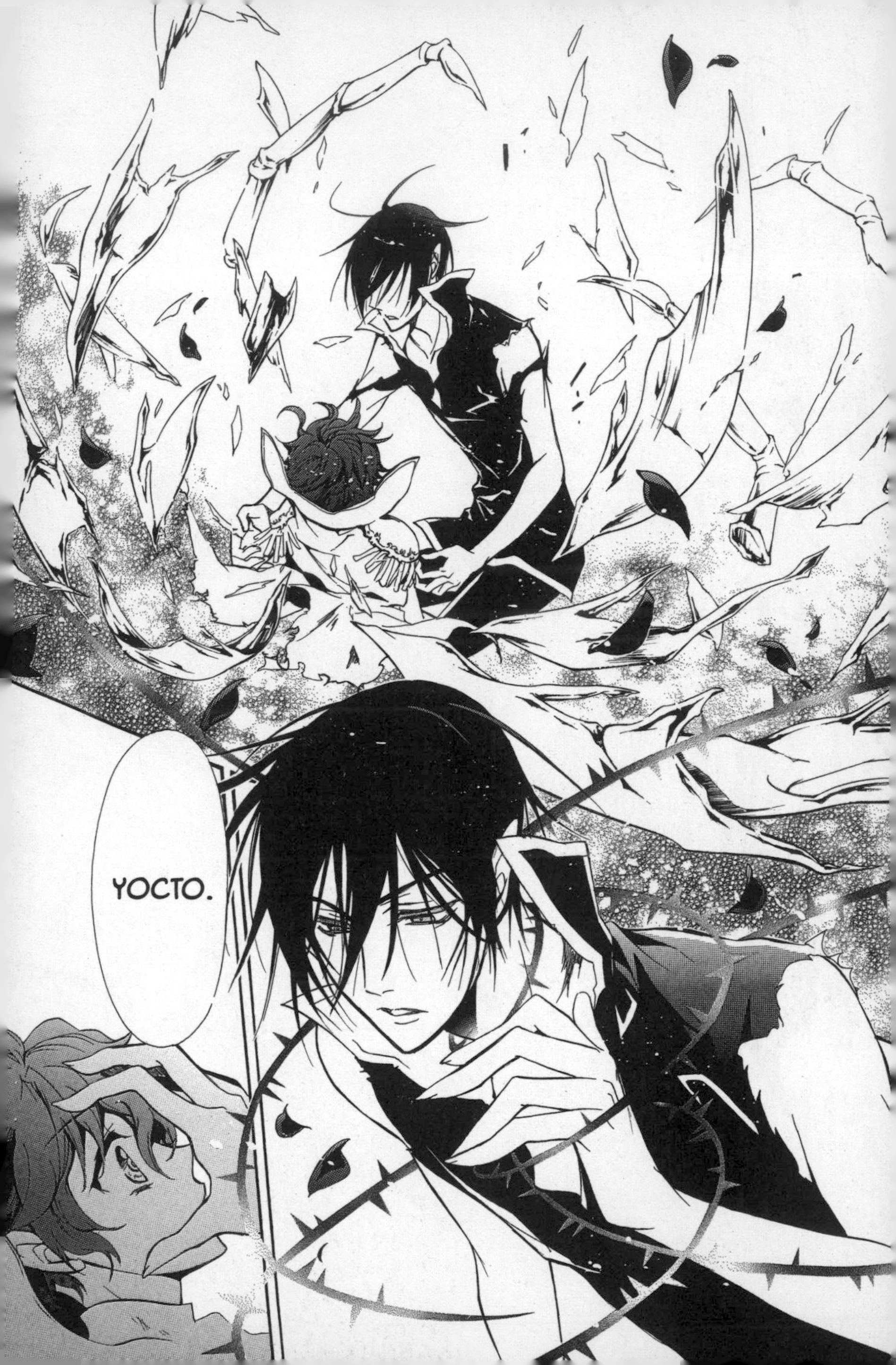
YOCTO.

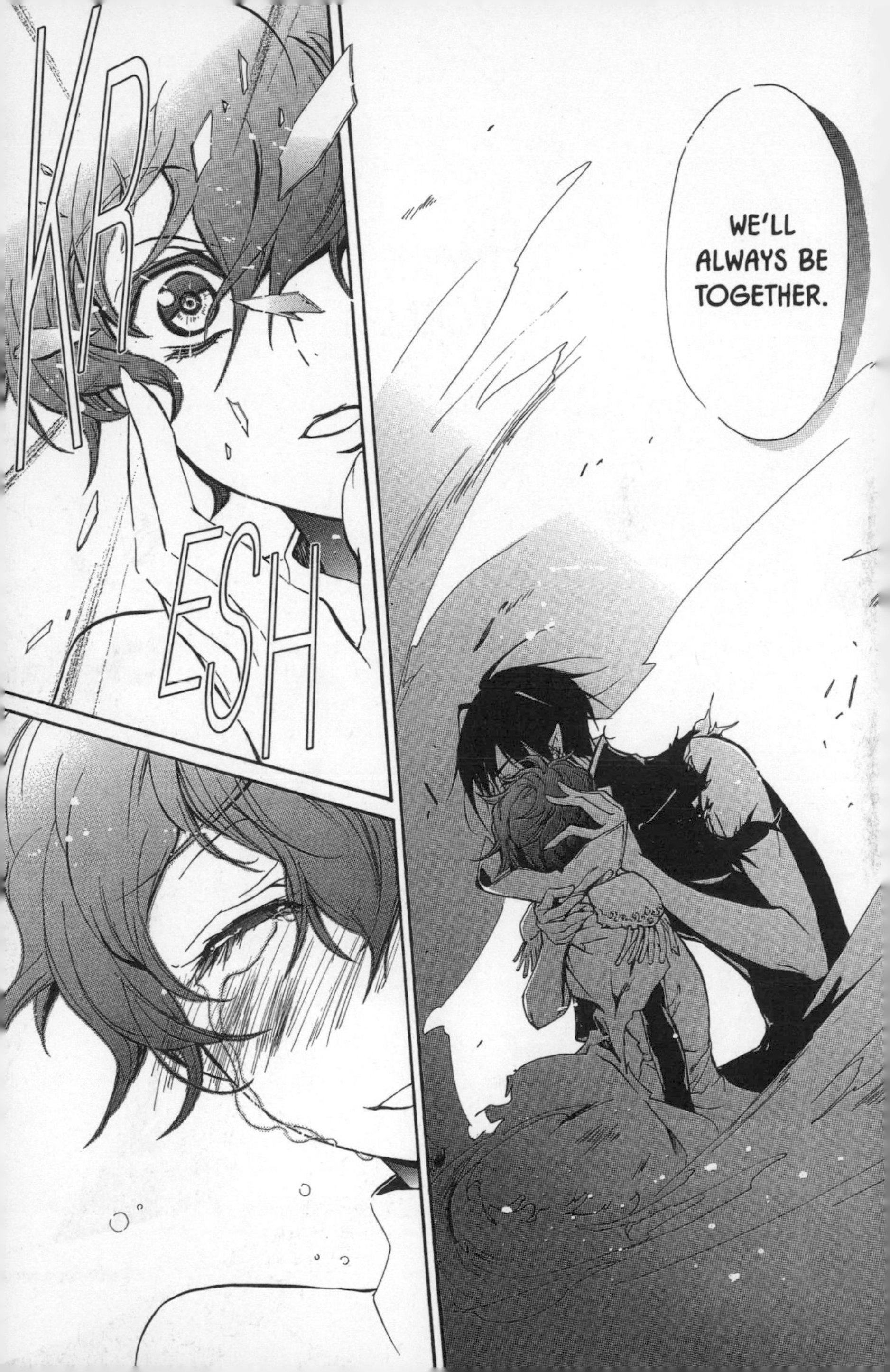
WE'LL ALWAYS BE TOGETHER.
KRESH

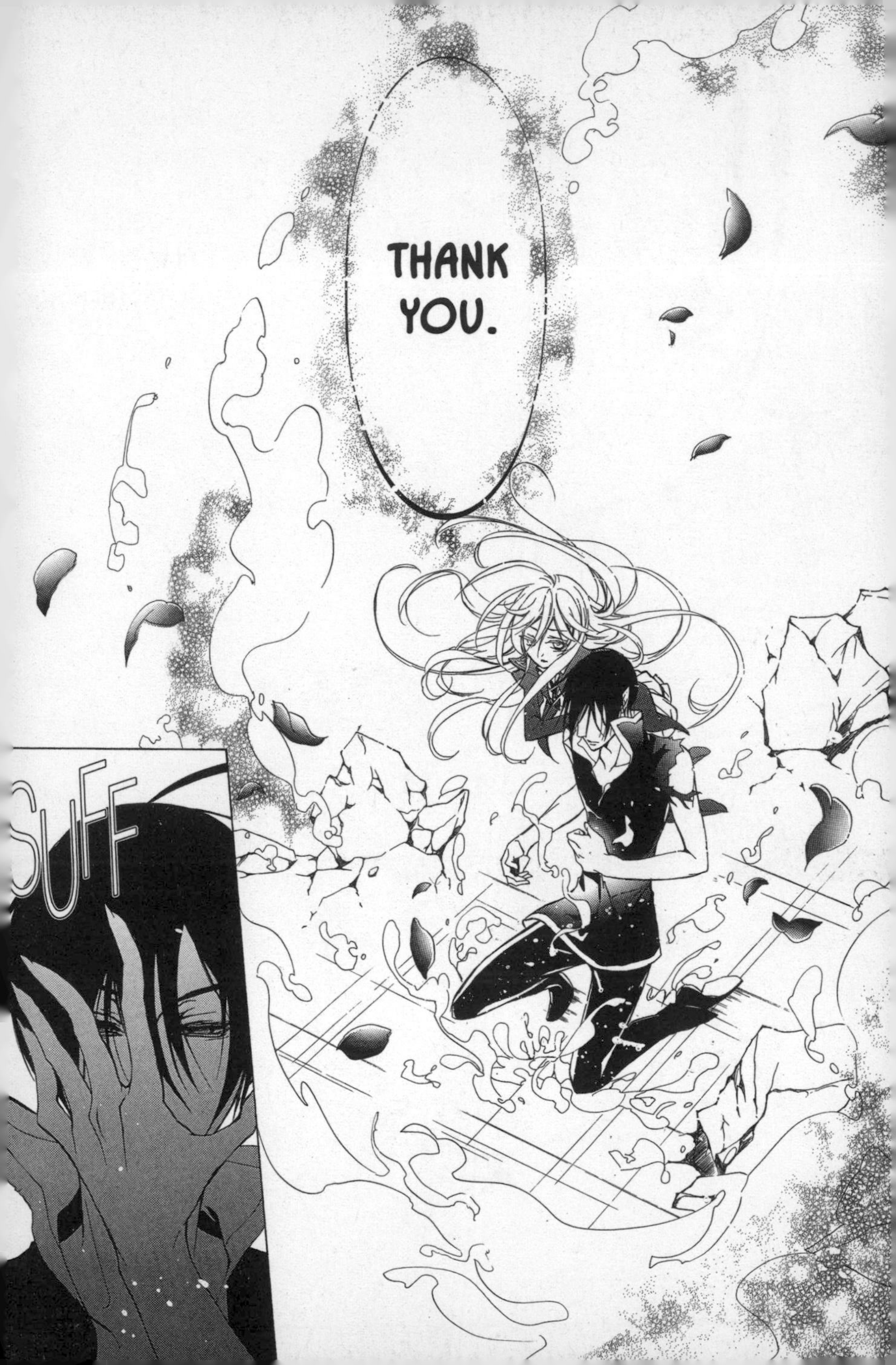
THANK YOU.
SUFF

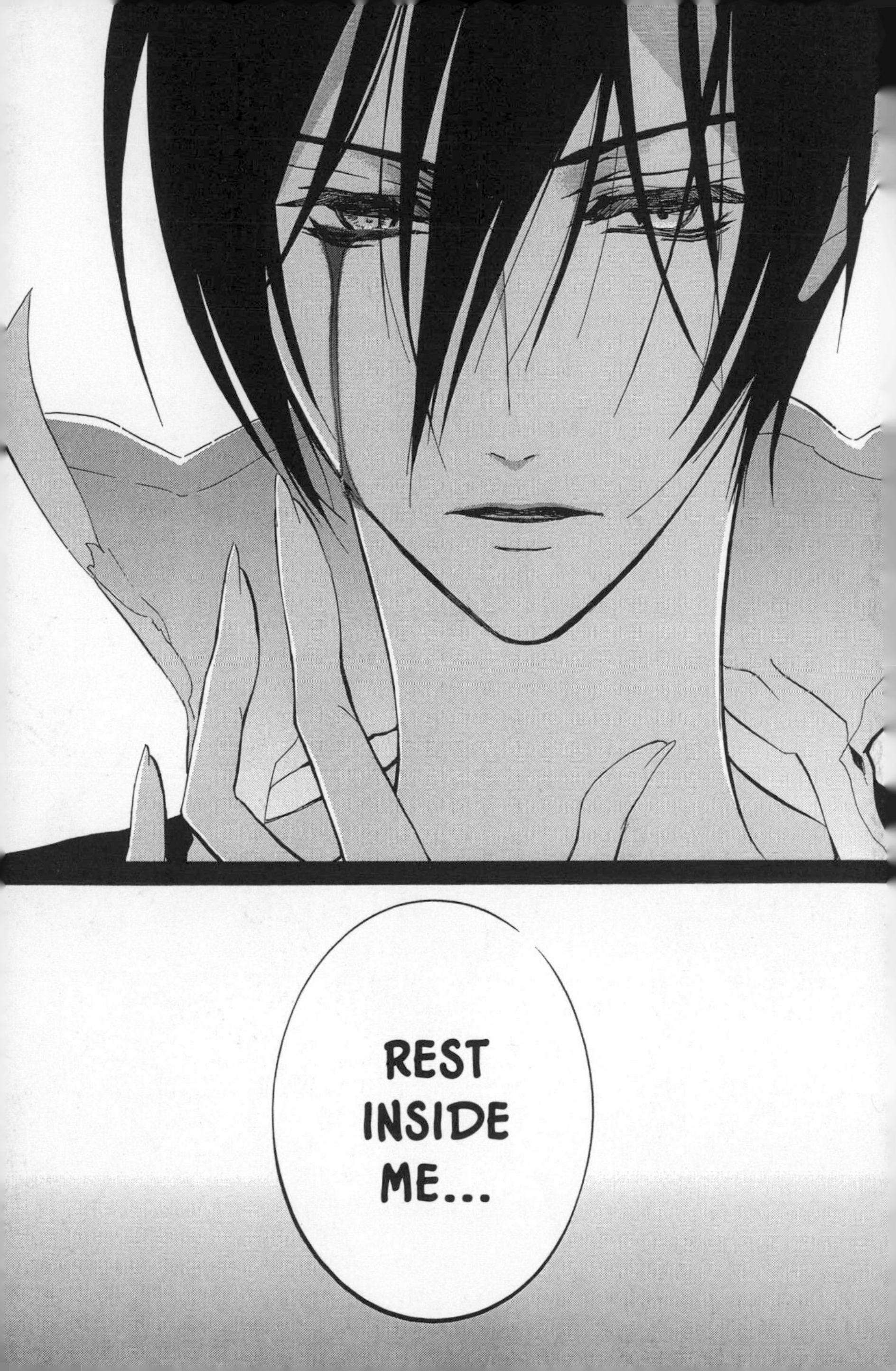
REST INSIDE ME...

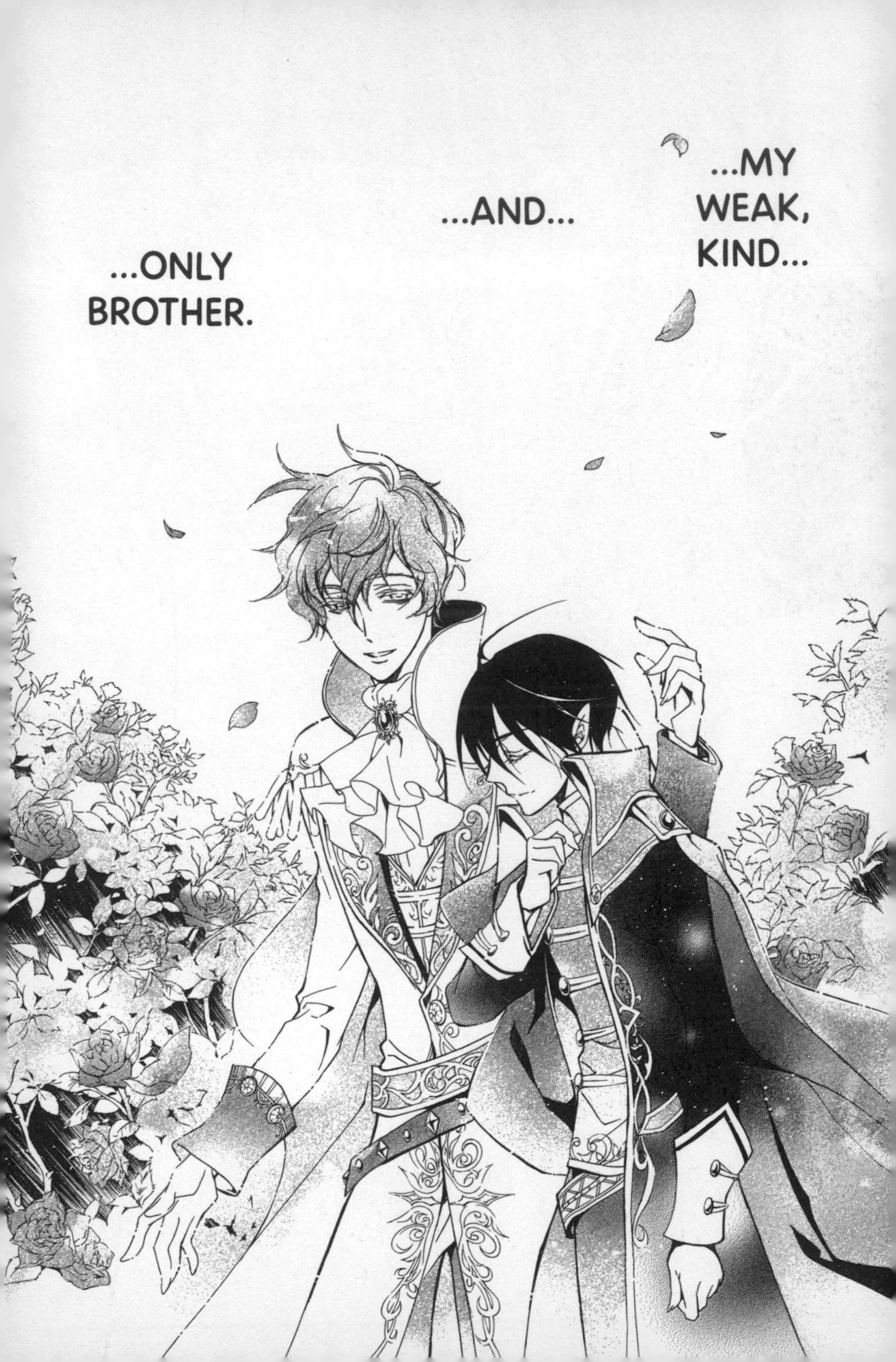
...MY WEAK, KIND...
...AND...
...ONLY BROTHER.

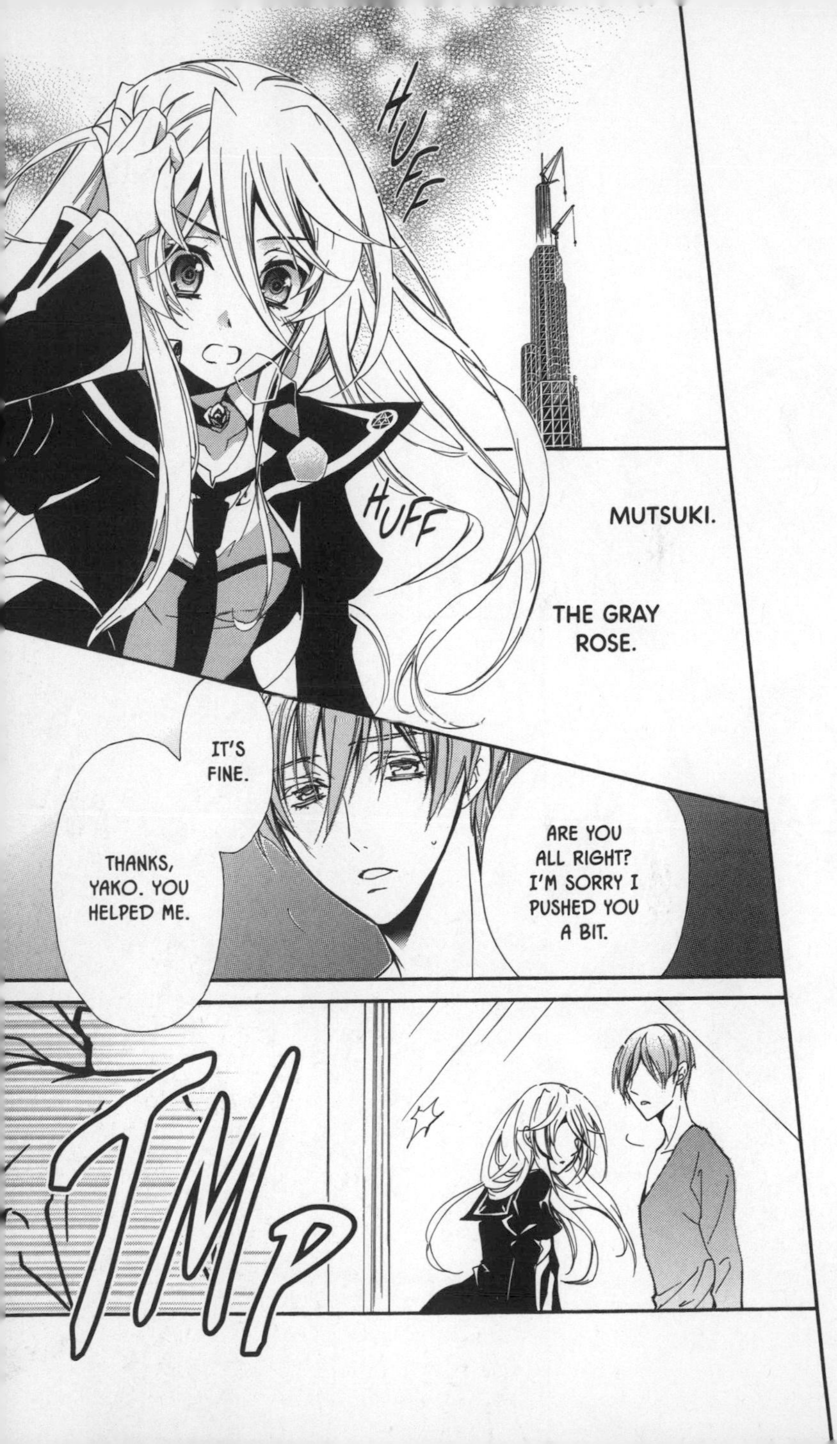
HUFF
HUFF
MUTSUKI.
THE GRAY ROSE.
ARE YOU ALL RIGHT? I'M SORRY I PUSHED YOU A BIT.
IT'S FINE.
THANKS, YAKO. YOU HELPED ME.
TMP

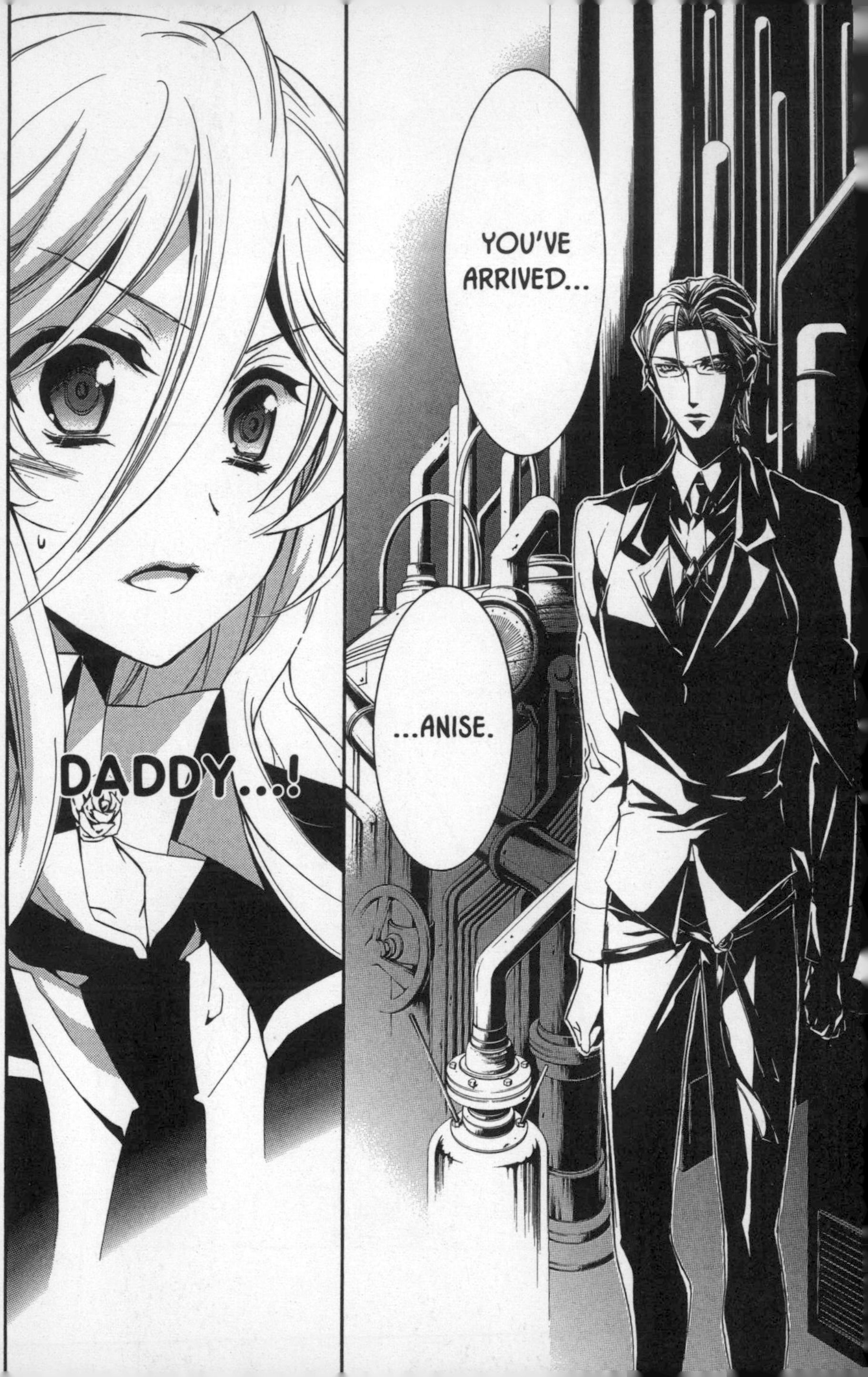
YOU'VE ARRIVED...
...ANISE.
DADDY...!

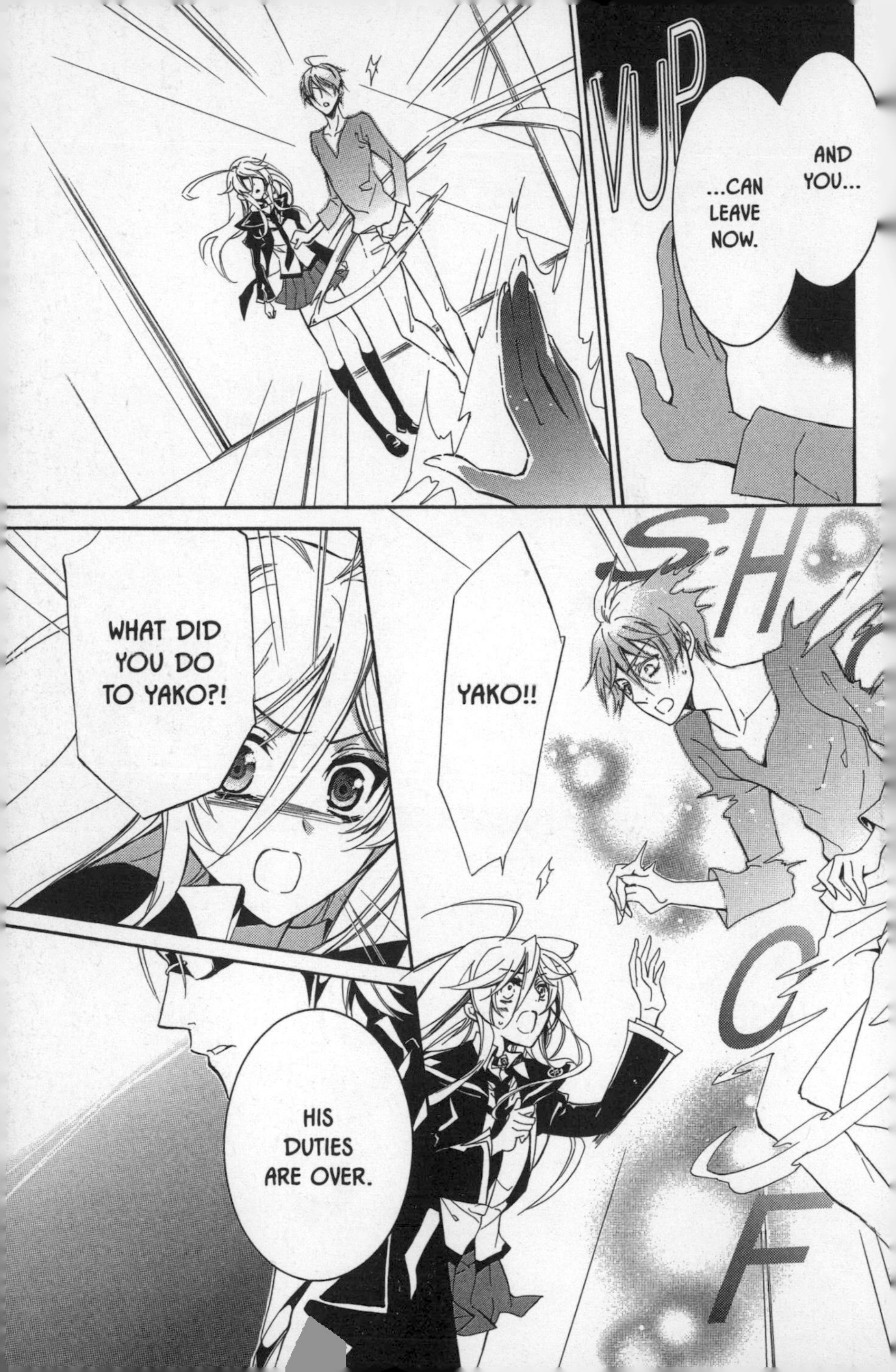
AND YOU...
...CAN LEAVE NOW.
VUP
SHOOF
YAKO!!
WHAT DID YOU DO TO YAKO?!
HIS DUTIES ARE OVER.

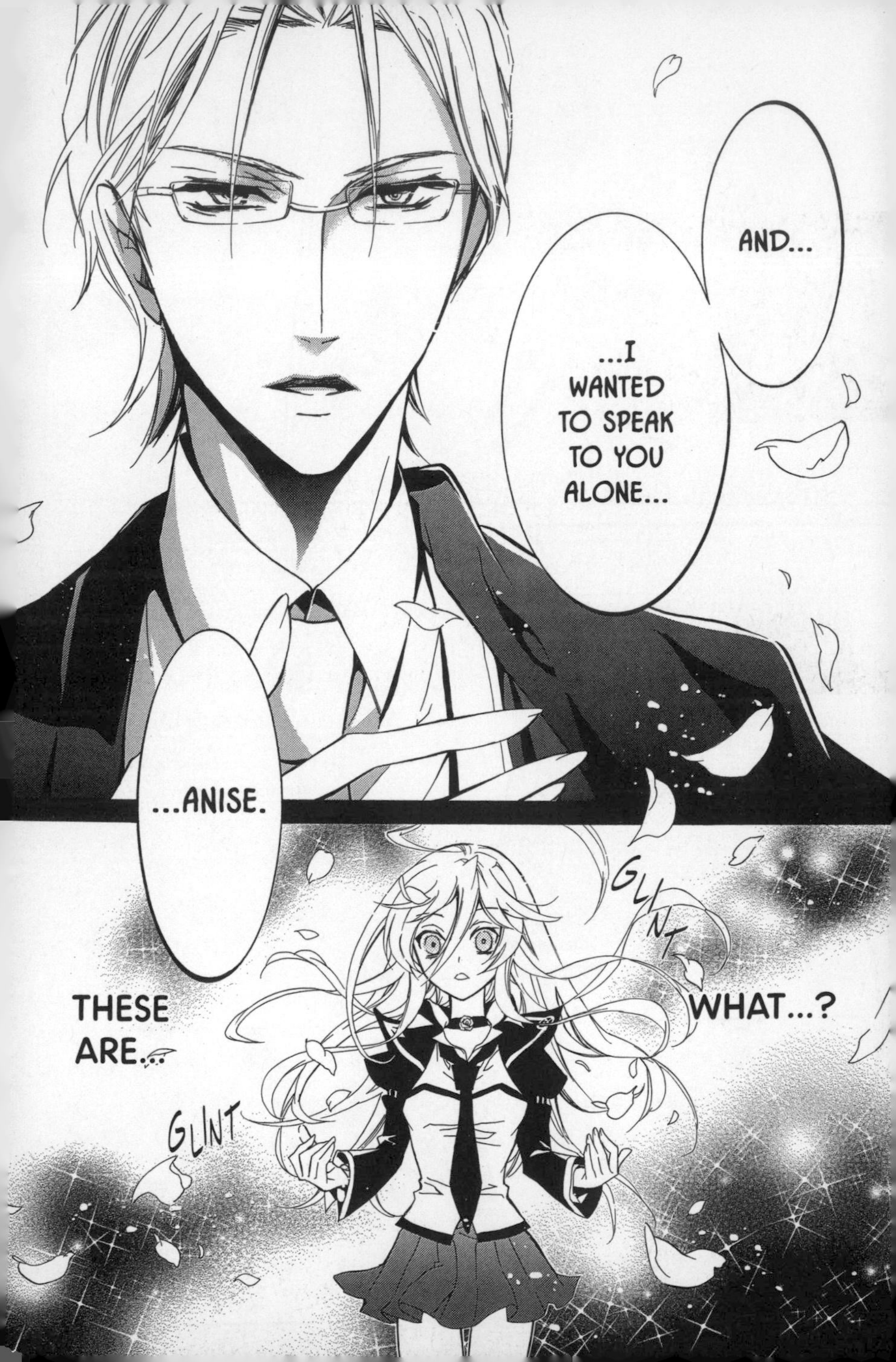
AND...
...I WANTED TO SPEAK TO YOU ALONE...
...ANISE.
GLINT
WHAT...?
THESE ARE...
GLINT

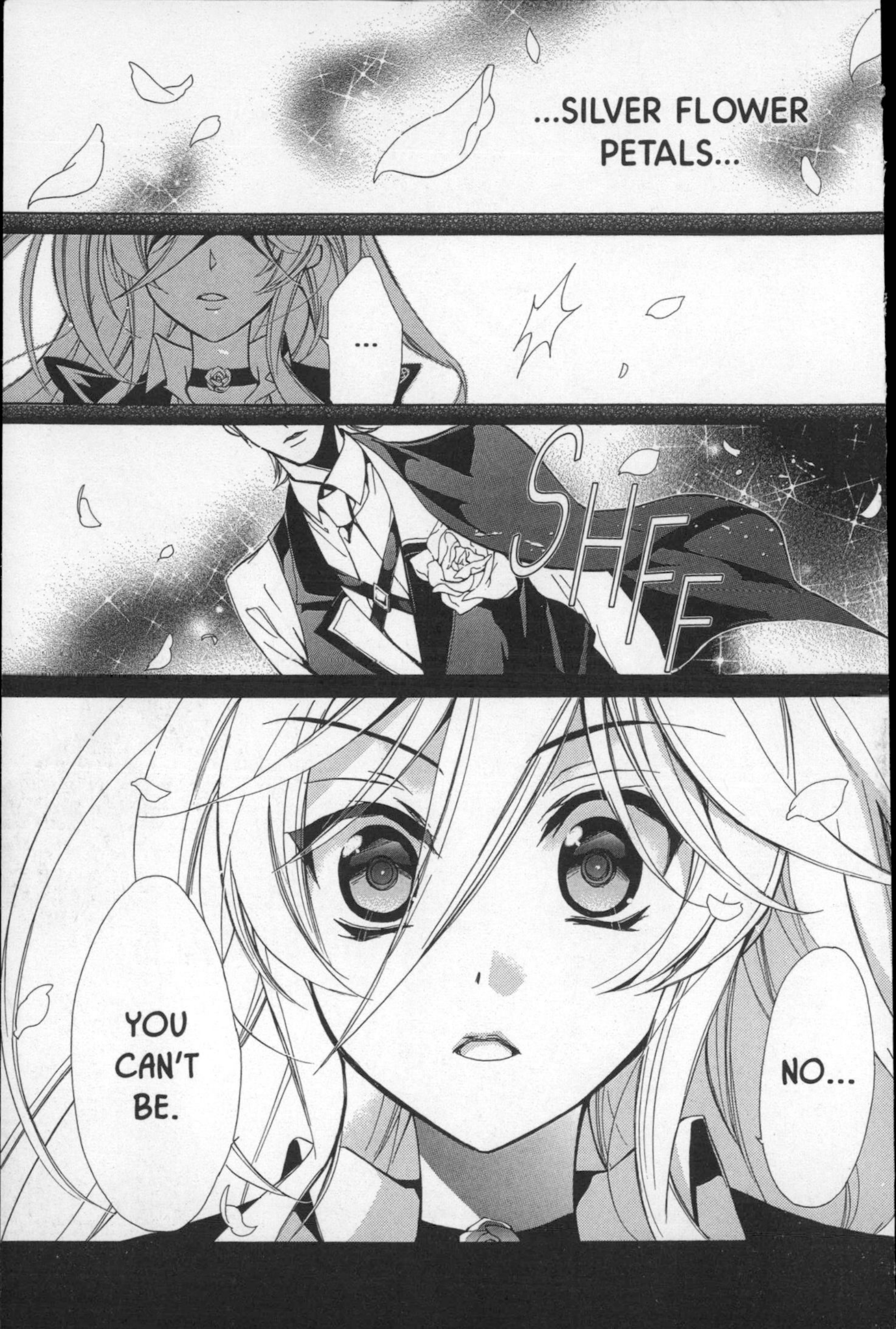
...SILVER FLOWER PETALS...
...
SHFF
NO...
YOU CAN'T BE.

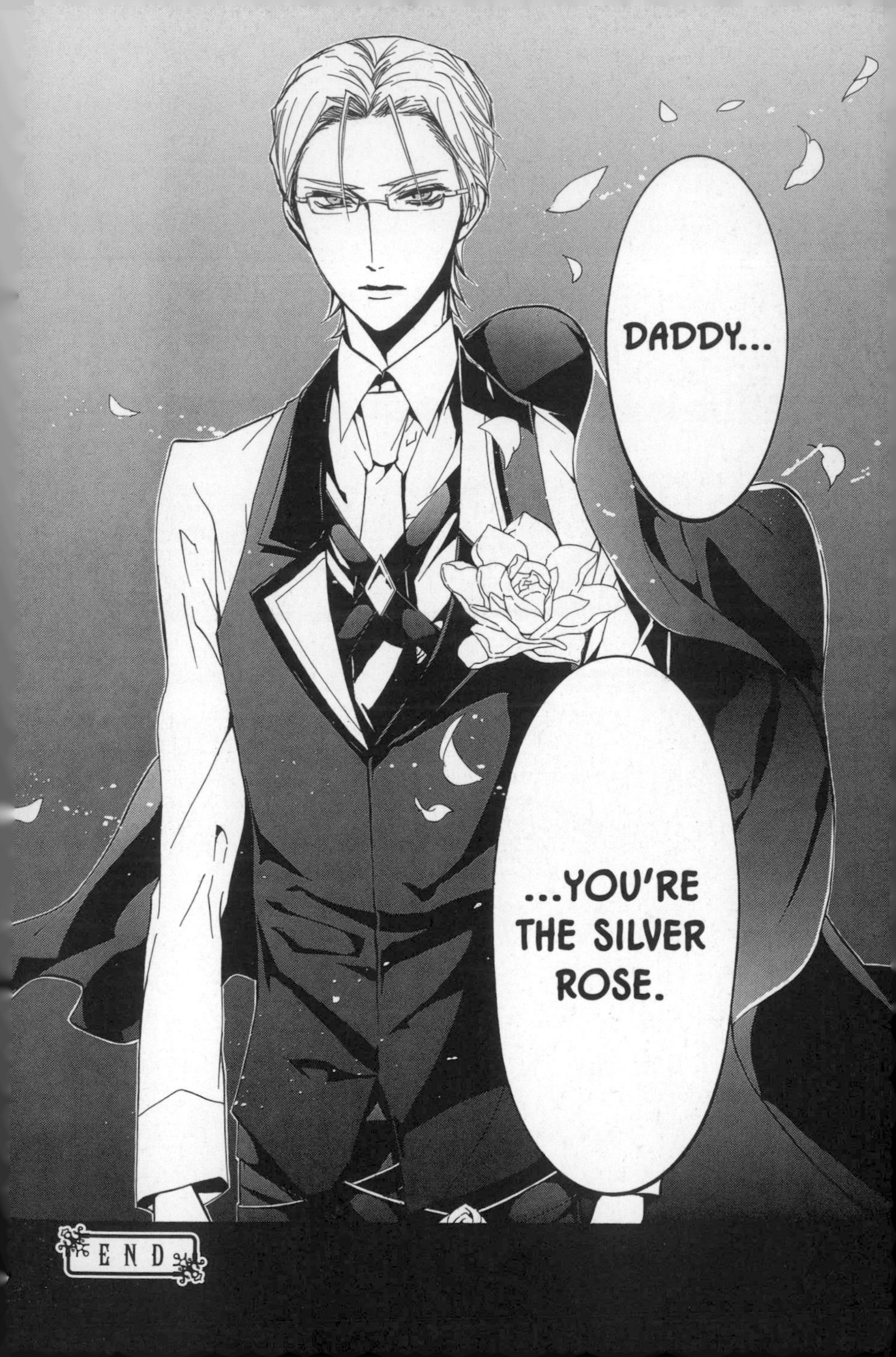
DADDY...
...YOU'RE THE SILVER ROSE.
END

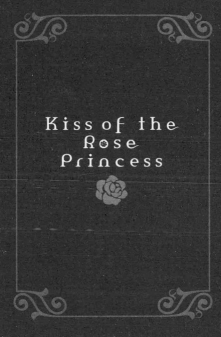

Kiss of the
Rose
Princess

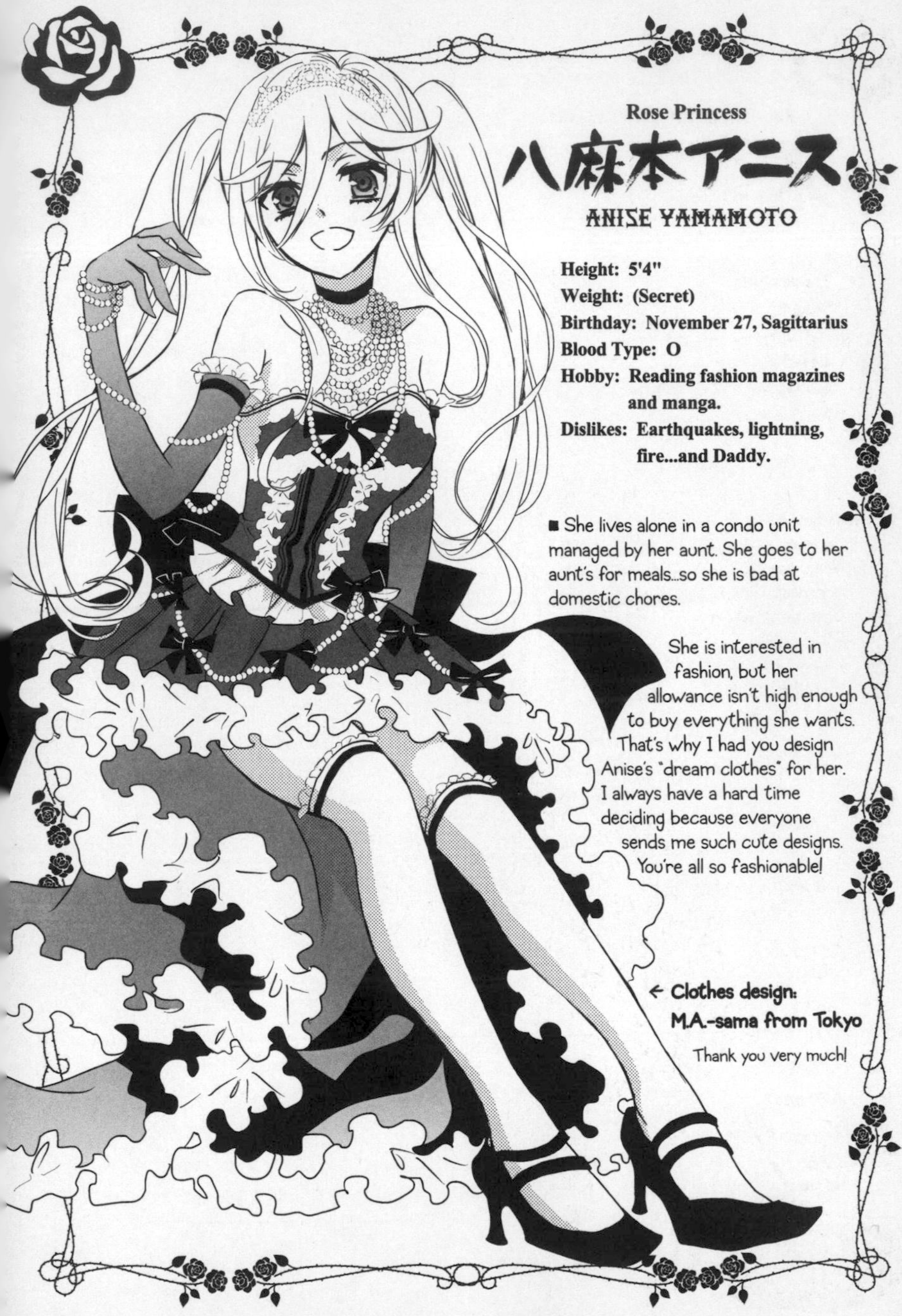

Rose Princess

八麻本アニス

ANISE YAMAMOTO

Height: 5'4"
Weight: (Secret)
Birthday: November 27, Sagittarius
Blood Type: O
Hobby: Reading fashion magazines and manga.
Dislikes: Earthquakes, lightning, fire...and Daddy.

■ She lives alone in a condo unit managed by her aunt. She goes to her aunt's for meals...so she is bad at domestic chores.

She is interested in fashion, but her allowance isn't high enough to buy everything she wants. That's why I had you design Anise's "dream clothes" for her. I always have a hard time deciding because everyone sends me such cute designs. You're all so fashionable!

← **Clothes design: M.A.-sama from Tokyo**

Thank you very much!

Fake Rose Knight: Gold Rose

来生ハルト

HARUTO KISUGI

Height: 5'10"
Weight: 130 lbs
Birthday: October 9, Libra
Blood Type: B
Hobby: Creating stand-up comedy skits.
Dislikes: Bugs.

He came back from Hong Kong and is currently staying at Schwarz's place. He's good at any kind of domestic chore, so he can be very handy.

Well then... See you in volume 9!!

Aya Shouoto

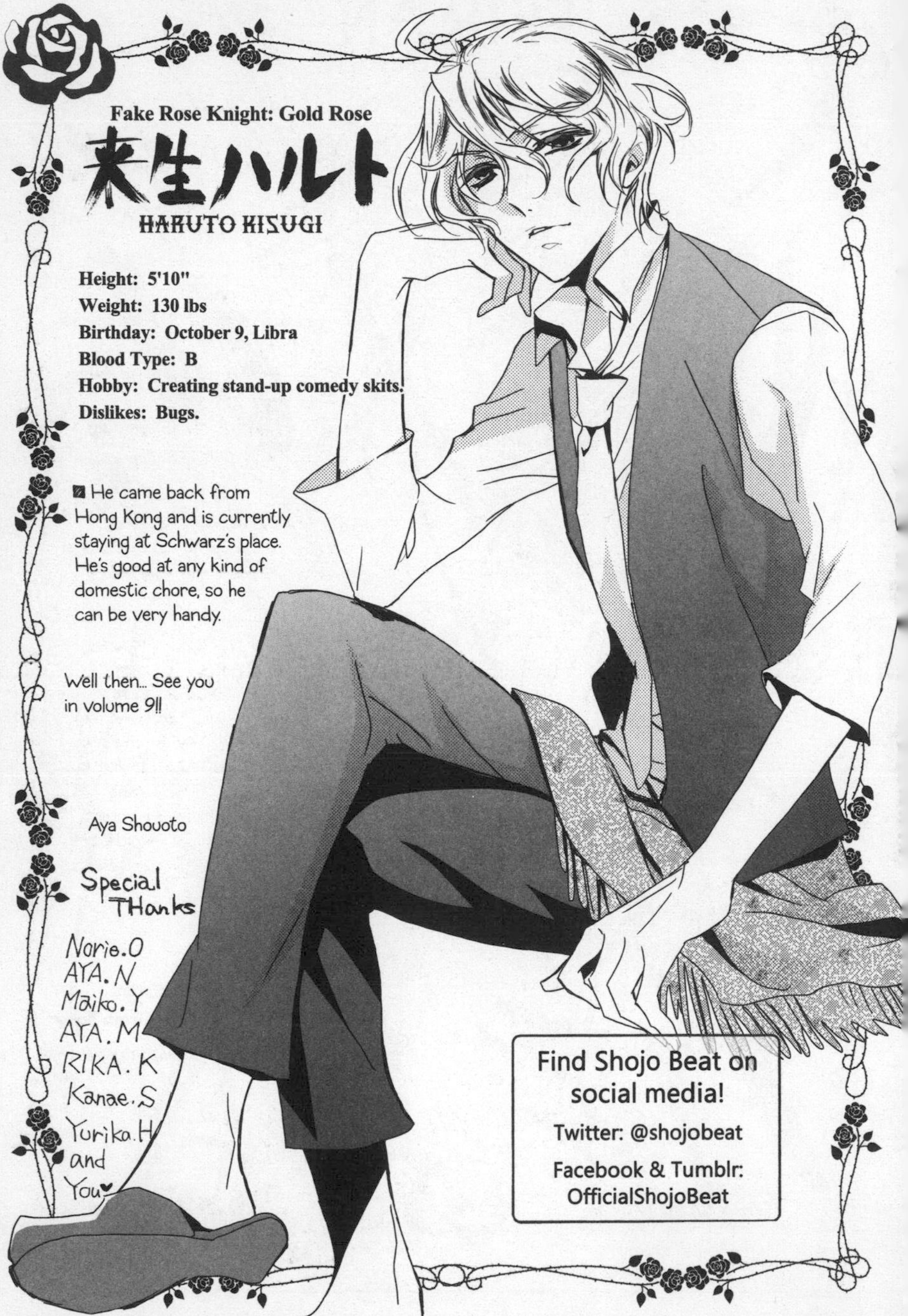

Special THanks

Norie.O
AYA.N
Maiko.Y
AYA.M
RIKA.K
Kanae.S
Yurika.H
and
You♥

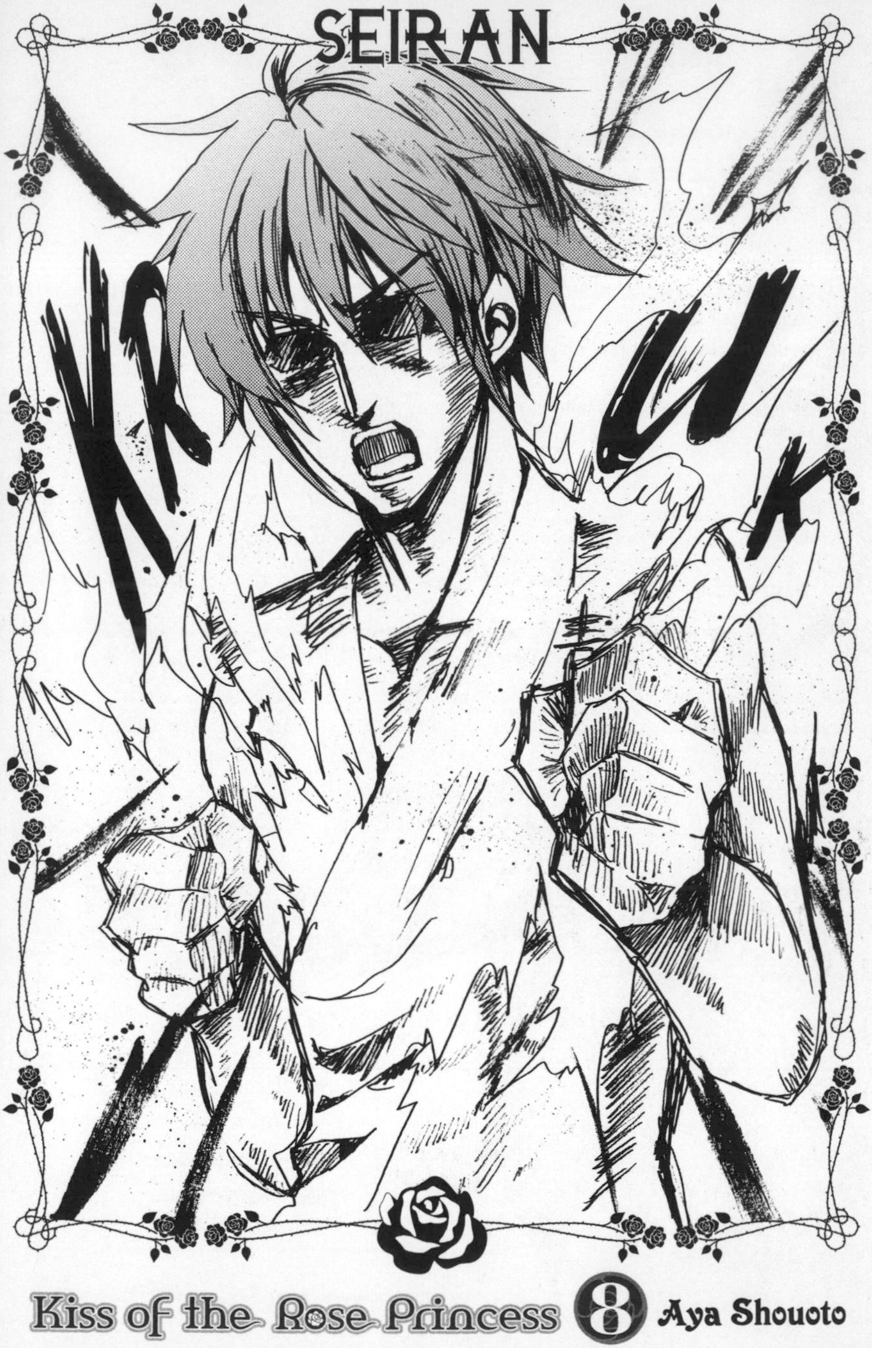
SEIRAN

Kiss of the Rose Princess 8 Aya Shouoto

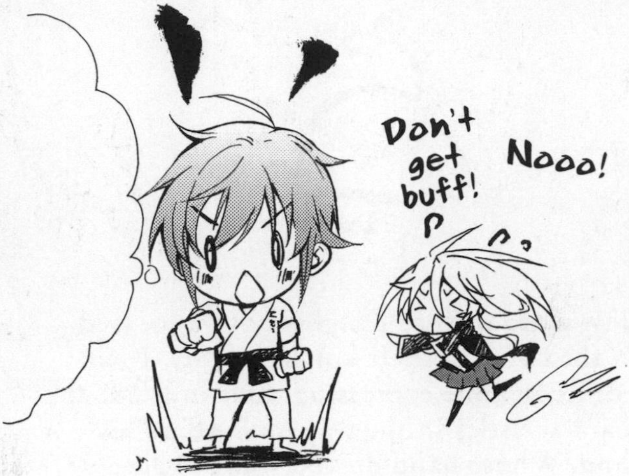
Don't get buff!
Nooo!

OSU OF THE ROSE PRINCESS

AYA SHOUOTO

Osu is a Japanese martial arts greeting often used in karate. It's also used to mean "yes" or "understood."

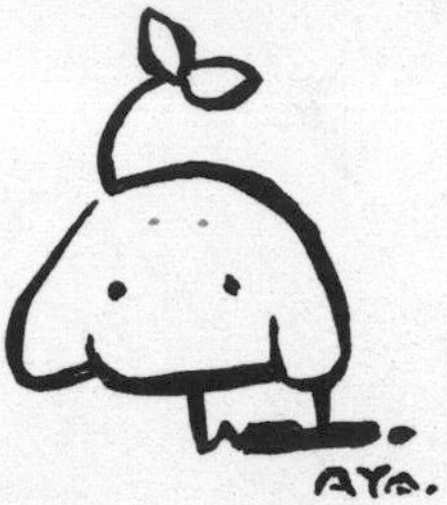
AYA.

Now all four Rose Knights have appeared on the cover in their knight outfits. I had a difficult time expressing their individual characteristics in the way each offers his hand. Whose hand do you want to accept?

-Aya Shouoto

Aya Shouoto was born on December 25. Her hobbies include traveling, staying at hotels, sewing and daydreaming. She currently lives in Tokyo and enjoys listening to J-pop anime theme songs while she works.

Kiss of the Rose Princess

Volume 8
Shojo Beat Edition

STORY AND ART BY
AYA SHOUOTO

Translation/Tetsuichiro Miyaki
Touch-up Art & Lettering/Inori Fukuda Trant
Design/Yukiko Whitley
Editor/Nancy Thistlethwaite

KISS OF ROSE PRINCESS Volume 8
© Aya SHOUOTO 2011
Edited by KADOKAWA SHOTEN
First published in Japan in 2011 by KADOKAWA CORPORATION, Tokyo.
English translation rights arranged with KADOKAWA CORPORATION, Tokyo.

Printed in the U.S.A.

Published by VIZ Media, LLC
P.O. Box 77010
San Francisco, CA 94107

10 9 8 7 6 5 4 3 2 1
First printing, January 2016

www.viz.com

Written by the creator of **High School Debut!**
MY love STORY!!
KAZUNE KAWAHARA Story
ARUKO Art

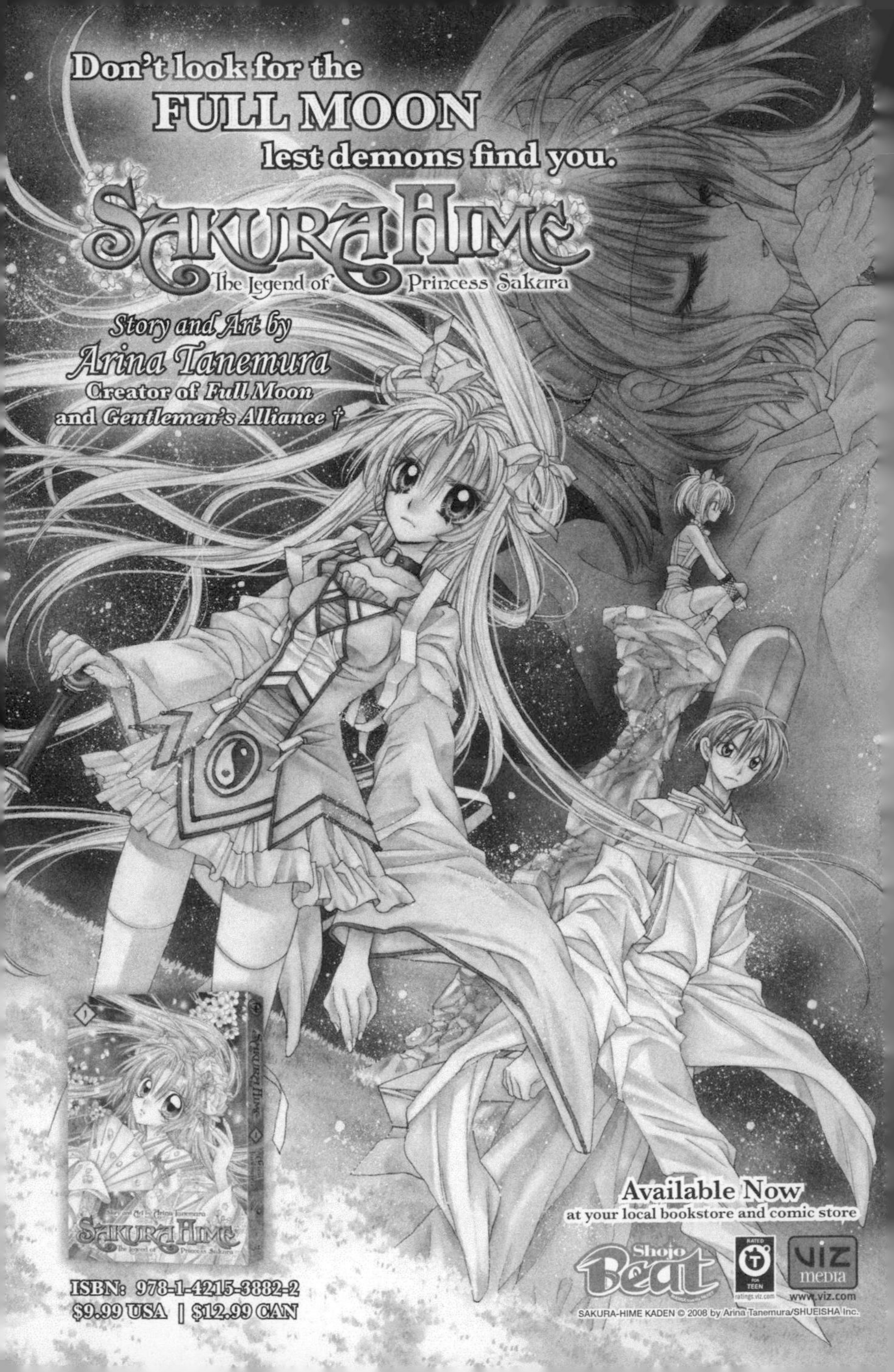
Don't look for the
FULL MOON
lest demons find you.
SAKURA HIME
The Legend of Princess Sakura
Story and Art by
Arina Tanemura
Creator of Full Moon
and Gentlemen's Alliance †
SAKURA HIME
The Legend of Princess Sakura
ISBN: 978-1-4215-3882-2
$9.99 USA | $12.99 CAN
Available Now
at your local bookstore and comic store
Shojo Beat
RATED T FOR TEEN
ratings.viz.com
VIZ media
www.viz.com
SAKURA-HIME KADEN © 2008 by Arina Tanemura/SHUEISHA Inc.

This is the last page.

In keeping with the original Japanese comic format, this book reads from right to left, so action, sound effects, and word balloons are completely reversed. This preserves the orientation of the original artwork. Check out the diagram below to get the hang of things, then turn to the other side of the book to get started!

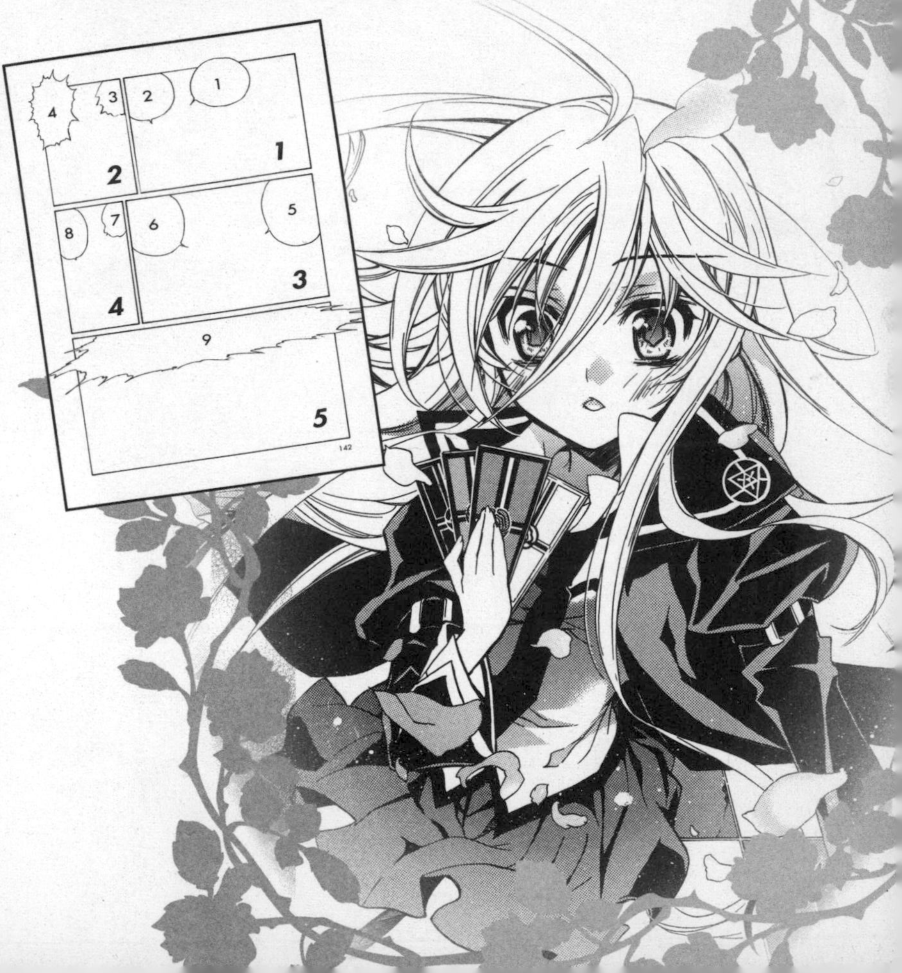
1
2
1
3
4
2
5
6
3
7
8
4
9
5
142